ECONOMIC REFORM AND DEVELOPMENT

By the same author

Dynamics of Agricultural Development
(in 3 Volumes)

About the Editors

Dr. K.S. Dhindsa is a Professor of Economics at the Punjab School of Economics, Guru Nanak Dev University, Amritsar (India). Dr. Dhindsa has a brilliant career, who after graduating from Punjab University, completed the post-graduate diploma in Economic Development from Glasgow University. Thereafter, he obtained his Master Degree from Leeds University (England). Then he went to London University where he successfully completed his Ph.D. degree. He is the author of two books entitled "India's Export Performance—Some Policy Implications" and "Indian Immigrants in United Kingdom : A Socio-Economic Analysis." He is also co-editor of a book entitled "Dynamics of Agricultural Development", (3 volumes). He has published a fairly large number of research papers in National and International Journals. For his post-doctorate he went to the School of Oriental and African Studies, University of London during 1989-91. He was the editor of Indian Journal of Quantitative Economics—A journal of international development, during 1994-96. He was the Dean of Faculty of Economics and Business during 1992-93 and was Chairman of Punjab School of Economics, Guru Nanak Dev University, during 1994-1996.

Dr. Anju Sharma is a lecturer in the Post Graduate Department of Economics, Khalsa College, Amritsar (Punjab). She obtained her M.Phil and Ph.D. (Economics) degree from Punjab School of Economics, Guru Nanak Dev University, Amritsar. She has carried out a variety of research in the field of economics. She is the author of a book entitled. "Dynamics of Cropping Pattern : A Regional Study of Punjab". She is also co-editor of a book "Dynamics of Agricultural Development", (Published in 3 volumes). A dozen of her research papers have already been published in reputed journals.

ECONOMIC REFORM AND DEVELOPMENT

Edited by

K.S. Dhindsa
Anju Sharma

CONCEPT PUBLISHING COMPANY, NEW DELHI-110059

Cataloging in Publication Data—DK
Courtesy: D.K. Agencies (P) Ltd. <docinfo@dkagencies.com>

Seminar: Emerging Trends in Indian Economy (1997 : Amritsar, India)
Economic reform and development / edited by K.S. Dhindsa, Anju Sharma.
p. cm.
Papers presented at the Seminar: Emerging Trends in Indian Economy, held at Amritsar during 28-29 March 1997 and Seminar: Economic Reforms in India, held at Jalandhar during 3-4 April 1998.
Includes bibliographical references.
Includes index.
ISBN 8180692736

1. India—Economic policy—1991- —Congresses. 2. India—Economic conditions—1947- —Congresses. I. Dhindsa, K. S. II. Sharma, Anju, 1970- III. Seminar: Economic Reforms in India (1998 : Jalandhar, India) IV. Title.

DDC 338.954 22

ISBN : 81-8069-273-6

First Published 2006

Published and Printed by
Ashok Kumar Mittal
Concept Publishing Company
A/15-16, Commercial Block, Mohan Garden,
New Delhi-110059 (India)

Phones : 25351460, 25351794
Fax : 091-11-25357103
Email : publishing@conceptpub.com

PREFACE

The Indian economy was characterized by Central Planning for industrial development and very little of foreign participation till the end of 1980s. This resulted in gross misallocation of resources and created a very large and inefficient public sector. However in 1991, the Indian economy was radically transformed by adopting new economic policy which included liberalization, privatization and globalization. Although the implementation of economic reforms was initially slow, but now these economic reforms seem to be irreversible. There are basically two major components of these reforms namely stabilization policies and structural adjustment programmes. A very powerful argument in favour of the reform is that it raises the long term growth rate of the economy. In order to implement economic reforms in various sectors of the economy, adequate attention needs to be immediately paid to the investment in necessary infrastructure, human resource development and social development that includes retraining of workers and safety nets. Efforts should be made by the government to reduce poverty and unemployment. The problem of fiscal deficit needs to be addressed both on the expenditure and revenue side. Interest payments and subsidies which are the two major components of government expenditure must be substantially curtailed. The financial sector is experiencing the winds of change even though the reforms in this sector are not complete. The unfinished agenda of economic reforms include institutional reforms, changes in labour laws, reforms of public enterprises etc.

In order to study various dimensions of economic reforms in India, two seminars were conducted. The first seminar 'Emerging Trends in Indian Economy' was held on 28-29 March, 1997 at Guru Nanak Dev University and the second seminar with a title 'Economic Reforms in India' was held on 3-4 April, 1998 at Layalpur Khalsa College, Jalandhar. Seventeen papers contributed by eminent economists invited from various parts of the country are included in this volume entitled

'Economic Reform and Development'. These papers are classified into three sections. Section I contains research papers on globalization, trade and investment. Papers in Section II deal with the impact of economic reforms on employment, poverty and regional disparities. Section III includes papers related to infrastructural development and institutional reforms.

We acknowledge our special thanks to all distinguished economists who have contributed high quality research papers in these seminars.

We are also thankful to the authorities of Guru Nanak Dev University and major industrialists both at Amritsar and Jalandhar who gave us financial support for the successful organization of these seminars. We are grateful to Mr. Jaskarn Singh and S.S. Chatha who helped us in organizing the seminar at Jalandhar. We also acknowledge our thanks to Professors G.S. Bhalla, Atul Sarma, K.N. Kabra and G.K. Chadha who gave us valuable suggestions in organizing this volume.

Certainly, the issues addressed in this edited volume would appeal policy makers, academicians, teachers and students who have the curiosity and desire to know more about India's economic reforms.

Last but not the least we are profoundly grateful to the publishers M/s. Concept Publishing Company for their whole-hearted co-operation in bringing out this book in a record time.

Amritsar

K.S. Dhindsa
Anju Sharma

CONTENTS

Section-II

Employment, Poverty and Regional Disparities **193**

Section-III

Infrastructural Development and Institutional Reforms **315**

LIST OF TABLES

ANNEXURES

KEYNOTE ADDRESS
INDIAN ECONOMY : MEANDERINGS OF FIFTY YEARS

After attaining Independence, India adopted democratic socialistic pattern of society. The architect of economic system under this democratic set-up, Jawahar Lal Nehru, the first Prime Minister of India, was considerably influenced by the Soviet Union's socialism. Although primarily a democratic republic, India, thus, absorbed some crucial elements of socialism in the management of its economy. Whereas in Soviet Union both production and distribution were socialistic in nature following in essence the philosophy of "from each according to capacity and to each according to need", the Indian model concentrated on the production side mainly. Whereas in USSR, prices were not allowed to play the role of balancing the supply and demand forces in the market and prices were determined arbitrarily to impart production rewards and effect arbitrary distribution decided upon by the central authority through central command system, India adopted a pattern of mixed economy, primarily dealing with production and on a very limited scale with trade. The consumption or distribution (Income distribution) was left to the trickle down effect through partially controlled market system.

Under the mixed economy the basic and heavy industry as well as key and sensitive production was appropriated to the public sector. Comparatively less important, yet industries demanding heavy investment, over which government opted for control, were put in joint ventures. All other ordinary industries and trade were left to the private sector. Yet government did not debar itself from entering into production lines and even trade which could be legitimately carried out by the private sector. Running of hotels, manufacture of watches, road transport, manufacture of cars and other consumer durables are a few of the examples, which could be beneficially and logically left to the private sector. Whereas in the Soviet Socialist system, the economy was frozen at a point of time and remained frozen for about seven decades with the central command system getting stronger, tighter and strangulating for the lower and states (soviets) level managements with no accountability to the public, the Indian Socialistic pattern nourished the public sector for attaining commanding heights. Whereas the Soviet system tightened its grip on production and distribution to make it inefficient and cost ineffective, breeding inefficiency in production and inequitability in distribution that rendered the integration of national economy with the world market irrelevant. The Indian economy though interacting selectively with the world economy in terms of exports and imports, remained primarily preoccupied with import substitution which led to adoption of second hand technology and high cost production that did not match international standards with respect to the quality of products. Under both systems, cost effective-ness, quality production, market competitiveness and role of prices as distributive agent and allocator of productive resources, suffered to the disadvantage of both the economies.

Under the pressures of imbalance of supply and demand of goods and services and also unaccountability of the central command system that did not cut its coat according to the cloth and expanded international commitments beyond the resources would permit, the Soviet system broke down first slowly and then suddenly that landed the economy and the society into a total chaos. All pervasive shortage of goods, specially food and necessities of life, mounting budgetary deficit, artificially managed high value of Rouble (Soviet-currency), rampant corruption, widespread dissatisfaction of the public and failure of the government management system, led to the breakup of the country into sixteen independent countries. The process of break down of the economy got speeded up because there was no private sector in existence as the public sector management system sagged down. Perforce the decision was made to privatize the economy. Yet, there was no laws, no market places, no agents, no wholesalers, no retailers and retail outlets and no government system to regulate the private market which are an essential requirement of the private sector and the free market to operate. Thus tight and frozen state of the economy had not thawing time and it just melted into anarchy and development of mafias, against which these economies are as yet struggling to stand up. Overnight, the alternative system which was considered even stronger in concept and functioning than the private or free economy of the western countries, flopped into the chaos characterizing these resultant states as underdeveloped or as developing economies.

Although India was also pursuing socialistic policies, yet its activity remained confined to production and trade and that too partially. Even as the state spread its arms to license, control, limit. regulate and influence the private sector, the private enterprise was allowed to grow with certain degrees of freedom. In spite of government having strangulating controls and limiting the private sector both in its spread and size, the private sector showed strong presence. No doubt, the license, permits and control as well as irrationally high tax rates and controls on foreign trade and exchange as well as financial sector, gave birth to black market and black money, yet the private sector not only survived these socialistic dispensations, but developed itself to be strong enough to respond positively and vigorously as the state controls showed signs of weakness and the government had to relax its hold to let the private sector play its role effectively.

It is here that when the situation developed that (1) inefficiencies of the public sector enterprises became an unbearable drain on the budgetary resources, (2) instead of contributing to the government resources, these enterprises ran into losses, (3) government, following socialistic policies, took over sick private units under the pressures of trade unions, which never revived to yield profits, (4) captive market became restless on the quantity and quality of goods and services offered by the public sector, (5) demonstrative effect of the international market in respect of goods and services available became visibly strong, (6) foreign debts mounted fast, repayments of foreign loans and discharging of international financial obligations became difficult, (7) budgetary and fiscal deficits of the state became unsustainable, (8) the foreign exchange reserves dried up to the extent that they were not enough for import needs of one week, (9) current account worsened, (10) inflation rate went up unprecedentedly, (11) imports exceeded exports unsustainably, (12) international investors shied away and (13) India looked like becoming a basket case in the face of escalating crude oil prices due to the effects of gulf war and three years continuous drought in the country, the review of the socialistic system being followed and the soft state policies pursued by the government came under some serious screening. In 1986-87 some steps were envisaged to liberalise the economy, yet soon the steps were retraced under the pressure of necessity of populist policies to appease and please the socialistic mindset of the politicians and leftist oriented vote banks.

Further, the situation deteriorated to the level that in 1990-91, it became extremely difficult for the government to meet its obligations to repay the international loans and interest due. At one stage the government started fiddling with the idea of defaulting on payments due. In fact, the government was given this advice by some otherwise quite serious policy makers. However, a good sense prevailed and government decided to pledge their gold stock and obtain resources from Central Bank of England to retire their obligations due. Credibility of the Indian economy and its government was so low that the pledged gold had to be physically lifted from India and put in the custody of Bank of England. This had two positive messages to convey: (1) India demonstrated its commitment to retire its debt obligations come what may, which added to the credibility of the country and its government, and (2) it did not dry up the sources of credit from the international community, governments and financial institutions. Rather this helped the inflow of direct investments and portfolio investments, when from the middle of 1991, the economy was thrown open and public sector started climbing down from its commanding heights.

It is during these years that Dunkle Draft concerning GATT made its appearance, which aimed at creating a level ground and conditions of fair play in the international trade in order to integrate the national economies with the international market. Indian mind yet was not prepared for this change. Socialistic orientation of four decades and vested interests, both bureaucratic and political, entrenched in public sector enterprises that operated in the captive market were looking like unsurmountable hurdles in the way of change to create and open and competitive market economy. The Document (Dunkle draft) which was a highly technical write-up was commented upon adversely without even seeing the document, much less reading it and even by illiterate leaders without understanding the nuances of it. Such was the psychological barrier in the mental frame of the national political leadership for the change from a partially controlled economy to the competitive market economy that had to be demolished. There was no alternative at this stage and fortunately the new minority government that came to power in the middle of 1991 could find a foothold and survive only if it brought about shift to free the economy from the socialistic stranglehold. There were many test cases before the policy makers at that stage. For instance in spite of stiff opposition to the Pepsi Foods Ltd., its functioning had introduced new production technology for tomato crop and had upgraded potatoes to render it suitable for processing, which helped the farming community in the hinterland of their factories considerably. Introduction of Pepsi Soft drink though on very demanding terms and conditions, had stopped an increase in prices of other local competing drinks along with the increase in the size of bottles. With the coming of Maruti Udyog, monopoly of Ambassador and Fiat cars had broken, which not only improved the fuel efficiency of the cars, but also forced the domestic entrenched companies to improve their models and share their captive market with the new comers.

Encouraged by these positive results of opening some of the sub-sectors to international competition and out of sheer necessity to save the economy from a break down, the new government, though a minority government unencumbered as it was, embarked upon a well thought out policy of liberalization, privatization and globalization of the economy. It was not an easy task, specially when there was to be encountered a stiff opposition in the parliament at every step, specially from the parties of the Left Front. Many of the Members of Parliament and ministers of the ruling coalition even were not feeling easy with the change, because they feared adverse influence of these policies on their vote banks, which were so far fed on socialist prescriptions and kept illiterate, ignorant and poor as they were. Yet credit goes to the supporting parties and right wing parties that the minority government last its full term and could pursue the changes introduced in a sustained manner, though quite in diluted form at later stages.

The process of liberalization involved (1) relaxing the norms and removal of licensing requirements for a large number of non-sensitive and non-core industries, reducing the reserved industries list drastically, (2) relaxing the reservation of production items for small industries and increasing the limits for investment in small and medium industry sub-sectors, (3) freeing the enterprises from limits of growth and expansions, (4) reducing the depredations of inspector raj, although government did not succeed fully in removing the old vestages in this respect, (5) speeding up of clearances of the projects where it was necessary and freeing the enterprises from licensing and approval requirements considerably, (6) allowing the multinational enter the Indian market through direct investments and collaborations with

Indian firms, (7) allowing portfolios investments from financial institutions, and (8) encouragement of Non-resident Indian (NRI) to invest in Indian firms, start their own ventures and effect deposits in Indian Banks and financial institutions.

This required removal of physical barriers to imports of commodities, inputs and capital goods and also rationalization of duties and tariffs, so that domestic firms and the industry as a whole remains competitive on one hand and gets the much needed necessary competition from foreign firms in order that they improve upon their competitive edge and introduce state of the art technology independently on their own and also in collaboration with foreign firms or multinationals. Simultaneously tax structure was rationalized to encourage investment, expansions and to promote sunrise enterprises and to be competitive in the international market, Industrial and trade sector reforms aimed at liberalization and globalization of the economy were accompanied by supporting financial sector reforms in order to provide the needed investment credit at reasonable cost and keep the rate of inflation under control. These two aspects have been and are crucial for sustained and faster growth of the economy i.e. (1) Reasonably priced investment credit and (2) low rate of inflation. no inflation rate at that time in 1991-92 was running around 17 per cent and interest rate on credit was running between 20 to 26 per cent. Even the deposit rates were 13 per cent and above in the organized sector and much above in the non-banking financial sector. Compared with this the interest rates and inflation were much lower in the competing countries. For instance the investment credit in USA was available at below 8 per cent and inflation rate around 3 per cent and even below. Therefore, the objective of financial sector reforms was to reduce the rate of inflation to one digit figure and much below as it is around 4 per cent today. Similarly prime lending rate being reduced to below 14 per cent and deposit rates to 10 per cent and below (Although deposit rate today is 12 per cent for very long term deposit). With the Central Bank attaining partial autonomy, now the endeavour is that government, rather than monetizing their fiscal drift, should borrow from the market at commercial rate and the bank keeps interest rates and inflation under control. Although situations have been developing when there was shortage of investment credit in the market due to excessive mopping up of funds by the government, yet financial sector did not come as an unsurmountable constraint on investment funds.

The government sector role has to be dominantly confined to the infrastructure development and social welfare growth. Private sector has to grow purely on commercial basis with the least and preferably without any burden on public exchequer in respect of subsidies, dole outs and concessions. The biggest constraint to investment growth today is the infrastructural constraints. Therefore, the first priority of the Central and State governments should be to develop infrastructure through public sector investment, collaborative commercially viable projects and through private sector investments based on generation of repaying capacity to retire the credit obtained. Of all the elements of infrastructure, the following five are the most crucial ones :

(1) Transport and Communication : This is becoming a major constraint to development of industry and trade and even agriculture. There is a direct and strong correlation between the quality as well as density of roads and development whether we examine this by countries, regions and states. Similarly quality, efficiency and adequacy of communication system is a prerequisite to growth and development of any area; region or the country. Thus, development of roads, railways, waterways, ports etc. and efficient communication system require first priority in country's investment programmes.

(2) Power : No primary, secondary or tertiary sector investments are possible in any area or place without the availability of adequate, regular and reasonably priced power, specially the electricity. This alongwith transport and communication system is posing the serious most constraint to private sector investments in India.

(3) Education : There is a generally accepted misconception that India has the advantage of availability of low cost labour. Though on a unit basis labour may be cheap, yet it is not a low cost labour when we use it as a denominator to factor productivity. Cheap labour if illiterate is always a costly labour, specially when such hoards of labour get unionized and hold the enterprises to ransom. It is, therefore, essential that for an accelerated growth the workers must be educated and skilled to handle their jobs competently and in the spirit of commitment. In addition to general education, the workers must develop technical skills enough to handle their jobs efficiently and cost effectively. In this respect India has lagged behind and the general type of education that is made available is not adequate and relevant to the needs of the socio-economic set-up we are heading for. Today more than two-third of our population is illiterate or is poorly and irrelevantly educated. The process of providing socially relevant education to the masses must, therefore, be initiated on a priority basis.

(4) Health : To be productive and efficient the worker must be healthy and robust. Not only that his family too must be healthy and living in hygienic environment. This requires provision of adequate public health and medical facilities. Illiterate workers with poor health can never prove to be efficient workers. In this respect Indian labour is one of the costliest labour in the world and does not provide any comparative advantage and competitive edge to the industry in the competitive world market. Provision of adequate public health facilities, hygienic living conditions, medical treatment and hospitalization facilities within the reach of the population is, therefore, a priority that must be accorded in our development planning.

(5) Production credit : Indian production and services sectors suffer from lack of sufficient absorptive capacity for commercially productive credit. In fact it is this lack of capacity to productively employ the institutional credit that is commercially viable and generates adequate repaying capacity, which is not allowing the economy to move on a higher growth path. For an economically feasible and commercially viable venture, there should be no need for subsidized capital and no need to provide for low interest priority sector lending. Cheap or subsidized capital is always used inefficiently and is mostly venture for a developing economy. The demand for commercially viable credit in India is low because of poorly developed infrastructural elements as discussed above. Any how once the four elements of constraints to economic growth and development are removed the demand for reasonably priced commercial credit will increase and growth in all the sectors will improve. The emphasis of development planning and policy should, therefore, be on removal of these five constraints to growth on a sustained basis to make the production process globally competitive.

The state, in addition to investment on infrastructure development, must then take up social welfare actively explicitly. In order to distribute the fruits of growth amongst wider population; specially the poorer and socially as well as economically handicapped segments of the society, state subsidies have a significant role to play. Yet, these subsidies to be effective must be (1) properly targetted to serve the really needy segments of society, and (2) of temporary nature in order to nurture the ventures and enterprises in their infancy till their growth becomes self sustained. There must not develop vested interests in obtaining subsidies for more than the minimum required period. Long drawn subsidies cripple rather than develop commercial viabilities of the enterprises and untargetted consumption subsidies create vested interest, who often do not deserve to be subsidized in the first place. Thus the second foremost function of the state at this stage should be to target and rationalize both the consumption as well as production subsidies and welfare activities in order to reach the genuinely needy segments of the society.

Thus Indian economy has come a long way through the past five decades and has changed in its form and content enough to leave behind the regime of controls, licences, inspections and restrictions and has come to operate in an open commercial environment of liberalization, privatization and globalization. The reforms have come to stay and are bound to proceed ahead faster and faster. There appears to be no going back irrespective of the change in governments. Yet, the policy frame of the government must concentrate on effective governance rather than operating the public sector production of goods like watches, bangles and hotels.

S.S. JOHL

INTRODUCTION

K.S. Dhindsa *and* Anju Sharma

After getting independence in 1947, India adopted democratic socialistic pattern of society and the government started development with Five-Year Plans. The main objective of the plans was to achieve higher rate of economic growth and thus higher level of national income and per capita income. Reduction in both income inequality and regional imbalances were other important objectives of the plans. Indian economy was greatly influenced by Soviet model of development in which the economy was regulated by the central authority and market forces were given very little role in determining the prices of the goods. In pursuing a socialistic pattern of society, some heavy and basic goods industries were reserved for the public sector, some other important industries were left to be jointly owned by public and private sector, while other less important industries were left only for private sector. Though Indian economy is said to be a mixed economy but the share of investment in public sector enterprises was above sixty per cent of the total investment. Within this framework, targets were allocated to production units of state enterprises and as regards private sector enterprises, targets were set to be achieved by investment licensing. In second Five-Year Plan, India followed import substitution policy called inward looking industrial policy. No doubt building up of heavy and basic industries like cement, iron and steel etc. built the base of Indian industries, but the continuous reliance on non-discriminatory industrial policy made Indian industry highly costly and uncompetitive in the world market. Imports were blindly replaced by domestic production without giving any thought to the gap between domestic and world prices for these products and this resulted in misallocation of resources, resulting in low rate of economic growth. Because of high level of protection, the industrialists did not pay any attention towards employing modern and improved techniques of production and this resulted in low productivity of Indian industries. Due to oligopolistic market structure and high production rate, the consumers had to pay higher prices for low quality products.

Due to slow growth of exports and in view of rapid increase in the demand for imports as a result of plan expenditure, the policy makers decided to embark on the road of industrialization through import substitution policy. Government also encouraged the small scale industries to generate employment and some manufacturing items were reserved exclusively for small scale industries. A relatively higher inflation rate together with rapid increase in demand for imports caused over valuation of Indian rupee which in turn discouraged exports and encouraged imports and thus created balance of payment crisis. During 1960 to 1980 India's export growth was much lower than world exports whose growth rate was in double digits. India's share in world exports remained below 0.5 per cent till 1991.

The total factor productivity in manufacturing sector also remained low due to various reasons i.e. restrictions on purchase of foreign technology, import restrictions, restrictions on labour laws and bureaucratic control in running public sector enterprises. Ban on import of many consumer goods forced Indian consumers to buy costly domestically produced goods. Tariff rates on goods whose imports were allowed were also very high. The growth rate of Indian economy also remained low because of inefficiency in running the state owned enterprises. Since public sector investment constituted around two-third of India's total investment, very low returns on public sector investment kept overall growth rate to a dismal rate. Because of red tapism and bureaucratic interference in running public sector enterprises, these units could not obtain commercial viability. Many government departments like State Electricity Boards and State Road Corporations were bearing huge losses and thus became a burden on national exchequer. Due to restrictive labour laws it has not been possible to fire workers in organized sectors. Thus overstaffing also contributed towards low productivity in the state owned enterprises. Both the quality and quantity of infrastructure was inadequate. The inflation started increasing during 1980s and reached 17 per cent in 1991. The complete financial sector including Insurance was under government control. Even in cities people had to wait for a year or so before getting the Telephone connections and the quality of Telephone services was also very poor. Roads were very congested, thus adding to fuel cost and time in transition. The result of such factors was that Indian economy experienced a very low growth rate of 3 to 4 per cent during the period from 1950 to 1980 and this consistent growth rate came to be known as 'Hindu Rate of Growth'.

In view of growing inefficiency in the public sector enterprises, rising fiscal deficits and deteriorating balance of payment situation, it was felt that change from the centrally planned economy towards a free market economy is necessary. Better and sustained performance of other Asian countries the so called 'Asian Tigers' also reflected that a shift from highly protected inward looking industrial policy to outward looking liberalised policy is inevitable for development. Rajiv Gandhi, soon after becoming Prime Minister categorically pointed out that his government will allow private entry into state owned enterprises. In order to initiate this process, some changes were introduced with regard to foreign trade policy, foreign equity and fiscal policy etc. All these changes were done for creating an uninhibited environment for private sector. Though this government embarked on the road of liberalisation but these reforms were very mild in nature. However, this helped in bringing the subject of economic reforms on political agenda for the very first time and set up the ground for future reforms. It also became clear to the policy makers that unnecessary controls are retarding the growth of Indian economy.

In 1991, the condition of India deteriorated to such an extent that government had to make bold decision of introducing economic reforms in various sectors of the economy, though the pace of these reforms was slow in the beginning. There is a need to analyse the factors which contributed towards the economic crisis of 1991 and which were largely responsible for a shift in India's economic policy. Towards the end of 1990s, debt ratios were quite high and foreign exchange reserves were just enough to meet two or three weeks imports. Due to very low foreign exchange reserves and mounting external debt, it was feared that India will become defaulter and would not be able to honour the external debt obligations. This greatly damaged the India's creditworthiness in the eyes of international lending agencies. Other events such as sharp increase in prices of oil due to Gulf war and sustained decline in foreign remittances especially from Gulf countries contributed to foreign exchange crisis. Rate of inflation was very high and the fiscal deficit as a percentage of GDP increased from 4.1 per cent in 1975-76 to 8.4 per cent in 1990-91. The rising overall deficit was the result of consistently rising government expenditure in relation to government revenue. The continuously increasing burden of subsidies, faster rising wage bills and interest payments put an intolerable burden on the Indian economy. Slow growth of tax revenue and lower rates of return from public sector investment resulted in resource crunch. No international agency was willing to grant loans to India. The IMF and World Bank agreed to give loans to India on certain conditions which were related to removal of government control in economic activities and to open up Indian economy in the rest of the world.

The economic reforms which Indian government introduced in 1991 can be broadly categorised in two parts. One is the Stabilisation Policics (SP) which were formed to manage demand side through bringing changes in fiscal and monetary policies of the government. The other category was related to Structural Adjustment Programmes (SAP) and thus relates to the supply side management of the economic system through bringing changes in policies related to trade and balance of payment regime and deregulation of economic activities. Important constituents of economic reforms can be grouped under three categories namely Liberalisation, Privatisation and Globalisation (LPG).

Liberalisation means liberating the Indian industry from the clutches of various unnecessary controls and restrictions which were creating hindrances in the development of these industries. Earlier for making investment in the private sector, license was required in which upper limit for production was mentioned. In case the manufacturers want to produce more than that fixed upper limit, again approval from the government was required. Privatisation implies transfer of ownership and/or management of an enterprise from public sector to the private sector. It is widely recognised that private ownership of production units is absolutely indispensable for accelerating the growth of the economy. Earlier investment in the public sector was considered to be the engine of self sustained growth. But past experience of public sector in many countries including India clearly demonstrates that the rate of return on invested capital in this sector is very low. Privatisation gives incentives to work hard because the profits from the invested capital remain in the pockets of individuals rather than government. Privatisation also allows competition, promotes efficiency and thus holds the costs down. The tendency towards disinvestment in the public sector is growing very fast all over the world. Under the disinvestment policy, the aim of the government is to transfer a part of ownership to private individuals. Globalisation means free movement of goods, services and factors of production like capital and labour across the world without any restriction. Thus globalisation includes removal of tariffs and quantitative restrictions in the form of quotas allowing free inflow and outflow of capital; permitting free flow of technology and removal of restrictions on foreign exchange. The main economic reforms introduced in different sector of the economy during the last decade i.e., after 1991 are highlighted below.

Firstly, radical changes have been made in the area of industrial policy by removing several barriers. Industrial licensing has been abolished for all industries except a small list of sensitive industries due to environmental and pollution considerations. The number of industries reserved exclusively for public sector has been reduced drastically. Electric power generation has been opened up to private investors including foreign investors. The telecommunication sector and air transport are also opened up to private sector. Access to foreign technology has been made much easier and the investment limits regarding the small scale and cottage industries have been revised. Earlier according to the Monopolies and Restrictive Trade Practices Act (MRTP), if any company having assets beyond Rs. 100 crore was used to be declared as MRTP company and it had to work under several constraints. Now the concept of MRTP has been done away with and while taking investment decisions these firms need not to take prior permission from the government.

Secondly, government introduced significant reforms in the field of taxation which were highly required for improving the working of this sector. The Taxation Reforms Committee headed by Raja Chelliah, renowned expert on taxation gave very useful recommendations like a move towards a simpler system of income and corporate taxes with moderate rates and fewer exemptions, progressive reduction in the level and range of custom duties, lower excise duties with substantial reduction of exemptions and a shift from specific to *ad valorem*. Keeping in view these recommendations, personal income tax and corporate tax rates and custom duties have been reduced significantly. Modified Value Added Tax (MODVAT) which gives tax credit on inputs has been extended to other items like textile, petroleum and capital goods. The bulk of the taxes have been changed from specific to *ad valorem* basis and the number of exemptions were greatly reduced. The long term objective of the government is to fully adopt value added tax (VAT) but its start could only be possible if government integrates tax on production which is imposed by the Central government and taxes on sales imposed by the State governments. The changes in taxation system will have to be accompanied by improvements in tax administration to realize full potential of tax reforms introduced since 1991.

Thirdly, for mobilising more resources for productive activities there was a pressing need to bring reforms in the financial sector. Based on Narsimha Committee recommendations, the Government of India announced a package of reforms in the financial sector. The Statutory Liquidity Ratio (SLR) and cash reserve ratio (CPR) would be reduced progressively and some steps have already been taken in this direction. To enhance competition in the banking sector, some new private banks have started working and the branches of the foreign banks have also been expanded. The commercial banks are allowed to fix the interest rates subject to the ceiling fixed by Reserve Bank of India. Recovery Tribunal has been set up to facilitate recovery from the defaulting borrowers. Bank branch licensing is liberalised and separate department has been set up for the supervision of banks. The Securities and Exchange Board of India (SEBI) is set up as an independent statutory authority for regulating the stock exchanges and supervising the major players in the capital markets. With the abolition of Capital Issue Control Act in May 1992, firms are now free to issue capital and price new issues according to market conditions.

Capital markets have been opened up for portfolio investment. Also Indian companies have been allowed to access international capital markets by issuing equity abroad through the mechanism of Global Depository Receipts. In the money markets many reforms are brought about. More participants like Mutual Funds. Primary Dealers were allowed to operate in the market. Minimum size of transaction in the call money is reduced to Rs. 5 lakh. Maturity period of Commercial Papers is reduced to 30 days from 3 months. New institutions such as Discount and Finance House of India (DFHI), Money Market Mutual Funds (MMMFs) are introduced to facilitate the growth of markets. No doubt the reforms in the financial sector are notable but still more needs to be done in this sector. By passing a law in which the bankers can sell the collateral (securities) against which loans have advanced is definitely right step in this direction. This will help in reducing non-performing assets (NPAs) of the banks which is quite high at the moment. There is also an urgent need to reduce credit to priorities sector that is being provided at subsidised rates. Furthermore, government borrowings from the Central Bank also needs to be reduced and this would be possible only if the fiscal deficit is brought down by reducing unproductive expenditure *i.e.* by reducing subsidies on fertilisers and power to the medium and large farms and by realising higher tax revenue both by avoiding tax evasion and by improving efficiency in the public sector enterprises.

Fourthly, keeping in view the objective of opening up Indian economy with rest of the world, government brought important structural reforms in the trade sector. To promote trade, tariff rates on capital goods, raw materials and intermediate goods are reduced substantially. In addition to custom duties; the quantitative restrictions on imports are also removed. Ban on the import of consumer goods is also lifted in 2001 and now the consumers are paying lower prices for better quality products. Devaluation of Indian rupee in the range of 20 to 25 per cent has also liberalised the trade. Imports were discouraged due to higher import prices resulting from devaluation and export got the stimulus in response to higher export value in terms of rupees. Also there was decanalization of some exports which were earlier permitted only through government trading agencies. In order to encourage exports, dual exchange rate was in force during the period 1991 to 1993 and in this system, market rate of exchange was kept for exports while official rate of exchange was used for imports and other items. This dual exchange rate system was unified by the end of 1993. With the amendments in Foreign Exchange Regulation Act (FERA) various restrictions which applied earlier to companies having equity 40 per cent or more were removed and now all companies are treated alike irrespective to the level of foreign equity. Restrictions on capital inflow of direct foreign investment and portfolio investment were also eased. Approval to companies having foreign equity is automatic in some cases while in others the approval from Foreign Investment Promotion Board (FIPB) is required. India has also signed the Charter of Multilateral Investment Guarantee Programmes and became its member. So there has been a significant liberalisation in trade sector.

Fifthly, keeping in view the present condition of public sector enterprises either bearing losses or earning very low returns, reform of these units is a critical requirement in the process of ongoing reforms. In public sector, companies have been given a clear indication that the further expansion plans must be financed either from internal resources or through raising funds from capital markets. Another important reform relates to the amendment of Sick Companies Act under which public sector companies within the purview of Board for Industrial and Financial Reconstruction (BIFR) are treated in the same way as the private sector companies. The board can also consider revival packages involving appointment of new managers and a fresh injection of capital. If no consensus can be reached for revival package, the BIFR is authorised to order the closure of such units. Disinvestment Commission has also been set up in this context. Disinvestment of these units will shift the resources towards other productive activities. The takeover of these enterprises by the private sector will bring better results because the private management will be in a position to retrench excessive staff and thus will reorganise production in an efficient manner. By having a look at the records of disinvestment during the last few years, one can easily point out that government has certainly fallen short of its target for disinvestment. Given the large size of public sector, efficiency of a large number of public sector enterprises needs to be improved considerably alongwith speeding up the process of disinvestment in certain cases. The government will have to take a bold decision of closing down some public sector units which are bearing losses and thus are a burden on national exchequer.

For bringing efficiency in public sector units, bureaucratic interference in the management of public sector units must be stopped. Appointments of various directors or heads must be done strictly on the basis of merit and handsome salaries and other perks must be provided for attracting talented persons to these units. This impression is generally confirmed from the potential NRI investors who maintain that in India, getting the approval for starting production units is not possible without giving bribery to the officials concerned at various stages. For eliminating this menace of corruption, bureaucrats and politicians at the helm of affairs must be severely punished. Considerable delay in the implementation of Disinvestment Commission's recommendations is giving a strict indication to investors who are potential buyers of disinvested capital. So rapid implementation of these recommendations is very much the need of the hour.

Sixthly, economic reforms must address the constraints on the efficiency and production in the agricultural sector. Production of various agricultural commodities in agricultural sector should be done in accordance with the demand for these commodities in the future. For promoting exports of agrobased products, production units of processing primary products should be set up at focal points in rural areas. As a result of sharp reduction in the tariff and non-tariff barriers, prices of the farming inputs will be lowered and this would result in improving terms of trade for agricultural sector. Rural credit, agricultural extension services, security of tenure; supply of improved seeds should be very much on the active agenda of the government. Protection to the industry has been substantially reduced. All government restrictions on movement of agricultural commodities across states have almost been removed. Subsidies given on fertilisers, water, and electricity to the medium and large farmers should be withdrawn. Thus money saved from the withdrawal of these subsidies can be invested for the development of rural infrastructure.

Seventhly, another important area which has so far not been paid adequate attention is the restrictive labour laws. In a labour abundant country like India there is no reason for keeping average wage rate higher than the average productivity of the workers. Presently the wage rates in the organised sectors are higher than the average productivity and relatively higher wage rates have detrimental effect on the production and exports of labour intensive products in case of which India has a comparative cost advantage. Moreover, higher wages also encourage the producers to adopt capital intensive technology, resulting in less opportunities for the employment of unskilled and uneducated workers. It is a general feeling among the business community that the employers must have the power to retrench workers and to close down the unviable production unit if it becomes necessary, otherwise it would be very difficult to compete effectively with other firms across the globe in an open environment. But in India labour laws provide complete job security to employees in the public sector. Even to the private sector there are restrictions on fire workers. The workers cannot be removed from jobs if their employment period in the concern exceeds over 240 days without the approval of the Labour Ministry. Thus for attracting higher domestic and foreign investment, some changes in these rigid labour laws are considered to be necessary. A National Renewal Fund has been set up to provide compensation to the workers if they become unemployed as a result of closing unviable production units. The workers retrenched from these units must be retrained so that they become capable of getting employment in other expanding sectors.

Finally, the reservation policy for small scale industries is another barrier in the way of achieving higher growth rates in India. It is true that small-scale industries are helpful in generating more employment opportunities in the short run but actually medium and large-scale firms provide greater opportunities because reinvestment rate of capital of such firms is generally higher than those of small firms. Also the reservation policy is harmful for efficient small firms which have the potential to grow at a faster rate and become significant exporters. Expansion of small-scale firms which are labour intensive would generate more employment opportunities. Thus significant changes in the present reservation policy can bring more efficiency in the resources used in these industries.

Supporters of the new economic policy point out that this policy has benefited the Indian economy in many respects. It has helped in increasing the flow of direct foreign investment and foreign exchange earnings. Besides this the rate of inflation has come down significantly in the past decade. Reforms allow readjustment of major macroeconomic imbalances of the economy and thus raise efficiency in the utilisation of resources. These will expose the Indian industrial sector to global competition and also provide access to foreign capital, technology and market access. New economic policy will also enhance the efficiency of the economy through better management, improvement in technology and closure of inefficient Public sector units. But reforms also pose certain challenges to the government. India has to keep its fiscal deficit at a low level. Red tapism, inefficiency, corruption, trade union activities etc. pose certain problems in the implementation of reforms. Since continuation of early gains in growth of various sectors depend on rapid expansion of the supporting infrastructure sector, development of this sector is another challenging job. Though some improvement in the infrastructure is done since 1991, but foreign investors still feel that India's infrastructure is poor both in quality and quantity. So, there is a desperate need to shift expenditure towards power, roads, ports, communication, education and health.

Firstly, power is a crucial element of infrastructure. But in India the gap between demand for and supply of power has increased due to the growth of industrial sector. Even in the household sector the shortage of power has affected a large number of poor people who cannot afford to buy generators or other alternative sources of electricity. The State Electricity Boards in India are incurring heavy losses especially due to power theft and the provision of providing free electricity to the farmers. To improve this situation and for providing adequate and regular power to the people, adequate amount of private investment is not coming forward because State Electricity Boards do not permit charging economically viable electricity rates from the people. So, in order to solve this problem some sort of agreement between Central and State governments about the pricing of electricity should be worked out.

Secondly, to encourage business at international level, ports capacity for handling export and import of goods need to be enhanced. Building up of adequate number of warehouses near the ports can help maintaining the strict delivery schedules for export destinations which again is very important in increasing the volume of exports.

Thirdly, the shortage of transport facilities is becoming a major constraint to the development of agriculture, industry and trade. Density and quality of roads is positively correlated with development. Since India's railways are already running at full capacity level, further expansion of this sector is the pressing need of today. Indian trains running at long distances are usually behind their schedule and this causes a great deal of inconvenience to the businessmen and passengers. Due to slow speed of both passenger and goods trains. the time to transit considerably increases on long distances. India's railway budget had been in deficit for most of the years due to various reasons. Therefore, special attention needs to be paid in this direction to promote business and to benefit general public. The freight rates and fare rates can be increased gradually so as to obtain higher revenue for further development of this sector.

Fourthly, adequate and reliable telecommunication facilities are indispensable for businessmen. No doubt, significant improvement in this sector has been done during the last few years. With the introduction of New Telcom Policy in 1999, the government has decided to introduce competition in this sector. Charges for both national and international calls have been reduced considerably and now the mobile services are not only available in cities but also in rural areas. Adequate telephone lines and telephone exchanges need to be set up for providing better services in rural areas.

Fifthly, the need for enhancing Human Capital is another pressing need. Education and health are the important elements of infrastructure in this context. For rapid economic growth people must be educated and trained to handle their jobs efficiently and effectively. In this field India is much far behind and the general education which people are getting from educational institutions is not relevant according to requirements of present socio-economic set-up of the country. So priority must be given to provide relevant education to the people which could help them in adjusting in the real environment. The quality of education in the schools, especially in the rural areas must attract the attention of policy makers.

To become productive and efficient the people should be in good health. For this purpose provision of sufficient public health facilities should be within the reach of the people. More hospitals should be opened in backward areas and they should provide medicines to the poor at subsidised rates.

Finally, on the fiscal front, corrective measures like cutting down current expenditure and better realisation of taxes through avoiding tax evasion are urgently needed. Fiscal deficit as a percentage of GDP and public sector fiscal deficit must be brought down. Not only this will release resources for productive investment, but will also increase the creditability of the Indian government in the eyes of international lending institutions and the potential foreign investors. For bringing the impact of different economic reforms to the policy makers, a detailed data at disaggregated level regarding all important variables must be made available to the researchers. This also brings out the necessity of collecting data and analysing this through great amount of high quality of research. At present a majority of Indian people are ignorant about the rationale behind reforms i.e. how these reforms would help not only rich but also the poor people in both rural and urban areas. The policy makers and academicians together must hold rallies and seminars throughout the country to bring awareness among the people regarding these economic reforms.

On the subject of economic reforms, two national seminars were conducted. The first seminar entitled 'Emerging trends in Indian Economy' was held on 28-29 March, 1997 at Guru Nanak Dev University, Amritsar and the second Seminar with a title 'Economic Reforms in India' was held on 3-4 April, 1998 at Layalpur Khalsa College, Jalandhar. In both the seminars, research papers on different aspects of economic reforms were invited from renowned scholars working with prestigious institutions of India. Out of three dozen papers, seventeen scholarly papers were selected to be included in this volume entitled 'Economic Reform and Development'. Broadly, this volume has been divided into three sections. Section I contains research papers on Globalisation, trade and investment. Papers which examine the impact of economic reforms on employment, poverty and regional disparities are contained in section II, and papers relating to infrastructural development and institutional reforms are kept in section III.

Arun Ghosh in his paper studies the implications of India's economic reforms in the context of globalisation involving free flow of scientific knowledge and technology, free movement of capital, labour, goods and services across countries. He pinpoints that the efforts of modern day globalisation would be to draw up the same rules of game for highly unequal partners. Trade Related Intellectual Property Rights (TRIPS) will protect the latest technology but these can prove to be the most harmful in the matter of patenting of life 'forms' which could lead to a great harm to millions upon millions of farmers across the world, by denying them the use of new varieties except at prohibitive prices. While GATT (1945) was set up to promote development through trade and to encourage competition, the Trade Related Investment Matters (TRIMs) agreement under GATT (1994) purports to encourage monopolies by ruling out interventions in the matter of amalgamation, mergers and anti-trust laws. The author also mentions that the globalisation of agriculture would make agricultural prices in India susceptible to wild fluctuations especially in case of staple crops and this would cause immense harm to millions of farmers. In 1994 GATT agreement, the rules of game have been changed by the highly advanced industrialised countries entirely in their favour and new issues like 'Human Rights', environmental pollution and other new GATT rules are calculated to work against the interest of developing countries. The author is of the opinion that we should rely on our domestic savings and technology to develop the country instead of borrowing short-term loans for long-term investments.

Atul Sarma in his paper entitled 'Restructuring of Public Enterprises in India' discussed the need and the constraints in the way of privatising public sector units in India. It is pointed out that it is the over-regulation and consequent operational rigidities that have led to the dismal performance of public sector enterprises. These enterprises in India are essentially driven by resource crunch and the disinvestment has been resorted to as a mode of privatisation as well as an instrument of fiscal adjustments. It is observed that while privatisation has been taken up as a part of the reform process, its pace has been very slow due to a number of reasons. In the process of restructuring public sector enterprises, Government of India has established a National Renewal Fund (NRF) to redeploy, retrain and rehabilitate the workers displaced in this process. But due to shortage of funds, a large number of people displaced could not adequately be retrained and redeployed, which has led to the skepticism in the privatisation of Public sector enterprises. Several existing legal acts are also responsible for impeding the process of privatisation. Also non-viable firms cannot sell their real estates under the urban ceiling act to settle their claims due to their creditors and make it easier for them to exist. Trade unions representing labour interest has a great source of income and job security. Even the consumers of the products of public enterprises have developed vested interest in the continuation of public enterprises for some of their products being available at subsidised prices. The author states that the cross-country experience suggests that ownership does matter and that for most activities it is not possible to achieve the same level of efficiency in a state owned enterprise as it is possible in a private enterprise. In the face of engulfing internal debt problems, the suggestion that the proceeds mobilised through disinvestment/ privatisation should be directed towards retiring internal debts has considerable merit. A large allocation of funds for education and health should be done by eliminating wasteful government expenditure and by making the entire public sector more efficient.

K.N. Kabra and V. Upadhyay in their paper have attempted to assess the impact of SAP on the black economy. It is pointed out that so long as punishment/penalties are light and elusive and the symbiotic equation with the public authorities remain intact, the black economy would continue to thrive. In this context, an attempt has been made to examine the emerging state of black economy with specific attention to VDIS 1997, which may be regarded as an integral part of SAP.

It has been claimed that the VDIS had not only succeeded in generating unprecedented amounts of revenue for the government but also had been able to make significant dent in the black economy in the country. The tax collection under the VDIS 1997 was Rs. 10,050 crore. However, the authors argue that there has been a shortfall of Rs. 3,000 crore in the normal yield from income tax during 1997-98. It means that income tax payers have substituted VDIS 1997 for normal tax payment by as much as nearly 30 per cent. This reduces the big claims about the grand success of it in terms of revenue collection. The study also shows that the biggest disclosures have come from either politicians of ill-repute who did not have any identifiable source of legitimate income or from ex-civil servants. The corporate sector has, by and large, kept itself out of this scheme. The authors further argue that the VDIS 1997 is sure to signal a negative message to honest tax payers and bring down tax compliance significantly for many years to come.

Preferential trading is assuming increased significance day by day at the regional levels. The SAARC members are also striving to change from preferential trading arrangement to free trade area upto 2005 but what would be its implications for India. In his paper South Asian Preferential Trading Arrangement : Implications of Trade Liberalisation for India', I. N. Mukherji has dealt with this issue. He starts with laying emphasis on the need of preferential trading and gives a brief history of the South Asian Regional Grouping. Then the impact of the trade liberalisation on India's imports has been analysed by assuming first free imports; secondly fifty per cent reduction in tariffs and then trade liberalisation in practice. It has been found that trade liberalisation in India would not be the cause of concern and it is unlikely to increase imports to the level which may be troublesome for domestic business. In fact there will be modest trade creation. However, the loss in the custom revenue will be significant. Therefore, a step by step movement towards SAFTA should be undertaken. Besides, India's trade with its partners is of primary and intermediate products So, the processing of these products can lead to more value-added and hence very likely to offset the loss in the custom revenue. Apart from this selective approach to Trade Liberalisation has been recommended. This will lead to the enhanced trade creation and minimised trade diversion as products are likely to create more trade being liberalised at first.

Atul Sarma and P.K. Mehta in their paper 'Prospects of Agro-Exports to European Union in The Emerging Environment' evaluate the prospects of agro-exports to European Union (EU) in the changed scenario after signing GATT (1994). In the beginning they have discussed economic reforms in general and then agro-exports in particular. Analysing the trade environment in European Union, the authors argue that a higher prospect is foreseen by the exporters in the post-unified Europe. To counter the protectionism in various forms in European Union, quality improvement and technological upgradation is must. The picture of the growth of Indian trade with European Union is presented to be dismal. It is unfortunate that in the global imports of European Union in 1993, India's share was only 1.21 per cent, inclusive of the increase in the liberalised regime. As far as the composition of trade is concerned, it is concentrated on a few goods and as much as 90 per cent or more is contributed by ten out of twenty of one product categories. Whereas the exports of vegetable products to European Union were highly concentrated in just three groups viz coffee, tea, oilseeds, lac and gum etc. accounting for 90 per cant of trade in this category, the exports of the prepared foodstuffs have shown some diversification. It is also brought forth that the exporters may benefit from the reduction in subsidy to agriculture in the developed countries including European Union but many non-tariff barriers on the diverse grounds will have to be faced. So the export prospects depend on the responsiveness of the exporters to changing environment and emerging challenges in the European Union Market. Furthermore, as the bulk of Indian exports come out of smaller units, their problems should also be addressed so that they can produce the products of international standard.

Arun Kumar in his paper talks about the domination of Transnational Corporations (TNCs) in the current global scenario. Under new economic policy, to facilitate transnational companies in India, FERA has been greatly diluted and restrictions on repatriation of dividends and requirements of indigenisation are almost eliminated. It is argued that the mechanism of transfer pricing to boost the collaboration profits would be resorted to. Further the WTO is supposed to govern international trade regime but is redefining national laws to suit TNCs. It puts most Third World nations on par with the advanced nations in the matters of trade like market access and national treatment to international capital. The author also points out that the global scene is dominated by the TNCs and a substantial number of them originate in the advanced nations. Consequently, the interest of the latter is furthered by them. It is in this sense that the IMF and World Bank represent the interest of the global capital irrespective of whether or not this coincides with the interest of the country being advised. TNCs would also adversely affect research and development in the Third World countries. If polluting technologies and production relocate in the Third World and advanced technology and clean products in the advanced countries, competition amongst the Third World countries can be used to keep the prices of these goods low for advanced countries while the prices of advanced products can be kept high through monopoly over technology. Terms of trade would shift against the Third World and lead to a drain from these economies. Under the proposed Exit policy, millions of people from middle and lower middle classes are stated to lose jobs. This will immediately reduce demand in the market and deepen recession. Indian industry facing loss of markets, unable to compete globally and facing an uncertain investment climate in India has increasingly turned to trading and speculative activities in the share market. If this trend permits, deindustrialisation and unemployment would arise.

I.N. Mukherji in his paper emphasises the need for harmonising a common investment area in South-Asia. Sectoral patterns and sources of foreign direct investment in different South Asian countries have also been discussed. The author also emphasises that while trade complementarities between SAARC member-states are limited, considerable production complementarities exist among the member-states. This points to the potential for setting up joint ventures among SAARC member-states. It is also pointed out that the provision of more fiscal concessions on a competitive basis for favouring Foreign Direct Investment (FDI) is not the answer to attracting more FDI because it is more influenced by stable macro economic environment, stable political regimes, transparent FDI regulations permitting simplification of procedures and approval process, enlarged market and adequate infrastructural facilities. The working group on investment established by SAARC Chamber of Commerce and Industry made various useful recommendations relating to mobilisation of investment, foreign direct investment and infra-regional investment opportunities. Elements of investment harmonisation include fair and equitable treatment of investment, free reparability of returns, limited current account convertibility, avoidance of double taxation agreement and procedure for settlement of disputes.

In their paper 'External Sector Reforms in India: An Evaluation', Dhindsa and Sharma discuss various external sector reforms such as import licensing policy, the tariff structure, export promotion incentives, foreign investment etc introduced in the economy after 1991. It is pointed out that as a result of external sector reforms, there was an improvement in overall balance of payments situation and the real effective exchange rate did not show any depreciation in the post reform period. Due to decrease in fiscal deficit, current account deficit has also declined. Both foreign exchange reserves and foreign investment have gone up considerably during the 1990s. So far the impact of economic reforms on employment is concerned, it is found that the growth rate of employment is much lower in the post-reform period as against the pre-reform period. Further it is observed that the combined deficit of the centre and states is still very high and this must be brought down to a lower level. In order to achieve a higher growth rate of the economy, attention needs to be paid towards institutional reforms, amendments in labour laws, further reduction in custom duties and more employment generation.

Shri Prakash in his paper has examined the theoretical inter-relationship between new economic policy and employment. It is observed that the growth of employment has declined both in public and private sector since 1991, though the deceleration of employment growth has been much more rapid in public rather than private sector. It is further pointed out that the objective of full employment planned to be achieved by the year 2002; warrants the complete reversal of trend in operation. The trend reversal will, however, require the development of labour and knowledge intensive technology of production rather than to import technologies or to invite multinational companies to establish the production facilities based on modern technologies in India. The empirical results thus validate our thesis that the Indian economy under the new economic policy has recorded employment less growth, which has further casualised and marginalised the poor. The author points out that during the current phase of liberalization and globalization, industrial output has grown at much lower rate than the expected rates. The growth of income during this period has largely been the result of autonomous agricultural development. Fortunately the Agricultural sector has been left alone by the new policy regime except the partial or full withdrawal of fertilisers, power and water subsidies enjoyed till then by agriculture. It is in fact difficult to mitigate mutually interrelated unemployment, partial unemployment, low wage employment and poverty in a labour abundant economy like India through investment by multinational companies in industries. Organized industries account for an extremely low proportion of output and employment. Thus the accelerated development of agriculture, irrigation and small scale industries using labour intensive techniques of production can only alleviate the twin problems of poverty and unemployment.

G.K. Chadha in his paper studied the recent trends in non-farm employment in India. For this study the author uses comparable NSS data from several rounds to estimate the impact of new economic policies on rural/urban and male/female employment. It is found that the recent years provide a disappointing employment scenario for the rural workers in general and rural female workers in particular.

Whatever additional employment came their way was largely confined to agricultural sector. Employment expansion in the construction activities that occurred during 1983-1988 noticed decline during the 1990s. This decline is attributed partly to the slackening pace of private investment in rural areas and partly to the shift of these activities from rural to urban areas. Moreover, unskilled and uneducated female workers are not fit for the new jobs available in non-farm sector. Thus the rural females seem to be getting highly marginalized in the matter of education, training and skill formation. The author points out that under the changing regime of globalisation and competitiveness, the future job markets in the non-agricultural sectors are sure to pose more and more difficulties for the rural workers especially among the rural females. Unless public policy intervenes effectively to break the educational barriers of this group of rural females. most of them would remain unemployed and poor.

In his paper entitled 'New Economic Policy and its Impact on Employment and Poverty of Scheduled Castes—Some Observations' Sukhadeo K. Thorat has made an attempt to assess the impact of far reaching economic reforms on economic conditions of scheduled castes in India. This is done by looking at the trends in few important aspects namely employment, unemployment, poverty and employment under reservation. It is argued that the contraction of public expenditure consequent upon the reduction in aggregate demand will bring reduction in employment level and increase in unemployment rates. The statistics on unemployment rates during pre- and post-reform periods also support this observation. It is well known that growing public expenditure was in part mainly responsible for rapid employment growth in rural non-farm sector during 1980s. The banking sector where the process of reforms has been slower than the government and public sector undertakings, the decline is yet not visible. The study also reveals that after the introduction of new economic measures which are privatisation and reduction in the role of government, the employment of scheduled castes has declined both in absolute numbers and in proportions. The scheduled castes not only suffer from various market failures more extensively than others, but additionally they also suffer from the market failures which arise out of caste and untouchability based discrimination. The study implies that given this type of market failures, what is indeed required is more state intervention and easy access to labour, land and capital markets and access to various social services more open to the discriminated groups i.e. the scheduled castes.

The study by Sucha Singh Gill and Jaswinder Singh deals with the impact of economic reforms on the rural poors in Punjab. It has been argued that various reform measures like reduction of industrial protection, fertilizers, subsidies and public investment in agriculture, increase in the issue price of Public Distribution System and decline in the allocation of anti-poverty central schemes have far reaching implications for rural areas dominated by agricultural activities. The study also reveals that marketisation of hitherto state-oriented economic activities has created a difficult situation for the poor people. The impact of the reform process on employment of agricultural labourers and artisans is neutral while the impact of these reforms on consumption standard is adverse. The workers have reduced the consumption of certain items and even they stopped the use of costly items like pulses, sugar, edible oil, butter and meat etc, which in turn will adversely affect the quality of workforce i.e. the real determinant of the growth of the nation. Various public safety net programmes initiated by the government to minimise the social cost of these reforms have shown dismal performance due to certain factors like ad hocism. uncertainty and lack of awareness, laxity on the part of administration and virtual absence of voluntary associations in rural areas. In such a scenario it is contended that the poor people in rural areas expect a greater and better role from the government in the public safety nets.

In a comprehensive paper, Ashok Mathur deals with the issue of regional disparities in development and economic reforms in India. Starting with some background facts on the concerned area, the author contends that on the eve of independence, India was not only an economically backward economy but one which was characterised by glaring regional economic disparities. The trends in regional income have more or less been found to be the same in various states. However, as far as the sectoral composition of income is concerned, the regional disparities in the primary sector are on the rise mainly due to the impact of seed-fertiliser technology which was more successful in the already agriculturally better-off areas. Contrary to this, the regional disparities in the secondary sector are on the decline. There has been disparities in the regional poverty scenario as well. In case of infrastructure sector, the disparities are much higher in case of roads as compared to those of other areas. Author also evolves some ways to analyse the impact of economic reforms in context to these regional disparities. So far as the foreign investment and backward area development is concerned, it is not expected to yield very fruitful results. It is mainly due to the urban consumer bias and capital intensive nature of foreign investment. The implications of the devolution of finance resources to different states by planning commission and furnace commission have also been evaluated. It has been found that devolution by finance commission has been more progressive than that by the planning commission. In the end it is emphasised that state intervention has also some important role to play in curtailing regional disparities in the social and industrial spheres.

D.N. Rao in his paper analyses the impact of economic reforms on health and environment. He emphasises that AIDS is emerging rapidly as a serious health problem among certain sections of the population. Malaria is also re-emerging in many areas. The index of environmental quality has declined sharply in almost all cities and major towns of India over the years, mainly due to water and air pollution caused by various industries and vehicle emission. The author further argues that health is a state subject in Indian constitution and urban health comes under the purview of local bodies. In India health care delivery system had turned iniquitous when access was measured by utilisation of public health services because access is limited to the workers from the organized sector and the richer section of the society. The poor people have to satisfy largely with traditional types of medicines or self-medication. Primarily health centres generally lack sophisticated modern equipments, skilled manpower and adequate quantity of drugs. Faced with the general all pervasive resource crunch, the health sector has been advocating various reform measures such as imposition of user charges in public hospitals, privatisation of health care provision, introduction of private health insurance including permission of entry of foreign health insurance companies and removal of drug price control. But the author argues that imposition of user charges in a society with large number of poors is highly iniquitous and is against the public finance principle of ability to pay. The social cost-benefit analysis of imported outdated polluting technology has to be done much more alertly. The menace of vehicular pollution has to be controlled. Rao pinpoints that the economic reforms process has left the health sector rudderless and some concerted policy has to be developed in this area also.

V. Upadhyay in his paper has made an attempt to analyse the performance of transport sector and identifies the problems being faced by this sector in India. Besides this, a critical evaluation of the solutions suggested to solve the problems of transport sector has also been done.

The author finds that there has been a massive traffic growth in India in recent years especially in case of road sector, whereas the share of railways in the total traffic has been declining continuously. Despite being energy inefficient, polluting and unsafe mode, the road transport is the dominant form of transport for the people and goods in India. The railways consider their first priority to provide efficient passenger services as a result of which their freight operations suffer. A very high increase in the freight rates in the recent years has tended to increase the inflationary pressures in the country. It is realized that inadequate transport infrastructure both in rural and urban areas is one of the major constraints in economic growth of India. Author explores the alternative sources of finance for the development of this sector. The government is putting greater reliance on leased resources to finance development and expansion of rail network. But it is argued that the growing resources to lease financing is certain to increase the interest burden on railways. It is also important to note that Private sector does not seem to be interested about these schemes especially in railways. However, the considerable liberalisation of the provisions relating to the transport sector is expected to attract a number of private players in the transport sector including the foreign entrepreneurs.

Sukhadeo K. Thorat in his second paper 'Some Theoretical Considerations in Reforms of Rural Institutions in India' discusses the theoretical framework to explain the role of institutions. While describing the process of institutional change, the author points out that the researchers have tended to take one view or the other. One view is that the institutional change is viewed as lagged response to the growth of productivity. The other viewpoint maintains that the institutions rather the technical changes are the dynamic source of economic development. The author adds that institutions could play effective role in economic growth if they are cost effective, equitable in terms of access and are fairly just in the distribution of income gains from economic activities. It is also pointed out that significant reforms of various rural institutions in India is essential and the working roles of rural bureaucracy and various other organisations and bodies need to be changed in such a way that its working becomes cost effective. Rural people should be provided information about various markets, particularly employment, credit, technologies, education etc. The rural organisations are generally controlled and used by powerful groups, the reforms or regulating provisions which would provide effective participation and also ensure due share to poor and deprived social group is, therefore, absolutely essential.

The paper by Karam Singh explores the role of Punjab agriculture in the future to meet the domestic demand for food products, potential for exports in the background of relative strength of Punjab agriculture in global economy, the scope for specialising high value commodities group in the agriculture and the infrastructure and institutional requirements to cope with the dynamics of challenges upcoming with the swings in the market scenario in the wake of domestic and global pressures and upbursts. The author is of the opinion that there is a scope for improving upon the average productivity at state level by raising the yield variability across districts, across villages and even across farmers. With liberalisation of Indian economy, the export competitiveness of its major agricultural commodities has also attracted the attention of policy makers and researchers. There is also a tremendous scope of value addition even in foodgrains, particularly of wheat products. The bread, buscuits and pasta products of wheat from outside Punjab have a better share of Punjab's domestic market than these products being processed to a large scale in Punjab. He further adds that entrepreneurial oriented high value exports include honey, mushrooms, Floriculture products, Vegetables and Fruits. We need to identify the pockets for each of these potential products and develop the necessary infrastructure and institutions to enhance the profitability, quality standards and export competitiveness for such products. It is also stressed that the growth of rural and non-farm sector is driven primarily by agricultural growth. The author also identifies certain areas for public investment in Punjab. The depressing situation of water resources, ecological degradation through the emergence of new pests and diseases, increased use of chemicals and unscrupulous disposal of agricultural and industrial wastes need urgent public attention.

Section-I

GLOBALISATION, TRADE AND INVESTMENT

1

INDIA'S ECONOMIC REFORMS IN THE CONTEXT OF GLOBALIZATION

Arun Ghosh

There is urgent need today to understand, first, the nature of world economic developments; and secondly, the pattern of economic reforms in India, with a view to ensuring that policy making and economic reforms in India are undertaken in India's interests. Some of the emerging compulsions in the light of which some compromises and adjustments may also become necessary would also be noted.

Economic Reforms

To begin with, it is necessary to understand what precisely the present contours of 'economic reforms' in India are, because there is considerable vagueness in statements made in this regard even by people in responsible positions. 'Economic reforms' relate to both 'external policies' and 'internal policies'; and they should be carefully distinguished (even though their effects are not always mutually exclusive).

Internal Economic Policy Reform

Let its first take up 'internal reforms'. These, again, can be classified into diverse types of reforms. For example, one could consider the following broad classification:

(a) 'Debureaucratization'—giving up 'discretionary controls' is the first (major) type of policy one can discuss in the context of economic reform. No one would object to the process of debureaucratization and the elimination of 'discretionary control'. As far back as 1979, the 'Committee on Controls and Subsidies' (of the Government of India) had recommended easing out of industrial 'licensing' and similar controls. All rigid, bureaucratic price and other controls would fall under this category.

(b) Frequently, this definition is extended, especially by the World Bank (and others influenced by what is usually described as 'neoliberal' economic thought), wherein public investment (even for infrastructure development) is decried. Under the philosophy of *laissez faire* and 'minimum government' as the best, in vogue especially after the advent of Ronald Reagan in the USA and Margaret Thatcher in Britain, even the World Bank (set up as the International Bank for Reconstruction and Development, and attuned in the past to lending to governments for infrastructure development) has now got used to the idea and concept of leaving all investment decisions to 'market forces, thereby discounting and discouraging the very process of planning. Indeed, the World Bank has late been urging the 'unbundling' of infrastructure ostensibly with a view to introducing competition, but in reality with a view to privatization of infrastructure facilities—an essentially 'ideological' stance. Of late, thus philosophy has been gaining ground in India, and has been treated as an essential ingredient of economic reform. One should add that the present 'Structural Adjustment Programme' (SAP) initiated by the World Bank has, in practice, gradually expanded, and now falls under this category, even though obviously the initial objectives of the SAP were different. The Structural Adjustment Policies initiated by the World Bank have been widely debated; and an early study, brought out by the Max Muller Bhavan and the HIVOS of Bangalore (1995) brings out the problems and internal contradictions between the 'objectives' of policy and the 'instruments' of policy adopted, succinctly. (See References). It is unnecessary to go over the entire spectrum of arguments here, to note that of late 'Structural Adjustment' is an integral part of the 'neoliberal' approach, leaving all economic decisions to the 'market forces'. The best recent exposition of both this philosophy and the consequent travails of developing countries—forced to adopt such policies—is given in a recent book by Biplab Dasgupta (1998).

(c) There is a third element of economic reform, which, in fact, was the genesis of the 'economic reform' programme initiated in India in June 1991. This relates to 'stabilization' of the economy, and is essentially concerned with the attainment of 'macroeconomic balance' in the economy. When India ran into a foreign exchange crisis in the summer of 1991, the IMF lent foreign exchange support, and one of the 'conditionalities' was 'stabilization' to be achieved through macroeconomic balance in the economy—essentially through government expenditure control but also involving monetary and credit policies, tax policies, etc. Significantly, this objective was soon forgotten in the light of the World Bank thrust for SAP; and indeed, more fundamental policy changes were introduced even though they were contrary to the objective of 'stabilization'. Perhaps one should also add that the past record of IMF intervention in bringing about 'stabilization' in developing countries has not been very happy. Indeed. even internal IMF appraisal brings out that barring, one or two exceptions, IMF intervention in some sixty odd countries has led to only deterioration in the economic condition in these countries, and as Biplab Dasgupta has pointed out, once in the grip of the IMF/ World Bank, developing countries have, in the past, seldom come out in a viable economic condition.

(d) Finally, again, as a part of SAP, diverse other types of policy changes have been introduced, in keeping with SAP objectives, and more particularly, in tune with the emerging philosophy of 'minimum government' and that the 'market knows best'. 'Economic reforms', which commenced with focus on 'debureaucratization' of the economy, and the progressive reduction of 'discretionary controls', has now taken on a totally different aspect, namely, that of SAP objectives, and more particularly, in tune with the emerging philosophy of 'minimum government' and that the 'market knows best'. 'Economic reforms', have now, taken on a totally different approach, namely, that all government intervention in the economy is 'pernicious'. It is forgotten that — no matter that policies are pursued — even 'non-intervention' (by government) is essentially tantamount to 'intervention' for the maintenance of the *status quo,* in a situation of extreme inequalities in the distribution of resource power and of income.

External economic policy reforms also fall into several distinct categories. These may be very briefly divided into :

(a) Trade liberalization, involving the gradual elimination of quantitative import restrictions and reduction of import duties, as well as the removal of export controls; and
(b) Liberalization of capital flows. This aspect, in turn, relates to two types of liberalization of capital flows: one of FDI and the other of short term capital flows.

Both these aspects would need to be discussed. Before doing so, however, it is necessary to explain the different aspects of 'globalization — as it is currently being pursued.

What is 'Globalisation'

There is, again, a great deal of misunderstanding in regard to the issue of 'globalization', and it may be useful to spell out different aspects of 'globalization', which are :

(a) Globalisation of 'knowledge' by way of free flow of not only scientific knowledge but also of technology across the world; for the history of the Industrial Revolution was essentially the history of inventions/innovations being copied— and production technology replicated — in what are now developed countries; and in Japan, 'reverse engineering' was freely practiced, with foreign engineers being employed initially to introduce the latest technological innovations borrowed from the West. The Japanese experience has been carefully documented by many different writers; an excellent comparative study is given by K. Ohkawa (1985);
(b) Free movement of labour across countries, a principle

universally followed until the second world war, but now totally banned; and highly selectively immigration allowed—temporarily—where labour shortage calls for the import of cheap, foreign labour;

(c) Free movement of capital which, until lately, consisted mainly of investment capital (or Direct Foreign Investment or DFI), but which now covers 'convertibility on capital account' making for large movements of short term capital — in enormous magnitudes — across borders; and

(d) Free movements of all goods across countries, for which there now exist serious restraints, not only in developing countries facing both teething problems as well as balance of payments problems, but also in highly developed countries, under all manner of subterfuges the latest being 'Human Rights' — *i.e.* the use of child labour and the use of low paid labour; possible danger to the 'environment' of production processes employed in newly developing countries; perceived health hazards and quarantine requirements (including 'packaging' specifications which are imposed primarily for 'protecting' domestic industry); and protection in the name of 'transition'—as in the case of Multi Fibre Arrangement—protection in the guise of anti-damping duties, etc.; and

(e) Of late, the diffusion of just one 'culture', including food habits even by way of 'junk foods' and drinks through the power of advertisement; through satellite television, and through means of very rapid communication through the telex, the 'fax' machine, 'e-mail', *et al.*, making the whole world 'conform' to just one pattern of life and thought.

Indeed, in a sense, because of recent developments in communications technology (as well as the speed of transport), the world can be truly described today as a 'global village'. The world is globalized today, whether one likes it or not, and local cultural mores are under threat. And yet, there is no, 'globalization' of either 'knowledge' or capabilities or 'incomes'.

And in that sense the world is deeply divided, not only politically but also economically. As stated earlier, there is no free migration of labour from one country to another. There are diverse entry restrictions in the matter of 'cheap imports' from developing countries. At the same time, the laws and practices, even the cultural mores of developed countries are taken as sacrosanct, to be imposed universally. The result is a deep division in the world, between the 'haves' and the 'have-nots', with a coalition of the 'haves' across national borders. The danger of a 20:80 divide in the world — with only some 20 per cent of available workers sufficing to produce all the material output required in the world—has been brilliantly outlined by Hans Peter Martin and Herald Schumann—Vienna and Berlin Bureau Chiefs of *De Spiegel*—recently (1997).

In one sentence , the effect of modern day 'globalization' would be to draw up the same rules of the game for highly unequal partners. It is as though a child were being asked to run a race against an adult; and this is the more piquant because the child is not to be allowed even access to 'knowledge'.

Importance of Trade and other Exchanges

Before commenting on specific issues, one point needs to be emphasized. In principle, all trade should be useful, and should benefit all participants. Just as division of labour within a country is likely to increase labour productivity and therefore output, so also international division of labour should help to increase world output, and therefore welfare, across the world.

Yet, the gains from trade are never equal; in particular, exchanges between unequals is fraught with grave danger. Alfred Marshall (1879) pointed out long ago the circumstances why, in real life, the gains from trade are never equal. Just as a cultivator who is forced to mortgage his produce to the money lender may gain nothing from the enforced exchange, just as there is no 'free' bargaining between a 'bonded' worker and his master, the highly disparate 'command over resources makes for unequal exchanges between those who have holding power and those who do not. The same principle applies, in different degrees, in regard to trade between nations where the ground rules for exchanges have been devised by one group of countries, to the detriment of the interests of other countries.

The above is particularly relevant in the context of the rules under the new GATT (1994), and the WTO which is supposed to enforce the new rules of the game in regard to all international exchanges.

A Word about the WTO

A brief word is necessary here in regard to the thrusts under the new GATT Agreements, signed on 15 December 1994 (which has come into effect from 1 January, 1995). The present essay is not directly concerned with the devastatingly one-sided Agreements which have been forced down the throats of developing countries, by the OECD countries generally and the USA in particular. Yet, they are relevant for any study of the contemporary world.

Some elementary features of the new trade rules now to be overseen by the WTO must be narrated here, because they represent the 'pernicious' nature of the new terms and conditions of 'globalization' which are to the detriment of all developing countries.

The new GATT may be summed up briefly as follows. Apart from focussing on the dismantling of 'trade barriers', the new rules focus on:

(a) Trade Related Intellectual Property Rights (TRIPS);
(b) Trade Related Investment Matters (TRIMs);
(c) General Agreement on Trade in Services (GATS);
(d) New dispensations in the matter of Agriculture;
(e) The Disputes Settlement Understanding; and
(f) New thrusts under the aegis of the WTO, calculated to help the industrially developed countries to exploit the resources and the markets of developing countries.

As already stated, the issue of the WTO is not directly within the scope of this essay. And yet, it is impossible to discuss the issue of 'globalization' and India's 'economic reforms' without at least some rudimentary understanding of the issues relating to the WTO.

The world had long recognized patent rights' of inventors/innovators, through the WIPO (World Intellectual Property Organization) which had been sanctified by the Paris and the Berne Conventions. But, by dragging this issue under the jurisdiction of the WTO, in effect what has happened is to replace private rights as International Legal Rights; and the rules of the game have been so framed as to deny developing countries access to 'knowledge'. The effect is bizarre; while the GATT is supposed to increase trade competition, the TRIPS encourages and fosters monopolies. Indeed, what is ironical is that while developed countries blame developing countries for environmental pollution—in fact, the truth is that today the USA alone accounts for 80 per cent of the CO_2 emissions in the whole world—the latest technologies which would help production processes to become less pollutive of the environment, are protected by TRIPS, and are priced beyond the reach of developing countries. Indeed, the TRIPS has the most pernicious impact in the matter of patenting of 'life forms' which is morally and ethically unacceptable, is violative of the UN Convention on Bio-Diversity, and would—if accepted in the form being pressed by developed countries—lead to enormous harm to millions upon millions of farmers across the world, by denying them the use of new seed varieties (except at extortionate prices), which will just not renew themselves, making the farmers dependent on seed imports at monopolistic prices, annually.

The TRIMS Agreement purports to lay down new rules of the game in the matter of the flow of capital; and while TRIMS purports to extend 'national treatment and 'Most Favoured Nation' treatment to all foreign investors, there are also provisions whereby *no conditions* are to be attached on any foreign investment (either by way of indigenisation or export commitment or payment restrictions or any other condition). In fact, foreigners are to have access to all sectors of the economy (except those specifically listed as excluded for reasons of national security); and capital should have total freedom of entry or exit.

In other words, no developing country can be allowed to *plan* investments; all investments must be "market determined"; and TNCs must have free entry/exit facilities in all countries.

Additionally, the OECD countries had circulated (in 1995) a draft of a Multilateral Agreement on Investment which purported, additionally, to abolish all has against amalgamations, mergers, all anti-Trust laws, in fact all provisions in the Company Law which may somehow restrict the free flow of foreign investment funds, no matter how invested. In other words, while GATT (1948) was set up to promote development through trade, and to encourage competition, the TRIMS Agreement under GATT 1994 purports to encourage monopolies, by ruling out interventions even in the matter of amalgamations, mergers, anti-Trust laws.

The GATS was specifically introduced (by US intervention) because, since the eighties, while the USA has been losing competitiveness in ordinary manufacturing activity, it has become highly efficient in services, especially financial services, owing to its leadership in 'information technology'. And, to the extent that the 'services market' is also to be thrown open, it redounds adversely on developing countries and their interests; although migration of labour is no longer possible, 'service' providers—as defined under the new rules—must be given access by all countries.

In the matter of Agriculture, a number of new guidelines have been introduced, "globalizing" agriculture; not only setting shunt (of 10%) on the totality of all subsidies (direct and indirect) but also enforcing (a) reductions in existing tariff levels in a manner calculated to permit developed countries to retain high tariff levels on agricultural imports; (b) ruling out quantitative import restrictions which had been used by developing countries to ensure 'food security', and security of at least minimum farm incomes; (c) ruling out public procurement (except at 'market prices' and through global tendering), thereby ruling against the setting of procurement prices and State purchases domestically, in the interest of food self-sufficiency; and finally, (d) "market access" (for imports from the world) upto 3 per cent of the total output (of, say, the totality of foodgrains).

The 'globalization' of agriculture would make agricultural prices in India susceptible to the (rather wild) fluctuations in prices of most staples; and would thereby cause immense harm to the 115 million farmers (as per the 1991 Census) in India. The conditions laid down would be prejudicial to the interests of the bulk of the population in a primarily peasant economy.

The new Disputes Settlement Understanding has also been drawn up in a manner calculated to help the strong and rich countries, to the detriment of the interests of all developing countries.

Finally the "new issues" now being raised—before the participating countries have had time to settle down to the new regime—relate to issues such as 'Human Rights' (and trade discrimination in order to enforce Human, Rights); environment pollution; public procurement (which is questioned as a "monopoly" and a "non-transparent" trading act), though the overall system actually helps to promote monopolies through TRIPS and TRIMS; and several other similar "new thrusts". All in all, the new GATT rules to be overseen by the WTO, are calculated to work against the interests of all developing countries.

How the WTO Issues are Relevant

How are the above thrusts under the WTO—the new "club" of the rich, powerful industrial countries—relevant to the present essay? These are the ground rules for globalization. There is no sharing of knowledge, no free movement of labour. Yet, there must be free movement of capital. There must also be diverse rules of trade and exchanges which impinge on the interests of newly industrializing countries. Even investment priorities cannot be laid down by developing countries; all investments must be 'market determined'. Article XVIII of GATT (1948) specifically allowed developing countries to impose trade restrictions for "economic development" and for balance of payments reasons. These provisions have now been watered down. GATT 1948 recognized the use of trade "for development"; this is no longer the case. In fact, even competition is no longer important: what is important is "market access". The rules of the game have been changed by the industrially developed countries entirely in their favour.

In other words, in a world of vastly divergent economic power, all are to be treated "equally". That. in itself, makes for inequality.

And, while the USA signed the Agreement subject to many provisos—the most important being that US laws can be changed only by the US Congress, and the WTO rules would apply in the USA only to the extent they are consistent with US laws—India (and other countries) have been forced to sign the Agreement without any provisos or preconditions. (To an extent, the Agreement is violative of the Indian Constitution insofar as subjects which are, under our Constitution, State subjects—like Agriculture—cannot be signed away by the Central Government unilaterally).

One way Globalization

Thus, when we keep talking of "globalization", and that we must globalize fast, we must understand "what shape the new international economic order is taking before we jump into "international waters". The WTO is just one facet—an important one—in this scenario. There are other, more sinister aspects to this emerging problem.

To understand the problem better, one must refer to the recent experience of the East Asian Tiger—South Korea—and the Southeast Asian NICs—Thailand, Malaysia and Indonesia—and see what lessons we can learn from their recent experience.

All four countries have shown remarkable growth between, say, 1960 and 1997. Indeed, they truly demonstrate the validity of the famous Akamatsu (1962) thesis of the "Flying Geese Paradigm" of development (See, Arun Ghosh, 1998). This essay cannot possibly go into details of that issue, nor of the devastation of all four economies in 1997 and early 1998 (Thailand, from mid 1996). Extensive literature exists today on: *(a)* the fantastic growth recorded by all these countries in recent years; *(b)* the structural transformation they have undergone; from primarily agricultural to essentially industrial countries; and *(c)* the (egalitarian) growth in incomes in all these countries until recently. And yet all four countries are now in deep distress. Indonesia considered by the London Economist as the most stable developing country, as late as November 1997—is the worst sufferer, with an annual inflation rate exceeding 30 per cent widespread unemployment; and the Indonesian Refinish at some 20 per cent of its value less than a year back. (With food riots already widely reported, with the recent political upheavals resulting from the widespread distress arising from rising unemployment and galloping food prices, Indonesia may even today after Sahara's exit—be compared to a volcano about to erupt). What happened to these countries? They all had domestic savings varying from 36 per cent of the GDP to 40 per cent of the GDP. One simple statistic will tell the story. Indonesia, with domestic savings at some 40 per cent of the GDP, had an investment rate of 46 per cent of the GDP. Indonesia depended on 'fickle', short term external capital, to push up the rate of growth of the economy.

And, that was the general pattern. All four countries borrowed abroad heavily; and their borrowings were largely short term. Foreign investors were glad to lead to these countries; and, in retrospect, if these countries were guilty–and they were guilty–of making long term investments with short term borrowings, the lenders were equally if not more culpable. Suddenly, investor confidence in Thailand suffered a shock; and the "contagion" spread quickly, fast to Malaysia, then to Indonesia, and finally to Korea.

Again, that story is not relevant this essay; what is relevant is the lesson for other developing countries. What is also relevant and interesting is the approach of the IMF, which has prescribed a medicine just the opposite of what was required. Two quotations are usefully given here in that context.

This is what the London *Economist* (24 January, 1998) has to say on the subject of "hot money flows":

> "Most economists are still wedded to the idea that international capital flows are desirable in principle... As the East Asian

> countries erased capital controls during the 1990s, they enjoyed huge inflow of foreign money, amounting to 5 to 10 per cent of GDP (see chart on text page), which went hand-in-hand with fast growth. With their subsequent crash, however, has come a recognition that freeflowing capital can throw up unforeseen difficulties. 'In retrospect', Alan Greenspan, the chairman of America's Federal Reserve; confessed last month, 'it is clear that more investment monies flowed into these economies than could be profitably employed at reasonable risk'. Investors are erratic, swayed by waves of excessive optimism followed by waves of excessive pessimism . ... These factors can mean that *market forces do not allocate capital perfectly around the world...*" (emphasis added).

Note the admission by the London *Economist,* the unfailing champion of the "market", that "market forces do not allocate capital perfectly".

Prof Jeffrey Sachs (Director of the Harvard Institute of Development) has pointed out that (a) the crisis in East Asia came from private markets, not from Government budgets; and that the problem started with "the irrational exuberance of mainly foreign investors"; and (b) that the "fiscal belt-tightening and high interest rates—a one-size-fits all remedy—are ill-suited for the economies of East Asia". Sachs has concluded that "The name of the game should be confidence mending, not orthodox austerity". The total irrelevance of IMF prescriptions indeed even of IMF analysis and predictions—is brought out vividly by Jayati Ghosh (1998), in her analysis of the IMF intervention in Thailand. Indeed, in Indonesia, tire IMF had to revise its prescriptions four times—and sign five Letters of Intent as to policies to be pursued—between 31 October 1997 and 7 August 1998, in less than ten months.

The Connection with India's Economic Reforms

Why have we spent so much time on the recent East Asian experience? That experience should sober us all, and make Indian economists think hard. And yet, the financial media in India has been pressing for more reform, more globalization, more inflow of external capital, indeed for Capital Account Convertibility, when that was the undoing of Thailand and Indonesia.

Three distinct points need to be made in this context. No one would object to doing away with "discretionary controls". In fact, reference has already been made to the High Level Committee on Controls and Subsidies (appointed by the Ministry of Finance), which had specifically recommended doing away with all discretionary controls, as far back as 1979.

But then, two other points stick out. First, infrastructure development must be the responsibility of the State; even Adam Smith the original exponent of the virtues of the market—was categorical on this point, when he said that "The third and last duty of the Sovereign or Commonwealth is that of erecting and maintaining those public institutions and those public works, which, though they may be in the highest degree advantageous to a great society, are, however, of such a nature that the profit could never repay the expenses to any individual or small number of individuals, and which it, therefore, cannot be expected that any individual or small number of individuals should erect or maintain" (Smith, 1776).

When India seeks foreign investment for the build-up of infrastructure, and when foreign investors seek a return of more than 30 per cent on their capital, what would be the price of infrastructure facilities after they are completed? And what will be the return to the economy after such investments? Economic theory (vide, Wicksell,1898, and Joseph Schumpeter, 1912) tells us that in a stationary state the rate of interest would be zero; and while Schumpeter goes on to examine the dynamics of development through "creative destruction" and innovation leading to the emergence of profits (and of interest on capital), Wicksell is more explicit: the rate of interest cannot be higher than the rate of growth of productivity that new investment would bring about. (In fact, that would give the ceiling of total return on capital, that is profit plus interest).

What is the rate of growth of the Indian economy that we expect? And what is the rate of interest/ profit expected by the foreign investor? The extortionate rates expected by them can be paid only be squeezing the savings of the rest of the economy.

It is herein that we derive two lessons. First, for infrastructure development, we cannot depend on private investment (let alone private foreign investment); and secondly, learning from recent East Asian experience, we must not borrow short term funds abroad for making long term investments.

Concluding Remarks

This essay has already become quite long. What conclusions do we draw? Insofar as economic reforms in India are concerned, while "debureaucratization" is all to the good, we cannot give up planning, we cannot do away with the allocation of investible domestic resources, we cannot but provide public funds for infrastructure development. Secondly, we cannot give up capital controls; and capital account convertibility would be a crazy policy to adopt. More importantly, we cannot woo foreign investors for infrastructure development, that would "drain away" the savings of the rest of the economy. Nor should we borrow short term funds for long term investments.

Human memory is short. In 1991, the foreign exchange crisis in India occurred principally because of the steady withdrawal of NRI funds (FCNR deposits) from October 1990 onwards. In fact, that is what broke the back of India's balance of payments, for the trade deficit had been brought down sharply, by early summer of 1991.

'Economic reforms', of course, extend way beyond the contours of policies discussed above. But, again, it is simply not possible to cover all aspects of the problem. Here, attention has been focussed on some of the most important elements. Once these essential issues are taken note of, other incidental policies emerge automatically.

One last point must be made, because it is an urgent one, only partially connected with the on-going economic reforms programme. That problem relates to the WTO and all its attendant thrusts. For that battle to be fought; India needs to canvass and obtain the support of all developing countries. And such support may still come—from Latin America on TRIPS, from Southeast Asia on TRIMS, from all peasant oriented agrarian countries on Agriculture—provided we are resolute, provided we canvass and mobilize support for a common cause.

But 'clarity' of ideas within the country, and importantly 'consensus' within the country is essential. There has been systematic 'disinformation' on these issues by both the financial media and, regrettably, even by the government in recent years. The new GATT Agreement of 1994 was never discussed even in the Parliament. There is need for a clearer perception in regard to these issues among the academia.

Finally, perhaps a last word is necessary. Each country must resolve to develop its people, through its own efforts. We need not be insular. In fact, in the modern world, it is impossible to be insular. We must benefit from knowledge and experience outside India. We must also 'trade" for there are resources (like 'oil') and other imports we need, for which we must pay for by the export of products in which we are competitive. Trade can and should be gainful to both parties. But, we must not only chart our own course, we must also pay the costs; we must rely on domestic savings to develop the country. We must build the technological knowledge base in the country through Research and Development efforts. And, going by the experience of nuclear and space technology, we do have the required manpower to do so.

REFERENCES

Bird, Graham (1995) : *IMF Lending to Developing Countries*, Routledge, London and New York.

Caulfield, Catherine (1996) Masters of Illusion : *The World Bank and Poverty Nations,* Macmillan, London

Chakravarthi, Raghavan (1990) : *Recoloniation : GATT Uruguay Round and the Third World,* 'Third World Network, Penang.

Des, B.L. (1996) : *Some Key Issues Relating to WTO*, Third World Network, Penang.

Dasgupta, Biplab (1998) : *Structural Adjustment, Global Trade and the New Political Economy*; Zed Books, London and Vistaar Publications, New Delhi.

Dhar, Biswajit (1995): *The Uruguay Agreements. A Critical Appraisal,* Research and Information System for Non-Aligned and other Developing Countries (RIS), New Delhi.

Dhar, Biswajit, Beena Pandey and Sachin Chaturvedi (1995) : 'Plant Variety Protection in India : An Appraisal', in *Biotechnology and Development Review,* No. 5, June-Dec.; RIS, New Delhi.

Drahos, Peter (1995) 'Global Property Rights in Information :'the Story of TRIPS at the GATT', in *Prometheus*, Vol. 13, No.1, June.

Economist, London: dt. 24 7.1997; double issue dt. 20.12.1997 and 2.1 1998, dt. 24.1.1998.

Feldstein, Martin (1998) : 'Asian Fallout The Heft's Errors', in *Foreign Affairs*, March-April.

Ghosh, Arun (1998) : *Asian Currency Turmoils and WTO Issues,* Centre for Study of Global Trade System and Development, New Delhi.

Ghosh Arun (1996): *The Proposed Foreign Investment Regime,* National Working Group on Parent Laws, New Delhi.

Glen, Biswajit, Beena Pandey and Sachin Chaturvedi (1995) : 'Plant Variety Protection in India: An Appraisal', in *Biotechnology and Development Review,* No. 5, June-Dec; RIS, New Delhi.

Martin, Hans Peter and Herald Schumann (1997): *The Global Trap*, Zed Books, London.

Ohkawa, K. and Ranis, G. with Messner, L. (Eds) (1985): *Japan and Developing Countries—A Comparative Analysis,* Basil Blackwell. Oxford.

Schumpeter, Joseph (1912) : *Theory of Economic Development* (translated from German by Redvers Opie), Oxford University Press, New York, 1961

Shobha Raghuraman, Heiko Sievers and Vinod Vyasulu (Eds) (1995): *Structural*

Adjustment, published for Max Mueller Bhavan and HIVOS, Bangalore, by McMillan India Ltd.

Smith, Adam (1776) : *An Inquiry into the Nature and Causes of the Wealth of Nations,* Everyman's Library, in two volumes, J.M. Dent & Sons, London, and E.F. Dutton, New York, 1910 (Reprint of 1931).

Wicksell, Knut (1898) : *Geldzins and Guterprise :* Translated from German by R.F. Kahn (1936) : *Interest and Prices : A Study of the Causes Regulating the Value of Money,* Macmillan, London, 1936.

2

RESTRUCTURING AND PRIVATISATION OF PUBLIC ENTERPRISES IN INDIA

Atul Sarma[1]

Within the broad contours of the public sector envisaged in the context of the planned development in India, public enterprises (PEs) have been used as a major instrument of policy. During the past four and a half decades of planning, the Union, state and local level governments established a large number of PEs of one form or another. These enterprises account for one-fourth of non-agricultural GDP and as much as 55 per cent of the economy's (excluding households) capital stock in 1993-94.[2]

Leaving aside its departmental undertakings, the Union Government had 246 enterprises (covering government companies and statutory corporations and six PEs under construction). PEs with a total investment of Rs. 1643.32 billion as on March 31, 1994. As against this, there were only five enterprises with an investment of Rs. 29 billion as on April 1, 1951.

Of 240 operational enterprises, 166 are enterprises manufacturing/producing goods while 74 are those rendering services. Fifty units among them are those sick units, which were taken over from the private sector.

Similar to the Centre, states have also set up a large number of PEs. However, the State Electricity Boards (SEBs) and State Road Transport Undertakings (SRTUs) are the largest ones among the State level public enterprises (SLPEs).

The total investment of SEBs of 25 states stood at Rs. 450 billion at the end of 1994-95. The total investment in the SRTUs was estimated at Rs. 39.84 billion at the end of 1994-95. The SLPEs have been set up to carry out diverse activities ranging from industrial development, agro-industries, mining and mineral development, fisheries development, small industries promotion, export promotion to financial assistance, and commodity trade and so on.

Road and power utilities apart, 25 states together established 954 SLPEs (against 51 in 1960) involving an investment of more than Rs. 382 billion as on March 31, 1992[3]. Many of the SLPEs are of small in size and operation. On the basis of the information available for 860 enterprises, these SLPEs include government companies (about 75 per cent), registered under the Indian Companies Act, those incorporated as public corporations, public authorities and statutory boards (about 10 per cent) and cooperative enterprises (about 15 per cent).

Considering the nature of activities, the SLPEs have been classified[4] into (i) Commercial enterprises, (ii) Commercial-cum-promotional enterprises, and (iii) Promotional enterprises. There were 436 SLPEs under the category (i), 312 under category (ii), and 127 under category (iii).

PERFORMANCE

To what extent the objectives with which the PEs were set up, have been achieved are not the subject of discussion here. Even so, a little discussion on returns on the massive investment made in the PEs is hugely relevant for the theme of the paper for more than one reason. First, the failure to realize adequate rate of return has contributed to the continued deterioration in fiscal balance of the government. Second the gap between investment requirement of the PEs and the availability of resources widened. More important, the fiscal crunch experienced since the late 1980s, has eventually driven restructuring and privatization of PEs in India.

The dismal financial performance of the Central PEs is shown in Table 2.1. Only 120 (75 manufacturing and 45 service) out of 240 operating enterprises earned positive net return of Rs. 97.21 billion in 1993-94. As against this, 117 (89 manufacturing and 28 service) enterprises incurred as much as Rs. 52.8 billion net loss in the same year. In aggregate 240 enterprises[5] earned net profit of only Rs. 44.35 billion which was a mere 2.78 per cent of the total capital employed and 8.11 per cent of the paid-up capital in 1993-94. What is more, among the profit making enterprises numbering 122, only 21 enterprises contributed more than one per cent of the aggregate net profit of the central PEs and these together made up 81.86 per cent of

Table 2.1 : Sectoral Performance Indicators of the Central Public Enterprises

Sl. No.	*Item*	*Manufacturing Enterprises*	*Service Enterprises*	*Total*
		1993-94	*1993-94*	*1993-94*
1.	No. of Operating Enterprises	166	74	240 $
1.1	Capital Employed (Rs. Cr.)	104120.6	55186.79	159307.4
1.2	Net Profit/Loss (Rs. Cr.)	3252.77	1182.01	4434.78
1.3	NP/Loss as per cent of CE (%)	3.12	2.14	2.78
1.4	Gross Profit/Loss (Rs. Cr.)	12109.87	6327.88	18437.75
1.5	Gross Profit as per cent of Capital Employed (%)	11.63	11.3	11.57
1.6	Paidup Capital (Rs. Cr.) #	45812.24	8860.65	54672.89
1.7	NP/Loss as per cent of Paidup Capital (%)	7.10	13.34	8.11
2.	Profit of Profit Making Enterprises (Rs. Cr.)	7599.45	2122.15	9721.6
2.1	No. of Enterprises	75	45	120
3.	Loss of Loss Making Enterprises (Rs. Cr.)	-4346.68	-940.14	-5286.82
3.1	No. of Enterprises	89	28	117
4.	No. of Enterprises neither making profit nor loss	2	1	3

$ In addition to these, six enterprises were under construction.
# Refers to as on 31-3-1994
Source : Public Enterprises Survey 1993-94, Vol. I, GoI.

the net profit earned by the profit making PEs. (Table 2.2) In terms of sectors, PEs belonging to Petroleum (55.2%) and power (14.2%) together accounted for about 70 per cent of the total net profit earned by the profit making PEs (Table 2.3) Thus if these two energy sectors are excluded, the net profit of the Central PEs was only around Rs. 13.5 billion

On the other hand, out of 117 loss making PEs, 79 have more than eroded their paid-up capital (Table 2.4) and 36 their total current assets (Table 2.5) through accumulated deficit. In several cases the accumulated deficit exceeded the paid-up capital many times. As a matter of fact, among 117 loss making PEs, there were only 7 PEs, which had no accumulated deficits.

The overall performance of SLPEs is still worse than the Central PEs. For example, the SEBs, which attracted large investments from states, instead of earning any return for states, made the states to bear ever growing commercial losses. Their combined losses were estimated to exceed Rs. 60 billion in 1994-95.[6] As a result, many of them are regular defaulters to the Central Power Agencies. For example, that

Table 2.2 : Relative Position of Profit Making Public Enterprises in their Aggregate Net Profit

Sl. No.	*Name of the Company*	*Net Profit (Rs. Lakh) 1993-94*	*Share in Total NP (%)*	*Cumu-lative Share*	*Rank*
1.	Oil & Natural Gas Corporation Ltd.	200939	20.563	20.56	1
2.	National Thermal Power Corporation Ltd.	105797	10.827	31.39	2
3.	Indian Oil Corporation Ltd.	77200	7.900	39.29	3
4.	Steel Authority of India Ltd.	54533	5.581	44.87	4
5.	National Fertilizers Ltd.	38911	3.982	48.85	5
6.	Mahanagar Telephone Nigam Ltd.	34416	3.522	52.38	6
7.	Gas Authority of India Ltd.	32054	3.280	55.66	7
8.	Hindustan Petroleum Corpn. Ltd.	30697	3.141	58.80	8
9.	Indian Railway Finance Corporation Ltd.	28352	2.901	61.70	9
10.	Northern Coal Fields Ltd.	22523	2.305	64.00	10
11.	Bharat Petroleum Corpn. Ltd.	21751	2.226	66.23	11
12.	Air India Ltd.	20190	2.066	68.30	12
13.	Power Grid Corporation of India Ltd.	18788	1.923	70.22	13
14.	Videsh Sanchar Nigam Ltd.	17610	1.802	72.02	14
15.	Shipping Corporation of India Ltd.	16758	1.715	73.73	15
16.	National Aluminium Company Ltd.	15672	1.604	75.34	16
17.	Power Finance Corporation	14906	1.525	76.86	17
18.	South Eastern Coal Fields Ltd.	13984	1.431	78.30	18
19.	Bharat Heavy Electricals Ltd.	13687	1.401	79.70	19
20.	Neyveli Lignite Corpn. Ltd.	11377	1.164	80.86	20
21.	Oil India Ltd.	9775	1.000	81.86	21
22.	Kudremukh Iron Ore Co. Ltd.	9391	0.961	82.82	22
23.	Indian Petro-Chemicals Corpn. Ltd.	8920	0.913	83.73	23
24.	Indian Telephone Industries Ltd.	8435	0.863	84.60	24
25.	Madras Refineries Ltd.	7939	0.812	85.41	25
26.	Rural Electrification Corpn. Ltd.	7110	0.728	86.14	26
27.	National Mineral Development Corporation Ltd.	7074	0.724	86.86	27
28.	National Hydro Electric Power Corpn. Ltd.	7054	0.722	87.58	28
29.	Cochin Refineries Ltd.	6825	0.698	88.28	29
30.	Central Coalfields Ltd.	6206	0.635	88.92	30
31.	Engineers India Ltd.	6031	0.617	89.53	31
32.	Housing & Urban Dev. Corpn. Ltd.	5902	0.604	90.14	32
33.	National Airport Authority Ltd.	5340	0.546	90.68	33
34.	M.M.T.C. Ltd.	5189	0.531	91.22	34
35.	Hindustan Aeronautics Ltd.	5031	0.515	91.73	35
36.	International Airports Authority of India	5022	0.514	92.24	36
37.	Rehabilitation Industries Corpn. Ltd.	3989	0.408	92.65	37
38.	Bharat Earth Movers Ltd.	3953	0.405	93.06	38
39.	Bongaigaon Refinery & Petrochemicals Ltd.	3791	0.388	93.45	39

Contd....

(Contd...)

Sl. No.	*Name of the Company*	*Net Profit (Rs. Lakh) 1993-94*	*Share in Total NP (%)*	*Cumu-lative Share*	*Rank*
40.	Cotton Corpn. of India Ltd.	3621	0.371	93.82	40
41.	Bharat Electronics Ltd.	3386	0.347	94.16	41
42.	Pawan Hans Ltd.	3357	0.344	94.51	42
43.	Western Coalfields Ltd.	3159	0.323	94.83	43
44.	Central Warehousing Corpn.	2907	0.297	95.13	44
45.	Garden Reach Shipbuilders & Engineers Ltd.	2509	0.257	95.38	45
46.	Telecommunications Consultants (India) Ltd.	2475	0.253	95.64	46
47.	State Trading Corpn. of India Ltd.	2264	0.232	95.87	47
48.	Hindustan Newsprint Ltd.	2247	0.230	96.10	48
49.	Hindustan Organic Chemicals Ltd.	2167	0.222	96.32	49
50.	Bharat Coking Coal Ltd.	2156	0.221	96.54	50
51.	Mahanadi Coalfields Ltd.	2127	0. 218	96.76	51
52.	Container Corporation of India Ltd.	2102	0.215	96.97	52
53.	Lubrizol India Ltd.	1914	0.196	97.17	53
54.	I. B. P. Co. Ltd.	1890	0.193	97.36	54
55.	Goa Shipyard Ltd.	1826	0.187	97.55	55
56.	Indian Railway Constn. Co. Ltd.	1695	0.173	97.72	56
57.	Bharat Aluminium Co. Ltd.	1527	0.156	97.88	57
58.	North Eastern Electric Power Corporation Ltd.	1476	0.151	98.03	58
59.	Balmer Lawrie & Co. Ltd.	1413	0.145	98.17	59
60.	Dredging Corporation of India. Ltd.	1267	0.130	98.30	60
61.	Fertilizers & Chemicals (Travancore) Ltd.	1241	0.127	98.43	61
62.	India Tourism Dev. Corpn. Ltd.	1221	0.125	. 98.56	62
63.	India Trade Promotion Organisation	1042	0.107	98.66	63
64.	Hindustan Vegetable Oils Corpn. Ltd.	1025	0.105	98.77	64
65.	Bharat Dynamics Ltd.	988	0.101	98.87	65
66,	Rail India Technical & Economic Services Ltd.	802	0.082	98.95	66
67.	Metallurgical & Engg. Consultants (India) Ltd.	705	0.072	99.02	67
68.	Electronics Corpn. of India Ltd.	648	0.066	99.09	68
69.	Mazagon Dock Ltd.	629	0.064	99.15	69
70.	National Backward Classes Finance & Dev. Corpn.	511	0.052	99.21	70
71.	Manganese Ore (India) Ltd.	508	0.052	99.26	71
72.	M S T C Ltd.	476	0.049	99.31	72
73.	Mishra Dhatu Nigam Ltd.	465	0.048	99.35	73
74.	Hindustan Zinc Ltd.	455	0.047	99.40	74
75.	National SC/ST Finance & Dev. Corpn.	409	0.042	99.44	75

Contd....

(Contd...)

Sl. No.	Name of the Company	Net Profit (Rs. Lakh) 1993-94	Share in Total NP (%)	Cumu-lative Share	Rank
76.	Ferro Scrap Nigam Ltd.	394	0.040	99.48	76
77.	Handicrafts & Handlooms Exports Corpn. India Ltd.	383	0.039	99.52	77
78.	Maharashtra Antibio. & Pharma. Ltd.	363	0.037	99.56	78
79.	Indian Oil Blending Ltd.	356	0.036	99.60	79
80.	Indian Renewable Energy Dev. Agency Ltd.	309	0.032	99.63	80
81.	ONGC Videsh Ltd.	283	0.029	99.66	81
82.	Andaman & Nicobar Isl. Forest & Plant. Dev. Corpn.	281	0.029	99.69	82
83.	Hindustan Teleprinters Ltd.	263	0.027	99.71	83
84.	Maharashtra Elektrosmelt Ltd.	239	0.024	99.74	84
85.	Hindustan Insecticides Ltd.	200	0.020	99.76	85
86.	Karnataka Antibiotics & Pharmaceuticals Ltd.	192	0.020	99.78	86
87.	Andrew Yule & Company Ltd.	186	0.019	99.80	87
88.	Central Mine Planning & Design Institute Ltd.	172	0.018	99.81	88
89.	National Film Dev. Corpn. Ltd.	140	0.014	99.83	89
90.	National Small Industries Corpn. Ltd.	131	0.013	99.84	90
91.	Hindustan Cables Ltd.	129	0.013	99.85	91
92.	Water & Power Consul. Services (India) Ltd.	126	0.013	99.87	92
93.	Bridge & Roof Co. (India) Ltd.	122	0.012	99.88	93
94.	Semi-conductor Complex Ltd.	121	0.012	99.89	94
95.	Central Cottage Industries Corpn. of India Ltd.	114	0.012	99.90	95
96.	Uranium Corporation of India Ltd.	104	0.011	99.91	96
97.	Modern Food Industries (India) Ltd.	73	0.007	99.92	97
98.	Bharat Heavy Plate & Vessels Ltd.	70	0.007	99.93	98
99.	Tungabhadra Steel Products Ltd.	69	0.007	99.94	99
100.	Bharat Refractories Ltd.	62	0.006	99.94	100
101.	Hindustan Latex Ltd.	54	0.006	99.95	101
102.	Projects & Equipment Corpn. Ltd. .	46	0.005	99.95	102
103.	Educational Consultants (India) Ltd.	45	0.005	99.96	103
104.	H. M. T. (International) Ltd.	44	0.005	99.96	104
105.	Biecco Lawrie Ltd.	43	0.004	99.97	105
106.	Southern Pesticides Corpn. Ltd.	40	0.004	99.97	106
107.	Indo Hokke Hotels Ltd.	36	0.004	99.97	107
108.	National Research Dev. Corpn. of India	35	0.004	99.98	108
109.	Bharat Bhari Udyog Nigam Ltd.	33	0.003	99.98	109
110.	Rajasthan Electronics & Instruments Ltd.	31	0.003	99.98	110
111.	Antrix Corporation Ltd.	23	0.002	99.99	111
112.	National Industrial Dev. Corpn. Ltd.	22	0.002	99.99	112

Contd....

(Contd...)

Sl. No.	*Name of the Company*	*Net Profit (Rs. Lakh) 1993-94*	*Share in Total NP (%)*	*Cumu-lative Share*	*Rank*
113.	HMT Bearings Ltd.	22	0.002	99.99	113
114.	Vignyan Industries Ltd.	18	0.002	99.99	114
115.	Lagan Jute Machinery Co. Ltd.	15	0.002	99.99	115
116.	Hooghly Printing Company Ltd.	14	0.001	99.996	116
117.	Hospital Serv. Consul. Corpn. (India) Ltd.	12	0.001	99.997	117
118.	Bharat Wagon & Engg. Co. Ltd.	11	0.001	99.998	118
119.	Food Corpn. of India	9	0.001	99.999	119
120.	Rajasthan Drugs & Pharma. Ltd.	3	0.0003	99.9996	120
121.	Indian Medicines Pharma. Corpn. Ltd.	3	0.0003	99.9999	121
122.	Air India. Charters Ltd.	1	0.0001	100.0000	122
	Total	977174			

Note : It includes only profit making enterprises.
Source : Public Enterprises Survey 1993-94, Vol.-I, GoI.

Table 2.3 : Relative Position of Profit Making Cognate Groups in their Aggregate Net Profit

Sl. No.	*Name of the Cognate Groups*	*Net Profit (Rs. Lakh) 1993-94*	*Share in Total NP (%)*	*Cumu-lative Share*	*Rank*
1.	Petroleum	394748	55.2	55.20	1
2.	Power	101356	14.2	69.37	2
3.	Financial Services	54610	7.6	77.01	3
4.	Telecommunication Services	52026	7.3	84.28	4
5.	Coal and Lignite	51145	7.2	91.43	5
6.	Industrial Dev. and Tech. Consultancy Services	23152	3.2	94.67	6
7.	Minerals and Metals	23104	3.2	97.90	7
8.	Trading & Marketing Services	12900	1.8	99.70	8
9.	Section 25 Companies	1721	0.2	99.94	9
10.	Tourist Services	394	0.1	100	10
	Total	715156			

Source : Public Enterprises Survey 1993-94, Vol.-I, GoI.

the NTPC's outstanding from the SEBs is a whopping Rs. 30 billion. Similarly, all the SRTUs taken together have also been showing rising commercial losses.

The remaining SLPEs, which too, involve massive states' investment of Rs. 385 billion till March 31, 1992 are also not in good health. These enterprises have been running into rising commercial losses, which stood at Rs. 8.45 billion during 1991-92.

Table 2.4 : Financial Position of the Loss Making Central Public Enterprises (Central Public Enterprises incurred loss during 1993-94)

Sl. No.	*Name of the Company*	*Total Paid-up Capital*	*Accum-ulated Deficit*	*Adjusted Paid-up Capital (1)-(2)*	*Accumulated Deficit as a % of Paid-up Capital : (%)*
1.	Elgin Mills Company Ltd.	110	30212	-30102	27465
2.	Weighbird (India) Ltd.	26	1931	-1905	7427
3.	Engineering Projects (India) Ltd.	800	57924	-57124	7241
4.	Cawnpore Textiles Ltd.	60	3765	-3705	6275
5.	Scooters India Ltd.	781	48112	-47331	6160
6.	Rehabilitation Industries Corpn. Ltd.	476	22806	-22330	4791
7.	Birds, Jute & Exports Ltd.	39	1110	-1071	2846
8.	Hindustan Steel Works Constn. Ltd.	2000	53398	-51398	2670
9.	National Bicycle Corpn. of India Ltd.	565	10551	-9986	1867
10.	Cycle Corpn. of India Ltd.	1187	21964	-20777	1850
11.	National Instruments Ltd.	608	9825	-9217	1616
12.	NTC (Gujarat) Ltd.	2484	39958	-37474	1609
13.	Bharat Process & Mechanical Engrs. Ltd.	486	7560	-7074	1556
14.	Artificial Limbs Mfg. Corpn. of India	197	2998	-2801	1522
15.	Bharat Ophthalmic Glass Ltd.	714	10155	-9441	1422
16.	Tannery & Footwear Corpn. of India Ltd.	1524	18742	-17218	1230
17.	NTC (Uttar Pradesh) Ltd.	3727	44844	-41117	1203
18.	NTC (Madhya Pradesh) Ltd.	3357	36553	-33196	1089
19.	NTC (West Bengal, Assam, Bihar & Ori.) Ltd.	4484	47302	-42818	1055
20.	U. P. Drugs & Pharma. Ltd.	92	968	-876	1052
21.	National Jute Manfs. Corpn. Ltd.	5480	54095	-48615	987
22.	Hindustan Shipyard Ltd.	7256	67920	-60664	936
23.	Brushware Ltd.	3	28	-25	933
24.	Bharat Brakes & Valves Ltd.	409	3688	-3279	902
25.	Braithwaite, Burn & Jessop Constn. Ltd.	193	1639	-1446	849
26.	Jute Corpn. of India Ltd.	500	4068	-3568	814
27.	Mining & Allied Machinery Corpn. Ltd.	3918	29566	-25648	755
28.	NTC (South Maharashtra) Ltd.	4805	35988	-31183	749
29.	Bengal Chemicals & Pharmaceuticals Ltd.	1371	9850	-8479	718
30.	NTC (Maharashtra North) Ltd.	5801	40719	-34918	702
31.	Triveni Structurals Ltd.	1024	6814	-5790	665
32.	Indian Airlines Ltd.	5515	36336	-30821	659
33.	Braithwaite & Co. Ltd.	1899	12300	-10401	648
34.	Smith Stanistreet. & Pharma. Ltd.	666	3868	-3202	581
35.	NTC, (Delhi, Punjab & Rajasthan) Ltd.	2843	16448	-13605	579
36.	Mandya National Paper Mills Ltd.	1775	10194	-8419	574
37.	Reyroll Burn Ltd.	150	852	-702	568
38.	National Bldg. Constn. Corpn. Ltd.	1995	10959	-8964	549
39.	Richardson & Cruddas (1972) Ltd.	1822	9859	-8037	541
40.	Nagaland Pulp & Paper Company Ltd.	4882	25040	-20158	513
41.	Orissa Drugs & Chemicals Ltd.	80	372	-292	465
42.	NTC (A. Pradesh, Karnataka, Kerala) Ltd.	5672	26122	-20450	461
43.	Burn Standard Company Ltd.	4240	18700	-14460	441

(Contd...)

(Contd...)

Sl. No.	Name of the Company	Total Paid-up Capital	Accum-ulated Deficit	Adjusted Paid-up Capital (1)-(2)	Accumulated Deficit as a % of Paid-up Capital : (%)
44.	Vayudoot	3617	15924	-12307	440
45.	British India Corpn. Ltd.	4466	19260	-14794	431
46.	Jessop & Co. Ltd.	3823	15676	-11853	410
47.	Bharat Pumps & Compressors Ltd.	2375	9618	-7243	405
48.	Rashtriya Pariyojna Nirman Nigam Ltd.	2984	11254	-8270	377
49.	Electronics Trade & Technology Dev.	500	1852	-1352	370
50.	North Eastern Regional Agri.Marketing	269	976	-707	363
51.	Bengal Immunity Ltd.	1674	5940	-4266	355
52.	Hooghly Dock & Port Engineers Ltd.	1430	4925	-3495	344
53.	Bharat Gold Mines Ltd.	5106	16908	-11802	331
54.	Fertilizer Corpn. of India Ltd.	64139	210563	-146424	328
55.	Mica Trading Corpn. of India Ltd.	808	2646	-1838	327
56.	Hindustan Fertilizer Corpn. Ltd.	68976	222785	-153809	323
57.	Projects & Development India Ltd.	3752	11719	-7967	312
58.	North Eastern Handicrafts & Handloom	137	407	-270	297
59.	Central Inland Water Transport Corpn.	8254	23941	-15687	290
60.	IISCO Ujjain Pipe & Foundary Co. Ltd.	300	840	-540	280
61.	Export Credit Guarantee Corpn. of India	5000	12183	-7183	244
62.	Heavy Engineering Corpn. Ltd.	28646	68992	-40346	241
63.	Hindustan Fluorocarbons Ltd.	1186	2790	-1604	235
64.	Indian Iron & Steel Co. Ltd.	38767	89270	-50503	230
65.	Damodar Cement & Slag Ltd.	1485	3381	-1896	228
66.	Tyre Corpn. of India Ltd.	6716	14366	-7650	214
67.	Hotel Corpn. of India Ltd.	4060	8351	-4291	206
68.	India Firebricks & Insulation Co. Ltd.	648	1280	-632	198
69.	Instrumentation Ltd.	2017	3695	-1678	183
70.	Bharat Leather Corpn. Ltd.	556	964	-408	173
71.	Utkal Ashok Hotel Corpn. Ltd.	114	185	-71	162
72.	Paradeep Phosphates Ltd.	12000	19286	-7286	161
73.	Hindustan Paper Corporation Ltd.	47935	68849	-20914	144
74.	Hindustan Prefab Ltd.	697	984	-287	141
75.	Tea Trading Corpn. of India Ltd.	1114	1497	-383	134
76.	Praga Tools Ltd.	1224	1455	-231	119
77.	Scooters India (Intrnal) gmbh W. Germ	8	9	-1	113
78.	Hindustan Photo Films Manfg.	15318	17031	-1713	111
79.	Delhi Transport Corpn.	0	137644	-137644	-
80.	Hindustan Antibiotics Ltd.	4034	4009	25	99
81.	Cement Corpn. of India Ltd.	39423	37720	1703	96
82.	Cochin Shipyard Ltd.	20118	19095	1023	95
83.	National Seeds Corpn. Ltd.	2062	1839	223	89
84.	Eastern Coalfields Ltd.	103900	89177	14723	86
85.	Visvesvarayya Iron & Steel Co. Ltd.	12692	8451	4241	67
86.	Central Electronics Ltd.	2545	1442	1103	57
87.	Madhya Pradesh Ashok Hotel Corpn. Ltd.	100	51	49	51
88.	Indian Additives Ltd.	1972	954	1018	48

(Contd...)

(Contd...)

Sl. No.	*Name of the Company*	*Total Paid-up Capital*	*Accum-ulated Deficit*	*Adjusted Paid-up Capital (1)-(2)*	*Accumulated Deficit as a % of Paid-up Capital : (%)*
89.	State Farms Corpn. of India Ltd.	2419	1153	1266	48
90.	Nepa Ltd.	6236	2892	3344	46
91.	Indian Drugs & Pharmaceuticals Ltd.	11550	5222	6328	45
92.	Mineral Exploration Corpn. Ltd.	5645	2528	3117	45
93.	Sambhar Salts Ltd,.	100	44	56	44
94.	Ranchi Ashok Bihar Hotel Corpn. Ltd.	72	29	43	40
95.	Rashtriya Ispat Nigam Ltd.	652754	260543	392211	40
96.	Madras Fertilizers Ltd.	10637	4116	6521	39
97.	C.M.C. Ltd.	1515	578	937	38
98.	NTC (Tamil Nadu & Pondichery) Ltd.	6091	1909	4182	31
99.	Hindustan Salts Ltd.	469	143	326	30
100.	Donyi Polo Ashok Hotel Ltd.	100	27	73	27
101.	Pyrites, Phosphates & Chemicals Ltd.	7467	2005	5462	27
102.	Assam Ashok Hotel Corpn. Ltd.	96	21	75	22
103.	Spices Trading Corpn. Ltd.	150	32	118	21
104.	Manipur State Drugs & Pharma. Ltd.	85	12	73	14
105.	Indian Rare Earths Ltd.	7122	665	6457	9
106.	Bharat Immunological & Biolo. Corpn.	1433	93	1340	6
107.	Hindustan Copper Ltd.	30520	1713	28807	6
108.	Coal India Ltd.	610484	23313	587171	4
109.	National Textile Corpn. Ltd.	45785	315	45470	1
110.	Konkan Railway Corporation Ltd.	47897	107	47790	0
111.	Sponge Iron India Ltd.	2808	0	2808	0
112.	Nuclear Power Corpn. of India Ltd.	220910	0	220910	0
113.	H.M.T. Ltd.	8773	0	8773	0
114.	Rashtriya Chemicals & Fertilizers Ltd.	55169	0	55169	0
115.	National Handlooms Dev. Corpn. Ltd.	1000	0	1000	0
116.	National Road Constn. Corpm. Ltd.	1000	0	1000	0
117.	Hindustan Vegetable Oils Corpn. Ltd.	771	0	771	0

Note :

1. Accumulated deficit is the sum total of losses over the years.
2. Net current assests/working capital is defined as total current assests minus current liabilities and provisions.
3. Total Current Assests :
   It includes raw materials, spare parts, work-in-progress, finished goods, other stores, sundry debtors, loans and advances, cash and bank balances/ deposits, other miscellaneous assests.

Table 2.5 : Asset Position of the Loss Making Central Public Enterprises (Central Public Enterprises incurred loss during 1993-94)

Sl. No.	*Name of the Company*	*Net current Assets/ Working Capital $ (lakhs)*	*Total Current Assets @ (lakhs)*	*Current Assets as a % of Working Capital (%)*
1.	Nagaland Pulp & Paper Company Ltd.	-14594	402	-3630
2.	Tannery & Footwear Corpn. of India Ltd.	-10615	443	-2396
3.	National Bicycle Corpn. of India Ltd.	-4358	219	-1990
4.	Delhi Transport Corpn.	-58834	2971	-1980
5.	Cycle Corpn. of India Ltd.	-8591	507	-1694
6.	Mandya National Paper Mills Ltd.	-6557	504	-1301
7.	Scooters India Ltd.	-30692	2606	-1178
8.	Rehabilitation Industries Corpn. Ltd.	-13687	1551	-882
9.	Hindustan Steel Works Constn. Ltd.	-28200	3534	-798
10.	Elgin Mills Company Ltd.	-14894	1982	-751
11.	Bharat Process & Mechanical Engrs. Ltd.	-4591	668	-687
12.	Bharat Ophthalmic Glass Ltd.	-6109	917	-666
13.	Hindustan Fertilizer Corpn. Ltd.	-143948	21740	-662
14.	Weighbird (India) Ltd.	-843	131	-644
15.	Utkal Ashok Hotel Corpn. Ltd.	-110	18	-611
16.	Vayudoot	-7020	1178	-596
17.	National Instruments Ltd.	-5539	973	-569
18.	NTC (Gujarat) Ltd.	-10127	2090	-485
19.	Bengal Chemicals & Pharmaceuticals Ltd.	-4163	966	-431
20.	NTC (Madhya Pradesh) Ltd.	-10446	2645	-395
21.	Fertilizer Corpn. of India Ltd.	-84137	29380	-286
22.	Smith Stanistreet & Pharma. Ltd.	-1250	454	-275
23.	Bharat Brakes & Valves Ltd.	-1704	830	-205
24.	NTC (West Bengal, Assam, Bihar & Orissa) Ltd.	-6563	3318	-198
25.	Richardson & Cruddas (1972) Ltd.	-4498	2466	-182
26.	NTC (Maharashtra North) Ltd.	-9134	5118	-178
27.	Artificial Limbs Mfg. Corpn. of India	-1144	712	-161
28.	Damodar Cement & Slag Ltd.	-2187	1396	-157
29.	Cawnpore Textiles Ltd.	-1074	727	-148
30.	Projects & Development India Ltd.	-6006	4638	-129
31.	Bengal Immunity Ltd.	-1421	1145	-124
32.	Bharat Gold Mines Ltd.	-4830	3961	-122
33.	Donyi Polo Ashok Hotel Ltd.	-7	6	-117
34.	Manipur State Drugs & Pharma. Ltd.	-28	27	-104
35.	Hotel Corpn. of India Ltd.	-3210	3181	-101
36.	Scooters India (Intrnl) gmbh W. Germany	-1	1	-100
37.	Birds Jute & Exports Ltd.	-191	193	-99
38.	NTC (Delhi, Punjab & Rajasthan) Ltd.	-3211	3290	-98

Contd....

(Contd...)

Sl. No.	*Name of the Company*	*Net current Assets/ Working Capital $ (lakhs)*	*Total Current Assets @ (lakhs)*	*Current Assets as a % of Working Capital (%)*
39.	Mining & Allied Machinery Corpn. Ltd.	-9694	10176	-95
40.	Orissa Drugs & Chemicals Ltd.	-125	132	-95
41.	Konkan Railway Corporation Ltd.	-6887	7283	-95
42.	IISCO Ujjain Pipe & Foundary Co. Ltd.	-948	1034	-92
43.	Reyroll Burn Ltd.	-274	330	-83
44.	Braithwaite & Co. Ltd.	-4805	5942	-81
45.	Tyre Corpn. of India Ltd.	-3312	4328	-77
46.	Brushware Ltd.	-12	16	-75
47.	Indian Drugs & Pharmaceuticals Ltd.	-8914	12222	-73
48.	Jessop & Co. Ltd.	-5396	9273	-58
49.	National Jute Manfs. Corpn. Ltd.	-4447	7690	-58
50.	Hindustan Paper Corporation Ltd.	-28784	51605	-56
51.	Hindustan Shipyard Ltd.	-15026	32017	-47
52.	U. P. Drugs & Pharma Ltd.	-117	259	-45
53.	Engineering Projects (India) Ltd.	-30504	101967	-30
54.	Hindustan Photo Films Manfg.	-2821	10316	-27
55.	Braithwaite, Burn & Jessop Constn. Ltd.	-797	3084	-26
56.	Bharat Leather Corpn. Ltd.	-95	376	-25
57.	Indian Iron & Steel Co. Ltd.	-17829	71723	-25
58.	Eastern Coalfields Ltd.	-22919	96992	-24
59.	Bharat Immunological * Biolo. Corpn. Ltd.	-69	304	-23
60.	Burn Standard Company Ltd.	-3209	15303	-21
61.	NTC (A. Pradesh, Karnataka, Kerala & Mahe) Ltd.	-2274	12587	-18
62.	Cement Corpn. of India Ltd.	-3205	26166	-12
63.	Bharat Pumps & Compressors Ltd.	-539	5136	-10
64.	Tea Trading Corpn. of India Ltd.	-103	1194	-9
65.	British India Corpn. Ltd.	-216	2582	-8
66.	Central Inland Water Transport Corpn. Ltd.	-405	5576	-7
67.	Hooghly Dock & Port Engineers Ltd.	-230	4992	-5
68.	Triveni Structurals Ltd.	-1673	41109	-4
69.	Heavy Engineering Corpn. Ltd.	-1349	45567	-3
70.	North Eastern Regional Agri. Marketing Corpn. Ltd	7	101	7
71.	Export Credit Guarantee Corpn. of India Ltd.	3800	32921	12
72.	Jute Corpn. of. India Ltd.	2371	16487	14
73.	Assam Ashok Hotel Corpn. Ltd.	8	54	15
74.	C. M. C. Ltd.	1495	9114	16
75.	Hindustan Copper Ltd.	7329	38411	19

Contd....

(Contd...)

Sl. No.	*Name of the Company*	*Net current Assets/ Working Capital $ (lakhs)*	*Total Current Assets @ (lakhs)*	*Current Assets as a % of Working Capital (%)*
76.	India Firebricks & Insulation Co. Ltd.	558	2645	21
77.	Indian Rare Earths Ltd.	2042	9582	21
78.	Hindustan Prefab Ltd.	790	3518	22
79.	Indian Airlines Ltd.	23453	100358	23
80.	Paradeep Phosphates Ltd.	9953	36261	27
81.	Rashtriya Pariyojna Nirman Nigam Ltd.	5789	20548	28
82.	NTC (South Maharashtra) Ltd.	10841	36023	30
83.	Nepa Ltd.	2314	7247	32
84.	Pyrites, Phosphates & Chemicals Ltd.	3438	10546	33
85.	National Bldg. Constn. Corpn. Ltd	19412	57887	34
86.	Nuclear Power Corpn. of India Ltd.	52206	150767	35
87.	Electronics Trade & Technology Dev. Corpn. Ltd.	1901	4996	38
88.	NTC (Tamil Nadu & Pondichery) Ltd.	5857	14207	41
89.	State Farms Corpn. of India Ltd.	1975	4005	49
90.	Hindustan Salts Ltd.	429	867	49
91.	Hindustan Antibiotics Ltd.	7001	13859	51
92.	Visvesvarayya Iron & Steel Co. Ltd.	11174	21669	52
93.	Indian Additives Ltd.	2680	5185	52
94.	Mineral Exploration Corpn. Ltd.	2725	5262	52
95.	Instrumentation Ltd.	7675	14802	52
96.	Sambhar Salts Ltd.	238	459	52
97.	Cochin Shipyard Ltd.	7705	14726	52
98.	Madras Fertilizers Ltd.	19135	35701	54
99.	Ranchi Ashok Bihar Hotel Corpn. Ltd.	59	108	55
100.	Praga Tools Ltd.	3310	6052	55
101.	Mica Trading Corpn. of India Ltd.	634	1158	55
102.	Hindustan Vegetable Oils Corpn. Ltd.	2462	4486	55
103.	Indian Road Constn. Corpn. Ltd.	34915	62281	56
104.	Central Electronics Ltd.	2992	5188	58
105.	National Handlooms Dev. Corpn. Ltd.	1321	2245	59
106.	Rashtriya Ispat Nigam Ltd.	41902	70243	60
107.	H. M. T. Ltd.	42276	69901	60
108.	National Seeds Corpn. Ltd.	2351	3475	68
109.	Rashtriya Chemicals & Fertilizers Ltd.	85483	126285	68
110.	North Eastern Handicrafts & Handloom Dev. Corpn.	235	315	75
111.	Coal India Ltd.	490168	653554	75
112.	Hindustan Fluorocarbons Ltd.	1371	1782	77
113.	National Textile Corpn. Ltd.	56919	70925	80
114.	Sponge Iron India Ltd.	831	998	83

Contd....

Sl. No.	*Name of the Company*	*Net current Assets/ Working Capital $ (lakhs)*	*Total Current Assets @ (lakhs)*	*Current Assets as a % of Working Capital (%)*
115.	Spices Trading Corpn. Ltd.	428	494	87
116.	Madhya Pradesh Ashok Hotel Corpn. Ltd.	14	16	88
117.	NTC (Uttar Pradesh) Ltd.	10033	4248	236

$ Net current Assets/Working Capital is defined as total current assets minus current liabilities and provisions.

@ Total Current Assets: It includes raw materials, spare parts, work-in-progress, finished goods, other stores, sundry debtors, loans and advances, cash and bank balance/deposits, other miscellaneous assets.

Similar poor financial performance is conceivable in the case of Municipal PEs numbering around 50 with an investment of about Rs. 30 billion. The database does not exist to throw much light on the actual performance of these PEs.

The growing gap between the pace of government expenditure and revenue and the resultant worsening fiscal imbalances since the late 1970s, on the other, led to restructuring PEs in the mid 1980s and privatisation and disinvestment in the post-reform period.

It is in this background that this chapter reviews the progress of the schemes of restructuring and privatisation of PEs. This also deals with a few important questions such as: Does ownership critically determine the performance of enterprise? (ii) What are the major barriers to restructuring and privatization of PEs? (iii) Can PEs be restructured in some ways which will be resisted the least in the prevailing political economy? and, (iv) Can such restructuring reduce fiscal burden while at the same time introduce new dynamism in public sector performance.

RESTRUCTURING IN THE PRE-REFORM PERIOD

The association between lack of autonomy of PE management and poor financial performance of PEs led to constituting several committees/commissions to review the working of PEs and to recommend appropriate measures for their reorganization and restructuring particularly since the 1980s.[7]

The Sengupta Committee which was appointed to review policy for PEs in the wake of the liberalisation process initiated in the mid

1990s have closely examined the constraints that have led to their poor performance. Apart from several recommendations in regard to improving the performance of PEs, the Committee made some major recommendations for restructuring the Central PEs. Without going into the details of different recommendations made the ones relating to restructuring on PEs may be noted.

First, for the purpose of defining the Government and PEs relations, the Committee classified the PEs owned by the Government of India but excluding departmental enterprises into two categories: Core & Non-Core. Core sectors as identified are: Coal; Lignite, Crude Oil, Petroleum and Natural gas, Power; Primary steel production; Primary production of Aluminium, Copper, Lead, Zinc and Nickel; Fertilizers and primary production of Petroleum and intermediaries.

It recommended that the plans, in regard to the investment planning, price fixation, financial management and similar other matters relating to the core sector should be integrated into the national plan.

On the other hand, the plans of the PEs in the non-core sector should be integrated into the national plan "only in an indicative sense" and such units would continue to be governed by the indicative and regulative framework of planning as applicable for all similar private sector units.

In this framework, the Committee recommended that PEs in the core sectors should be reorganised into Holding Companies (HCs) under the administrative control of the concerned sectoral Ministry. A HC should have independent subsidiary companies under the Company Law. HC in a particular core sector would serve as a link between government and PEs for the purpose of financing of the investments, setting target, budgetary performance, evaluation and project proposals etc. The basic idea is to combine in a harmonious manner both the accountability and operational flexibility by distancing the subsidiary companies from the direct government control.

As for the PEs in the non-core sector, the Committee recommended that the PEs should be re-organized into a few HCs and some Apex Companies, on the basis of a careful exercise.

Another important recommendation for providing operational flexibility to PEs relates to entering into Memorandum of Understanding (MOU) between HC and the Government for a five year period in regard to its plans for Investment, Production, Capacity utilisation, Profits, Dividend etc. on a mutually agreed basis.

As follow-up measures of the recommendations of this Committee as also others appointed to examine one or another aspects of PEs, several steps were taken to give operational flexibility to the undertakings while at the same time maintaining a balance between their autonomy and accountability.

To cite a few examples, since April 1986, the powers for incurring capital expenditures delegated to the Boards of Central PEs were enhanced to Rs. 50 million as recommended by the Arjun Sengupta Committee. Similarly, the schemes/projects costing above Rs. 50 million but not above Rs. 200 million were to be considered by the Expenditure Finance Committee while investment proposals above Rs. 200 million by the Public Investment Board/Cabinet. Another important change relates to the reduction of Government Directors on the Boards of Public Undertakings to one. Again, recognising the need of continuity at the top level in an industry, the tenure of five years has been given to Chief Executives and functional directors appointed by government[8].

MEMORANDUM OF UNDERSTANDING

For the purpose of enhancing operational efficiency of PEs and to strike a balance between autonomy and accountability as recommended by the Arjun Sengupta Committee; the concept of the MOU[9] was introduced in the mid-eighties and re-emphasized in the IPR of 1991. In pursuance of this, an increasing number of PEs from four in 1987-88 to 100 in 1994-95 (Table 2.6), entered MOU with their respective administrative ministry.[10] The MOU usually covers financial targets, government clearances, investment decisions, delegation of powers by the government, incentives to be given and foreign exchange.[11]

HOLDING COMPANY

The introduction of the concept of HC[12] can be seen as the most drastic step towards restructuring PEs in the 1980s. The logic of HC lies in introducing an intermediate level of management *i.e.* the Board of the HC between the Ministry and the subsidiary companies. The Board of the HC would also carry out the job of coordination between the subsidiary companies. This would minimise the interface between the Ministry and the subsidiary companies. Being persuaded by this logic, the concept of Holding Company was put in operation.

Table 2.6 : Public Enterprises and Memorandum of Understanding

Year	*Number of PEs Signing MOU*
1987-88	4
1988-89	11
1989-90	18
1990-91	23
1991-92	72
1992-93	98
1993-94	101
1994-95	100

Note: The actual number of PEs covered would be larger as some PEs have subsidiaries under them.

Source:S.L. Rao (1996, ed.): Reforming State-owned Enterprises, NCAER, New Delhi.

But this had not led to improving the returns on the capital invested in the PEs. It is because the basic constraints stem from the framework of the political economy within which these enterprises work. The erosion of their autonomy in the name of accountability has gone too deep to the changed by mere signing of a MOU[13] or forming HC.

PRIVATISATION

The aggressive privatisation carried through in the UK, France and some other developed countries in the 1980s had little impact on India's Public Sector Reform Policy[14] Only in the context of unsustainable budget deterioration experienced by 1990-91, privatisation formed part of economic reforms initiated since the mid1991-92.[15] It may be mentioned however, that several official committees did consider and recommend one or another type of privatisation ever since 1955.[16]

Before taking up the privatisation attempts in the 1990s, its different connotations may be noted. Privatisation covers at least three ways of altering the relationship between the state and the private sector[17] These are :

(i) denationalisation, which involves transfer of ownership of public sector assets to private sector. This may be partial or full depending on whether a part or the whole of the equity of a PE is transferred.

(ii) deregulation or liberalisation which leads to opening up the areas or sectors reserved hitherto exclusively for the public sector; and
(iii) contracting out which involves franchising to private firms the production of goods and services, which are under the financial control of the government

Public sector reforms in the 1990s covered privatisation in all three manners, though the scale varied. In fact, privatisation is an important part of the IPR of 1991[18], it has carved out a new approach to the public sector, which includes privatisation and concentration on strategic and high tech areas.

The IPR of 1991[19] and its subsequent amendments have mostly abolished the industrial licensing, which necessitated permission from the government for new investment and capacity expansion. It has removed the entry barriers in the manufacturing sector for all industries irrespective of the levels of investment other than a few specified ones, which will remain to be subject to compulsory licensing. Simultaneously, MRTP has been restructured to focus on preventing monopolistic or anti-competitive business practices and restrictive unfair business practices or abuse of market powers to gain excess profits.

In contrast to layers of reservation in the past, the IPR of 1991 and its subsequent amendments reduced the sectors exclusively reserved for the public sector to only six which relate to Defence, Atomic energy, Minerals for Atomic energy, Coal, Mineral Oils and Railway Transport. Thus it has provided the private sector much larger scope for its participation in industrial activities.

The policy has also clearly recognised that "many PEs have become a burden rather than an asset to the government and that the original concept of public sector has also undergone considerable dilution over the years." The policy declared that:

> "Government will strengthen these PEs which fall in the reserved areas of operation or are in the high priority areas or are generating good or reasonable profits. Such enterprises will be provided a much greater degree of management autonomy through the system of memorandum of understanding. Competition will also be induced in these area, by inviting private sector participation. In the case of selected enterprises, part of government holdings in

the equity share capital of these enterprises will be disinvested in order to provide further market discipline to the performance by PEs. There is a large number of chronically sick PEs incurring heavy losses, operating in a competitive market and serve little or no public purpose. These need to attended to".

It is in this policy perspective that the privatisation of the existing PEs should be considered.

Central PEs

As mentioned earlier, privatisation of PEs in India is essentially fiscal crisis-driven. This is clearly reflected in the fact that privatisation schemes largely constituted in disinvestment policy.[20] The government started disinvesting its share holding beginning from 1991-92. In this year, the government realised Rs. 30.4 billion by disinvesting its share holding in 30 PEs and this accounted for 8 per cent of its holdings in these enterprises. The government continued to disinvest in the subsequent years and realised a total of Rs. 105 billion by 1994-95 by way of disinvesting its holdings to the public sector financial institutions, mutual funds and general public (Table 2.7).

Even with successive doses of disinvestment, the government of India holdings in these PEs remained in the range varying from 51.8 per cent (in Madras Refineries Ltd) to 99.03 per cent (in Kundermukh Ore Company Ltd) at the end of 1995.[21]

The extent of holdings that the government owns determines its control in the management of PEs. With 26 per cent ownership the government can exercise limited control over special resolution brought in general body meetings of the enterprise, with 51 per cent, it can have effective control while a 100 per cent ownership will ensure full control over the PE.

It is clear from the extent of disinvestment, the government has made so far that it has adopted the policy of privatisation through partial transfer to its equity holdings in different PEs and not through total transfer of its ownership. However, the government of India constituted in February 1992 a Committee on Disinvestment of Shares in public sector enterprises. Its terms of reference include[22]: "To advise on limits on the percentage of equity to be disinvested in respect of such public sector enterprises."

In brief, the Committee recommended that the government should

Table 2.7 : Year-wise/Central Public Enterprise-wise details of Shares Disinvestment since 1991-92

Sl. No.	*Name of the Public Enterprises*	*Percentage Central Govt. Holding*					
		1.7.1991	*31.3.1992*	*31.3.1993*	*31.3.1994*	*31.3.1995*	*31.12.1995*
1.	Andrew Yule & Company Ltd.	71.30	62.80	62.80	62.80	62.80	62.80
2.	Bharat Earth Movers Ltd.	100.00	80.00	80.00	80.00	60.08	60.08*
3	Bharat Electronics Ltd.	100.00	80.00	80.00	80.00	75.86	75.86
4.	Bharat Heavy Electricals Ltd.	100.00	80.00	79.54	79.46	67.72	67.72
5.	Bharat Petroleum Corpn. Ltd.	100.00	80.00	70.00	69.62	66.20	66.20
6.	Bongaigaon Refinery & Petrochemicals Ltd.	100.00	80.00	74.60	74.59	74.47	74.47
7.	Cochin Refineries Ltd.	61.16	55.04	55.04	55.04	55.04	55.04
8.	Container Corporation of India Ltd.	100.00	100.00	100.00	100.00	80.00	76.92$
9.	C.M.C. Ltd.	100.00	83.31	83.31	83.31	83.31	83.31
10.	Dredging Corporation of India Ltd.	100.00	98.56	98.56	98.56	98.56	98.56
11.	Engineers India Ltd.	100.00	100.00	100.00	100.00	94.01	94.01
12.	Fertilizers & Chemicals (Travancore) Ltd.	98.69	97.46	97.35	97.35	97.35	97.35
13,	Gas Authority of India Ltd.	100.00	100.00	100.00	100.00	96.63	96.63
14.	Hindustan Cables Ltd.	100.00	96.36	97.97	97.97	97.97	97.97
15.	Hindustan Copper Ltd.	100.00	100.00	98.88	98.88	98.88	98.88
16.	Hindustan Organic Chemicals Ltd.	100.00	80.00	80.00	80.00	56.90	56.90*
17.	Hindustan Petroleum Corpn. Ltd.	100.00	80.00	70.00	69.72	60.25	60.25*
18.	Hindustan Photo Films Manfg.	100.00	87.47	87.47	87.47	87.47	87.47
19.	Hindustan Zinc Ltd.	100.00	80.04	75.93	75.93	75.92	75.92
20.	H.M.T. Ltd.	100.00	95.14	90.32	90.32	90.32	90.32
21.	India Tourism Dev. Corpn. Ltd.	100.00	100.00	100.00	100.00	90.00	90.00
22.	Indian Oil Corporation Ltd.	99.88	99.88	99.88	99.88	96.08	96.08
23.	Indian Petro-Chemicals Corpn. Ltd.	100.00	80.00	80.97	62.40	62.40	62.40

Contd....

(Contd....)

Sl. No.	Name of the Public Enterprises	Percentage Central Govt. Holding					
		1.7.1991	*31.3.1992*	*31.3.1993*	*31.3.1994*	*31.3.1995*	*31.12.1995*
24.	Indian Railway Constn. Co. Ltd.	100.00	99.74	99.74	99.74	99.74	99.74
25.	Indian Telephone Industries Ltd.	99.65	79.72	77.79	77.67	77.02	77.02
26.	Kudremukh Iron Ore Co. Ltd.	100.00	100.00	100.00	100.00	99.03	99.03
27.	Madras Refineries Ltd.	84.62	67.70	67.70	51.80	51.80	51.80
28.	Mahanagar Telephone Nigam Ltd.	100.00	80.00	80.00	80.00	67.18	65.73$
29.	National Aluminium Company Ltd.	100.00	97.28	87.20	87.19	87.15	87.15
30.	Mineral & Metal Trading Corp.	100.00	99.33	99.33	99.33	99.33	99.33
31.	National Fertilizers Ltd.	100.00	97.72	97.66	97.66	97.65	97.65
32.	National Mineral Development Corporation Ltd.	100.00	100.00	98.38	98.38	98.38	98.38
33.	Neyveli Lignite Corpn. Ltd.	100.00	95.42	93.86	94.19	94.19	94.19
34.	Oil & Natural Gas Corporation Ltd.	100.00	100.00	100.00	100.00	98.00	97.94$
35.	Rashtriya Chemicals & Fertilizers Ltd.	100.00	94.36	92.50	92.50	92.50	92.50
36.	Shipping Corporation of India Ltd.	100.00	81.49	81.49	81.49	80.12	80.12
37.	State Trading Corpn. of India Ltd.	100.00	92.02	91.02	91.02	91.02	91.02
38.	Steel Authority of India Ltd.	100.00	95.01	89.49	89.45	89.04	88.93$
39.	Videsh Sanchar Nigam Ltd.	100.00	85.00	85.00	85.00	85.00	85.00
40.	Industrial Dev. Bank of India	100.00	100.00	100.00	100.00	100.00	72.14

* These companies had floated public issues, percentage of Govt. holding after proposed public issue is not known.
$ Figures are provisional, as the shares sold in Oct. 1995 are yet to be transferred in favour of successful bidders.
Source: Economic Survey 1995, Govt. of India, p. 121.

disinvest less than 49 per cent of its equity in PEs in the sectors reserved for the public sector and more than 74 per cent in other PEs,

However, these recommendations, which were made in April, 1993 had little impact on the actual disinvestment levels in the subsequent years.[23] In fact, the disinvestment of the capital stock of PEs as shown in Table 2.7 has not so far altered the ownership pattern giving effective control to the private sector. (Maruti Udyog Limited is one case in which the government and its private sector counterpart have 50:50 stake).

Some PEs have, however, resorted to floating public issue as a technique of altering ownership pattern. In the recent past, Indian Petrochemicals Limited (IPCL), Balmer Lawrie Limited, State Bank of India (the largest commercial Bank in India), Oil and Natural Gas Commission issued fresh share capital reserving 5 per cent of their issue for their employees.[24]

Some PEs such as National Thermal Power Corporation (NTPC), Steel Authority of India (SAIL), etc. have made public issues even in the foreign capital markets by floating Euro-Dollar Issues.[25] There are other PEs, which have undertaken preparatory measures towards disinvestment.

Some enterprises such as Indian Airlines and Air India have converted themselves from public corporations to government companies, which have greater flexibility for public issues and restructuring. The State Bank of India Act and the Banking Companies Act have been amended so as to enable the public sector banks to have access to capital market.

Some changes have also been introduced in regard to capital restructuring of loss making units to facilitate pricing and price preferences, wage policy, giving access to capital market and so on.

Similarly, recapitalisation has been done for some enterprises. For example, Steel Authority of India is now required to find funds for its growth, maintenance and working capital in decontrolled competitive environment.

Again, some enterprises such as Electronic Corporation of India and the Indian Drugs and Pharmaceutical Ltd. have closed down their loss making activities.

In the same spirit, Indian Railways, Posts and Telegraphs, Air Corporations; etc. have made a move to give up their loss making activities unless these are subsidised by the government in full.

The Indian Telecom sector has been going through a process of dramatic restructuring since 1984. It has attempted to restructure itself from the initial status of a departmental undertaking adopting a mix of privatisation schemes: Creating Corporation, accessing capital market, opening up for the private and foreign investors' participation in basic and value added services etc.

A telecom regulatory authority has already been set up as an autonomous body to oversee the policy and regulatory aspects such as price regulations, norms for consumer satisfaction, fixation of license fee, revenue sharing with DOT by the private operators.

From the above illustrative micro-level discussion of the Central PE reforms, it is clear that a number of PEs have attempted privatisation of one form or another. Till March 31, 1995 seven of them have completed as planned, nine others have initiated one or another scheme of privatisation and 21 have already planned for privatisation[26] (Table 2.8). A variety of techniques have been adopted in this regard, which includes private sale, lease, management contract, joint ventures and partial disinvestment. Among these, however, partial disinvestment seems to be the most preferred instrument of privatisation. Table 2.9 throws further light in regard to the sectors in whch the PEs have undertaken privatisation.

As to disinvestment as technique of privatisation, the question of adequacy of capital market to support such programmes without crowding out the private sector assumes a great importance. One estimate show that the Indian capital market can raise something around $20 billion each year by way of new issues.[27] The present mobilisation through the capital market is just half the amount. There is thus potential for much larger mobilisation for supporting a higher level of disinvestment.[28] This potential is further enhanced by the possibility of mobilisation through Euro-Dollar issues as have been done by about 15 Indian corporate enterprises to the tune of $3 billion in 1993-94.[29]

Another preparatory measure towards privatisation of chronically loss making enterprises/sick units relates to the amendment of the Sick Industrial Companies (Special Provisions) Act, 1986 (SICA) in December 1992 in the framework of the new industrial policy. The 1992 amendment in the SICA has extended its provisions to cover sick public sector units as well.

Up to December 31, 1995, 138 PEs (59 Central and 79 State PEs) were referred to the BIFR.[30] It dismissed 26 PE cases as non-maintainable, sanctioned revival schemes for 29, recommended

Table 2.8 : Survey of Privatisation by Stages of Completion in respect of the Central Enterprises

Sl. No.	*Cases*	*Planned*	*Underway*	*Completed*
1.	Central Enterprises			X
2.	Oil & Natural Gas Commission Corporation		X	
3.	Indian Iron & Steel Co. Sale		X	
4.	Bharat Heavy Electrical Mkting	X		
5.	Telecom (Cellular phone)		X	
6.	Telecom Rural Exchange	X		
7.	Small Oil Fields	X		
8.	Indian Petro. Chem. Open Public			X
9.	17 Central Enterprises Disinvested		X	
10.	National Textile Mills of Eastern India	X		
11.	Coal India Finance by Multinational	X		
12.	Hindusthan Latex Ltd.	X		
13.	Madras Port	X		
14.	Richardson & Cruddas (Madras) to be closed	X		
15.	Public Sector Banks	X		
16.	National Power Corp. allow Private party set up power plant		X	
17.	Indian Railways Privatise Catering			X
18.	Doordarshan Metro Channel			X
19.	Private Participation in Coal Washeries	X		
20.	Pvt. Ownership of Oil Pipe Lines	X		
21.	Hindustan Copper Ltd. to issue PCDs		X	
22.	100% Equity of Sick CPEs for Private party	X		
23.	Air India and Indian Air Lines Corporation		X	
24.	H. Petro Chem & Multinational tie up for Sulphur Plant			X
25.	Indian Railways to throw open all services to private sector	X		
26.	Mazgaon Dock to be disinvested	X		
27.	Pvt. Sector to be allowed to deal ports	X		
28.	PTT Power plant of Coal India Ltd. to Pvt. Sector	X		
29.	Paral. Corporation & Hindusthan Fertilizer Corporation to be hived off.	X		
30.	Mahan. Telephone & Videsh Sanchar Nigam to raise fund from Capital market	X		
31.	IDBI goes Public			X
32.	Indian Oil Corp. deals with Pvt. party for marketing	X		
33.	500 Unviable Bank branches to be closed	X		
34.	Hindustan Machine Tools restructured	X		
35.	Railways lease cargo open		X	X
36.	Scooter India sale		X	
37.	Bicycle Corporation for sale			
	Total	21	9	7

Source : Compiled by Mishra, R. K., Institute of Public Enterprise, Hyderabad.

winding up to the concerned High Court in 14 and was considering the rest. But the problem is that the BIFR takes enormous time to decide the intensity of sickness of the sick units that have been referred to it.

In order to streamline its disinvestment programme[31], the Government of India set up (on August 7, 1996) a Disinvestment Commission.[32]

Yet another preparatory step towards restructuring of PEs is the creation of a National Renewal Fund (NRF). Its objective is to redeploy, retrain and rehabilitate the workers displaced in the process of restructuring PEs. While a large corpus is required for the NRF, only a small allocation of about Rs. 30 billion has been made so far. As a result, a large number of workers displaced could not adequately be retrained and redeployed. This has led to skepticism of the privatisation programmes of PEs.

State Level Public Enterprise Reforms

The privatisation efforts of the state governments can be appreciated better if these are viewed in the context of the following broad features of SLPEs:[33]

(i) Dominant two sectors, *viz.* Power and Road transport accounting for about 75 per cent of investment and labour force, are in the nature of utilities. They are, therefore, to meet certain social obligations. While doing so they are required to provide 'cross-subsidisation'.

(ii) Being public utilities, both these sectors are governed by Central legislative framework. More importantly, Planning Commission, Central Electricity Authority, Ministry of Surface Transport and quinquennial Finance Commission promote 'yardstick competition' by making inter-state comparison of physical and financial performance as part of plan/monitoring exercise.

(iii) The SLPEs other than those in these two dominant sectors are of competitive nature, although some of them are promotional.

(iv) The Central Government holds equity in most of SLPEs other than power and road transport either directly or indirectly through Industrial Development Bank of India;

Central Warehousing Corporation of India; National Seeds Corporation etc. Such enterprises are, in effect, a joint sector between the Centre and State Governments.

(v) Some of these joint sector enterprises such as State Finance Corporations were also set up under a national level special legislative framework.

(vi) About 15 per cent of the equity in SLPEs other than power and road transport are in promotional category.

These features of SLPEs suggest two important things: First, SLPEs owed their existence more to historical factors and pragmatic considerations than to ideological reasons of 'commanding height'. The second, which partly follows from the first, is that public purpose and social and welfare considerations weighed heavily in setting up a number of SLPEs. The latter obviously act as a constraint on states' ability to privatise. In addition, the restructuring of the enterprises in the joint sector, which is in a way 'close loop system', does not entirely rest with the state's initiatives. Lack of access of NRF to the states has also constrained the implementation of Voluntary Retirement Schemes in their over-staffed PEs till recently.

Even so, restructuring and privatisation of PEs are clearly on the agenda of most states. It is because states operate under very rigid budget constraints, far more than the Union Government. Under the fast deteriorating budget balance, states do not have resources to provide budgetary support to their PEs. On the other hand, the SLPEs do not have access to tax free bonds or to external commercial borrowing as in the case of central PEs. On the top of it, SLPEs other than those in power and transport operate in a competitive market. As a result, it is not possible for state governments to use administered price, price preference etc. to help the survival of their PEs without affecting budget.

Being placed as they are, the states had to choose between the allocations to its sovereign functions and merit goods such as education, health, drinking water etc. and continue to bear the budgetary burden arising from the loss making SLPEs.

It is this resource crunch that has driven the state initiatives in privatisation. Adequate data are not available to assess the exact dimension of actual privatisation the states have undertaken. On the basis of information available for 17 out of 25 states and one Union territory in a scattered manner, an illustrative discussion is proposed

Table 2.9 : Survey of Privatisation Transaction by Sectors in respect of the Central Public Enterprises

Sl. No.	*Case*	*Dept.*	*Other PEs*	*Pri-mary*	*Secon-dary*	*Tertiary*	*Modality*	*Any Other Information*
1.	31 PSUS	Undertaking	Cos.		x	x	Sale of Share	To MFs and Trust
2.	ONGC		Corp.		x		Corp.	For Pvt.
3.	ISCO		Co.		x		Sale	Mukund took up Bid due to political persons it was held up
4.	Telecom	Undertaking			x	x	Pvt-Par.Parti'n	Green Field Pvt.
5.	Oil Fields		Cos.		x		Sale	
6.	17 PSUs	Undertaking	Cos.		x	x	Sale of Shares	To MF and Trusts
7.	NTC Eastern India		Corp.		x			Assets disinvestment
8.	CIL		Co.	x			JV	With Multinationals
9.	HIL		Co.		x		Sale of Assets	Planned
10.	Madras Port		Trust			x	Lease	Planned
11.	Richardson & Cruddas		Co.		x		Closer	Planned
12.	DDES					x		
13.	Railways Pvt. Catering	Undertaking				x	Fragmentation	Completed
14.	DD Metro	Undertaking				x	Private Sale	Of time slot (completed)
15.	CIL		Co.	x			J V	Planned
16.	Hindustan Copper		Co.	x			New Issue	Underway
17.	AI and IA		Corp.			x	Convr. into Company	Completed
18.	HPCL		Corp.		x		J V	ION KTC
19.	Railways Services	Undertaking				x	Leasing/Fragm.	
20.	Mazagaon Dock		Trust			x	Disinvestment	
21.	PTT Power of CIL		Co.	x			Sale of assets	
22.	FCI & HFC		Co & Corp.		x		Closer	Planning,
23.	MNTC & VSNL		Co.			x	Public Issue	Planning
24.	IDBI		Corp.			x	Convr. into Company	

Contd....

(Contd....)

Sl. No.	Case	Dept.	Other PEs	Pri-mary	Secon-dary	Tertiary	Modality	Any Other Information
25.	IOC Mkting		Corp.		x		Pvt. of Internal Operation	
26.	PSO Banks		Cos.			x	closer	500 unviable Bank for Closer
27.	NHT		Co.		x		Restructuring	
28.	Rlys. Space Cargo	Undertaking					Leasing	
29.	Scooter India		Co.		x		Sale of assets	
30.	Bicycle Corp.		Co.		x		Sale of assets	

X = ... in the sector; Co.=Company; Corp.=Corporation; Undertaking= Deptt. Undertaking.
Source : Compiled by Mishra, R. K., Institute of Public Enterprise, Hyderabad.

Table 2.10 : Privatisation of State Level Public Enterprises by Stages of Completion

S. No.	*State*	*Planned*	*Underway*	*Completed*	*Total*
1.	Andhra Pradesh	2	-	1	3
2.	Arunachal Pradesh	-	1	-	1
3.	Assam	2	-	-	2
4.	Bihar	23	-	-	23
5.	Goa	-	-	-	-
6 .	Gujarat	-	1	-	1
7.	Haryana	1	1	-	2
8.	Himachal Pradesh	-	-	-	-
9.	Jammu & Kashmir	-	-	-	-
10.	Karnataka	-	6	-	6
11.	Kerala	2	18	-	20
12.	Madhya Pradesh	1	1	-	2
13.	Maharashtra	5	1	-	6
14.	Manipur	-	-	-	-
15.	Meghalaya	-	-	-	-
16.	Mizoram	-	-	-	-
17.	Nagaland	-	-	-	-
18.	Orissa	7	5	7	19
19.	Punjab	3	-	-	3
20.	Rajasthan	-	1	-	1
21.	Sikkim	-	-	-	-
22.	Tamil Nadu	1	1	-	2
23.	Tripura	-	-	-	-
24.	Uttar Pradesh	-	3	1	4
25.	West Bengal	3	-	-	3
26.	Delhi	1	-	-	1
	Total	50	39	9	98

Note : This does not contain the. information regarding Orissa.
Source : Compiled by Mishra, R. K., Institute of Public Enterprise, Hyderabad.

to indicate the type of privatisation efforts the different states have initiated.[34]

In contrast to the central government, which has preferred disinvestment most as the instrument of privatisation of PEs, state governments seem to have favoured joint ventures more particularly in the power sector. Several states such as Arunachal Pradesh, Assam, Karnataka, Kerala, Rajasthan, Madhya Pradesh, Tamil Nadu have planned or already commenced such joint ventures.

Table 2.10 gives an aggregate picture of privatisation of SLPEs by stages of completion as it stood on March 31,1994. It shows that

Table 2.11 : Privatisation of State Level Public Enterprises by Stages of Completion/ Case-wise

Sl. No.	*State*	*Planned*	*Underway*	*Completed*
1.	Andhra Pradesh	APSFC/APIDC	—	HAL
2.	Arunachal Pradesh	—	Power Plant (JV)	—
3.	Assam	Refinery/Hydro Project	—	—
4.	Bihar	23 loss making Units	—	—
5.	Gujarat	—	Gas Unit (lease)	—
6.	Haryana	Hydal Power Project	Sugar Mill	—
7.	Karnataka	—	5 Power Projects NGEF (Disinvestment)	—
8.	Kerala	Kayankulam Power Project/Kerala Auto Way	Keltron(sales)/17 PE Disinvestment	—
9.	Madhya Pradesh	Power Project	S.M. Iron & Steel (JV)	—
10.	Maharashtra	5 Sugar Coop/Power	S R T C	—
11.	Orissa	OLCOP & OT MILLS IPICOL Cements Mushroom plant	Kalinga Steel Latex Plant	Charge Chrome Sugar Mills Sewa Paper BTM Gangapur Plant
12.	Punjab	Cattle Dev./Road/ Sugar Mill	—	—
13.	Rajasthan	—	Didwana Chemicals (lease)	—
14.	Tamil Nadu	TNCC	T.N. Hospital (JV)	—
15.	Uttar Pradesh	—	UPCC/Auto Tractors/ Power Plant	UPTRON
16.	West Bengal	Jute Mills/Schools & Hospitals/Ramman-I Project	—	—
17.	Delhi	DESU	—	—

Source : Compiled by Mishra, R.K., Institute of Public Enterprise, Hyderabad.

17 states together privatised nine SLPEs, initiated privatisation process for 39 SLPEs and planned privatisation for 50 till March 31,1994. Most states have commenced and a few completed review of their portfolio of SLPEs to decide upon the appropriate instrument for their restructuring.

States adopted a wide variety of instruments for restructuring and privatisation of their SLPEs: Joint venture, disinvestment, sale of assets, merger, winding up, management contract, franchising etc., (Table 2.11)

Considering the fact that only 98 out of the total of 954 SLPEs outside power and transport sectors have been touched so far in one way or another, privatisation efforts cannot be expected to have any major impact. Even so, the following important points have clearly emerged :

(1) Contrary to the general perception, states' efforts for restructuring their PEs are considerable. It is noteworthy that some of the less advanced states such as Orissa, Rajasthan, Assam and Kerala have made greater stride in this regard. In fact, Orissa and Rajasthan, two least advanced states of the Indian Union, have been pursuing very aggressive privatisation programmes. Orissa's privatisation programme is reported to have yielded encouraging results particularly in the power sector turning it from a deficit to a power surplus state.

(2) While the partial disinvestment is observed to be the most perferred modality of privatisation for the central PEs, joint ventures have been more widely opted instrument at the state level. More importantly, it is the states, which have succeeded in completely privatising some of their PEs. ACC, Babcock, Allwyn Nissan Limited, Auto Tractors Limited, East Coast Breweries and Distilleries Limited, Goa Telecommunications Limited. Goa Time Movers, Haryana Breweries Limited, Orissa Mining Corporations' Charge Chrome Plant and Rajasthan State Tanneries, which have been completely privatised, are all SLPEs. In contrast, the Central Government made an unsuccessful attempt to privatise fully the Indian Iron and Steel Company (IISCO) and Scooters India Limited.[35]

(3) As compared to the Central Government; states seem to be more innovative in their choice of appropriate instrument for privatisation.

(4) In the cases of complete transfer of SLPEs to the private sector, the states have demonstrated impressive skill in dealing with labour resistance to ownership transfer. Andhra Pradesh in the case of Hyderabad Allwyn Ltd. employing 12000 workers and Orissa in the case of Gahgapur Mill employing 1200 workers provide good examples. This is particularly impressive because states did not have access to the NRF for retraining and re-employing the retrenched workers.

(5) On the basis of two detailed case studies in UP, Bajaj (1994) has observed that PE privatisation encounters a number of

obstacles such as developing a coherent strategy, choosing enterprises, valuation of assets, funding credible entrepreneurs capable of successfully running the enterprises. What is more, the entire privatisation process has to be transparent.

(6) State's stride in their privatising efforts should be viewed in the following context. As mentioned earlier, for a number of SLPEs, in which Central PEs have stake, states on their own cannot take any initiatives. Again, states being closer to voters can be expected to be more susceptible to labour resistance. Besides, a large chunk of SLPEs is of promotional type.

Legal Barriers to Privatisation

The pace of privatisation should be viewed in the context of the constitutional as well as the existing Central Legislative frameworks.[36]

The Supreme Court of India's interpretation of Article 12 of the Constitution of India treating PEs as an extension of the state has made the management decisions amenable to the filing of writ petitions thus obstructing the implementation of management policies. In fact. there are about 4000 writ petitions pending in different courts of India. These relate to appointments, promotions and various other decisions of the management.[37] This indicates another dimension of legal barrier that the PE management encounters in their decision making process under the existing legal framework.

The Industrial Disputes Act, 1947 stipulates that industries that employ more than 100 workers will have to seek the permission of the government before retrenching workers. The earlier government proposed an exit policy allowing industries employing upto 300 workers to retrench workers without seeking the permission of government but did not pursue for lack of political will.

Similarly, the loss making private and public large and medium industrial companies falling under the First Schedule of the Industries (Development and Regulation) Act, 1951 (with initial investment in plant and machinery being of Rs. 5 million or more and the number of workers being 50 or more) are to be referred to the BIFR under SICA, 1986. But when sick units are referred to the BIFR, inordinate delay is involved in arriving at a decision. In the meantime, loss accumulates.

Again, the provisions under the Companies Act 1956[38] in regard to merger of sick units with healthy ones or firm liquidation involve long drawn process.

In short, all these Acts as legal barriers as much to CPEs as to SLPEs. It is in this legal environment that the pace of PE restructuring and privatisation should be considered.

Further, the privatisation of PEs as undertaken in some form or other beginning from the early 1990s will change their status from monopolist and duopolist to competitive enterprises. But they will not entirely be free to take decisions in regard to operation, pricing and product mix since the interest of the society and state has to be protected. There is, therefore, an urgent need to formulate an appropriate regulatory mechanism for the PEs, particularly the dominant ones, as has been initiated in the case of Insurance, Telecommunications etc.

SUMMING UP

Historically, PEs were set up with multiple objectives as part of the ideology of placing the public sector at the commanding height of the Indian economy in the planning process. The Parliament/State Legislature as representatives of people is the owner of PEs in the ultimate analysis.

To ensure accountability, therefore, the government has built a complex network of administrative and parliamentary monitoring and controls. This led to the erosion of autonomy of the PEs curbing their operational flexibility for running them as commercial concerns. This contributed, in no small measure, to their poor financial performance.

Several committees including Parliamentary Committee on public undertakings, reviewed from time to time different aspects of management system and controls and the performance of PEs and recommended appropriate measures for improving their performance.

In pursuance of their recommendations, some half-hearted measures of reforms relating to central PEs were, indeed, introduced. These varied from reforms towards striking a balance between autonomy and accountability to reorganisation of enterprises in the form of HCs and negotiating MOUs in the period prior to the current reform programme. HC concept and MOU can be regarded as the two most important instruments of restructuring PEs in this period.

These reforms, though merely scratched at the surface, were helpful but never adequate to ensure reasonable rate of returns on the massive capital employed in these enterprises. On the basis of crosscountry experience, Sunita Kikery has observed: "This kind of reforms and attempts tended to yield very minimal results at the end of the day."[39] In any case, such reforms were mostly confined to the central PEs and not extended to cover the SLPEs.

PE reforms as part of the current reform programme were drastically different both in contents and directions. This is essentially driven by resource crunch. With fast deteriorating budgetary balance, on the one hand, and rising expenditure commitments of government, on the other, the required budgetary support was no longer available to the PEs. More importantly, disinvestment has been resorted to as an instrument of fiscal adjustment.

Being faced with much more rigid budget constraints, states have also taken up privatisation programme for their PEs. In fact, states have employed a wider variety of instruments to privatise their enterprises. A few of them are highly innovative in designing and implementing some instruments of privatisation. In fact, it is the states which have truly privatised some of their enterprises.

Dereserving all but six sectors for the public sector under the July 1991 IPR, the Government of India has greatly widened the role of the private sector in the Indian economy and thus made an important stride towards privatisation.

In short, while privatisation has been taken up as part of the reform process, its pace has been slow. There are a number of reasons for this. Several barriers as explained earlier impede privatisation. The legislative framework as provided under the Industrial Disputes Act, the Urban Land Ceiling Act (abolished recently), the Companies Act or the specific statutes under which were established the PEs, the Sick Industrial Companies (Special Provision) Act and the actual functioning of the BIFR instituted thereunder acted as legal barriers.

Similarly, the Supreme Court interpretation of Article 12 of the Constitution treating PEs as an extension of the state has narrowed down management options.

The privatisation of even the chronically loss making enterprises has to be referred to the BIFR which, in turn, takes enormous amount of time in deciding upon the course of action for the referred concerns.

On the other hand, closure, winding-up or liquidation of enterprises also involves a long-drawn process given the existing framework of the Companies Act.

Another major barrier to privatisation is labour resistance. An appropriate exit policy framed after combining both labour and management interests would remove an obstacle of vital importance.

There also exist several obstacles in operationalising privatisation. These arise from "developing a coherent strategy, choosing enterprises, valuation of assets, finding credible entrepreneurs capable of successfully running the enterprises"[40] and making the entire privatisation process transparent. Some cases of privatisation completed in the past five years suggest, however that even these barriers are not insurmountable.

The most important barrier to privatisation is the unholy alliance of different interest groups. Policy makers consisting of politicians and bureaucrats, use PEs both as a source of personal aggrandisement as well as a means of patronage. Trade Unions representing labour interest have a great stake in PEs as a source of income and job security. Even consumers of the products of PEs have developed vested interests in the continuation of PEs, for some of their products being available at subsidised prices. The alliance of these different interest groups systematically built up resistance to privatisation. It is no wonder, therefore, the pace of privatisation is tardy even in the face of unsustainable fiscal deficits.

In defence of PEs, it is argued that ownership does not necessarily determine the performance of an enterprise. It is true that the number of private sick and weak units is as large as 2,35,868 with the amount outstanding Rs. 1225.9 billion at the end of September 1992. It is also true that the nationalization of a number of sick units (50 units at the Central PE level) in the private sector contributed to an extent to the growth of PEs.

But then in the changing economic environment, PEs will lose their vitality anyway if they fail to continuously upgrade and modernise the technologies and become competitive. It does not look feasible that the required investment will be available as budgetary support from the government is shrinking in the face of deteriorating budgetary balance and changing priorities of government in favour of pure public goods and merit goods.

The cross-country experience suggests that "ownership does matter and that for most activities it is not possible to achieve the same level of efficiency in a state-owned enterprise as it is possible in a private enterprise".[41] It is because the nexus between rent seeking politicians and risk-averse and power (and not surplus) maximising bureaucrats can stifle any drastic attempts to reform PEs towards successfully running commercial concerns as they did in the past.

This suggests that privatisation particularly in the non-core sectors has to be high on the agenda of the government both at the Centre and states. Cross country experience brings out: "The high costs and poor performance of SOEs (State-owned Enterprises) and the modest and fleeting results of reform efforts have turned many governments towards privatisation. Other reasons include shifting development theory and ideologies in the face of mounting SOE losses, the collapse of communism in Eastern Europe and the Soviet Union and some success of early privatizers such as United Kingdom."[42]

In the Indian context, the unsustainable fiscal deficits and the shift in the development paradigm and ideology in favour of greater market reliance. the major political parties of India have broadly endorsed privatisation particularly the non-core and non-strategic PEs as part of public sector reforms.

The pace of reforms wil', however, critically depend on a number of factors. Just to cite a few :

An appropriate regulatory mechanism has to be put in place in recognition of the fact of monopoly and duopoly enjoyed by many a PE being faced with a competitive situation in the privatisation process.

A legal framework, which cases the transfer of government ownership, has to be created through appropriate amendments of the existing laws that hinder the process of privatisation.

In this regard, it is encouraging to note that steps have recently been taken to bring about the required changes under the Companies Act, 1956. Similarly, Telecommunication and Insurance regulatory bodies have already been set up.

It is important to recognise that the opposition to privatisation coming from left ideologies political parties and intellectuals is real. To buttress this, there is a habit of thinking that has developed from long years of dominating position of the public sector in the Indian economy. The current practice of disinvestment scantily spread across a select number of PEs, has met with a valid criticism. The proceeds from disinvestment have merely been used for fiscal adjustment which does not contribute to any long run improvement in macro balances of the economy

In view of resistance to privatisation, it is important to evolve a well-thought out and persuasive scheme of privatisation clearly setting at rest all different types of scepticism and apprehensions. Such a scheme should be based on the following considerations :

(i) It is socially undesirable to bear the high cost of low return earning and loss making PEs which have been contributing, in no small measure, to the unsustainable fiscal deficits of the government;

(ii) A large number of PEs without the required budgetary support will anyway languish in a competitive environment;

(iii) The liquidation of assets, which were acquired largely with borrowed funds and partly with tax payers money cannot be seen as being frittered away without making any contributions to the fiscal health of the economy. A sound fiscal policy is that the liquidation of assets should lead to the liquidation of equivalent liabilities.

(iv) A clear position on the use of proceeds through the privatisation process will be helpful in providing options for alternative uses of public money between fattening the vested interest groups in the process of maintaining the languishing PEs and contributing towards a sound fiscal health.

In short, a persuasive scheme of privatisation has to combine the appropriate modality and its transparent execution with the exact scheme of deploying the proceeds from disinvestment/divesting towards long term macro-economic improvement.

Keeping these in view, two alternative suggestions merit serious considerations. One relates to deploying the proceeds from disinvestment to retiring internal debt and the other to debt: equity swaps. In essence both the suggestions recognise the seriousness of the internal debt trap the country is heading towards, and averting it by utilising the proceeds from privatisation.

The debt build-up has undoubtedly assumed an alarming proportion in the country. The total internal liabilities of the Government of India alone stood at 52.1 per cent of GDP at the end of 1995-96 (BE). Interest liability thereon accounted for 9.7 per cent of GDP and claimed 47.3 per cent of its total gross revenue. In the face of engulfing internal debt problem, the suggestion[43] that the proceeds mobilised through disinvestment/privatisation should be directed towards retiring internal debt has considerable merit.

The other suggestion[44] relates to debt-equity swaps. It has been argued as follows. With the phasing down SLR security requirements by the Reserve Bank of India from 38.5 per cent in 1990 to the current level of 25 per cent, an overhang of SLR securities in excess of the required level in the banking system is estimated at about Rs. 250 billion. If a mechanism were created for banks to swap SLR for the government holding in PEs, this would be beneficial to government in terms of reduction of its debt and to the bank for revitalising securities portfolios by the substitution of debt for government equity. In the process, the outstanding government debt would get reduced and correspondingly interest liability would decline. Other macro economic benefits would be: A mechanism of debt equity swaps would improve the overall liquidity in the system resulting from the elimination of overhang of government securities. And, PE shareholders will be widely distributed in the process. Another benefit would be that even a limited sale of PE holdings to institutional buyers might result in efficient pricing but without generating liquidity pressures in the market.

Recognising the need for an explicit policy on deployment of proceeds from disinvestment, the budget for 1996-97 has proposed to use the proceeds to step up the expenditure on education and health and "for creating a fund to strengthen PEs." This option is undoubtedly superior to the one followed so far *i.e.* deploying the proceeds for fiscal adjustment. But, it does not guarantee any medium and long term improvement in the fiscal health of the economy, as dictated by sound principles of public finance. A large allocation for education and health is no doubt desirable but this should be done by eliminating wasteful government expenditures and by making the entire public sector more efficient. The point that may be flagged is that an appropriate scheme of using the proceeds from disinvestment for liquidating internal liabilities, which will contribute to the overall improvement in the fiscal health of the economy will serve the purpose of forging a wide measure of public acceptability.

NOTES

1. The author is grateful to Dr. Pradeep Kumar Mehta for providing editorial support, Mr. Prem Chand Pandey for his very helpful research support and Mr. S.A. Srinivas for his secretarial assistance Thanks are also due to Dr. Y. Venugopal Reddy, Dr. Rajeshwar Rao, Dr. R.K. Mishra and Dr. Bibek Debroy who spared time to provide some useful information and suggestions.
2. World Bank (1994): "India: Recent Economic Developments and Prospects" Report No. 12940-IN, Washington D.C. As cited in Gupta Anand (1996): "The Political Economy of Privatisation", paper presented at the One Day

Colloquium on Policy Analysis *"Public Sector Restructuring and Labour Reform : Progress and Prospects"*, NCAER, New Delhi, July 2, p. 1.

3. The discussion on the SLPEs is based on the data presented in the study: Mishra, R.K., *et al.,* (1992) Financial Contributions of State Level Public Enterprises in India, Volumes 1 & 2 (Unpublished), Institute of Public Enterprises, Hyderabad.
4. The alternative classification could be in terms of financial and non-financial SLPEs.
5. These include three PEs, which neither made any profits nor any losses.
6. Report of the Tenth Finance Commission, (1994), p.11. There is, however. inter-state differences in the performance of the SEBs of Andhra Pradesh, Gujarat, Madhya Pradesh, Maharashtra, and Tamil Nadu, recorded a cumulative profit, the SEBs of Bihar and Assam, had cumulative deficits of more than Rs. 10 billion each. See *The Economic Times*, 16 March, 1994.
7. Committee on Public Undertakings (COPU) 49th Report, (1981-82): Economic Administrative Reforms Commission Report (1983-84); Report of the Committee to review Policy for Public Enterprises (1986); Economic Advisory Council Report (1986), COPU's 32nd Report (1987-88); Report of 8th Plan Working Group on the management of Public Enterprises (1989), Standing Conference of Public Enterprises (SCOPE), (1989), Approach Paper to the White Paper on Public Enterprises, SCOPE (1990), Blue Print of SCOPEs, White Paper on the Public Sector.
8. Still the average tenure of a chief executive is about three to three and a half years only because by the time Directors are appointed as Chief Executives they are left with limited service due to superannuation, Hakeem, M.A. (1995): "PSUs : Not an extended Arm of Govt.," *Financial Express*, Sep. 5.
9. Iyer, R.R.: *"The Memorandum of Understanding System—Indian Experience"*, in S.L. Rao (1996, ed.), *op. cit.,* pp. 48-86.
10. The first to enter MOU was ONGC with the Ministry of Petroleum and Natural Gas in March 1987. The five others to follow it were: Steel Authority of India, Bharat Heavy Electricals, Ltd. Coal India Ltd., National Thermal Power Corporation and National Textile Corporation.
11. But the MOUs are not regarded as a very powerful instrument of restructuring mainly because "often MOUs are monitored at the level of CEOs and CMDs and do not percolate down to the lower level of management. See, Tommy, V.K. (1995): 'Need for a Paradigm Shift, *Financial Express,* Sept. 21.
12. A HC controls other companies which are its normally subsidiaries. For concept and evaluation, see, Canada, U.D.: "The Holding Company Concept and Its Use", in Rao, S.L. (1996, ed.) op. cit, pp. 87-100.
13. Ahluwalia, I.J. (1996): "Economic Reforms in India: Issues Ahead". Part 1, in Ahluwalia, I.J. and Albert Berry, *Perspectives: Focus on Indo-Canadian Business and Economic Issues,* the Conference Board of Canada, p. 12. Also see, Jena, P.K. (1995): "Privatisation : Not the best bet" *Financial Express* Dec. 26.
14. The other experts have made similar observations as well. See, for example. Hakeem, M.A. ; "Reforms has bypassed Public Sector", *Financial Express,* June 5.

15. From an average surplus of 1.8% of GDP on the current fiscal position, of the Central Government in the second half of the 1970s, the deficit increased to 3.3% in 1990-91. The gross fiscal deficit of the Central Government rose from 3.2% of GDP in 1975-76 to 6.2 % in 1980-81 and to 8.4% in 1990-91
16. For example, COPU (1955) was the first to recommend disposal of atleast 25% of the share capital of PE, Krishna Menon Committee also held a similar view. The Mohamad Yunus, Panel recommended for partial privatisation of both Indian Airlines and Air India. The spirit of privatisation was reflected in the Narasimham Committee (1984) Arjun Sengupta Committee's (1984) recommendations, and in the Long-term Fiscal Policy (1985). The budget for 1991-92, prior to the budget for the same year by the newly installed Congress Government. announced disinvestment of 20% of the equity capital of selected PEs in favour of financial institutions and mutual funds in public sector. See. Das, D.K. & Bhagat (1994, ed.) : *Economics of Privatisation : Issues and Options*, Deep & Deep Publications, New Delhi, p. 51.
17. For greater details, see, Kay, J.A., and D.J. Thompson (1986), Privatisation : A Policy in Search for a nationwide, *Economic Journal*, Vol. 96, pp.18-32. Also see, Mani, Sunil (1992), New Industrial Policy: Barriers to Entry Foreign Investment and Privatisation, *Economic and Political Weekly*, Vol. 27, No. 35; pp. 86-94.
18. The observation made by Isher J. Ahluwalia runs contrary to this because of the narrow interpretation she has associated Privatisation with Ahluwalia. I.J. (1996) *op. cit* p. 13.
19. Reddy, P.L. and V. Vithal Babu (1996) compiled India Trade and Investment Guide (New Policies, Guidelines organisation. (1991-96), p. 7.
20. It has been argued that necessary legal framework is a pre-condition for successful privatisation. See, Sachdeva, Gulshan (1996): 'Privatising for the Future". *Economic Times*, May 4.
21. In some quarters, it has been argued that offering bits and pieces of PEs doesn't make sense as long as government retains a majority stake. The limited privatisation will not lead to change in management style to improve efficiency, see, Kanth Sri (1995). "Whither Privatisation". *Economic Times (Corporate Dossier)* Dec. 8-14
22. The other terms of reference of the Committee are:
    (i) To devisec criteria for selection of Public Sector Enterprises for disinvestment during 1992-93;
    (ii) To suggest the target clientele including mutual funds, Financial Institutions, Banks, Employees, Resident Investors, Non Resident Indians, Foreign Institutional Investors;
    (iii) To make suggestions on the *modus operandi* of disinvestment, whether through public sector offers or private placements;
    (iv) To lay down the criteria for valuation of equity shares of public sector enterprises;
    (v) To make recommendations on any other subject matter germane to the disinvestment plan. For details. See Government of India (1993), Ministry of Finance, Committee Disinvestment of Shares in Public Enterprises.
23. However, on the basis of such recommendation, the UF government is considering disinvestment up to 74% of equity in selected cases, such as STC and MMTC. See *Financial Express,* March 29, 1996.

24. The concept of employee share holding to the extent of 5% of the fresh issue was mooted in 1986 with the objective of promoting greater participation resulting from their being stakeholders. It may be mentioned that in the disinvestment carried through so far, employees are given 5% share.
25. The share holding of Euro issues rests with a depository created in the form of trust, which exercises the voting rights. Thus the Euro issues are intended to assure a high dividend to the foreign investors but not voting rights to them and low cost capital to the domestic company.
26. For detailed discussion on the issue, see Mishra, R.K. Volume on Privatisation in India. in the seminar on *Restructuring of State Level Public Enterprises* (June 30-July 1, 1995), Institute of Public Enterprises, Hyderabad (unpublished) pp. 267-268 see also Mishra, R .K. and R. Nandagopal "Capital Market and Privatisation of Public Enterprises," in *ibid.* For the case of India see, Sankar, T.L. and Y. Venugopal Reddy (1989, ed.): *Privatisation Disinvestment of Ownership of Public Enterprises*, IPE, Silver Jubilee Publication, pp. 133-139.
27. Mishra, R.K., *op. cit.*, p. 268.
28. An exercise in computable general equilibrium framework shows that public sector investment in India has not crowded out private sector investment. See, Pradhan B.K., D.K. Ratha and Atul Sarma (1990): "Complementarity between Public and Private Investment in India", *Journal of Development Economics*, 33, pp. 101-106.
29. This would, however, require a significant improvement in the currently prevailing unfavourable conditions in the capital market and appropriate pricing of the instruments both in the domestic and foreign markets to avoid the situations like the fiasco of VSNL issue and frequent postponing of the issues of the PEs in the domestic capital market. Equally important for the success of such efforts is the infusion of institutional credit at a much higher level in the capital market through the banking system.
30. Under the SICA total of 2497 private and public sector companies were referred to the BIFR from its inception to the end of December 1995. Out of the 1756 references registered, the BIFR dismiss 383 cases as non-maintainable, sanctioned/approved revival schemes in 530 cases and recommended 407 cases to the concerned High Courts for winding up.
31. Incidentally, the government has stressed that the proceeds through disinvestment would be utilised in health and education, apart from strengthening other PEs.
32. The broad terms of reference of the Disinvestment Commission are:
    - (i) To draw up a long-term disinvestment programme within five to ten years for PEs referred to it;
    - (ii) To determine the extent of disinvestment as well as mode (domestic, international capital markets / auction / private sale to identified investors, etc.) in each PE;
    - (iii) To prioritise PEs referred by the Core Group;
    - (iv) To recommend a mix between primary and second divestment; and
    - (v) To select financial advisers and ensure employee participation in the sale process. For details, see, *Economic Times,* 8 August, 1996.

33. Largely based on unpublished notes, prepared by Reddy, Y. Venugopal.
34. These observations are based on unpublished notes prepared by Reddy, Y. Venugopal and Dutta, Abhijit, privatisation of SLPEs in India—A Survey into the 'Happenings' in the Volume on Seminar on Restructuring of State Level Public Enterprises (June 30 to July 1, 1995) op. cit., pp. 138-201.
35. For greater details see Gupta, Anand (1996), The Political Economy of Privatisation in India Presented at the One Day Colloquium on Policy Analysis: Public Sector Restructuring and Labour Reform : Progress and Prospects, New Delhi, July 2, p.11.
36. Chapter 5B of the Industrial Disputes Act, 1947, which was in 1976, provides that the employer, before retrenching even a single worker has to obtain prior permission of the government. This permission is not given for populist reasons. For detailed discussion, sec Chary, H. *et al.*, "Simplification of Labour and Procedures", in Menon, N.R.M. and Bibek Devroy (1995, ed.): Legal Dimension of Economic Reform, Allied Publishers, p. 21.
37. Mishra, R.K. "Privatisation in India" in the volume, *op. cit.* p. 267.
38. The Finance Minister has just (August 30, 1996) constituted a committee consisting of industry representatives, economist and bureaucrat as members to prepare draft amendments to the Companies Act, 1956.
39. Kikery, Sunita, Framework of the Methods of Privatisation of the State-owned Enterprises in Rao, S.L. (1996, ed.), Reforming State-owned Enterprises, NCAER, p. 222.
40. Bajaj, J.L. (1994), *op. cit.*, p. 128.
41. Ewing, Andrew, Improving the performance of state-owned enterprises in Rao, S.L. (1996, ed.), op. cit., p. 37.
42. Kikeri, Sunita, John Nellis and Mary Shirley, "Privatisation: Lessons from Market Economics", The World Bank Research Observer. p. 247.
43. Sahota, I.S., Chelliah, R.J. and several other noted economists have expressed this view repeatedly.
44. For detailed exposition see Parekh, Deepak S. (1996) Annual General Meeting Statement. Infrastructural Lease Financial Services Limited, *Economic Times* (Delhi Edition), July 19.

3

THE BLACK MONEY, THE SAP AND THE VDIS

Kamal Nayan Kabra and *V. Upadhyay*

The Structural Adjustment Programme (SAP) was initiated statedly in order to overcome some of the glaring shortcomings and omissions of the earlier policy regime. Among these, excessive bureaucratisation as a consequence of burdensome regulations and restrictions on private initiative to save, invest and innovate find a prominent place. Similarly high rates of taxation, particularly on individuals and corporate incomes and wealth were also considered counter-productive. Such factors gave rise to a collusive relationship between politicians and administration on the one hand, and the businessmen on the other. The net result of these features of the statist policy regime was to foster the growth of a burgeoning black economy.

These factors were often pointed out and a strong case was made for doing away with these features in order to cleanse the system of the scourge of black economy, popularly known as the menace of black money. Thus it was maintained that to the extent the SAP does away with the factors responsible for the black economy, it will remove some of the basic distortions from price-market-mechanism and unshackle the processes of growth. More particularly the features of SAP like deregulation and debureaucratisation, a regime of low and reasonable tax rates, removal of restrictions on investment, imports and innovations and generally setting the prices right were expected to deal some decisive blows against the black economy. It is in this context that one has to view various policy changes, initiated under the SAP for curbing the growth of black economy and enabling people to come clean. The Voluntary Disclosure of Income Scheme (VDIS) 1997 may well be regarded as the culmination of such policies initiated for removing market distortions caused by statist policy regime. This was in addition to the battery of schemes introduced immediately in the aftermath of reinvigorated pursuit of SAP in 1991.

The above are among the propositions spelling out the stated rationale for the VDIS which we intend to examine in the following. However, SAP had another important dimension. This may be considered in relation to the short-term fiscal stabilisation dimension of the SAP. As a part of this policy based on neo-classical resurgence it was intended to increase the role of market forces and to roll back the state. In the period immediately preceding the full-blooded imposition of SAP in 1991, the fiscal health of the economy was in terrible mess. Fiscal deficit of unprecedented and unmanageable proportions was narrowing down the options of the state in many ways. Hence the SAP intended to reduce fiscal deficit and introduce an element of stability in the macro economic landscape. Reducing tax rates was a part of the philosophy of SAP and expanding the tax base did not appear feasible both on account of administrative and political factors. Then, democratic pressures restricted the scope for cutting down revenue expenditure. Thus one option was to reduce capital account and social welfare expenditure in order to reduce fiscal deficit. Another option to this framework was to fall back upon the huge and growing reserves of black wealth and current flows of black incomes for increasing public revenue. The Voluntary Disclosure of Income Scheme, 1997 seems to owe itself to a certain extent to this factor. In fact, we would argue that this seems to be the main rationale for the VDIS.

The VDIS promised to kill two birds with one stone. On the one hand, it would increase the revenue and, on the other, atleast create the illusion of flushing out and curbing black incomes and wealth. This may be regarded as a major short run-revenue objective of the VDIS-1997, which may well be regarded as an integral component of the SAP. Granting of a royal, friendly treatment to the operators of the dirty, unclean economy has a long history going back to the 1950s.

Almost coinciding with the inauguration of the Indian republic, a series of 'voluntary' disclosure of income schemes for coaxing out the undeclared, unofficial and illegal incomes were introduced. By now the first half-century of our independence has seen nine such schemes, as though to keep up with the number of five year plans. It must, however, be recognised that there was a gap of fourteen years between the first and the second such effort to induce out into the legal framework the hoarders of black incomes and wealth and enable people to make a clean breast of it all atleast partly and for the time being. Thus fiscal history dotted with an unending series of attempts to unearth "black" incomes and wealth.

Given this background and the fact that the VDIS-1997 is an integral part of the policy package known as the SAP, we intended to examine the emerging state of the 'black' economy under the SAP dispensation with specific attention to an examination of the VDIS. To begin with, in the following section we try briefly to assess the essential character of the financial market's scam of the early 1990s and explore its linkages with the earlier and current phase of liberalisation. Following from this, section II is devoted to an overall examination of the early 1990s attempts for coming to terms with several forms of our black economy. The counter-productive results of these measures seemed to have been lost on the policy-makers. This background enables us to take up the question of the impact of the SAP regime on the black economy in section III showing how by means of combination of the sins of commission and omission and probably on account of its inherent nature, the SAP strengthened the sinews of our underground economy, taking us towards a version of crony capitalism. An eloquent vindication of our view was seen in the form of the VDIS1997 which we examine in the section IV in terms of the essential features of the scheme, its rationale, implementation and results and overall evaluation. We conclude by adumbrating in the concluding section some preconditions and steps conducive to reduction of the menace of the black economy.

I

India has seen over the last five decades the emergence of an interconnected network of informal illegal systems working in the interstices of the formal legal system. According to the Joint Parliamentary Committee which inquired into the irregularities in securities and banking transactions, "During the period from July 1991 to May 1992 the most glaring proof of the nexus between the irregularities in banks and the overheating of the stock market (which) came to light and that there was a sharp increase in securities transactions during the corresponding period of the banks involved in serious irregularities related with the scam".

The whole nation was shell shocked by the magnitude (at minimum Rs. 4024.45 crore), brazen devices, involvement of a large number of public agencies, nexus of the scamsters with the highest fora on the government and as the Joint Committee puts it, "some evidence of collusion of big industrial houses playing important role' in the scam. The Joint Committee was categorical in maintaining that the scam was the result of "liberalisation without adequate safeguards". It seems possible to go a little further and maintain that "capital market liberalisation contributed in a variety of ways to the perpetration of the worst and the most complex bank fraud committed since Independence". The systems failure remained a non-starter because in the absence of the policy changes and changed permissive growth-at-any-cost environment of business associated with liberalisation, neither the motor power, nor the amounts involved, nor the stock market's wild bull run would have become available to the scamsters. As an RBI functionary maintained, the scam was based on three important policy changes. Many PSUs, flush with market mobilised funds and bit by the high profitability bug of the SAP era, needed to invest in lucrative channels huge funds raised by them from the capital market. The stock market was in the grip of a bull frenzy thanks to capital market "reforms" like free equity pricing, reduced capital gains, tax, entry of FIIs wealth tax exemption, etc. They obtained the PSUs funds by means both fair and foul for stoking the bull fires. The funds were made available by the banks as a result of the fiat to increase dividend payments by 50 per cent in order that the fiscal deficit target of the stabilisation component of the SAP could be met and the threat of implementing Narasimhan Committee's recommendations could be averted. Hence they entered the PSU funds under Portfolio Management Services and, in order to obtain this kind of returns went into the grip of the over-speculating brokers, by lending to the brokers against non-existent and fake securities.

The bull phase was taken by the Finance Minister as an early indication of the SAP, who, contrary to the assessment of the SEBI chief that it was speculative boom (based on the illegal transfer of money market resources to the capital market), maintained that 'the market can never go wrong" and that a falling economy cannot have a rising market. Thus the SAP regime created conditions and pressures for the scam to emerge and flourish, neglected their supervisory and corrective role, tried to cover up and block it and derail a thorough inquiry into it, failed to take action against the main scamsters (the Action Taken Report was essentially a cover-up) and even after a thorough exposure, they are persisting with the same policies, particularly in the financial sphere.

Despite such a rude shock, the managers of liberalisation did not take steps to see how, why and by whom such shenanigans may be perpetrated in various fields and how to check them in the tracks in order particularly to prevent the degeneration of state-supported marketisation- privatisation drive into crony capitalisation east Asian countries (for a detailed account, see, Kabra, 1992).

II

The serendipity of the financial markets scam could well have been taken as an early warning of the dangerous possibilities of letting the market forces have a free run in a situation in which the oligopolistic market operators in India's highly skewed economy were sitting atop huge accounted of unaccounted wealth and had control over regular inflows of illegal, unclean incomes, as sizeable, according to some estimates (Gupta, S. 1991) as the open, legal GDP. Whether by design or as a response to the fiscal and BOP problems, intensified liberalisation under SAP coincided with four amnesty schemes in the 1991. More or less on the heels of taking steps to implement the MOU with the World Bank in 1991, these schemes, with varying features but with the common running thread of a soft kid-glove approach for bringing out into the open, legal framework a good deal of the wealth and incomes form the "black" economy were initiated. These schemes were :

(i) Gold Bond Scheme,
(ii) India Development Bonds,
(iii) Foreign Remittance Immunity, and
(iv) Voluntary Disclosure Scheme

It may be noted that the Bearer Bond Scheme (which was called a scheme to provide the black economy with its own "black" currency) of 1981 was to mature shortly. This need for cash outgo too may have increased the huge to roll over the scheme, *albeit* with a new name. The essence of these schemes was to legalise various types of unaccounted resources on very favourable terms of distinctive feature to induce in foreign exchange and gold which had been accumulated by the black operators and acquired astronomical proportion. This was a clean reflection of these schemes real intent to respond to a severe external liquidity crisis, which faced India in 1991. It was made possible to utilise the income and wealth disclosed under these schemes for further investment/gifts/use, etc. As a result 41.26 tonnes of gold (a tiny fraction not only of the total gold stock estimated at around seventy thousand tonnes but also of the annual gold demand of over 400 tonnes) and Rs. 4462.5 crore of black savings/ income (again a tiny part of the total estimated black economy) moved into the legal, declared framework.

It is clear that these schemes could not go any meaningful distance towards cleansing the system. This goes to strengthen the hypothesis that the hope to overcome at least partly the short-run revenue and foreign exchange crunch seems to have been the main motives for these schemes. Their impact on the existing and future black economy hardly entered the calculations of the policy-makers. It means insofar as the "black" economy is concerned we remain at square one. Let it not be forgotten that a major factor responsible for the 1991 foreign exchange liquidity crisis was the huge amount of stashing away of wealth in foreign lands. Similarly but for tax evasion, there would have been no fiscal crunch. Do these schemes, therefore, amount to rewarding those who perpetrate serious national crisis? Are there some element in the SAP which either directly or indirectly contribute to curbing the black economy? After a fairly long spell of intensified SAP, what has happened to the size, forms and spread of the black economy?

Answers to such questions may well be imagined on the basis of massive and brazen misuse of these supposedly anti-black economy schemes which in effect increased the depth and diaspora of the unclean economy. It is reported that current black incomes were used to buy gold for investment under the gold-bond scheme, thus not only laundering of illegitimate incomes and wealth, but higher returns too were ensured. In order to lure the NRIs to "invest"in these schemes, high level delegations, headed by the Minister of State for Finance toured abroad and the officials were told to be "tolerant' towards tax-offenders and "remove fears from the minds of the public", (read taxdodgers). The Finance Minister justified this approach (even the misuse of the schemes by departing from the laid down conditions) on the ground that "it would be wholly counter-productive if simultaneously those who took advantage of the two schemes were to be prosecuted". However, the possibility of using hawala transactions for remitting unclean incomes and obtaining them back through the amnesty scheme was officially recognised. A former chief minister of a state has been hard put to explain Rs. 100 crore received by her in this form. Thus it was recognised at the official level that "substantial fraudulent claims of immunity" were made in a large number of cases, with or without the collusion of bank managers. Instead of immobilising and unearthing the hoards of past number two wealth in order to usher in an era free of corruption and rent-of authority, the amnesty schemes are likely to have generated additional "black" incomes and wealth, ensured tax-free returns on them, created the possibilities of their unrestricted circulation and sent signals that the authorities are ready to surrender to the power of the dirty economy, wherever financial difficulties overwhelm them.

III

As is well-known the phenomenon of tax evasion, violation of economic laws and regulations mainly in the area of industry and foreign trade have been considered responsible for the growth of very large sized black economy and its exponential growth. In this sense the SAP was regarded as a method of removing some of the root causes of the black economy. The main elements of the SAP like getting the prices right and letting the market allocate resources on the basis of the criterion of relative profitability, low rates of taxes and freer flow of goods services and capital across international borders and greater open internal and external competitiveness were expected to remove or weaken the basic reasons behind black economy.

Thus there are doubts about the prospects of completing the agenda of the SAP. Leaving these doubt apart one may ask a question as to what is the nature of the new regime and society which results as a consequence of a successful introduction of the SAP? This is apparent that under the new regime many of the things, which were earlier considered illegal and/or unacceptable, now stand recognised as perfectly legal and acceptable. For example, on account of the low rates of income, wealth and company taxes the market economy loses one of its most potent and practical instrument for *ex post facto* equity in the distribution of income and wealth. Even the growth of public revenue from these taxes can hardly sustain the hypothesis of supply side economies about a more than proportionate growth in revenue. The absolute increase in revenue may be related more to higher nominal income than to better tax compliance. Such low rates of taxes may or may not be equal or lower than to the cost of holding black incomes and wealth and the cost of occasionally converting such black incomes into white. The point remains that so long as the prospects of detection are weak, punishment/penalties are light and elusive and the symbiotic equation with the public authorities remains intact, the black economy would continue to thrive.

Similar would be the case with respect to external trade. What was earlier not allowed to be imported and was treated as contraband or was allowed to come into the country in a very restricted manner through import licences and with heavy import duty are now allowed to come into the country openly, legally and cheaply. This again is a change not in the actual behaviour of the economy, but in the fact that the line is drawn at a different level: what was illegal import, like for example of gold and silver has now been legalised.

Similar traits can be seen with respect to black incomes generated by the corporate sector whether financial or industrial. You remove restrictions on the remuneration packages offered to the corporate bosses, and you find that what was illegally siphoned off by way of corporatisation of private expenditure, now becomes legitimate, tax-deductible company expenditure. Nothing has changed in reality except that the law now recognises as legal what was earlier deemed to be illegal. It is an example of revolution by redefinition. In practice there are a number of examples of such practices which we have been reported during the period 1991 to date. In fact, the draft bills prepared by the UF Government like the Companies Bill FEMA (in place of FERA), the Money laundering Bill new Income Tax law, etc. are examples of accommodation shown to those who were sought to be regulated but who managed to circumvent and bypass these laws. Naturally, with a law in conformity with the actual market processes, there would be little need for its violation and hence illegal economic activities concerning these matters would have ceased.

Even after over six years of liberalisation, India has not been able to live down her reputation as one the most corrupt markets (yes, market and thankfully not the nation) even according to some votaries of liberalisation. *Fortune quotes* a Hong-Kong based firm 'Political and Economic Risk Consultancy Ltd.' which rated India at seven on a corruption score board (presumably out of 10), as third most corrupt market in Asia, after China and Indonesia, where bribes add to operating costs. In order to provide some vignettes of multifarious illegalities, corrupting our economic and political system, we pick up on a random basis some reports from the press. It may be noted that detected and reported cases are but a fraction of the totality of the fraud and illegality prevalent in our system giving rise to the worry "are we going the Italian way?" We try to organise some select glimpses of this information in such a manner that the cases can be related to specific dimensions of the structural adjustment programme. Obviously no claims of being exhaustive or referring necessarily to the most glaring of these cases are made.

Let us first take the case of how external liberalisation is marked by multifarious scams. This is an area in which very many far-reaching changes concerning trade, foreign exchange, technology transfer, capital movements (direct foreign investment, portfolio investments by foreign institutional investors and investments by the NRIs), foreign banks, reduction in tariffs and very liberal promotion of export-orientation were witnessed. This is an area which has been full of illegalities like duty-evasion (smuggling), under or of over invoicing, capital flight, illegal money transfer through Hawala, large-scale money, laundering, including by the narcotic mafias, black markets in foreign currency, fraudulent declarations of the value and description imports and exports, misuse of various schemes of export promotion, commissions and kick backs in bulk imports and exports of canalised items as also of public account imports.

With more opening up, deregulation, marketisation and promise of liberal returns, did there come about a change among the participants, both national and international, away from the illegal; clandestine transaction? A study by John Zdanowicz, of the Florida International University estimated that owing to over and under invoicing capital flight from India to USA amounted to nearly 8 billion during 1992 notwithstanding current account convertibility. So blatant are these practices that exercise bicycles normally priced at over $100 per piece were billed at about half a dollar each.

Importer-friendly scheme of value-based advanced licensing (VABAL) which significantly enlarged the duty exemption scheme was introduced in April 1992. It was to grant great flexibility to the licence except the items listed in the sensitive list. The obligation was to export equivalent value, either before or after imports.

Many instances of the misuse of such a business-friendly measure have come to light indicating the nature of the market response. Fictitious exports of things like ball pens, bricks and broken plastic buckets would be made, to be dumped in high seas. Value equivalent would be flown out through hawala for laundering unaccounted wealth.

The importing party may be a related or front concern. The money would come back as export proceeds, equivalent to the value of VABAL Materials which have either high import duty or prima in home markets would be imported for sale in the home market. Trade performance of this period represented in part the return of the flight capital.

Recently, cases came to light when false bills of entry were used for sending out huge amounts (Rs. 456 crore and Rs. 100 crore in two cases) from a Mumbai Bank to Hongkong. It came to light as the Hongkong authorities alerted their Indian counterparts of rather large transactions, which they suspected could be drug mafia money. It also brought out lack of co-ordination between the Reserve Bank of India exchange Banker and the customs authorities. Thus money laundering and convertibility on trade account are getting mixed up. If the recommendations of a recent RBIs Taraporewala Committee on capital account convertibility are accepted, illegal transfer of savings or illegally-obtained incomes by Hawala or under the over-invoicing would become redundant. The illegal wealth would legally find place in safe hands and India would witness the worst replay of the 1997s Thai and Indonesian crisis.

Red-carpet has been rolled out for portfolio investment by FIIs in India's primary and secondary capital market and preferential capital gains treatment has been offered with a view to impart at least some stability to the hot money flows. However, the FIIs are flowing in and out of the share market without attracting capital gains tax or profit taking as they take advantage of our tax treaty with Mauritius to avoid their tax liabilities. It is estimated that 95 per cent of profit booking by the FIIs was done through Mauritius. This is well-known and yet no corrective has been introduced in order not to displease the FIIs and huge revenue losses and mockery of our laws are accepted as the price of this uneven playing field policy vis-a-vis foreign capital.

This is indicative of the MNCs scant respect for the laws of the host countries. How Nestle fosters monopoly by production arrangements with Campco, evades excise duty and has been accused of under-weighing is not untypical of the MNCs profiteering. The ITCs excise dispute based on charges of evading over Rs. 800 crore still seems to be hanging fire and even litigation could not spare them of the obligation to deposit over Rs. 300 crore. Though the charges against Enron of paying kickbacks in the one-rejected Dabhol project may be difficult to establish, two things are clear. The company did massive cost escalation to which its own subsequent scaling down of the project cost bears testimony. The expenditure of about Rs. 64 crore for "educating" Indians about its projects can easily be treated as a case of "creative accounting" to cover up building "useful" support for their Indian operations. The first ever conviction by SEBI of the top executives of Hindustan Lever on charges of insider trading for booking illegal profits is an indication of the persisting behavioural patterns.

The notorious Jain Hawala scandal, a fortuitous peep into the widespread and mufti-faceted cancer of our system, in an interlinked case of international money laundering, money transfer, commissions and kickbacks based awarding of public sector contracts (including foreign companies) mainly wage infrastructure and defence contracts involving top politicians and bureaucrats. Most blatant anti-national linkages with the terrorists and narco-terrorism bares the worst criminal aspects of these pay-offs. It is true that the evidence collected by the CBI has not been judged to be adequate by the law courts. But such are the ways of the number two economy that it rarely leaves sufficient legally-admissible evidence. However, many of the accused have admitted the acceptance of money from the Jain brothers, which lends credence to the existence of scam. All these lend voluminous support to the Vohar Panel findings of politicians-criminals support from the underground economy. The implications of the Hawala scam are particularly ominous for the power sector as it involved two power ministers and a number of bureaucrats. How the public sector has been informally privatised and made to go in for inflated cost plant and equipment, making a mockery of competitiveness and efficiency through opening up, makes the cost of Hawala many times more than Rs. 64 crore.

How large policy-based imports too have been misused to cause huge loss to the public exchequer and the collection of bribes, commissions and illegal gains on the basis of insider information is illustrated by the notorious sugar scam of 1994, when the decision to import sugar was delayed by four months which, according to the Parliamentary Standing Committee on Civil Supplies and Public Distribution cost the nation Rs. 638 crore. This excludes the bribes which could have been collected for delaying the decisions, which led to sugar price hike going upto Rs. 10 to Rs. 12 per kg and the alleged profits by some insiders who entered into forward contracts abroad and made a killing. What is highlighted by such cases is that under liberalisation, the politicians are collecting rent of authority for using their discretion in determining the timing, sequence, areas and extent of liberalisation.

In response to a question in Parliament, the Finance Minister admitted that lately there has been some increase in economic crimes but he did not consider it alarming in view of the level of economic activities and their rapid expansion. Some examples from the fiscal, mainly tax arena can provide a glimpse of the emerging nature of tax regime after tax cuts, greater faith in the tax payers and simplification of tax laws etc. which form part of Fiscal Policy Liberalisation.

Modvat was introduced as an effective antidote to tax evasion. But many instances of the misuse of Modvat by irregular, unintended availing of Modvat credits (revenue loss Rs. 1823 crore; in another case false Modvat claims worth about Rs. 100 crore from mini-steel mills were detected) by devices like claiming credit without documents, claiming Modvat credit twice, availing of customs duty as Modvat credit. Against about Rs. 300 crore due to the government from the exporters as Modvat credit only Rs. 140 crore worth of Modvat credit has been reversed according to a press report in October 1995. Increased Modvat use from about 12 per cent in 1986-87 to over 30 per cent now is generally related to slow-down in excise revenue.

Tax evasion indicators like those from searches and seizures can be supplemented by the Comptroller and Auditor General's Report on tax administration. According to such a report under assessment of taxes and revenue loss aggregated to Rs. 673.93 crore during 1994-95. Similar mind-boggling figures have been reported for import and export duties. In the case of customs duties as many as 591 exemption certificates were in force leading to forgone duty of Rs. 2798 crore, which is nearly 10.47 per cent of total customs receipts. Similarly, excise duty exemptions numbering 309 are in force leading to revenue loss of Rs. 9360 crore. During 1994-95, total of 4830 raids unearthed assets worth Rs. 577 crore.

Defaults in income tax payments involve astronomical figures. As on 31st March 1995, the major tax defaulters included Harshad Mehta (Rs. 3647.93 crore), Hiten Dalal (Rs. 1271.33 crore), Bhupen Dalal (Rs. 729.71 crore), Ashwin Mehta (Rs. 608.17 crore) and so on. Eight foreign banks have defaulted the payment of Rs. 750 crore. The sum total of such defaults would easily exceed the proposed annual outlay on poverty-alleviation programmes.

Refusing to learn the lessons of the 1991-92 financial markets scam several prominent PSUs like SAIL, Nuclear Power Corporation, ONGC, OIC are reported to be placing their fund, flouting government directive, with the banks that have neither the stipulated capital base, nor credit rating. This kind of exposure can be highly destabilising as the PSUs had around Rs. four to five thousand crore for short time investment. Another source of trouble in the financial sphere is that against 670 registered non-banking financial companies, there are estimated to be 39 thousand unregistered ones who escape observing the RBI norms. It is reported that many companies are depositing their working capital funds borrowed from the banks without NBFCs. Little wonder, "the other incomes" of the companies show very good results. With liquidity at a premium, the NBFCs are bending every rule in the book, like collecting unsecured fixed deposit by paying commission of around 5 per cent.

Bank frauds, whose number increased steadily since 1991, have become endemic as shown below:

No. detected	*Amount involved*	*(Rs. Crore)*
1991	1559	65.41
1992	1717	145
1993	2273	320.32
1994	2266	200.07

It may not be out of place to refer to a major state level scam. Fraudulent and unauthorised withdrawals from the treasurers by the Animal Husbandry officials of Bihar, going on for the last 15 years, has become a corruption case of epic proportions. The figures for the last eight years are as under:

Bihar's Fodder Scam (Rs. Crores)

Year	*Budgetary Provision*	*Actual Withdrawal*
1987-88	33.70	6.92
1988-89	37.78	6.13
1989-90	42.21	8.65
1990-91	54.92	29.29
1991-92	59.10	70.72
1992-93	66.94	87.77
1993-94	74.14	125.03
1994-95	74.40	170.61

It seems that neither the executive, nor the legislature comes down upon such an unbelievably large fraudulent, kleptomaniac operations, which ought to have surfaced at so many points in the course of budgeting, its sanction, scrutiny, revision, audit etc. especially in a state which was in the throes of a severe financial crunch.

The frequency and magnitude of financial markets scams after liberalisations seem to have increased compared to the situation prior to liberalisation when the public sector dominated the financial markets. This makes one wonder that if capital account convertibility and other financial sector 'reforms' are implemented, what would be our defence against the enactment of the East Asian Drama on our stage. This warning is worth heeding because we too are attracting large quantities of hot money flows into our stock exchanges, are contracting lots of short term external debts and are trying to finance long term infrastructure projects on the basis of short term credits and investments. These transactions are extremely sensitive to that elusive entity called market confidence, which is highly contagious, and need not bear any specific relationship with the real sector's performance.

IV

Perhaps as a recognition, at least implicitly of the inability of the SAP to undo the basis and results of the unclean economy and the need to raise resources from this segment of the economy for overcoming the current fiscal constraint the authorities have to take some steps which while raising revenue may give the impression of scaling down the black economy. Therefore, quite expectedly, the government announced the Voluntary Disclosure of Income Scheme in June 1997. Its declared objective was to raise revenue and curb the black economy in the country. In this section we discuss in details the main features of the VDIS'97 and examine its rationale, implementation and results. In the concluding section, along with an overall evaluation of the VDIS'97, we suggest some steps which in our view are vital in any purposeful struggle against the ever-growing menace of the black economy.

The VDIS'97 allowed individuals to convert 'black' income or wealth into 'white' on payment of 30 per cent tax, the rate for corporations was 35 per cent. The persons or corporations making declarations were granted immunity from all prosecution under the Income Tax Act, the Wealth Tax Act, the FERA and the Companies

Act. All particulars contained in a declaration (under the scheme) are to be treated as confidential. The scheme has provided that any information given under it could not be called for presentation before any court. It is to be noted here that income declared under the scheme was taxed at the current highest applicable rate (i.e. 30 per cent) and not the highest rate prevailing in the year of tax evasion. While the government had announced similar schemes in past also. in the new scheme the tax on disclosed income was levied at the lowest ever rate of 30 per cent. The tax rate of 30 per cent applicable to the disclosures was, according to Revenue Secretary, no more than the cost of "managing black money". There was "no penalty, no surcharge and no interest" for not disclosing income in the past. In addition, several loopholes (discussed later in detail) were deliberately built in the scheme, which made effective rate of taxation on certain assets (jewellery, bullion, silver utensils etc.) much lower than the announced rate of 30 per cent.

As discussed above, the VDIS'97 should be viewed as an integral part of the SAP. The SAP aimed at removing market distortions caused by the presence of huge parallel economy. The VDIS'97 was supposed to be an important step in that direction. Raising revenue in the short-run was another equally important goal of the VDIS'97. The overall framework of the SAP included the long-term fiscal policy announced in the mid-80s under which rates of taxation were lowered in several successive steps (see Table 3.1). To increase revenue with lower rates of taxation, it was necessary to expand the tax base in the country which, however, was not found feasible because of political compulsions and perceived weaknesses of administrative machinery. The net result of these policies was an unprecedented increase in fiscal deficit, which was against the basic tenets of the SAP. In order to bring fiscal imbalances under control, the government sources seem to have come to the view that it was left with no option, at least in the short-run, other than tapping the black economy resources for raising revenue.

The government made all possible efforts to make the VDIS'97 a success. However various guidelines issued under the scheme lacked clarity which had a deterring effect on potential declarations in the initial phase of the scheme. The drafting of the scheme was very poor which left scope for different interpretations. To clear confusion over various provisions of the scheme, the Central Board of Direct Taxes had to issue clarifications time and again.

Table 3.1 : Rates of Personal Income Tax : 1987-88 to 1998-99

(In percentage)

S.No.	*Taxable income*	*Assessment years*								
		1987-88 and 1989-90	*1990-91*	*1991-92 and 1992-93*	*1993-94*	*1994-95*	*1995-96*	*1996-97*	*1997-98*	*1998-99*
1.	On the first Rs. 18,000	Nil	Nil	Nil	Nil	Nil	Nil	Nil	Nil	Nil
2	On the next Rs. 4,000	25	20	Nil	Nil	Nil	Nil	Nil	Nil	Nil
3.	On the next Rs. 3,000	25	20	20	Nil	Nil	Nil	Nil	Nil	Nil
4.	On the next Rs. 3,000	30	30	20	Nil	Nil	Nil	Nil	Nil	Nil
5.	On the next Rs. 2,000	30	30	20	20	Nil	Nil	Nil	Nil	Nil
6.	On the next Rs. 5,000	30	30	30	20	20	Nil	Nil	Nil	Nil
7.	On the next Rs. 5,000	30	30	30	20	20	20	Nil	Nil	Nil
8.	On the next Rs. 10,000	30	30	30	20	20	20	20	15	10
9.	On the next Rs. 10,000	40	40	40	30	30	20	20	15	10
10.	On the next Rs 40,000	40	40	40	30	30	30	30	30	20
11.	On the next Rs. 20,000	50	50	50	40	40	30	30	30	20
12.	Over Rs.1,20,000	50	50	50	40	40	40	40	40	20+

\+ 30 % when income exceeds Rs. 1,50,000.

Note : Certain incomes of non-resident Indians are taxable at the flat rate of 20 per cent (for details *see* para 179.1)

contd.

Union Surcharge on Income Tax

a. For the assessment year 1987-88 : Nil

b. For the asessment years 1988-89 and 1989-90 : 5 per cent of income tax if total income exceeds Rs. 50,000 (no surcharge is payable in the case of a non-resident).

c. For the assessment year 1990-91 : 8 per cent of income-tax if total income exceeds Rs. 50,000 (no surcharge is payable in the case of non resident)

d. For the assessment years 1991-92 and 1992-93 : 12 per cent of Income Tax if taxable income exceeds Rs. 75,000 (no surcharge is payable in the case of non-resident)

e. For the assessment years 1993-94 and 1994-95 : 12 per cent of income tax if taxable income exceeds Rs. 1,00,000 (no surcharge is payable in the case of non-resident)

f. For the assessment years 1995-96 and 1996-97 and beyond : NIL.

Source : Compiled from various sources like Budget Papers.

The Voluntary Disclosure of Income Scheme which was announced on June 18, 1997 (vide Ministry of Finance Notification No.10373) created a major controversy on that day itself over the clarification of the Chairman of the CBDT that even those persons who were facing inquiry on the violation of FERA but were not served with detention order were eligible to take recourse to the VDIS to convert their black money into white. The Finance Minister had to issue a clarification the next day that no unusual benefits would be conferred under the VDIS to persons facing enquiries, proceeding or prosecution (see the *Tribune*, June 20, 1997).

Potential declarants feared that income out of sales turnover declared under the VDIS would be subject to sales tax up to 15 per cent in addition to the 35 per cent income tax which companies were required to pay under the scheme. To allay these fears about levy of sales tax by state governments, the Finance Ministry announced that "there is no question of state governments being able to use information furnished under VDIS as evidence to levy sales tax... VDIS is a creation of an Act of Parliament and the Act clearly provides that all information, including income disclosed, shall remain confidential" (see The *Times of India*, Dec. 30, 1997).

The VDIS'97 was described as a grand success not only by the Finance Ministry but also by some experts and business commentators as well. It was claimed that the VDIS'97 had not only succeeded in generating unprecedented amounts of revenue for the government but also had been able to make a significant dent in the black economy in the country. A significant proportion of black economy; it was claimed, had been channelised into the productive system. These claims need to be examined more closely.

The tax collection under the VDIS'97 was Rs. 10,050 crore through 4,66,031 declarations implying that the average declaration per person amounted to nearly Rs. 7 lakh. It implies that about Rs. 33,000 crore of black incomes and wealth were disclosed. According to the Finance Ministry, 77.5 per cent of the total resources secured under the scheme would accrue to the states, rest of the funds would be at the disposal of the Central Government. The Central government's funds would be used to finance the Common Minimum Programme and the infrastructure needs of the nation.

Like the VDIS'97, there have been several schemes in past also aimed at tapping black money. The VDIS'97 is, however, being described as the most successful of all the schemes: tax collections under the VDIS'97 are more than the tax collections under all the earlier schemes put together. Although there is some apparent truth in this statement, a closer examination of various tax amnesty schemes shows that results of the VDIS'97 have not been very different from those of earlier schemes. Table 3.2 shows the amounts of tax collected under various tax amnesty schemes since independence (with the exception of the special bearer bonds schemes of 1981 which was very different in nature). Tax collections in current prices and in 1980-81 prices are given in column 2 and 3, respectively. As can be seen from the table, although the differences in the amounts of tax collections in current prices under various schemes are enormous, these are greatly reduced when the nominal figures are adjusted to price change, or, are viewed in the context of current, comparable estimated size of the black economy.

The table also gives for various amnesty schemes tax-collections to GDP ratio in percentage terms. This ratio shows an increasing trend over time. The low value of this ratio for the VDIS'85 is probably due to the fact that the VDIS'85 came only a few years after the special Bearer Bonds Scheme of 1981 whereas in case of other schemes, there was a gap of about 10 years between two successive schemes. The value of this ratio (in percentage terms) is 0.75 for the VDIS' 97, which is higher than the values for earlier schemes but is not very drastically different from them.

Table 3.2 : Tax collection under various VDS Scheme

Scheme		*Tax collection in current prices* (*Rs. crore*)	*Tax collection 1980-81 prices* (*Rs. crore*)	*Tax collection as % of GDP*
(1)		*(2)*	*(3)*	*(4)*
VDS1951		10.9	51.60	0.109
VDS 1965		50.3	156.45	0.192
VDS 1976	(Income Tax)	249.0	348.30	0.293
	(Wealth Tax)	7.7	10.77	0.009
VDS 1985	(Income Tax)	338.0	261.38	0.147
	(Wealth Tax)	70.7	47.66	0.026
VDS 1997		10,050	2566.67	0.750

Source : For figures in column (2), Ministry of Finance, Govt. of India.

It would be more pertinent here to calculate the ratio of tax collections to the size of the black economy. We have not attempted this exercise on account of the non-availability of reliable estimates of the size of black economy over time. It is, however, generally agreed that the rate of growth of the black economy in our country has been higher than the rate of growth of GDP. It is, therefore, not unreasonable to argue that the ratio of tax collections under various amnesty schemes to the size of the black economy has remained more or less constant. As shown later, there has been a shortfall of Rs. 3000 crore in the normal yield from income tax during 1997-98. It means the income tax payers have substituted VDIS'97 for normal tax payment by as much as nearly 30 per cent. This puts paid to the tall claims about the grand success of it in terms of revenue collection. (Interim Budget 1998-99, The *Economic Times,* March 26, 1998).

The estimates of black income vary from 20 per cent to 50 per cent of GDP. Taking a figure of 40 per cent, black income in the current year would be around Rs. 5,60,000 crore. Almost the entire black income (80 per cent according to some estimates) accrues to the rich (the upper most decile of our population) and, therefore, would be taxable. Informal sector incomes are usually small and within the exemption limit (i.e. non-taxable) and, therefore, are not part of the black economy. Even if only 50 per cent of total black income is taxed at the rate of 20 per cent, it would generate additional revenue of Rs. 56,000 crore, through income tax in the current year.

Uncovering black income and bringing it into tax net was, however, not the sole objective of the VDIS'97. The scope of the VDIS'97 was much wider it covered both black income as well as black wealth accumulated over past year. The Parliamentary Standing Committee on Finance and Black Money estimated that the amount of black money in 1994-95 was of the order of 300,000 crore (at 1980-81 prices) or Rs. 1,100,000 crore at current prices in comparison to GDP of Rs. 945,615 crore at current prices in 1994-95. It would not be unreasonable to think that the volume of black wealth and black income in the country now is equal to GDP (i.e. in the region of Rs. 1,400,000 crore) if not more. The voluntary disclosure of Rs. 33,000 crore worth of assets and income touches only a fringe of the problem, amounting to no more than 2.3 per cent of the estimated black income and wealth. The VDIS'97 has thus clearly failed in making a serious dent in the parallel economy, even in terms of revenue contribution.

Lowering of rates of taxation does not automatically reduce tax evasion. There is not direct link between them. People do not pay taxes voluntarily. Even with a low tax rate, there is an incentive to evade if chances of detection are low and penalties on detection are not severe enough more so as a result of the tax liabilities likely to arise in future year after year. Often the cost and risks involved in tax evasion are very low which encourages tax evasion. For the corporations, black income earned from tax evasion provides a competitive edge in the market It serves as an arsenal against rivals. Compliance with tax laws can only be increased if the sanctions in the law against infringements are made credible.

There has been, as mentioned earlier, a continuous scaling down of tax rates in India for quite some time now. If incidence of income tax is best measured by the average tax rate, one would see that our rate-structure is very low and has come down to very low levels (see Table 3.3). This has had not desirable effect in terms of containing tax evasion is evident from the fact that during the era when the tax rates were sizeably scaled down, all the estimates of the black economy show a disproportionate, quantum jump in the size of the black economy, its infiltration in newer areas and adoption of new, additional tricks for the purpose. Moreover, there has been no increase in tax payments by rich income groups relatively to lower income groups. As a matter of fact, as can be seen from Table 3.4 the share of income tax paid by relatively rich income groups in total income tax collections has been declining continuously over time. Table 3.4 provides details of high income (Rs 5 lakh and above) returns for the period 1985-86 to 1992-93. The number of high income returns increased from 5.3 thousand in 1985-86 to 19.8 thousand in 1992-93, however, in terms of percentage of total returns, the increase was very marginal.

Table 3.3 : Conversion of Marginal Income Tax Rates into Average Rates : 1987-88 to 1998-99

Total Income	*Assessment Years*								
	1987-88 to 1989-90	*1990-91*	*1991-92 and 1992-93*	*1993-94*	*1994-95*	*1995-96*	*1996-97*	*1997-98*	*1998-99*
20,000	2.50	2.00	Nil	Nil	Nil	Nil	Nil	Nil	Nil
23,500	5.85	4.68	1.27	Nil	Nil	Nil	Nil	Nil	Nil
26, 500	8.30	6.98	3.39	Nil	Nil	Nil	Nil	Nil	Nil
29, 000	10.17	8.96	4.82	0.68	Nil	Nil	Nil	Nil	Nil
32, 500	12.30	11.23	7.23	2.76	1.53	Nil	Nil	Nil	Nil
37, 500	14.66	13.73	10.26	5.06	4.00	1.33	Nil	Nil	Nil
45,000	17.22	16.44	13.55	7.55	6.66	4.44	2.22	1.66	1.11
55,000	20.45	19.81	17.45	10.72	10.00	7.27	5.45	4.09	2.72
80,000	26.56	26.12	24.50	16.75	16.25	13.75	12.50	11.25	7.50
1,10,000	31.13	30.81	29.63	21.27	20.90	18.18	17.27	16.36	10.90
1,35,000	34.62	34.37	33.40	24.74	24.44	21.48	20.74	20.00	12.59
1,50,000	36.16	35.93	35.06	26.26	26.00	23.23	22.66	22.00	13.33
3,00,000	43.08	42.96	42.53	33.13	33.00	31.66	31.33	31.00	21.66

Source: For figures in column (2), Ministry of Finance, Govt. of India.

For simplifying the calculation we exclude surcharge where and when applicable, standard deduction and tax rebates on various approved investments. The two by and large may 'probably cancel out the impact of each other on the average rates.

Table 3.4 : Income Tax payable by rich income groups (Returned income Rs. 5 lakh or above)

Assessment Year	*No. of returns in thousands*	*Returned Income (Rs. Crore)*	*Tax payable (Rs. Crore)*
1985-86	5.3 (0 2)	5706 (40.5)	3177 (70.1)
1986-87	6.8 (0 2)	7277 (36.9)	3011 (62 7)
1987-88	8.1 (0.2)	10274 (40.9)	4063 (62.7)
1988-89	8.0 (0.2)	4883 (22.9)	2471 (45.6)
1989-90	14.2 (0.3)	7233 (27.8)	3130 (50.1)
1990-91	16.2 (0.3)	7938 (26.8)	3429 (49.1)
1991-92	18.0(0.3)	7531(21.6)	3616(44.1)
1992-93	19.8 (0.3)	7848 (21.1)	3767 (42.3)

Note : Figures in parentheses are percentages of total number of returns, returned income and total tax payable for the respective years.

Source : Directorate of Income Tax, *All India Income Tax Statistics for assessment year 1985-86 to 1992-93.*

Such cases accounted for 21.1 per cent of total returned income in 1992-93 in comparison to 40.5 per cent in 1985-86. More importantly, cases in this category accounted for 42.3 per cent of total tax payable in 1992-93 in comparison to 70.1 per cent in 1985-86. This clearly shows that tax payments by the rich have been continuously declining in relative terms. This is despite the fact that the economic reforms process started in 1985 has led to inequitous growth in the economy benefiting the rich at the cost of common people. The phenomenal rise in conspicuous consumption (luxury cars, etc.) during this period is a clear indication of that trend.

Burden of taxation on the salaried person, on the other hand, is increasing since salaried employees cannot escape the tax net because of TDS. As can be seen from Table 3.5 gross tax payable from salaries shows significant growth not only in absolute terms but also in terms of percentage of total gross income tax over the period 1985-86 to 1992-93. Gross tax payable from salaries accounted for 9.2 per cent of total gross income tax in 1992-93 in comparison to 5.4 per cent in 1985-96. With greater scope for evading non-salary incomes this ratio indicates heightened incidence of evasion on non-salary incomes, which normally should have increased to a greater extent than salary incomes.

Disclosure schemes in fact promote dishonesty by rewarding tax evaders. Under the VDIS'97, income or assets declared by individuals were taxed at the rate of 30 per cent, the rate for corporations was

35 per cent. However, as has been shown by several analysts, the effective rate of taxation after taking into account various factors works out to be much lower.

Table 3.5 : Gross Income Tax from salaries

Assessment Year	*Gross Income Tax Payable from salaries (Rs. Crore)*	*Gross Income Tax payable from salaries as % of total gross Income Tax by all classes of the payers*
1985-86	287	5.4
1986-87	243	4.1
1987-88	435	5.6
1988-89	440	6.8
1989-90	836	9.2
1990-91	974	9.4
1991-92	1029	7.5
1992-93	1219	9.2

Source : Directorate of Income Tax, *All India Income Tax Statistics for Assessment Years 1985-86 to 1992-93.*

If the declared assets were jewellery, bullion or silver utensils, the effective rate of taxation was only about 10 per cent. This was made possible because the VDIS'97 was full of loopholes, which were exploited by "smart' declarants fully to convert high-value jewellery (including even recently bought jewellery) into "white" for a pittance. One special feature of the scheme was that no bill, voucher, etc. was required to prove the date and source of money used to purchase jewellery or bullion. A simple affidavit indicating the date of purchase was accepted by the tax authorities on face value. Individual declarants were asked to pay income tax at the rate of 30 per cent (35 per cent in the case of corporation) of the value of the declared items at the time of purchase. A cut-off date of April 1, 1987 (the rationale for which is known only to the mandarins presiding over the Ministry of Finance) was set for items purchased earlier than that date. By manipulating dates of purchase, the individuals or corporations making disclosures declared the minimum possible values for jewellery and other items and thus were able to reduce their tax liabilities to very low levels. In addition, benefits of indexation were available in case of subsequent sale of assets under the VDIS. This aspect is illustrated with the help of the following example developed by Mr. A. Das. Let us say an

Indian citizen, X, who had purchased one kg silver jewellery on April 1, 1987, at the then price of Rs. 4,794, decided to declare the asset under the VDIS. X sold off the jewellery on June 23, 1997, for Rs. 6850 per kg at the going price. The cost of indexation for X shot up to Rs. 10,387 for 1997-98. Under the VDIS, the tax payable by X amounted to Rs. 1,438 (30 per cent of Rs. 4794, or the cost of purchase). X, however, incurred a capital loss of Rs. 3,537 since the cost of indexation was far higher than the sale proceeds. Thus tax savings due to capital loss was Rs. 707, that is 20 per cent of capital loss. Effective cash outflow hence was only Rs. 731 (tax payable minus tax saving due to capital loss). The effective tax rate in this case works out to only 10.67 per cent. (See Das. A, "For smart one VDIS tax rate can be 10 per cent", *Indian Express,* July 7, 1997).

Dholakia has estimated the aggregate value of assets declared under the VDIS'97, based on his estimate of the weighted average appreciation in asset values, to be Rs. 122,000 crore at current prices, as against the officially indicated nominal value figure of Rs. 33,000 crore. 'Thus, the effective rate of tax directly payable under the VDIS turns out to be only 8.2 per cent, rather than the nominal rate of 30 per cent announced in the scheme. The overwhelming response of the tax-payers and the resulting unprecedented success of the VDIS'97 in terms of tax collections are, to a large extent, attributable to such an incredibly low rate of effective tax payable on the actual amounts declared under the scheme' (Dholakia, B.H. "VDIS'97: A Macro Economic Assessment", *The Economic Times,* Jan 15, 1998).

The effective rate of taxation is lower than the nominal rate of 30 per cent for one another important reason also. Under the current scheme, a person pay tax only on wealth accumulated (in the form of various assets) from past income, but no tax on past income spent on consumption (luxurious or otherwise). For example, if a person say had income of Rs. 10 lakh in 1996-97 and he blew most of it on foreign travel. In 1997-98 he has no assets to show and thus pays no tax. Had, on the other hand, he paid tax honestly in 1996-97, his tax liabilities would have been substantial.

Honest tax-payers feel cheated when they see tax-evaders getting off scot-free by paying small token sums under the disclosure scheme. By rewarding declarants for late disclosures, schemes such as the VDIS'97 put a premium on dishonesty. According to T.N. Pandey, the VDIS'97 was harshly discriminatory against honest taxpayers. On the income on which they paid tax ranging from 60 to 40 per cent on due dates their unscrupulous brethren are paying tax at 30 per cent. And even this 30 per cent is a misnomer inasmuch as such persons must have earned much more than the tax (paid by tax deferral, which is using the taxes due to the government and not paid for earning more income). Such measures may give some revenue at a very heavy social, ethical and other costs, but cannot provide a solution to the ever increasing menace of tax evasion and black money'. (see *Business Standard,* June 6, 1997).

The VDIS'97 is sure to signal a negative message to honest tax payers and bring down the tax compliance significantly for many years to come. Past experience shows that repeated disclosure schemes have adverse impact a regular tax collection. The experience of the past year (i.e. 1997-98) has not been any different. The revised estimates presented in the interim budget for 1998-99 show that in 1997-98 there were major shortfalls in tax collections (of Rs. 14,236 crore). The total tax revenue during 1997-98 were Rs. 99,158 crore against Rs. 1,13,394 crore projected in the 1997-98 budget. The income tax collections were short by Rs. 3000 crore, corporation tax collections fell short by Rs. 500 crore. Income tax revenue were not only short of the budgeted amount but were even lower than the collections in 1996-97. These figures clearly show the disastrous effect of the VDIS'97 on regular income tax and corporation tax collections. Because of the enormous attention given by the income tax department to the Voluntary Disclosure of Income Scheme in 1997-98, the regular tax-collection work was completely ignored.

The former Finance Minister, Mr. P. Chidambaram's claims that lower tax rates would yield higher collections thus clearly stands rejected.

(In Rs. crore)

	1996-97 R.E.	*1997-98 B.E.*	*1997-98 R.E.*
Income Tax	18,843	21,700	18,700
Corporation Tax	19,010	21,860	21,360

Source: The Hindu, March 26,1998,

The euphoria displayed by the Finance Ministry following the collection of Rs. 10,050 crore under the VDIS'97, now it appears, was completely misplaced. The government, particularly the tax administration, are responsible, to a good degree, for stagnating tax revenue and rapid growth in the size of the black economy. In fact, instead of a tough, no nonsense attitude towards tax-dodgers and their collaborators in the revenue administration machinery, a new kind of partnership between the two seems to be emerging. After all, both as a matter of general perception and based on the circumstantial evidence of the existing size and exponential growth of the unclean economy, it stands to reason to suspect that by means of extortion or for overlooking tax evasion and its multi-fold expansion for a consideration, the personnel of the tax departments play a critical role. To the extent the complex, ambiguous and lengthy tax laws and procedures are such as to permit, tolerate or encourage the tax evaders, the tax administration cannot absolve itself of a certain identifiable degree of responsibility for genesis of 'black' income and wealth and their operation in the economy. The 'new' ambience and bonhomie following the VDIS is something, which may turn out to be counter productive if the past experience is any guide.

The available information suggests that some of the biggest disclosures have come from either politicians of ill-repute who did not have any identifiable source of legitimate income or have come from their close relatives or from ex-civil servants. The corporate sector has, by and large, kept itself out of the scheme. This by itself is an indication that most resourceful well-organized segment has decided to ignore this scheme. How such illegal income and wealth get reproduced on an extended scale, spreads into other sectors, corrupts politics, administration and law-making are well-known.

A handful of very large declaration, going to dizzy levels of upto Rs. 500 crore, mean very many declarations would be below the arithmetic mean. Those who have 'saved' taxes for decades have experienced a virtual tax exemption. Thus honesty and good citizenship have been penalised. Leave alone the immorality of it all even the hard cash calculus of sound and viable fiscal policy suggests that strong incentives have been created for generating black income and their conversion into hidden, generally unproductive assets. The VDIS declared incomes and wealth would be grist to the black economy mill.

Overall right from the conception to execution and the gloating over its putative 'success' the VDIS appears to be a very black economy-friendly scheme. It believed in many circles that a lot of tainted money has been laundered under this scheme, going beyond the purview of amnesty granted, for example, wealth and income obtained by corrupt practices too seem to have been declared as no means of checking such a malpractice was provided. Unless a thorough audit is ordered in order to ensure that criminal and other offences related incomes and wealth have not been white-washed under the scheme, it is difficult to believe that the scheme has not been counter-productive. An effective onslaught against the black economy requires reorientation of policies and plans away from subserving the cause of growth *per se* to an active concern with various qualitative aspects of growth as the primary concern. This is not a place to discuss an alternative policy agenda for this purpose. However, it may be mentioned that for the success of the attempts to unearth and reduce the scope for further generation of such incomes and wealth, it is very important that the schemes be transparent, accountable and reduce both the means and incentives for accelerating the growth of this segment of the economy, whatever inducements are offered have to be a once-for-all variety, invoking exemplary, different penalties for post-amnesty indulgence in black transactions (which would need systematic computerised collating of data from various sources) Scheme which neglects these tenets may well be regarded as scams in their own right. They represent collusive relationship between the illegal economy and economic administration.

REFERENCES

Business Standard, June 6, 1997.

Das, A., "For smart one VDIS tax rate can be 10 pc", *Indian Express*.

Dholakia, B.H. " VDIS'97 : A Macro Economic Assessment," *The Economic Times*, Jan. 15, 1998.

Directorate of Income Tax, *All India Income Tax Statistics for Assessment Years 1985-86 to 1992-93*.

Government of India, Ministry of Finance, Notification No. 10373. *The Voluntary Disclosure of Income Rules*, 1997, June 9, 1997.

Kabra, Kamal Nayan, *The Black Economy in India, Problem & Policies* Delhi, 1982, Chanakya.

Kabra, Kamal Nayan, "Voluntary Disclosure Immoral" *Kaleidoscope*, Feb. 1998.

The Economic Times, March 26, 1998.

The Hindu, March 26, 1998.

The Times of India, Dec. 30, 1997.

The Tribune, June 20, 1997.

4

SOUTH ASIAN PREFERENTIAL TRADING ARRANGEMENT

Implications of Trade Liberalisation for India

Indra Nath Mukherji

Introduction

Preferential trading is one of the mildest forms of an integrative arrangement. Under the arrangement, the Contracting States (CS) offer a preferential margin with respect to trade barriers in relation to their MFN rates. CS having disparate levels of development as well as trade regimes find this an acceptable instrument for initiating regional trade liberalisation. Such an arrangement nevertheless provides the building blocks towards accelerated regional trade liberalisation culminating in a free trade area within a defined time frame. Under a free trade area the CS eliminate all trade restrictions on their mutual trade, while maintaining restrictions in their trade with non-CS at a level they deem appropriate. When all CS decide on a common external tariff, then the arrangement translates itself in a more cohesive customs union. The most comprehensive integrative arrangement arises in the nature of a common market when all CS agree not only to allow free movement of goods and services, but all the factors of production including capital and labour. The Agreement on South Asian Preferential Trading Arrangement (SAPTA) which has been made operational since December 8, 1995, thus symbolises the beginnings of the very first stage of an integrative arrangement among the member countries of SAARC.

The idea of regional cooperation in South Asia was first mooted in May 1980. Following consultations amongst the countries of the region, Foreign Secretaries of the seven South Asian Countries (SACs), viz. Bangladesh, Bhutan, India, Maldives, Nepal, Pakistan and Sri Lanka met for the first time in Colombo in April 1981. This was followed, a few months later, by the meeting of the Committee of the Whole, which identified five broad areas of regional cooperation. The Foreign Ministers, at their first meeting in New Delhi in August 1983, formally launched the Integrated Programme of Action (IPA) through the adoption of a Declaration on South Asian Regional Co-operation (SARC). At the first summit held in Dhaka on 7-8 December, 1985, the Charter was adopted establishing the organisation of South Asian Association for Regional Co-operation (SAARC).

The IPA presently covers thirteen agreed areas of co-operation. The first attempt towards moving into core areas of trade and economic co-operation was the commissioning by the SAARC Secretariat, a *Regional Study on Trade, Manufactures and Services*. The study was completed in 1991 outlining a number of recommendations for promoting regional co-operation in the core economic areas. The Council of Ministers at its Ninth Session in Male in July 1991, endorsed the study and decided to set up a high level Committee on Economic Co-operation (CEC).

At the Colombo Summit in December 1991, the Heads of State or Government of SAARC approved the establishment of the Inter Governmental Group (IGG) to seek agreement on an institutional framework under which specific measures for trade liberalisation among SAARC Member States could be advanced. The IGG met twice to evolve a Draft Agreement on SAARC Preferential Trading Arrangement (SAPTA).

The CEC at its third meeting in New Delhi in November 1991, recommended that the Draft Agreement on SAPTA, with a few modifications, be approved by the Council of Ministers at its next Twelfth Session in Dhaka. Subsequently, the Council of Ministers signed the framework agreement on SAPTA in Dhaka on 11 April, 1993, the signing of SAPTA was a landmark achievement of the Seventh SAARC Summit held in Dhaka (SAARC 1993: 6-7). The New Delhi Summit held from 2-4 May, 1995, formally approved the proposals for preferential trade worked out by the IGG and later endorsed by the SAARC Foreign Ministers. With all the member countries having ratified the agreement, the same came into force on December 7, 1995, the date which marks the end of the first decade of SAARC's existence.

In view of the very modest or symbolic nature of regional trade liberalisation achieved in the First Round, the CS are looking forward to more far reaching trade liberalisation in course of the Second Round. At the end of two-day meeting of SAARC Commerce Ministers held from 7-8 January, 1996, a joint communique reiterated a commitment to accelerate the SAPTA process and to the realisation of the South Asian Free Trade Area (SAFTA) as the goal preferably by the year 2000 but not later than 2005.

With a view to launching the Second Round, the IGG met in Colombo during 14-15 March, 1996, and subsequently between 7-8 September in Islamabad. The IGG met for the third time between 25-26 October, 1996, in New Delhi to finalise the National Schedule of Concessions (NSC) under the Second Round which was placed before a meeting of CEC to be held between 28-29 October, 1996. The NSC for the Second Round was concluded at the Fourth Meeting of the Inter Governmental Group (IGG) held in Kathmandu from 29-30 November, 1996. It was decided that all necessary procedures would be completed so that the Schedules as finalised during the second round enter into force by March 1, 1997.

Impact of Trade Liberalisation on India's Imports: Trade Creation/ Trade Diversion and Revenue Implications

Assuming Free Imports

An attempt has been made in this section to offer some estimates of possible trade creation, or trade diversion as also the revenue implications following import liberalisation in India on imports from all its partner countries in the SAARC region, excluding Bhutan.The reason for excluding Bhutan is that India has free trade with Bhutan. The data set used for this analysis is the top fifty products imported by India from other Contracting States (CS) of SAPTA. These products accounted for India's total imports from Bangladesh, Maldives and Nepal, and over 97 per cent of its imports from all CS in the region during 1994-95 at the highest level of disaggregation, viz. at eight digit classification under the Harmonised Systems (HS).

On the basis of assumed import demand elasticities, two possible scenarios are postulated: (1) 100 per cent reduction of tariff's or free trade, and (2) a fifty per cent reduction in duties on existing MFN tariffs and para tariffs. The assumed price import demand elasticity is based on a study by Bhuyan (referred to in Rehman *et al.* (1980). The study by Bhuyan had estimated price elasticity of import demand for each member country from the SAARC region for each SITC section. The import data used in this study was based on HS system at a disaggregated level. In order to obtain the corresponding SITC category, another study (W.R. Cline *et al.*, 1978) was referred to which showed the correspondence between each HS section and SITC class. The relevant chapters of the disaggregated HS codes helped us to identify the relevant section under the HS classification from which the relevant SITC classification was matched.

This study further assumes: (1) countries under discussion are small open economies and hence are price takers in world markets, that is, the elasticity of export supply is infinite and hence import prices will fall by the full amount of the cut in tariffs, (2) imports and domestic goods are assumed not to be perfect substitutes that is, the import demand function will not be shifted by the change in import competing countries. Given the above assumptions, the increase in quantity imported of commodity is given by :

CMQi=b *MQCi * CTRi/100/(1+TRi) where
i = each top 50 product at eight digit HS code,
MQCi = initial import immunity of product i.
CMQi = increase in import quantity of product i,
TRi = initial tariff rate on product i,
CTRi = change in tariff rate on product i,
b = price elasticity of import demand,
Thus new import (NIi) following tariff reduction = (CMQi + MQCi)* UVCi,
UVCi = unit value import cost of product i,
RDPi = Potential revenue difference on product i = – Ni * CTRi/100
(assuming revenue foregone on base year as well as on additional imports which could have been substituted from rest of the world.)
RDi = actual revenue difference and is given by:—(MQCi* UVCi)* CTRi/100.

Under the assumption of non-competing domestic substitutes, trade creation is assumed to take place when as a result of tariff reduction, more is imported from the partner country and provided further that the unit cost of the product is lower in the partner country than that prevailing in the rest of the world. Conversely trade diversion is expected to arise if following tariff reduction, more is imported from the partner country where the unit cost of the product is higher than that in the rest of the world. Thus, the unit cost difference with respect to any product is given as :

PDi=(Mvwi/Mqwi)—(Mvpi/Mqpi) where:
Mvwi - India's net import value of product i from rest of the world;
Mqwi = India's net import quantity of product i from the rest of the world,
Mvpi = India's import value of product i from partner country,
Mqpi = India's import quantity of product i from partner country.

Trade creation takes place if PDi is positive. Trade diversion takes place when PDi is negative. Thus trade creation (TCi) for product i takes place when:
TCi = PDi* CMQi (when PDi is positive)
Conversely, trade diversion (TDi) takes place for the i-th product when:
TDi = PDi * CMQi (when PDi is negative)

When trade creation and trade diversion effects are summed up over the top fifty products, we get an overall estimate for all the selected products which gives a near total estimate of India's total imports from the region.
Net trade creation /diversion is thus given by:
$\Sigma TCi - \Sigma TDi$

A positive value denotes net trade creation while a negative value denotes net trade diversion. Having examined the methodology of estimation adopted in this study, we highlight the main results of India's free imports (total elimination of customs duties) on imports from all partner countries (excluding Bhutan) has been presented in Table 4.1

It will be observed that in case India opted for full tariff reduction in favour of top fifty products (which accounts for almost near total imports from the region), additional imports from Bangladesh would be no more than Rs. 321 million or 27 per cent of India's imports from Bangladesh. There would be potential revenue loss of about Rs. 380 million, actual revenue loss of Rs. 298 million and trade diversion of Rs. 24 million. The potential revenue loss will be greater than the actual loss since.

Table 4.1 : India's Import from SAARC : Increase in Import, Revenue Difference, Trade Creation/Diversion, assuming Free Import (Rupees) : 1994-95

Variables	*Bangladesh*	*Maldives*	*Nepal*	*Pakistan*	*Sri Lanka*	*SAARC*
MVC	1,196,349,412	7,251,080	1,005,287,988	1,657,557,341	800,228, 621	4,666,674,442
CMV	320,901,621	2,890,172	300,526,467	327,113,835	248,266,858	1,199,698, 953
(CMV/MVC) *100	27	40	30	20	31	26
NI	1,517,251,033	10,091,252	1,305,814,455	1,984,671,176	1,048,495,479	5,866,323,395
RDP	-569,498,727	-5,305,380	-597,808,696	-1,050,744,785	-535,102,088	-2,758,459,676
RDP*	-379,665,818	-3,536,566	-398,539,131	-700,496,523	-356,734,725	-1,838,972,764
RD	-447,660,786	-3,812,676	-436,834,165	-862,307,281	-404,618,910	-2,155,233,818
RD*	-298,440,524	-2,541,784	-291,222,777	-574,871,521	-269,745,940	-1,436,822,545
TC/TD	-23,557,531	-208,170	1,291,614	11,911,000	34,515,906	23,952,819

Source : Estimated from Monthy Statistics of Foreign Trade of India (Imports), March 1995, DGCI & S, Kolkata.

Note : MVC = Base Year Value.
CMV = Increase in Import Value.
NI = New Import (MVC + CMV).
RD= Revenue Difference (difference in revenue consequent to tariff reduction).
RD* = Given and use tariff concessions, we assume two-thirds of estimated value.
RDP = Potential Revenue Difference.
RDP* = Two-thirds of estimated value of RDP.
TC/TD = Trade Creation / Trade Diversion.

In case of Maldives the increase in imports would be Rs. 2.9 million or 40 per cent of India's total imports from Maldives, the potential revenue loss would be Rs. 5 million actual revenue loss of Rs. 2.5 million, end trade diversion of Rs. 0.2 million.

In case of Nepal India's imports would expand by Rs. 300 million or 30 per cent, the potential revenue diference would be Rs. 398 million, actual revenue loss of Rs. 291 million and trade creation of Rs. 1.2 million.

India's import from Pakistan would increase by Rs. 327 million or 20 per cent, the potential revenue loss would be Rs. 700 million, actual revenue loss of Rs. 575 million and trade creation Rs. 1.2 million

India's imports from Sri Lanka would increase by Rs. 248 million, or by 31 per cent, the potential revenue loss would be Rs. 535 million, the actual revenue loss would be Rs. 270 million, trade creation would be Rs. 35 million.

For the SAARC region as a whole, the increase in imports would be 26%, potential revenue loss Rs. 1839 million, actual revenue loss Rs. 1436 million, and net trade creation Rs. 24 million.

For the purpose of illustration, a detailed product-by-product analysis of trade creation, trade diversion assuming free trade, increase in imports and revenue foregone under alternative assumption in the context of Indo-Pak trade has been presented in Annexure I.

Assuming Fifty Per Cent Reduction in Tariffs

In Table 4.2 we have presented the next possible scenario where it is assumed that India decides to offer a 50 per cent cut in its tariff in favour of its SAARC partner states. Summary results are presented in Table 4.2.

In such a situation India's imports from Bangladesh would increase by Rs. 186 million or by 16 per cent, the potential revenue loss would be Rs. 172 million, actual revenue loss Rs. 125 million, and trade diversion would be Rs. 13 million.

India's import from Maldives would increase by Rs. 1.6 million or by 23 per cent, the potential revenue loss would be Rs. 2.4 million, actual revenue loss Rs. 0.9 million, and trade diversion would be Rs. 0.1 million.

Table 4.2 : India's Import from SAARC : Increase in Import, Revenue Difference, Trade Creation/Diversion, assuming 50 per cent Reduction in Tariff (Rupees) : 1994-95

Variables	*Bangladesh*	*Maldives*	*Nepal*	*Pakistan*	*Sri Lanka*	*SAARC*
MVC	1,196,349,412	7,251,080	1,005,287,988	1,657,557,341	800,228, 621	4,666,674,442
CMV	185,780,145	1,685,572	181,435,854	198,532,383	149,600,521	717,034,475
(CMV/MVC) *100	16	23	18	12	19	15
NI	1,382,129,557	8,936,652	1,186,723,842	1,856,089,724	949,829,142	5,383,708,917
RDP	-259,472,758	-2,363,248	-267,749,716	-490,401,532	-241,833,250	-1,261,820,504
RDP*	-172,981,839	-1,575,341	--178,499,811	-326,934,355	--161,222,167	-841,213,512
RD	-188,188,103	1,406,142	-169,084,450	-371,903,655	-162,773,982	-890,544,048
RD*	-125,458,735	937,428	-112,722,967	-247,935,770	-108,515,988	-593,696,032
TC/TD	-13,412,354	-124,145	-622,306	7,530,810	20,442,121	13,814,126

Source : Estimated from Monthly Statistics of Foreign Trade of India (Imports), March 1995, DGCI & S, Kolkata.

Note : MVC = Base Year Value.
CMV = Increase in Import Value.
NI = New Import (MVC + CMV).
RD= Revenue Difference (difference in revenue consequent to tariff reduction).
RD* = Given and use tariff concessions, we assume two-thirds of estimated value.
RDP = Potential Revenue Difference.
RDP* = Two-thirds of estimated value of RDP.
TC/TD = Trade Creation / Trade Diversion.

The increase in India's imports from Nepal would increase by Rs. 181 million or by 18 per cent, the potential revenue loss would be Rs. 178 million, and trade diversion would be Rs. 0.6 million.

Reduction in tariff by 50 per cent is expected to increase India's imports from Pakistan by Rs. 199 million or by 12 per cent, cause potential revenue loss of Rs. 327 million, actual revenue loss of Rs. 248 million, and result in trade creation of Rs. 7.5 million.

India's imports from Sri Lanka is expected to increase by Rs. 150 million or by 15 per cent, cause potential revenue loss of Rs. 161 million, actual revenue loss of Rs. 108 million and result in trade creation of Rs. 20.4 million,

For the SAARC region as a whole, a 50 per cent reduction in customs duty by India is expected to increase imports by Rs. 717 million, or by 15 per cent, cause potential revenue loss of about Rs. 841 million, actual revenue loss of Rs. 594 million, and lead to trade creation of Rs. 13.8 million.

For the purpose of illustration, a detailed product-by-product analysis of trade creation, trade diversion assuming free trade, increase in imports and revenue foregone under alternative assumptions in the context of Indo-Pak trade has been presented in Annexure II.

It thus appears that under the assumptions indicated above, a move by India towards a partial or full fledged free trade area is unlikely to cause a very dramatic increase in imports. Thus Indian businessmen need not be excessively alarmed at the prospect of imports from neighbouring countries surging in so as to adversely affect the Indian domestic industries. However, it is also true that a move towards a full elimination of customs duties is likely to impact more adversely on customs revenues, particularly in the short run. This could be a matter of concern for the Indian government. However, a partial decline in customs duties (such as a 50 per cent reduction assumed as a possible case), is unlikely to impact as adversely in terms of customs revenue since augmented imports to some extent compensates for the diminished revenue realisation. It may be noted further that while reduction in tariffs causes trade diversion with Bangladesh, Maldives and Nepal (in case of 50% tariff reduction for Nepal), trade creation with Pakistan and Sri Lanka offsets this *as a result of which there is net positive trade creation with the region as a whole*. However it may also be observed that this modest trade creation is overwhelmingly offset by revenue loss which the Indian government will encounter as a result of moving towards nil customs duties with its neighbours. *Hence a gradual decline in customs duties is preferable to a one shot movement towards zero tariffs with its trading partners in the region.*

While the static effects of trade liberalisation points to immediate welfare loss since loss in customs revenue far outweighs the modest gains in terms of trade creation, one may also look at the positive dynamic effects that could result in value added in manufacturing as a result of reduction in customs duties and its resulting favourable effects on growth in manufacturing output and employment. As we have noted above, primary commodities and intermediate goods have a large share in India's regional trade. Hence a reduction in customs duties in respect of such products is likely to improve the value addition as well as the profitability of such industries. The long term impact of consequent growth in manufacturing output could offset the static effect of loss in customs revenue.

The loss in welfare effects can be further minimised by selectively liberalising imports in respect of products that are expected to create more trade. In Table 4.3 we present a list of products that could create more trade, being cheaper for India to import from Bangladesh as compared to imports from the rest of the world and further the share of which being imported from partner country is no more than 75 per cent of India's world imports.

It may be observed that in case India liberalises its imports selectively in favour of products with trade creation potentialities, then the total trade creation under the assumption of free trade would be Rs. 10.4 million, while in case of the alternative assumption of 50 per cent tariff reduction the trade creation would be only 6.1 million. The products likely to result in the largest gains include: granules, bovine leather, other alums, other finished tanned leather, marble, other ash and residue, etc.

The possibilities of trade creation in case of selective liberalisation of imports from Maldives under the two possible scenarios is presented in Table 4.4.

It may be seen that trade creation in case of free imports from Maldives could create trade to the extent of Rs. 0.3 million while in case of fifty per cent reduction in customs duties the trade creation would be Rs. 0.2 million. The products that could create more trade include other ferrous waste, shelled almonds, aluminium waste, and cowries.

In Table 4.5 we have presented a list of products with trade creation possibilities with Nepal in case of reduction or elimination of tariffs.

It may be observed that in case of free trade, the trade creation would be 0.2 million, and in case of fifty per cent reduction of duties,

Table 4.3 : List of products among top fifty imported by India from Bangladesh with possible Trade Creation and Value Share less than 75 per cent

Code	*Description (in brief)*	*Unit*	*Value share%*	*TC-I*	*TC-II*
00	Granules Chipping & Powder of MA	Ton	71.54	2231724	1305348
09	Bovine Leather Full Grains—Others	Kg	9.72	2214874	1217182
09	Other Alums	Kg	23.53	1101614	700753
09	Other Finished Tanned Leather From G	Kg	11.49	934396	513496
00	Marble & Travertine Crude/Rough	Ton	1.06	660480	388032
00	Other Ash & Residue Contng Miai	Kg	0.13	505862	299551
01	Chrome And Semi-Chrome Goat Su	Kg	27.15	505235	277650
03	Second Hand or Used Motor Cars	No	0.25	261357	261357
00	Other Fers Prdcts & Iron in Pll	Ton	5.26	396924	243276
02	Prchmnt Drsd Lthr of Othr Fnsh	Kg	18.14	415032	228081
09	Others (Ecaussine etc.)	Ton	37.04	284382	166530
01	Shrimp (Scampi) Macrobactium Fr	Kg	70.49	300951	159046
09	Other Fabrcs Impgrntd Lamntnd	Kg	1.72	145728	95473
09	Steel others		0.02	114140	68484
09	Other Bovine Anml Hids Bark Tn	Kg	10.84	87972	55048
09	Other Prpd Lthr of Goat or Kid	Kg	12.92	77950	42838
02	Journals & Periodicals	Kg	0.18	61800	33960
01	D.C. Motors	No	0.23	43320	27075
01	Printed Books	Kg	0.24	26102	14353
01	Lether Of Othr Anmls (Except S)	Kg	1.97	25458	13991
00	Othr Printd Books etc. of HD	Kg	0.01	17664	10350
00	Outer Soles & Heels of Rbber/P	PR	0.05	17808	9772
	Total			10430773	6131646

Source : Estimated from Monthly Statistics of Foreign Trade of India (Imports), March 1995, DGCI & S, Kolkata.
TC-I = Trade Creation assuming 100 % Reduction in Customs Duties.
TC-II= Trade Creation assuming Fifty percent Reduction in Tariff.

Table 4.4 : List of Products among Top Fifty Imported by India from Maldives with Possible Trade Creation and Value Share < 75 per cent

HS Code	*Description (in Brief)*	*Unit*	*Value Share %*	*TC-I*	*TC-II*
72044909	Other Ferrous Waste, Other	Kg	0.03	242220	146433
08021200	Shelled Almonds Frsh or Dried	Kg	0.15	50226	33660
76020000	Aluminium Waste & Scraps	Kg	0.01	24990	14070
05080003	Cowries	Kg	8.62	2124	1122
	Total			319560	195285

Source : Estimated from Monthly Statistics of Foreign Trade of India (Imports), March 1995, DGCI & S, Kolkata.

Note : TC-I = Trade Creation Assuming Free Import.
TC-II = Trade Creation Assuming Fifty per cent Reduction in Customs Duties.

Table 4.5 : List of Products among Top Fifty Imported from Nepal with Possible Trade Creation and Value Share < 75 %

HS Code	*Description (in Brief)*	*Unit*	*Value Share %*	*TC-I*	*TC-II*
53031001	Jute Raw (Excl Bimlipatam & Mes)	Ton	7.91	1608890	915546
41061903	Wet Blue Chrome Tanned Goat Le	Kg	26.95	2727615	1498959
54033900	Other Yarn, Single	Kg	18.22	910537	548929
41041039	Other Chrome Tanned Leather	Kg	14.42	953028	523737
38061009	Rosin and Resin Acids—Other	Kg	9.94	265640	167400

Source : Estimated from Monthly Statistics of Foreign Trade of India (Imports), March 1995, DGCI & S, Kolkata.

Note : TC-I = Trade Creation Assuming Free Import.
TC-II = Trade Creation Assuming Fifty per cent Reduction in Tariff.

Table 4.6 : List of Products among Top Fifty Imported by India from Pakistan with possible Trade Creation and Value Share < 75%

HS Code	*Description (in Brief)*	*Unit*	*Value Share %*	*TC-I*	*TC-II*
08021100	Almonds Frsh or Dried in Shell	Kg	2.54	10627830	7221465
26201900	Other Ash & Residue Contng Mai	Kg	1.48	4296162	2544054
12119026	Ayurvedic & Unani Herbs N.E.S	Kg	8.48	4038496	2435920
51012900	Other Degresd Wool Nt Crbnsd No	Kg	0.49	2780544	1555632
52093909	Other Fabric of Yarn of Cotton	Sqm	1.85	1350600	8145650
13019009	Other Natural Gums	Kg	19.12	938816	566272
60012900	Looped Pile Fabrics of other Tx	Kg	10.47	838656	505890
51012100	Degresd Shorn Wool Nt Crbnsd No	Kg	4.05	840072	469992
08021200	Shelled Almonds Frsh or Dried	Kg	9.1	723347	457388
17019902	Cane Sugar Refind	Ton	4.37	533627	321912
12119039	Plants & Parts E.G. Seeds, Fruits	Kg	4.39	525888	317196
4102909	Other Bovine Leather & Equine Leath	Kg	1.89	408376	224423
51032001	Waste of Sheep's & Lamb's Wool	Kg	5.46	272778	164532
13019019	Other Resins	Kg	15.38	260172	156924
13019029	Other Gum Resin	Kg	23.23	190239	114744
08022100	Hazelnuts In Shell, Frsh or Dri	Kg	48.06	110064	66384
54033900	Other Yarn, Single	Kg	1.24	81121	48898
51032009	Other West of Wool (Excl Sheep's)	Kg	3.73	73312	44220
74040001	Waste & Scrap of Copper	Kg	0.22	66392	40024
71031019	Other Semi Precious Stone	Crt	0.19	54528	32888
41043902	Chrome Uppers	Kg	8.25	24540	13486
07131000	Peas(Pisum Sativum) Dried	Ton	0.07	130	78
	Total			29035690	18116972

Source : Estimated from Monthly Statistics of Foreign Trade of India (Imports), March 1995, DGCI & S, Kolkata.
TC-I = Trade Creation Assuming Free Import.
TC-II= Trade Creation Assuming Fifty per cent Reduction in Tariff.

the trade creation would be 0.2 million. The products likely to create trade include: jute raw, wet blue chrome, other yarn, other chrome tanned leather, and rosin and resin acids other.

Selective trade liberalisation with Pakistan is likely to result in larger trade creation as may be seen in Table 4.6.

Under the assumption of free imports, India's trade creation with Pakistan would be Rs. 32 million while under the assumption of fifty per cent reduction in tariffs, the trade creation would be Rs. 21 million. The products contributing to trade creation the most would be almonds, other refined sugar, other ash and residue, ayurvedic and unani herbs, other degreased wool, other fabrics, other natural gums, looped pile fabrics, etc.

The largest gain from selective import liberalisation by India would arise in case of its import liberalisation in favour of Sri Lanka as may be seen in Table 4.7.

It may be observed that under the assumption of free trade, trade creation would be Rs. 40 million while under the assumption of fifty per cent reduction in tariffs, the trade creation would be Rs. 24 million. The products likely to contribute most in trade creation include: other refined sugars, defective sheet of iron and steel, remelting scrap ingots, waste and scrap of copper, and unbleached kraft, zinc waste and scrap, 6-hexanelactam, graphite crystalline, etc.

Trade Liberalisation in Practice

Since this study was undertaken, two Rounds of Negotiations have been concluded. It has now been acknowledged that the First Round (hereafter SAPTA-I) was no more than a symbolic in gesture. No more than 226 products were offered concessions of which 100 were in favour of least developed countries (LDC). This could have resulted in intra-regional trade liberalisation of no more than 6 per cent. This share could have been even less if account were taken of common products offered concessions under other arrangements. The depth of tariff cuts are significant only in case of India which could help in levelling down the country's relatively high tariffs.

India's preferential imports under SAPTA-1 amounted to about US $ 12 million, more than half of it coming from Bangladesh. India's preferential imports from Pakistan came next in importance, being 20 per cent of the total. In terms of liberalised trade coverage, India received concessions in respect of US $ 40 million, most of it being offered by Sri Lanka, followed by Nepal. However as noted above,

Table 4.7 : List of Products among Top Fifty Imported by India from Sri Lanka with Possible Trade Creation and Value Share < 75%

HS Code	*Description (in Brief)*	*Unit*	*Value Share %*	*TC-I*	*TC-II*
25041001	Graphite Cystalline (Flakes)	Kg	50.77	7570392	5119032
72044901	Defct. Shet of Iron & Steel		1.11	7907918	4632889
84186909	Parts of Refrigerator others...	No	0.82	6963451	4082023
72044909	Defect. Shet of Iron other...		2.09	5019976	2803372
85152109	Elec. or Laser Equip. Automatic	No	16.7	2142836	1607127
74040002	Wst & Scrp of Copr Aloys (Eg Br)	Kg	1.04	2131824	1249464
74040001	Waste & Scrap of Copper	Kg	2.23	1717875	1006848
13019049	Other Balsam/Oleoresins	Kg	19.04	1399980	840000
73110002	Low Pressure Cylin. (Working)	Kg	22.7	1324116	794448
72045000	Remelting Scrap Ingots	Ton	12.96	821568	481536
29337100	6-Hexanelactam (Epsilon Caprol)	Kg	1.65	823795	446880
47071000	Wste and Scrp of Unblechd Kraf	Kg	11.46	562938	424185
47073000	Wste and Scrp of other Papr/Pap	Kg	3.84	269079	202757
52081149	Unspecified Descriptions Millm	Sqm	59.84	272376	163440
79020000	Zinc Waste and Scrap	Kg	14.54	254901	149398
54021002	Yarn of other Nylon	Kg	2.13	191520	114920
39021000	Polypropylene	Kg	0.07	175380	89040
26140003	Rutile	Kg	28.8	171878	76390
15131900	Coconut (Copra) Refined Oil	Kg	55.14	97359	65833
87084000	Gear Boxes	Kg	3.26	112357	52528
17019909	Other Refnd Sugar Includ. Cent	Ton	1.11	21248	12416
87089900	Otr Prts & Accsrs of Vhcls of H	Kg	0.03	1786	1072
	Total			39954553	24415598

Source : Estimated from Monthy Statistics of Foreign Trade of India (Imports), March 1995, DGCI & S, Kolkata.

Note : TC-I = Trade Creation assuming Free Import.
TC-II = Trade Creation assuming Fifty per cent Reduction in Tariff.

that since the tariff cuts were high by India in relation to its partners, the revenue foregone by India was more than 80 per cent of the total revenue foregone by all CS. Most of this revenue foregone by India was in favour of Bangladesh (Mukherji 1995)

The exchange of trade preferences under SAPTA-1 suffers from the limitation that a large number of products offered concessions by CS are not being imported at all from the region. These products are likely to be subject to non-tariff measures or to export controls. Thus the negotiations did not adopt any trade coverage criterion, nor did it address itself to the more intractable non-tariff measures.

Having taken the decision to transform SAPTA to SAFTA by the end of this century, or latest by 2005, more far reaching negotiations were launched under SAPTA-II. The National Schedule of Concessions (NSC) were signed on November 30, 1996. The customs notifications giving effect to the negotiations were targeted to be released by March 1, 1997. An account of the products offered concessions under SAPTA-II is illustrated in Table 4.8.

Table 4.8 : Number of Products offered concessions under SAPTA-II

Favouring / *Offered*	*BD*	*BHU*	*IND*	*MLD*	*NPL*	*PAK*	*SL*	*Total*
BD		2	222 (a)	2	26 (b)	13	7	272
BHU	1	—	—	—	10(c)	33	3	47
IND	513 (c)	—	—	1 (c)	—	375	22	911
MLD	3	9 (c)	—	—	3 (c)	—	2	8
NPL	41 (d)	38 (c)	—	12 (c)	—	172	14	277
PAK	26 (c)	10 (c)	230	—	99(c)	—	21	386
SL	16 (c)	—	22	3 (c)	4 (c)	53	14	112
Total	600	50	474	18	142	646	83	2013

Source : SAARC Secretariat.

Note : Each tariff line is counted as one product. Hence there is some minor discrepancy with the numbers listed serially under NSC

(a) According to products listed serially under NSC: 204 products of which 11 for LDC.

(b) 16 products listed serially in NSC: of which 11 for LDC.

(c) For LDC only.

(d) Of which 25 for LDC.

It will be observed that under SAPTA-II as many as 2013 products have been offered concessions of which 764 have been offered exclusively in favour of LDC. India has offered the maximum number of concessions numbering 911 products (favouring mainly Bangladesh), followed by Pakistan (386 products). In return, India has received concessions in respect of 474 products. The largest number of products conceded concessions have been in Pakistan (646 products) followed by Bangladesh (600 products). It will be seen that India and Nepal have not exchanged any concessions under SAPTA-II since presumably they have earlier exchanged more extensive and significant concessions under a bilateral framework.

As argued earlier, the product coverage approach in order to be meaningful, must underline a trade coverage concept as an essential adjunct. In order to test this, we have analysed below from a list of top fifty products for the year 1995-96, how many of these come under the list of concessions conceded under SAPTA-I and SAPTA-II. This has been presented in Table 4.9.

The results of the sorted data scan reveals that there has been poor bilateral exchange between India and Bangladesh during SAPTA-II as the concessions offered to Bangladesh on the basis of trade flows covers two lowly ranked products amount the top fifty with modest export flows from India. Under the trade flows for the year 1994-95 only one product exchanged under SAPTA-I had been identified -viz. urea, (ranked No. 2 in India's bilateral imports from Bangladesh during 1994-95). This product did not figure at all in India's list of top 50 during 1995-96.

The trade coverage concept has been applied relatively more appropriately in India's trade negotiations with Pakistan and Sri Lanka. It may be noticed that some top ranking products offered concessions by India include: grapes dried (rank 3), beans-others (rank 5), and resin-gum (rank 8). Among the top ranking products received concessions by India—all under SAPTA-II include meal of soyabean—bean solvent extracted.—defatted (rank l), other colouring materials (rank 7), oil-cake of soyabean—bean, solvent extracted—defatted variety (rank 11), reactive fellows (rank 12), reactive greens (rank 19) etc. The data reveals that the trade coverage in respect of products in which India will be getting concessional imports from Pakistan will be higher than what Pakistan will be receiving from India.

India will be receiving concessions in respect of five product under the top fifty being exported to Sri Lanka. Some of the high ranking products include: steel billets (rank 15), cotton yarn-grey (rank 20), cotton yarn-others (rank 31) etc.—all negotiated under SAPTA-II. In contrast, India's offer of concessions that figure among the top fifty products being imported by India were all negotiated under SAPTA-I. Some of the top ranking products being imported by India from Sri Lanka include: copper waste (rank 11), pine oleoresins (rank 15), betel nut whole (rank 16), etc. It may be observed that not a single top ranking product was offered concessions under SAPTA-II.

Regarding the nature of tariff cuts, it may be observed that these have been quite deep when offered by India in favour of LDC, such

Table 4.9 : Concessions Offered and Received by India to/from Bangladesh, Sri Lanka and Pakistan in SAPTA-I & II contained under Top 50 Products Trade during 1995-96 (Value in Rs. Thousand)

Products	*Rank*	*Description*	*Concessions Offered To*			*Concessions Received From*		
(H.S. Code)			Bd	Pak	Sl	Bd	Pak	Sl
23040003	1	Meal of Soyabean Solvent Extracted	—	—	—	—	776236	—
080620	3	Grapes Dried	—	68907	—	—	—	—
071390	5	Beans—Others	—	58519	—	—	—	—
12099109	6	Vegetable Seeds for Planting Nes	—	—	—	—	73915*	—
320300	7	Other Colouring Materials	—	—	—	—	72981	—
130190	8	Resin-Gum	—	33252	—	—	—	—
23040002	11	Meal of Soyabean Solvent Extracted	—	—	—	—	48539	—
74040002	11	Copper Waste & Scrap of Cop. Alloys	—	—	21856*	—	—	—
32041601	12	Reactive Fellows	—	—	—	—	43866	—
72249004	13	Steel Billets	—	—	—	—	—	137256
13019048	15	Plants—Pine Oleoresins	—	—	17365*	—	—	—
08029001	16	Betelnut whole	—	—	17296*	—	—	—
32041603	19	Reactive Greens	—	—	—	—	32099	—
32041602	20	Reactive Oranges	—	—	—	—	30207	—
52051101	20	Cotton Yarn—Grey	—	—	—	—	—	92841
32041605	21	Reactive Blues	—	—	—	—	28360	—
13019049	22	Plant—Other Balsam and Oleoresins	—	—	11939*	—	—	—
12119035	25	Plants—Camboge Fruit Rind	—	—	9557	—	—	—
12119049	26	Plants—Others	—	—	—	—	140490	—
12119015	28	Plants—Psyllium Husk	—	—	—	—	11787	—

Contd.

(Contd.)

Products (H.S. Code)	Rank	Description	Concessions Offered To			Concessions Received From		
			Bd	Pak	Sl	Bd	Pak	Sl
13019029	29	Other Gum Resins	—	—	8221*	—	—	—
32041604	30	Reactive Violets	—	—	—	—	11021	—
52051109	31	Cotton Yarn—Others	—	—	—	—	—	70635
121110	32	Liquorice Roots	—	4228	—	—	—	—
320411	32	Disperse Dyes and Preparations	—	—	—	—	10342	—
28030002	33	Carbon Black for Rubber Industries	—	—	—	—	—	69118
40151100	33	Articles of Apprl & Clothing—Surgical	—	—	5275*	—	—	—
291822	36	Accetyl Salicylic Acids and its Salts	—	—	—	—	8837	—
39042202	38	Polyvinyl Chloride (PVC)	—	—	—	—	—	61834
490199	39	Printed Books—Others	103	—	—	—	—	—
490110	39	In Single Sheets, Whether or not folded	—	2203	—	—	—	—
760611	40	Electrolytic Plants or Sheets	—	—	—	—	8332	—
670290	41	Artificial Flowers	90	—	—	—	—	—
13019009	42	Plants—Other Natural Gums	—	—	3384*	—	—	—
09081001	47	Nutmeg—In Shell	—	—	2792*	—	—	—
32041109	48	Disperse Yellow—Others	—	—	—	—	5221	—
08029003	49	Nuts, Areca	—	—	2726*	—	—	—
09041103	50	Black Pepper Garbled	—	—	—	—	4994*	—

Note : The concessions exchanged are generally to 8-digit HS. Classification here some products have been highlighted at a disaggregated 8-digit level.

* Indicates concessions exchanged under SAPTA-I

No concessions were exchanged between India and Nepal in SAPTA-II

Only one product was offered concessions by India to Maldives under SAPTA-II

There have been no negotiations between India and Bhutan, bilateral trade being free.

Source : Monthly Statistics of Foreign Trade of India (Exports/Imports), March 1996, DGCI & S, Kolkata.

as Bangladesh. Generally when the MFN rate has been 50 per cent, the preferential rate has been 50 per cent of the MFN rate. When the MFN rate has been 25 per cent, the concessional rate has been 25 per cent of the former. In case of non-LDC, the preferential rate has generally been 10-15% of MFN rate. The concessions offered by Bangladesh to India (as also to all non-LDC), as also by Pakistan to India (as also to all non-LDC) has been 10 per cent of MFN rates. Sri Lanka's MFN rates in respect of products offered concessions to India (hence to all non-LDC) which were already low (10 per cent), was made totally free.

One notable feature of the NSC has been the specification of non-tariff measures (NTM) whenever applicable. In case of LDC, India has offered the relaxation of NTM. This is a novel feature of SAPTA-II negotiations as this problem had been eluded in SAPTA-I and in similar earlier agreements such as the Bangkok Agreement. This may be expected to favour specially the LDC who are likely to be the beneficiaries of such measures.

In both the Rounds India's offer of concessions been more in terms of both trade coverage as well as reductions in customs revenue. Further, since India has, in addition, permitted relaxation of NTMs in favour of LDC, *the trade regime in India is likely to be better harmonised with those of its partner CS, at least at the regional level.*

Concluding Observations

The liberalisation of trade in India need not be a matter for concern by Indian business and industry. Free trade is unlikely to lead to such a spurt in imports as to cause any major problem for the domestic business. On the contrary, there could be net trade creation, albeit a modest one, which would benefit the user industries and ultimately, the consumers. The loss in customs revenue by the Indian government would however be relatively more in relation to the modest trade creation. Hence a step by step movement towards SAFTA as envisaged under SAPTA is along the lines suggested in this study. In this context it must also be noted that since a large share of India's trade with its partners is in primary and intermediate products, the user industries could add more value and profitability on their produce as a result of fall in customs duties. Looked at in the dynamic context of growing manufacturing output, the loss in customs revenue could be largely offset. This study has further demonstrated that trade creation could be enhanced and trade diversion minimised by adopting a selective approach to trade liberalisation, whereby initially products likely to create more trade being liberalised.

NOTE

1. This paper draws on some of the findings of a project, "South Asian Preferential Trading Arrangement—Identifying Products in India's Regional Trade", Sponsored by International Development Research Institute, Ottawa, Canada and published in *Asia Pacific Development Journal,* ESCAP, Bangkok, Vol. 5, No. 1, June 1998.

REFERENCE

Monthly Statistics of Foreign Trade of India (Imports/Exports), Director General of Commercial Intelligence and Statistics (DGCI & S), Ministry of Commerce, Government of India.

ANNEXURE—4.I

India's Import of Top 50 products from Pakistan : Increase Imports, Revenue Difference, Trade Creation/Diversion, assuming Free Imports

H.S. Code	Description (in Brief)	Unit	SITC SETC	Pei	MVC (Rs) (1994-95)	VS (%)	MQC (1994-95)	UVC (Rs.)	NUVW (Rs.)	NUVWTR (Rs.)	DIV (Rs.)	TR (%)	CTR (%)	CMQ	CMV (Rs.)	NI (Rs.)	RDP (Rs.)	RD (Rs.)	TC/TD (Rs.)
1	2	3	4	5	6	7	8	9	10	11	12	13	14	15	16	17	18	19	20
8041003	Dry Dates Hard Chhohara Or Kh	Kg	0	-0.5	577635120	88.6	38509008	15	15	20	0	32	-32	4667759	70016385	647651505	-207248482	-184843238.4	0
17019909	Other Refnd Sugar Including Cent	Ton	0	-0.5	333703125	1.86	28125	11865	12777	19421	912	52	-52	4811	57082515	390785640	-203208533	-173525625	4387632
17019902	Cane Sugar Refind	Ton	0	-0.5	15374180	4.37	11860	12963	13226	20104	263	52	-52	2029	26301927	180043107	-93622416	-79945413.6	533627
8062001	Raisins	Kg	0	-0.5	104224588	25.57	2004319	52	52	121	0	132	-132	570194	29650088	133874676	-176714572	-137576456.2	0
55169400	Other Mixed Woven Fabrics or Ar	SQM	6	-1.22	94787775	99.73	1263837	75	55	84	-20	52	-52	525756	39431700	134219475	-69794127	-49289643	-10515120
13019003	Asafoetida	Kg	0	-0.5	47334500	64.01	378676	125	119	181	-6	52	-52	64774	8096750	55431250	-28824250	-24613940	-388644
12079100	Poppy Seeds Win Broken	Kg	0	-0.5	44142624	92.64	3678552	12	11	17	-1	52	-52	629226	7550712	51693336	-26880535	-22954164.48	-629226
8062009	Sultanas & other Dried Grapes	Kg	0	-0.5	35763658	41.67	674786	53	38	88	-15	132	-132	191965	10174145	45937803	-60637900	-47208028.56	-2879475
8021100	* Almonds Frsh or Driedin Shel	Kg	0	-0.5	34869432	2.54	894088	39	84	178	45	112	-112	236174	9210786	44080218	-49369844	-39053763.84	10627830
54033300	Other Yarn of Cellulose Acetate	Kg	6	-1.22	20311291	94.99	223201	91	81	123	-10	51.8	-518	92616	8428056	28739347	-14886982	-10521248.74	-926160
26201900	other Ash & Residue Conting Mai	Kg	2	-1.6	15803700	1.48	1436700	11	17	25	6	45.2	-45.2	716027	7876297	23679997	-10703359	-7143272.4	4296162
8025000	Pistachios Fresh Or Dried	Kg	0	-0.5	15180730	6.68	170570	89	78	119	-11	52	-52	29176	2596664	17777394	-9244245	-7893979.6	-320936
52051109	Mercerized Unspecified	Kg	6	-1.22	13677072	59.72	164784	83	55	84	-28	52	-52	68550	5689650	19366722	-10070695	-7112077.44	-1919400
08021200	* Shelled Almonds Frsh or Dried	Kg	0	-0.5	13585380	9.1	119170	114	143	246	29	72	-72	24943	2843502	16428882	-11828795	-9781473.6	723347
25010002	Rock Salt	Ton	2	-1.6	12679863	100	16319	777	777	1103	0	42	-42	7728	6004656	18684519	-7847498	-5325542.46	0
41042905	Bovine Leather Otherwise...		2	-1.6	12705012	4.15	1411668	9	9	11	0	22	-22	407555	3667995	16373007	-3602062	-2795102.64	0
41042909	Bovine Leather Other....		2	-1.6	12730599	1.89	1414511	9	10	12	1	22	-22	408376	3675384	16405983	-3609316	-2800731.78	408376
08042002	Figs Dried	Kg	0	-0.5	12008295	35.75	307905	39	38	58	-1	52	-52	52668	2054052	14062347	-7312420	-6244313.4	-52668
8131000	Apricots, Dried	Kg	0	-0.5	10860121	62.08	264881	41	39	59	-2	52	-52	45309	1857669	12717790	-6613251	-5647262.92	-90618
12111000	Liquorice Roots Frsh/Dried W/N	Kg	0	-0.5	9606352	93.78	1200794	8	7	11	-1	52	-52	205399	1643192	11249544	-5849763	-4995303.04	-205399
41043909	Bovin Lethr Ful Grain Other...	Kg	2	-1.6	8306118	2.75	922902	9	9	11	0	22	-22	266446	2398014	10704132	-2354909	-1827345.96	0
51012900	Other Degresd Wool NT Crbnsd No	Kg	6	-1.22	6825654	0.49	206838	33	85	108	52	27	-27	53472	1764576	8590230	-2319362	-1842926.58	2780544
52094200	Denim (Yarns of Different Colou)	SQM	6	-1.22	6292380	70	67660	93	28	43	-65	52	-52	28147	2617671	8910051	-4633227	-3272037.6	-1829555
09093001	Cumin Black (Kalijiri)	Kg	0	-0.5	5659872	64.42	353742	16	13	17	-3	32	-32	42878	686048	6345920	-2030694	-1811159.04	-128634
09094000	Seeds of Caraway	Kg	0	-0.5	5432952	85.53	194034	28	32	42	4	32	-32	23519	658532	6091484	-1949275	-1738544.64	94076
08091000	Apricots Fresh	Kg	0	-0.5	5081930	34.69	133735	38	22	33	-16	52	-52	22876	869288	5951218	-3094633	-2642603.6	-366016

(Contd..)

(Contd...)

52085909	Fabric of Cotton—Others...	SQM	6	-1.22	4722264	9.5	65587	72	49	74	-23	52	-52	27284	1964448	6686712	-3477090	-2455577.28	-627532
51012100	Degresd Shorn Wool NT Crbnsd N	Kg	6	-1.22	3926484	4.05	135396	29	53	67	24	27	-27	35003	1015087	4941571	-1334224	-1060150.68	840072
84733009	Parts & Accessories—Others		7	-0.89	3643137	0.09	1097	3321	1885	2645	-1436	40.3	-40.3	281	933201	4576338	-1844264	-1468184.211	-403516
8134009	Others (Except Dried Citrus Fruits	Kg	0	-0.5	3064094	88.74	71258	43	30	46	-13	52	-52	12189	524127	3588221	-1865875	-1593328.88	-158457
12119026	Ayurvedic & Unani Herbs N.E.S.	Kg	2	-1.6	2765028	8.48	460838	6	22	33	16	52	-52	252406	1514436	4279464	-2225321	-1437814.56	4038496
51032009	Other Wst of Wool (Excl Sheep's)	Kg	6	-1.22	2819680	3.73	176230	16	17	26	1	52	-52	73312	1172992	3992672	-2076189	-1466233.6	73312
12119039	Plant & Parts e.g. Seed—Others	Kg	0	-0.5	2794920	4.39	279492	10	21	32	11	52	-52	47808	478080	3273000	-1701960	-1453358.4	525888
41042904	Bovine Leather E.I. Tanned...		2	-1.6	2170000	4.33	310000	7	7	9	0	22	-22	89499	626493	2796493	-615228	-477400	0
52093909	Fabric of Cotton-Others...	SQM	6	-1.22	1947990	1.85	64933	30	80	122	50	52	-52	27012	810360	2758350	-1434342	-1012954.8	1350600
13019009	Other Natural Gums	Kg	2	-1.6	1714080	19.12	214260	8	16	24	8	52	-52	117352	938816	2652896	-1379506	-891321.6	938816
74040001	Waste & Scrap of Copper	Kg	6	-1.22	1640000	0.22	40000	41	45	68	4	51.8	-51.8	16598	680518	2320518	-1202028	-849520	66392
51032001	Waste of Sheep's & Lamb's Wool	Kg	6	-1.22	1420705	5.46	109285	13	19	29	6	52	-52	45463	591019	2011724	-1046096	-738766.6	272778
8022100	Hazelnuts in Shell, Frsh or Dri	Kg	1	-0.5	1340550	48.06	26811	50	74	112	24	52	-52	4586	229300	1569850	-816322	-697086	110064
60012900	Looped Pile Fabrics of Other Tx	Kg	6	-1.22	1312000	10.47	16000	82	208	316	126	52	-52	6656	545792	1857792	-966052	-682240	838656
41051902	Finished Leather of Vegetable	Kg	2	-1.6	1293700	1.5	129370	10	7	9	-3	22	-22	37350	373500	1667200	-366784	-284614	-112050
13019019	Other Resins	Kg	0	-0.5	1351984	15.38	168998	8	17	26	9	52	-52	28908	231264	1583248	-823289	-703031.68	260172
12123001	Apricot Kernels	Kg	0	-0.5	1250092	100	21188	59	59	90	0	52	-52	3624	213816	1463908	-761232	-650047.84	0
13019029	Other Gum Resins	Kg	0	-0.5	1271032	23.23	158879	8	15	23	7	52	-52	27177	217416	1488448	-773993	-660936.64	190239
41061909	Other Finshd Tannd Lthr From G	Kg	2	-1.6	917750	0.94	91775	10	8	10	-2	22	-22	26496	264960	1182710	-260196	-201905	-52992
71031019	Other Semi Precious Stone Uncu	CRT	6	-1.22	852020	0.19	16385	52	60	91	8	52	-52	6816	354432	1206452	-627355	-443050.4	54528
7131000	Peas (Pisum Sativum) Dried & S	Ton	0	-0.5	843600	0.07	100	8436	8462	9477	26	12	-12	5	42180	885780	-106294	-101232	130
54033900	Other Yarn, Single	Kg	6	-1.22	781908	1.24	8499	92	115	175	23	51.8	-51.8	3527	324484	1106392	-573111	-405028.344	81121
41043902	Chrome Uppers	Kg	2	-1.6	765000	8.25	85000	9	10	12	1	22	-22	24540	220860	985860	-216889	-168300	24540
	Total				1657557341										327113835	1984671176	-1050744785	-862307281	11911000

Note : For source, notes and abbreviations see Annexure-I

Note : The following items has been deleted from the above list of 50 items because the quantity cannot be specified.

(i) Record No. = 46, Code no. = 99930002, description= 'Returned goods'. MVC (1994-95) = Rs. 940778.

* Tariff rate on these items is given in Rs./unit. We have calculated percentage custom duty as : (Tariff rate per unit/country unit value)* 100, to which another 2% is added as special customs duty.

Source : Monthly Statistics of Foreign Trade of India (Imports), March 1995. DGCI & S. Kolkata.

ANNEXURE—4.1 *(Contd.)*

Note to Abbreviations and Estimation

SITC	=	Standard Industrial Trade Classification (Col. 4) Correspondence between H.S. Classification and SITC Classification obtained from W.R. Cline *et al.*, "Trade Negotiations in the Tokyo Round—A Quantitative Assessment" (1978). Table B-1, p. 252.
PEI	=	Price elasticity of imports (Col 5) estimated by Bhuyan A.R. "Economic Integration in South Asia : An exploratory Study, Dacca : Dacca University, 1979, quoted by M.A. Rahman *et al.*, in "The Trade Effects of A South Asian Customs Union : "An Expository Study", in the Pakistan Development Review (Spring, 1891).
MVC	=	Base year import value from specified partner country (col. 6).
VS	=	Value share—The share of the specified partner country in the world import of the identified product (col. 7).
MQC	=	Quantity of Import from specific partner country (Col. 8).
UVC	=	Unit value of Import from specified partner country obtained by dividing value by quantity imported (Col 9) = (Col 6/ Col 8).
NUVW	=	Net Unit value of Import from the rest of the world—obtained by dividing value by quantity after netting the same from specified partner country (Col 10).
NUVWTR	=	Net Unit value from the rest of the world plus tariff rates : gives the landed price of Imports from the non- member states [Col. 11 = Col. 10 (1 + TR)].
DIV	=	Difference in unit value (Col. 12 = Col. 10 – Col. 9).
TR	=	Tariff rates in percentage (Col 13).
CTR	=	Change in tariff rate (Col 14).
CMQ	=	Change in quantity imported (Col 13 : see text for method of estimation).
CMV	=	Change in Import value (Col 16 = Col 9 × Col 15).
NI	=	New Import [Col 17 = Col 9× (Col 8 + Col 15)].
RDP	=	Revenue Difference Potential = Col 18 = (Col 17× Col 14/ 100).
RD	=	Revenue Difference = Col 19 = (Col 6× Col 14/100).
TC/TD	=	Trade Creation/Trade Diversion = Col 15 × Col 12; see text for details of estimation.

ANNEXURE—4.2

India's Import of Top 50 Products from Pakistan : Increase in Imports, Revenue Difference, Trade Creation/Diversion, assuming Fifty per cent Reduction in Tariff

H.S. Code	Description (in Brief)	Unit	SITC SETC	PEI	MVC (RS) (1994-95)	VS (%)	MQC (1994-95)	UVC (Rs.)	NUVW (Rs.)	NUVWTR (Rs.)	DIV (Rs.)	TR (%)	CTR (%)	CMQ	CMV (Rs.)	NI (Rs.)	RDP (Rs.)	RD (Rs.)	TC/TD (Rs.)
1	2	3	4	5	6	7	8	9	10	11	12	13	14	15	16	17	18	19	20
08041003	Dry Dates Hard (Chohara Or Kh)	Kg	0	-0.5	577635120	88.6	38509008	15	15	17	0	32	-16	2655794	39836910	617472030	-98795524.8	-86047714	0
17019909	Other Refnd Sugar Including Cent	Ton	0	-0.5	333703125	1.86	28125	11865	12777	16099	912	52	-26	2902	34432230	368135355	-95715192.3	-77810433	2646624
17019902	Cane Sugar Refind	Ton	0	-0.5	153741180	4.37	11860	12963	13226	16665	263	52	-26	1224	15866712	169607892	-44098051.9	-35847362	321912
08062001	Raisins	Kg	0	-0.5	104224588	25.57	2004319	52	52	86	0	132	-66	398449	20719348	124943936	-82462997.8	-55113458	0
55169400	Other Mixed Woven Fabrics of AR	SQM	6	-1.216	94787775	99.73	1263837	75	55	69	-20	52	-26	317123	23784225	118572000	-30828720	-18460923	-6342460
13019003	Asafoetida	Kg	0	-0.5	47334500	64.01	378676	125	119	150	-6	52	-26	39070	4883750	52218250	-13576745	-11037195	-234420
12079100	Poppy Seeds W/N Broken	Kg	0	-0.5	44142624	92.24	3678552	12	11	14	-1	52	-26	379533	4554396	48697020	-12661225.2	-10292939	-379533
08062009	Sultanas & Other Dried Grapes	Kg	0	-0.5	35763658	41.67	674786	53	38	63	-15	132	-66	134144	7109632	42873290	-28296371.4	-18911657	-2012160
08021100	Almonds Frsh or Dried in Shell	Kg	0	-0.5	34869432	2.54	894088	39	84	131	45	112	-56	160477	6258603	41128035	-23031699.6	-16022064	7221465
54033300	Other Yarn of Cellulose Acetate	Kg	6	-1.216	20311291	94.99	223201	91	81	102	-10	51.8	-25.9	55835	5080985	25392276	-6576599.48	-3944649	-558350
26201900	Other Ash & Residue Contng Mai	Kg	2	-1.601	15803700	1.48	1436700	11	17	21	6	45.2	-22.6	424009	4664099	20467799	-4625722.57	-2517550	2544054
08025000	Pistachios Fresh of Dried	Kg	0	-0.5	15180730	6.68	170570	89	78	98	-11	52	-26	17598	1566222	16746952	-4354207.52	-3539772	-193578
52051109	Mercerized Unspecified	Kg	6	-1.216	13677072	59.72	164784	83	56	69	-28	52	-26	41348	3431884	17108956	-4448328.56	-2663749	-1157744
08021200	Shelled Almonds Frsh or Dried	Kg	0	-0.5	13585380	9.1	119170	114	143	194	29	72	-36	15772	1798008	15383388	-5538019.68	-4243454	457388
25010002	Rock Salt	Ton	2	-1.601	12679863	100	16319	777	777	940	0	42	-21	4534	3522918	16202781	-3402584.01	-1922958	0
41042905	Bovine Leather Otherwise...		2	-1.601	12705012	4.15	1411668	9	9	10	0	22	-11	223972	2015748	14720760	-1619283.6	-1175819	0
41042909	Other		2	-1.601	12730599	1.89	1414511	9	10	11	1	22	-11	224423	2019807	14750406	-1622544.66	-1178187	224423
08042002	Figs Dried	kg	0	-0.5	12008295	35.75	307905	39	38	48	-1	52	-26	31768	1238952	13247247	-3444284.22	-2800029	-31768
08131000	Apricots, Dried	kg	0	-0.5	10860121	62.08	264881	41	39	49	-2	52	-26	27329	1120489	11980610	-3114958.6	-2532304	-54658
12111000	Liquorice Roots Frsh/Drid W/N	kg	0	-0.5	9606352	93.78	1200794	8	7	9	-1	52	-26	123891	991128	10597480	-2755344.8	-2239958	-123891
41043909	Others	kg	2	-1.601	8306118	2.75	922902	9	9	10	0	22	-11	146425	1317825	9623943	-1058633.73	-768712	0
51012900	Other Degresd Wool NT Crbnsd No	kg	6	-1.216	6825654	0.49	206838	33	85	96	52	27	-13.5	29916	987228	7812882	-1054739.07	-788188	1555632
52094200	Denim (Yarn of Different Colour)	SQM	6	-1.216	6292380	70	67660	93	28	35	-65	52	-26	16977	1578861	7871241	-2046522.66	-1225515	-1103505
09093001	Cumin Black (Kalijiri)	kg	0	-0.5	5659872	64.42	353742	16	13	15	-3	32	-16	24396	390336	6050208	-968033.28	-843126	-73188
09094000	Seeds of Caraway	kg	0	-0.5	5432952	85.53	194034	28	32	37	4	32	-16	13382	374696	5807648	-929223.68	-809321	53528
08091000	Apricots Fresh	kg	0	-0.5	5081930	34.69	133735	38	22	28	-16	52	-26	13798	524324	5606254	-1457626.04	-1184978	-220768
52085909	Others	SQM	6	-1.216	4722264	9.5	65587	72	49	62	-23	52	-26	16457	1184904	5907168	-1535863.68	-919714	-378511
51012100	Degresd Shorn Wool NT Crbnsd N	kg	6	-1.216	3926484	4.05	135396	29	53	60	24	27	-13.5	19583	567907	4494391	-606742.785	-453408	469992
084733009	Parts & Accessories—Others		7	-0.893	3643137	0.09	1097	3321	1885	2265	-1436	40.3	-20.1	164	544644	4187781	-841743.981	-624346	-235504

(Contd......)

(Contd...)

8134009	Others (Except Dried Citrus Fruit)	kg	0	-0.5	3064094	88.74	71258	43	30	38	-13	52	-26	7352	316136	3380230	-878859.8	-714469	-95576
12119026	Ayurvedic & Unani Herbs N.E.S.	kg	2	-1.601	2765028	8.48	460838	6	22	28	16	52	-26	152245	913470	3678498	-956409.48	-481405	2435920
51032009	Other Wst of Wool (Excl Sheep's)	kg	6	-1.216	2819680	3.73	176230	16	17	21	1	52	-26	44220	707520	3527200	-917072	-549162	44220
12119039	Others	kg	0	-0.5	2794920	4.39	279492	10	21	26	11	52	-26	28836	288360	3083280	-801652.8	-651706	317196
41042904	Bovine Leather E.I. Tanned...		2	-1.601	2170000	4.33	310000	7	7	8	0	22	-11	49184	344288	2514288	-276571.68	-200828	0
52093909	Others	SQM	6	-1.216	1947990	1.85	64933	30	80	101	50	52	-26	16293	488790	2436780	-633562.8	-379392	814650
13019009	Other Natural Gums	Kg	2	-1.601	1714080	19.12	214260	8	16	20	8	52	-26	70784	566272	2280352	-592891.52	-298430	566272
74040001	Waste & Scrap of Copper	Kg	6	-1.216	1640000	0.22	40000	41	45	57	4	51.8	-25.9	10006	410246	2050246	-531013.714	-318506	40024
51032001	Waste of Sheep's & Lamb's Wool	Kg	6	-1.216	1420705	5.46	109285	13	19	24	6	52	-26	27422	356486	1777191	-462069.66	-276697	164532
08022100	Hazelnuts in Shell, Frsh or Dri	Kg	1	-0.5	1340550	48.06	26811	50	74	93	24	52	-26	2766	138300	1478850	-384501	-312585	66384
60012900	Looped Pile Fabrics of Other Tx	Kg	6	-1.216	1312000	10.47	16000	82	208	262	126	52	-26	4015	329230	1641230	-426719.8	-255520	505890
41051902	Finished Leather of Vegetable	Kg	2	-1.601	1293700	1.5	129370	10	7	8	-3	22	-11	20526	205260	1498960	-164885.6	-119728	-61578
13019019	Other Resins	Kg	0	-0.5	1351984	15.38	168998	8	17	21	9	52	-26	17436	139488	1491472	-387782.72	-315249	156924
12123001	Apricot Kernels	Kg	0	-0.5	1250092	100	21188	59	59	74	0	52	-26	2186	128974	1379066	-358557.16	-291491	0
13019029	Other Gum Resins	Kg	0	-0.5	1271032	23.23	158879	8	15	19	7	52	-26	16392	131136	1402168	-364563.68	-296373	114744
41061909	Other Finshd Tannd Lthr from G	Kg	2	-1.601	917750	0.94	91775	10	8	9	-2	22	-11	14561	145610	1063360	-116969.6	-84935	-29122
71031019	Other Semi Precious Stone Uncu	CRT	6	-1.216	852020	0.19	16385	52	60	76	8	52	-26	4111	213772	1065792	-277105.92	-165944	32888
07131000	Peas (Pisum Sativium) Dried & S	Ton	0	-0.5	843600	0.07	100	8436	8462	8970	26	12	-6	3	25308	868908	-52134.48	-49098	78
54033900	Other Yarn, Single	Kg	6	-1.216	781908	1.24	8499	92	115	145	23	51.8	-25.9	2126	195592	977500	-253172.5	-151856	48898
41043902	Chrome Uppers	Kg	2	-1.601	765000	8.25	85000	9	10	11	1	22	-11	13486	121374	886374	-97501.14	-70799	13486
	Total				1657557341										198532383	1856089724	-490401532	-371903655	7530810

Note : RD = Revenue Difference = Col 18= [(Col 6 × Col 14/100) + (Col 17 * Col 13/200)]. For other estimation, abbreviations and source see Annexure-I

RDP = Revenue Difference Potential = Col 17* Col 14/100

The following items has been deleted from the above list of 50 items because the quantity cannot be specified

Source : As in Annexure I

(i) Record No. = 46, Code no. = 99930002, description= 'Returned goods', MVC (1994-95) = Rs. 940778.

5

PROSPECTS OF AGRO-EXPORTS OF EUROPEAN UNION IN THE EMERGING ENVIRONMENT

Atul Sarma[1] and *Pradeep Kumar Mehta*

In the wake of an almost complete break with the past, from a physical control regime to a market-driven one, the thrust of development policy since mid1991[2] has been on the integration of the Indian economy with the rest of the world and modernisation and upgradation of technology. The objectives of the reforms in essence are to restore macro economic balances in the short run and to move the economy to a higher trajectory of growth in the medium to longer terms.

These goals are sought to be achieved by creating a market-friendly environment for enhancing competitive strength and integrating the Indian economy in the global system. In this new regime, unlike past, export performance plays a critical role of the engine of growth.

Policy Reforms since Mid-1991

The policy reforms during the past five years[3] dismantled the licensing system for most industries, granted automatic approval for technical agreements in priority sectors and in sectors which involve no foreign exchange outflow, encouraged foreign investment by allowing majority equity participation[4], allowed private foreign portfolio investment, introduced current account convertibility in phases, modified MRTP and FERA to remove an important barrier to growth.

The import policy in the post-reform period has been reformulated to minimise the role of quantitative restrictions and tariffs[5] and, to lessen the dispersion of rates. The peak tariff rates were lowered from the level of 255 per cent to 50 per cent in 1995-96. The import of most capital goods, raw materials and intermediaries was freed as long as foreign exchange for their imports is obtained from the market and duties on these were reduced substantially. The import of consumer manufacturers was also opened upto a limited extent under the Special Import License (SIL). The negative import list was drastically pruned. Most end-use exemptions and exemptions from countervailing duties were eliminated.

In addition, several steps were introduced for export promotion. Attempts were made to offer export credit at internationally competitive rates. Banks were directed to adhere to the stipulated target for export credit (10 per cent of net bank credit). The setting up of private bonded warehouses to facilitate importing and warehousing of the goods and paying custom duties only at the time of clearing them for consumption was allowed. Green channel facility for speedy clearances to certain categories of exporters and importers was offered. The scheme of SIL was introduced to reward exporters for superior performance and quality maintenance. It permitted import of certain specified products, many of which were on the restricted list, at zero duty. A new category of Super Star Trading House was created to reward big exporters[6].

Further, exporters benefited immensely from the various exporter friendly changes in the schemes relating to imports for export production. For example, in the case of Advance Licenses, actual user obligation was removed making them freely transferable subject to certain conditions. Similarly, input-output norms were announced on rising number of products and the list of sensitive items was substantially pruned. Likewise, the EPCG scheme was expanded to cover service producers (such as professionals), third party exports, deemed exports and even second hand capital goods. Export obligation thereunder was lowered. The scheme even facilitated import of capital goods etc. on zero custom duty. The EPZs and EOUs schemes, which were introduced in the early1980s, were also simplified and extended to newer activities such as agriculture and service sectors inclusive of trading, re-export after repackaging and labelling and repair, reconditioning, re-engineering etc. Now no prior permission is required for inter-unit transfer between EPZs. The procedures for third party export by EOUs/EPZs have been simplified.

Again, exporters have been offered tax free treatment to their export income as against a 45 per cent tax on the companies' income from domestic sales.

The export activities were further benefited from procedural simplification and rationalisation[7].

Recently, government attention has been drawn towards infrastructural constraints. This has led to initiating a number of schemes to improve the basic infrastructure with direct private and foreign investment.

Policy Reforms for Agro-exports

One of the important policy shifts in the course of reform process relates to agro-exports. Prior to mid-1991, the export of agro-items was subjected to quantitative restrictions and/or canalisation ever since the foreign exchange regulations were imposed. The volume of agro-exports was dependent on a number of internal factors such as domestic demand and inflationary pressure in the economy. As a result, India was never treated as a regular and dependable source of agro-products.

Following the change in government's perception, in this regard, in the recent years, a number of restrictive policies relating to agro-exports were relaxed for encouraging such exports. These include: decanalisation of a number of items, abolition of minimum export prices, for example, in the case of basmati rice; reduction of minimum export price in the case of non-basmati rice; permitting export of sunflower seeds and superior quality of wheat to a limited quantity, allowing agro-based EOUs to avail duty free capital goods imports even if they export only 50 per cent of their output; enlarging the definition of capital goods so as to include the need of the agro-sector, scrapping of most restrictions on coffee marketing etc. Incentives are also given to horticulture, tissueculture and floriculture products, in addition to vegetables and fruits.

These and similar such measures would play a significant role in promoting exports of many Indian agro-products like basmati rice and coffee which enjoy a premium in the international market because of their superior natural qualities. It is expected that in the near future India would emerge as a major foodgrain exporter with an export of 2.5 million tonnes of non-basmati rice and two million tonnes of wheat earning a record of Rs. 25 billion of foreign exchange in 1995-96. The export of non-traditional agro-products like flowers etc. is also expected to register a faster growth in years to come.

Indian efforts towards promoting agro-exports would be further complemented by the successful conclusion of the Uruguay Round of multilateral trade negotiation which has attempted at reducing protection and subsidisation of agricultural products particularly in developed countries[8].

All this suggests that the recent policy changes were intended to create a trading environment for enhancing the competitive strength of Indian exports, inclusive of the agro-products, in international markets by way of reducing protection as also by creating an export friendly environment. This was sought to be done more through improving the incentive structure in terms of market determined exchange rates, concessional tariffs on export-linked imports and simplification and rationalisation of the procedures as a departure from the past policy of export subsidy. The price incentives offered by the government were size neutral, which was a distinct departure from the past policy favouring smaller units.

Our interaction with the selected exporters (162 in total) from ten different cities from different regions of the country during 1993 and 1994 revealed that the exporting community was, by and large, bullish and optimistic about the policy changes[9]. Exporters perceived the need for evolving a strategy to face the new challenges thrown up by the new regime and the changing international trading environment. In this respect, they were looking for enhancing productivity gains; change in product-mix and diversification towards new lines of production.

European Union (EU) is one of our major export markets accounting for one-fourth to one-fifth of total export. Further, given the vast difference in the levels of development and resource endowments of India and the EU, bright export prospects can be expected in many items including agro-based items. Keeping these in view, in this chapter an attempt has been made to explore the possibility of agro-exports to the EU in the light of past performance of Indian agro-exports in the European market. At the outset, an attempt has been made to bring out the recent developments in the trading environment in the EU and their implications on Indian exports.

Trading Environment in European Union

Since mid 1980s, the EU has been passing through rapid policy changes towards economic integration of 12-member states[10]. The EU has already left behind the magic date of 31 December, 1992, which was set as the target date for completion of the unified single European

Market. The unified market was aimed at removing the physical, technical and fiscal barriers for the movement of goods and services across the member nations. The unification process led to a number of fundamental changes in the EU trading environment many of which have important bearings on Indian exports.

For example, the removal of controls at the borders between member-states has lowered the cost of distribution within the EU by way of reducing waiting time at the borders and the cost of handling of formalities. Further, the abolition of the internal borders rendered impossible to enforce the national quotas while the global quotas at the EU level became difficult following the Uruguay Round multilateral trade agreements. It is likely, therefore, that the demand for protection from foreign competition would be increasingly met through anti-dumping and safeguard measures[11].

Furthermore, the unification of the EU market is expected to increase the extent of competition within the market because of lower prices of domestically produced goods resulting from lesser inefficiencies and a quicker rate of technical innovation. This would make the import of competing goods, particularly from the developing countries, difficult. In contrast, an increase in imports may also take place, particularly of income elastic products, as the unification is expected to boost growth prospects of the EU member nations.

One of the important changes resulting from the unification is the mutual recognition of technical norms and standards and common minimum health and safety requirements. This will enable overseas suppliers to sell the same product in every member-state resulting in economies of scale associated with larger scale production. Most developing countries, however, feel that the emerging technical, health and safety regulations may form effective and stronger trade barriers, intentional or otherwise, these being higher than the preunification levels in most cases, The European standards for food and engineering products, for example, are particularly relevant for many Indian exports.

Information on production processes in developing countries and its consequences on labour, environment and health is gathered and widely circulated among the EU consumers who are concerned about these aspects and insist on guarantees against some practices such as those relating to environment and animal friendliness of the products; use of child labour and prison labour, their effects on consumer's health, the working conditions of labour etc. Such concerns are reflected, for example, in the norms relating to maximum pesticides residue in food products and high hygienic standards for every step of the production process from the handling of the catch to the final packaging and testing of fish to be imported in the EU. All these also constitute powerful trade barriers to Indian exports.

Our interaction with the selected exporters, who were exporting to the EU, has revealed that the exporters foresee a bright prospect in the post-unification Europe mainly because of the reduction in information and infrastructural cost and expected growth in EU economies and likely import expansion. At the same time, they were concerned about the growing protectionism in various forms in the EU. To face the growing competition in the EU, they were aiming at quality improvement and technological upgradation, in addition to aggressive marketing and price rationalisation.

Growth and Composition of Indian Export to the EU

Despite EU being an important and growing trade partner of India, India remained a marginal player in the EU market accounting for only 1.21 per cent of EU global imports in 1993, though, increased under the liberalised regime from 0.67 per cent in 1985. The EU imports from India during 1983-93 grew at a rate of 9 per cent per annum against 3.9 per cent per annum from all the Extra-EU sources. This indicates emerging competitive strength of Indian exports *vis-a-vis* its competitors from the rest of the world.

Indian exports to the EU are characterized by excessive dependence over a few product categories: as much as 90 per cent or more has been contributed by only ten out of 21 product categories. What is more, five top product categories (*viz.* Textiles, Leather, Diamonds, Vegetable products and Footwear) alone contributed 70 per cent or more, though an extent of diversification is discernible over the years.

All the four categories of agro-products (*viz* Vegetable products, Prepared foodstuffs, Fats & oils and Animal products) were among the top 10 categories in 1976 but over time two of them went out due poor performance (Table 5.1). Except Animal products, all of them have suffered from negative to marginally positive growth since 1976. The combined share of these four categories has, therefore, declined from 21.75 per cent in 1976 to 12.56 per cent in 1993. Still Vegetable products occupied fourth place and Animal products tenth one in 1993, jointly accounting for a little less than 10 per cent of total EU imports from India.

Table 5.1 : Composition and Growth of the Primary Imports from India by EU

(Per cent)

Sl. No.	*Commodity Description*	*1976*	*Rank*	*1983*	*Rank*	*1991*	*Rank*	*1993*	*Rank*	*Annual Growth rate 1976-93*	*1976-82*	*1983-93*
1.	Veg. Products	18.49	2	11.56	3	5.81	4	6.13	4	1.48	1.53	1.46
2.	Pre. foodstuffs	12.76	4	11.13	4	3.65	9	3.06	10	-1.71	-0.87	-2.05
3.	Animal Products	1 .43	10	2.33	7	3.28	10	2 .74	11	13.26	13.90	12.99
4.	Fats & oils	1.82	8	1.33	12	0.82	14	0.63	15	2.17	5.74	0.70
	Sub-total	21.75		26.35		13.55		12.56				
	Total	100		100		100		100		8.25	6.42	9.03

Having observed the export behaviour of primary products at aggregate level in brief, an attempt can be made to analyse the export performance of agro-based items, *viz.* Vegetable products and prepared foodstuffs, at a disaggregate level in somewhat more details.

Vegetable Product and Prepared Foodstuffs

In 1976, Vegetable product exports to EU were highly concentrated in just three groups, *viz.* Coffee, tea etc., Oil seeds, and Lac and Gum etc., together accounting for almost 90 per cent of the export under this product category (Table 5.2). Over the years, new vegetable products emerged in the export basket, indicating a considerable degree of diversification. While Coffee, Tea etc. remained consistently dominant (42 per cent in 1993) among the nine Vegetable product groups, Edible fruits gradually emerged as a significant group contributing more than one-fourth of the total exports of this category in 1993. Further, Cereals and Edible vegetables also made significant improvement, though to a much lesser extent, particularly in the post-liberalisation period. On the other hand, Oil seeds and Lac and gum etc. which were important exports of this product category in 1976, substantially lost their respective shares.

In contrast, the Prepared foodstuffs exports, which also consisted

Table 5.2 : Distribution and Growth of the Product Groups within the Primary Product Categories of EU Imports from India

(Per cent)

Code	*Commodity Description*	*Share*				*Average Annual Growth*		
		1976	*1983*	*1991*	*1993*	*1976-93*	*1976-82*	*1983-93*
	Vegetable Products	**100**	**100**	**100**	**100**	**1.48**	**1.53**	**1.46**
09	Coffee, tea etc.	54.43	68.01	42.36	42.30	-1.27	3.80	-3.33
08	Edible fruits	4.78	8.77	22.82	27.76	12.85	9.75	14.18
10	Cereals	0.31	3.26	10.14	9.29	23.17	70.31	7.47
12	Oilseeds	21.40	4.11	12.21	8.66	1.98	-16.23	10.78
13	Lac & gums etc.	12.43	10.39	7.35	5 06	-1.74	-0.86	-2.11
07	Edible vegetables	4.09	1.86	2.31	4.62	2.21	-8.88	7.28
06	Live trees & other plants	0.41	0.89	1.59	1.51	8.30	5.63	9.44
14	Vegetable planting materials	2.13	2.62	1.16	0.76	-2.66	15.98	-9.57
11	Products of milling	0.03	0.10	0.05	0.05	7.26	19.39	2.53
	Prepared Foodstuffs	**100**	**100**	**100**	**100**	**-1.71**	**-0.87**	**-2.05**
23	Residues & waste of food industries	62.63	53.31	49.70	52.46	-2.27	-3.19	-1.89
24	Tobacco	26.32	27.98	23.17	22.39	-3.95	2.13	-6.40
17	Sugar & confectionery	9.10	11.59	17.54	13.00	2.45	-25.07	16.85
20	Preparations of vegetables, fruits	0.88	2.32	4.30	5.02	10.50	23.11	5.59
19	Preparations of cereals	0.38	1.01	2.20	2.33	10.92	26.17	5.07
21	Misc. edible preparations	0.20	0.49	1.39	2.26	9.38	10.52	8.91
16	Preparation of meat	0.48	2.13	1.41	1.96	3.56	4.96	2.98
22	Beverages	0.00	0.01	0.24	0.57	25.60	40.21	19.92
18	Cocoa & preparations	0.01	1.15	0.07	0.02	-3.87	127.17	-33.06

of nine product groups, became more diversified in the subsequent period. Only three product groups, *viz.* Residue and waste from the food industry, Tobacco and its manufactures, and Sugar and Confectionery, had a major market presence contributing around 98 per cent of the total exports of this category in 1976 which declined to 88 per cent in 1993. While these product groups maintained their respective dominance in the export basket, the former two lost some ground over the years. The remaining six groups, thus, improved their respective shares, to a varying extent, over the years. Nevertheless, only one among them, *viz.* Preparations of vegetables, fruits etc., emerged as a significant group contributing five per cent of the total export from this category in 1993.

It is interesting to note that three of the product groups *viz.* Preparations of vegetables and fruits, Preparations of cereals and Miscellaneous edible preparations improved their significance continually and rather sharply between 1976-1993 from 0.9 per cent to 5 per cent, 0.4 per cent to 2.3 per cent and 0.2 per cent to 2.3 per cent respectively. One can note that these very items have also gained significance over time within the Vegetable products' category. A similar observation can be drawn from the analysis of the annual growth performance of the groups under the two agro-based food categories. Under the the Vegetable product category, Cereals exports (23.2 per cent) and Edible fruits (12.9 %) recorded a high growth during 1976-93, while Coffee, Tea etc., showed a negative growth of 1.3 per cent. Even Edible vegetables export recorded a fairly high growth (7.3 per cent) in the post-liberalisation period. It is noticeable that the export of Live trees, which is not yet a significant export group to the EU, was growing at the rate of 9.4 per cent per annum in the post-liberalisation period as against 5.6 per cent in the preceding period.

In the prepared foodstuff category as well, preparations of vegetables, fruits etc, preparation of cereals and miscellaneous edible preparations exhibited a growth of around 10 per cent per annum during 1976-93, though the growth rates in the post-liberalisation period decelerated to a varying extent. In contrast, two of the dominant Prepared foodstuffs groups, *viz.* Tobacco and Residue and waste from food industry, exhibited negative growth indicating poor performance. Only Sugar and Confectionery could turn to positive growth in the post-liberalisation period from a high negative growth in the preceding

Table 5.3 : Distribution of Product Sub-Groups (at 4-digit Level) within Groups of Agro-based Products

(Per cent)

Sl.	*Code*	*Commodity Description*	*1993*
1		**Vegetable Products**	
1.1	06	Live trees and other plants	100
1.1.1	0604	Foliage and parts of Plants	74.17
1.1.2	0602	Other live plants, cuttings	10.46
1.1.3	0603	Flowers : cut, buds, dried etc,	10.18
1.2	07	Edible Vegetables	100
1.2.1	0712	Vegetables : dried, whole, slice	38.05
1.2.2	0714	Manioc, arrowroot and salep	34.15
1.2.3	0713	Vegetables : dried leguminous	19.15
1.3	08	Edible fruits	100
1.3.1	0801	Nuts : coconuts, Brazil and cashew	79.43
1.3.2	0802	Other nuts : fresh/dried etc.	15.74
1.4	09	Coffee, tea etc.	100
1.4.1	0902	Tea	61.12
1.4.2	0901	Coffee : husks and skins	27.06
1.5	10	Cereals	100
1.5.1	1006	Rice	98.34
1.7	12	Oilseeds	100
1.7.1	1211	Locust beans seaweeds	41.54
1.7 2	1202	Ground-nuts : not roasted	30.81
1.7.3	1207	Oilseeds and oleaginous fruits	19.17
1.8	13	Lacs and gums etc.	100
1.8.1	1302	Vegetable saps and extracts	74.31
1.8.2	1301	Lac, gums, resins	25.69
2		**Prepared Foodstuffs**	
2.2	17	Sugars and confectionery	100
2.2.1	1701	Cane or beet sugar	63.80
2.2 2	1703	Molasses resulting from sugar	35.97
2.5	20	Preparations of vegetables, fruits	100
2.5.1	2008	Fruit, nuts and other edible parts	63.41
2.5.2	2001	Vegetables, fruits and nuts	24.70
2.8	23	Residues and waste of food industries	100
2.8.1	2306	Oil-cake and solid residues, excluding oil	89.54
2.9	24	Tobacco	100
2.9.1	2401	Tobacco refuse and unmanf.	99.52

period. Such behaviour of agro-based groups reflects the strong competitive edge that India might have in the EU market in vegetables, fruits and cereals.

A further disaggregation of exports under the four dominant product groups of Vegetable products reveals that 98 per cent of Cereal exports, 79 per cent of Edible fruits exports and 61 per cent of Coffee, Tea etc. exports in 1993 were contributed by just one sub-group in each, *viz,* Rice; Nuts: coconuts, Brazil and cashew; and Tea respectively (Table 5.3). However, the exports under Edible vegetables were more diversified: two sub-groups, *viz.* Vegetables dried, whole, sliced etc. and Manioc, Arrowroot and Salep contributed more than one-third each of the group total and Vegetables (dried leguminous) contributed one-fifth.

Similarly, two of the four dominant groups under the prepared foodstuffs showed the prominence of one sub-group in each: Refuse and unmanufactured tobacco (99.5 per cent) in the Tobacco group and Oil-cakes (89.5 per cent) in Residues and waste from food industry. In the remaining two dominant groups of this category, the prominence of the top sub-group was somewhat less, *i.e.* around 64 per cent. There were Cane or Beet sugar in the Sugar and Confectionery group and Fruit preparations in preparations of vegetables, fruits etc.

It appears, therefore, that in most of the dominant agro-based groups, the concentration over a few sub-groups was very high.

All these products groups were also dominant, though not in same order, among the EU global imports of vegetable products and Prepared foodstuffs. This is evident from the estimates of Complementarily index and Similarity index[12], as shown in Table 5.4, both of which increased over time in the case of Vegetable products.

Table 5.4 : Complementarity and Similarity Indices between EU Imports from India and Extra-EU Countries

Year	*Complementarity Index*		*Year*	*Similarity Index*	
	Vegetable Products	*Prepared Foodstuffs*		*Vegetable Products*	*Prepared Foodstuffs*
1976	0.65	0.85	1976	52.70	56.08
1983	0.72	0.92	1983	48.96	66.95
1991	0.79	0.86	1991	64.31	61.61
1993	0.81	0.89	1993	67.66	65.76

Note : Computed at 2-digit Import compositions within the categories.

Table 5.5 : Distribution and Growth of India's Market Share in EU Imports from Extra-EU Countries

(Per cent)

Code	*Commodity Description*	*Market Share*				*Average Annual Growth*		
		1976	*1983*	*1991*	*1993*	*1976-93*	*1976-82*	*1983-93*
	Vegetables Products	**1.88**	**1.41**	**1.53**	**2.10**	**0.30**	**-3.94**	**2.14**
09	Coffee, tea etc.	4.64	3.36	3.63	4.92	-0.21	-5.44	2.08
08	Edible fruits	0.52	0.53	1.00	1.82	7.37	0.86	10.24
10	Cereals	0.02	0.39	2.90	3.86	33.71	79.28	18.19
12	Oilseeds	2.04	0.26	0.90	0.78	0.80	-21.76	12.14
13	Lac and gums etc.	28.29	13.65	8.24	7.55	-6.65	-9.60	-5.37
07	Edible vegetables	0.73	0.24	0.23	0.64	-1.79	-15.80	4.78
06	Live trees and other plants	0.99	0.80	0.75	0.81	-1.27	-7.18	1.33
14	Vegetables plaiting materials	10.86	8.05	2.51	2.94	-6.89	7.51	-12.36
11	Products of milling	0.10	0.52	0.22	0.30	5.80	24.77	-1.29
	Prepared Foodstuffs	**2.51**	**1.78**	**1.15**	**1.15**	**-5.49**	**-9.71**	**-3.65**
23	Residues and waste of food industries	5.27	2.33	2.00	2.04	-5.95	-16.21	-1.27
24	Tobacco	4.35	3.89	1.75	1.65	-8.25	-4.26	-9.87
17	Sugars and confectionery	2.02	3.27	2.43	1.80	-0.83	-27.55	13.18
20	Preparations of vegetables, fruits	0.17	0.40	0.33	0.47	4.98	16.07	0.63
19	Preparations of cereals	1.13	2.08	1.13	1.07	-1.76	11.99	-7.03
21	Misc. edible preparations	0.21	0.30	0.52	0.65	3.23	-2.63	5.80
16	Preparation of meat	0.13	0.41	0.13	0.19	-2.80	-5.03	-1.85
22	Beverages	0.00	0.00	0.05	0.10	22.99	30.85	19.83
18	Cocoa and preparations	0.00	0.20	0.01	0.00	-4.29	111.36	-31.43

In Prepared foodstuffs, their values were quite high. All this indicates that, by and large, the dominant product groups of Indian exports in both the product categories were closely linked to the dominant global imports of the EU.

Consequent upon this compatibility, India's market presence in different dominant Vegetable product and prepared foodstuffs groups in the EU global import ranged between 0.6 per cent to 4.9 per cent (Table 5.5). In some of the dominant groups of the vegetable product category, the market share increased over the years. But in the case of Prepared foodstuffs, the market share of most of the dominant groups tended to decline though remained above one per cent.

The most impressive growth in market share was reflected in Cereal exports (from 0.02 per cent in 1976 to 3.9 per cent in 1993). A similar tendency was also noticeable in the case of Edible fruit sexport. The market shares of both Cereals (18.2 per cent) and Edible fruits (10.2 per cent) were growing at a faster pace as compared to other groups of this category (except oilseeds) in the post-liberalisation period. In the case of the other two important Vegetable products as well, the growth in market share was positive in the post-liberalisation period in contrast to the negative growth in the preceding period. Considering the market share of both these categories in the EU global import being low, there seems to be growth potential.

It appears that the recent exchange rate reform induced significant and positive impacts on the exports of most of the vegetable export groups but not on any of the top three dominants prepared foodstuffs groups (Table 5.6). Interestingly, it had a significant and positive impact on the exports of the three prepared foodstuffs groups, the share of which was found to be rising sharply over the years. In all three, however, the coefficient was less than unity.

Among the groups of Vegetable products, Edible vegetables has the highest elasticity. To be more specific, one per cent change in the foreign exchange rate resulted in a two per cent change in the export of Edible vegetables and almost unit change in respect of Edible fruits and Cereals. On the other hand, this instrument had little impact on the most dominating traditional export, which is Coffee, Tea etc. This shows that the newer exports are more responsive to the exchange rate reforms than traditional ones.

With regard to price and income responsiveness of these exports, it is found that within the dominant vegetable product groups, Edible vegetables and Cereals are price elastic in the EU market but Edible fruits and Coffee are not (Table 5.7). Similarly, Edible fruits and

Table 5.6 : Exchange Rate Elasticities of the Agro-based Product Groups

Meth. of Esti.	*Code*	*Commodity Description*	*Cons-tant*	*EXCH*	R^{-2}	*D-W Statis-tics*
ARI		**Vegetable Products**	**10.74**	**0.45* (3.26)**	**0.63**	**1.54**
OLS	09	Coffee, tea etc.	10.81	0.12 (1.16)	0.34	2.19
ARI	08	Edible fruits	7.05	0.86* (11.72)	0.95	1.54
OLS	10	Cereals	7.63	0.89* (8.42)	0.87	2.12
OLS	12	Oilseeds	7.94	0.68* (2.63)	0.37	1.76
ARI	13	Lac and gums etc.	9.05	0.25* (4.77)	0.63	2.05
ARI	07	Edible vegetables	2.98	1.98 (2.07)	0.60	1.42
ARI	06	Live trees and other plants	5.49	0.60* (5.63	0.81	1.59
OLS	14	Vegetables plaiting materials	10.14	-0.44* (-2.99)	0.44	1.39
ARI	11	Products of milling	4.90	0.33 (1.9)	0.86	2.06
ARI		**Prepared Foodstuffs**	**13.37**	**0.11 (0.25)**	**0.19**	**1.39**
ARI	23	Residues & waste of food industries	12.94	0.17 (0.51)	0.18	1.38
ARI	24	Tobacco	10.41	-0.20 (-0.68)	0.31	1.55
ARI	17	Sugars and confectionery	11.23	0.07 (0.03)	0.14	1.41
ARI	20	Preparations of vegetables, fruits	7.25	0.60* (8.92)	0.89	1.79
ARI	19	Preparations of cereals	6.50	0.50* (5.52)	0.75	1.91
ARI	21	Misc. edible preparations	3.39	0.99* (4.66)	0.71	1.80
ARI	16	Preparation of meat	4.59	0.64 (0.96)	0.39	1.54
ARI	22	Beverages	-0.67	2.12** (3.47)	0.57	1.65
ARI	18	Cocoa and preparations	10.88	-2.15* (-3.89)	0.68	1.65

Note : * and ** Represent significance at the one and five per cent confidence level respectively.
The figures in the brackets are the T-Values of the coefficients.

Table 5.7 : Relative Price and Income Elasticities

Meth. of Esti.	*Code*	*Commodity Description*	*Cons-tant*	*(I PM/ EXPM)*	*GDP-CUR*	R^{-2}	*D-W Statis-tics*
ARI		**Vegetable Products**	**-3.98**	**-1.11***	**0.13**	**0.62**	**1.74**
				(-5.14)	**(0.16)**		
OLS	09	Coffee, tea etc.	-0.82	-0.45	-0.3	0.60	1.87
				(-1.23)	(-1.56)		
ARI	08	Edible fruits	-11.40	-0.67	0.75	0.78	1.48
				(-1.38)	(2.84)		
OLS	10	Cereals	-33.40	-1.28	3.58	0.88	1.89
				(-2.01)	(8.21)		
OLS	12	Oilseeds	-1.96	-1.22*	-0.36	0.55	1.73
				(-4.35)	(-0.55)		
ARI	13	Lac and gums etc.	1.33	-0.24	-0.35	0.18	1.76
				(-1.35)	(-2.25)		
ARI	07	Edible vegetables	-5.48	-1.26*	-0.44	0.93	1.73
				(-12.9)	(-0.21)		
ARI	06	Live trees and other plants	-2.25	-0.43	-0.31	0.41	1.57
				(-0.86)	(-1.41)		
OLS	14	Vegetables plaiting materials	4.32	-0.44	-0.88	0.75	1.50
				(-1.82)	(-2.28)		
ARI	11	Products of milling	-11.52	-0.8*	0.69	0.49	1.99
				(-3.21)	(2.9)		
ARI		**Prepared Foodstuffs**	**2.20**	**-2.82***	**-0.96**	**0.93**	**2.04**
				(-13.25)	**(-13.01)**		
ARI	23	Residues and waste of food industries	-0.18	2	-0.35	0.55	1.73
				(2.11)	(-1.32)		
ARI	24	Tobacco	2.13	-0.57	-0.69	0.77	1.57
				(-1.09)	(-2.25)		
ARI	17	Sugars and confectionery	-2.27	-1.96*	-0.34	0.53	1.94
				(-4.52)	(-0.48)		
ARI	20	Preparations of vegetables, fruits	-13.02	0.28	0.91	0.88	1.98
				(0.73)	(7.17)		
ARI	19	Preparations of cereals	-3.89	-0.65	-0.37	0.24	2.23
				(-1.65)	(-0.14)		
ARI	21	Misc. edible preparations	-8.30	-1.09*	0.36	0.71	2.09
				(-6.49)	(1.75)		
ARI	16	Preparation of meat	-6.42	-0.09	-0.43	-0.59	1.82
				(-0.11)	(-0.97)		
ARI	22	Beverages	-30.23	-1.82*	2.77	0.71	2.09
				(-6.31)	(5.69)		
ARI	18	Cocoa and preparations	-15.04	-0.1	0.66	0.50	1.85

Note : * represent significance at the one per cent confidence level respectively. The figures in the brackets are the T-Values of the coefficients.

Cereals are income elastic while the other two groups are not. This shows that the demand for Edible fruits and Cereals will grow faster with the increase in income level in EU but Indian exports of Cereals will be sensitive to the prices offered by Indian exporters. Income responsiveness is low in the case of the dominant groups of Prepared foodstuffs *viz.* Tobacco (0.9) and preparation of Vegetables etc. (0.7). Only Sugar and its preparations are found to be highly price elastic group (2.0).

Examining the comparative advantages of these few dominant export groups of Vegetable products in Table 5.8, it is found that the Relative Export Share (RES) of Edible fruits and Cereals was rising over the years and became more than 100 in the post-liberalisation years from less than 100 in the preceding years. Although the RES of Edible vegetables remained below 100 even in 1993, it started rising in the post-reform period. In the case of Coffee, however, this was declining though stood far above 100. Similarly, the RES of Oilseeds and Lac etc. too declined sharply. The RCA followed broadly the same pattern and was above 100 in the post-liberalisation period in all the dominant groups except Edible vegetables.

This can be said even in the case of prepared foodstuffs, in which all the top three dominant groups had above 100 value of the RES though it declined over the years. The comparative advantages, as reflected in RCA, also declined over the two periods for both of them. In fact, both for Sugar and Tobacco, it fell below 100 in the periods 1983-93 from above 100 in 1976-83.

On the whole, it appears that in the wake of the liberalised policies comparative advantage has emerged for newer vegetable products items like fruits, cereals and, to a lesser extent, for vegetables.

The inter-temporal export growth of Edible fruits and Cereals in the post liberalisation period was largely explained by their competitive strength which was growing over the years (Tables 5.9). But in the case of Coffee, Tea etc. India lost competitive edge. In Edible vegetables, too, India lost some of its advantage. The Commodity Composition effect of the Coffee, Tea etc. among the few dominant groups was positive and highly dominant particularly in the post-liberalisation period. Looking across the groups under the Vegetable product category, India seems to enjoy competitive strength in most cases, though to a varying extent, in the post liberalisation period.

The above discussion clearly suggests that among the various

Table 5.8 : Relative Export Indices and Revealed Comparative Advantages of the Agro-based Product Groups

Code	*Commodity Description*	*Relative Export Indices*				*Revealed Comparative Advantage*	
		1976	*1983*	*1991*	*1993*	*1976-83*	*1983-93*
	Vegetable Products	**211**	**210**	**159**	**174**	**210**	**158**
09	Coffee, tea etc.	521	503	377	406	495	367
08	Edible fruits	59	80	104	150	94	216
10	Cereals	2	58	301	319	749	1032
12	Oilseeds	228	39	94	64	23	85
13	Lac and gums etc.	3171	2042	855	624	1678	407
07	Edible vegetables	82	35	24	53	25	66
06	Live trees and other plants	111	119	78	67	123	52
14	Vegetables plaiting materials	1218	1204	260	243	1198	146
11	Products of milling	11	79	23	25	326	16
	Prepared Foodstuffs	**281**	**267**	**119**	**95**	**260**	**65**
23	Residues and waste of food industries	590	349	207	169	278	125
24	Tobacco	487	582	182	136	638	84
17	Sugars and confectionery	227	489	253	149	771	97
20	Preparations of vegetables, fruits	19	60	34	38	122	32
19	Preparations of cereals	126	311	117	89	538	57
21	Misc. edible preparations	24	44	54	54	63	60
16	Preparation of meat	14	61	13	16	165	10
22	Beverages	0	1	5	8	1	56
18	Cocoa and preparations	0	29	1	0	1632	0

Table 5.9 : Competitive Strength of the Indian Exports to the EU Market under the Product Groups of Agro-based Product Categories : 1983 and 1993 (Shift Share Approach)

Code	*Commodity Description*	*World Trade Effect (%)*	*Commodity Effect (%)*	*Market Effect (%)*	*Competitive Effect (%)*	*Total of all Effects (%)*
	Vegetable Products					
09	Coffee, tea etc.	-314	623	-50	-159	100
08	Edible fruits	14	-7	0	93	100
10	Cereals	15	-37	-1	123	100
12	Oilseeds	24	-34	0	110	100
13	Lac and gums etc.	-133	82	5	146	100
07	Edible vegetables	21	-15	-6	101	100
06	Live trees and other plants	34	64	-17	19	100
14	Vegetables plaiting materials	-66	65	1	99	100
11	Products of milling	-172	65	96	111	100
	Prepared Foodstuffs					
23	Residues and waste of food industries	-122	204	-18	36	100
24	Tobacco	-108	137	39	31	100
17	Sugars & confectionery	-182	27	31	224	100
20	Preparations of vegetables, fruits	76	-21	4	41	100
19	Preparations of cereals	64	245	61	-270	100
21	Misc. edible preparations	20	-1	38	43	100
16	Preparation of meat	-130	24	70	136	100
22	Beverages	2	-1	0	99	100
18	Cocoa and preparations	-45	53	1	92	100

Vegetable product groups, Edible vegetables, Edible fruits and Cereals were having rising market shares in the EU. On the other hand, the remaining two, *viz.* Coffee, Tea etc. and Oilseeds seem to have lost the market advantage over the years, though the latter lost much more and much faster.

In the case of Prepared foodstuffs, all the top three dominant groups continued to enjoy, though at a reduced level, competitive strength; as well as comparative advantages, despite the unfavourable market conditions as reflected in income elasticity.

It is useful to recall that the agro-based primary products were subjected to export restrictions. Only in the new policy regime, agriculture and agro-processing exports have been encouraged.

Following the shift of policy in favour of agro-processing exports, together with substantial foreign direct investment in the food processing sector, exports from the primary sector, such as edible fruits, vegetables and cereals, as well as some of their preparations, can be expected to improve their performance significantly and yield still better results in the course of time.

Even some of those products which are yet not significant, may also hold out a great promise for emerging as an important contributor to the Indian exports to the EU. For example, India is seriously exploring the export potentials in potted green plants and orchids, for which there exist in the EU a market as large as two billion dollars worth[13].

As a matter of fact, these two product categories, *viz.* Vegetable products and Prepared foodstuffs, have already been identified as 'very major thrust areas' with special emphasis on fruits[14], vegetables, cut flowers, etc. The Ministry of Commerce anticipates export of agricultural and allied products to increase from $3.26 billion in 1992-93 to $5 billion in 1996-97.

Indian exporters may also benefit from the reduction in subsidy to agriculture in developed countries and from the integration of global trade in agro-based items in the GATT framework following the implementation of the Uruguay Round.

But then, many of the agricultural product groups face non-tariff barriers originating from the Common Agricultural Policy (CAP) of the EU[15]. Furthermore, barriers in newer forms, specifically high and rigid health and safety standards, have also emerged in the EU market. They include the norms of maximum pesticide residue, packaging regulations etc. It has been feared that these standards can act as powerful barriers to almost any agricultural exports from India including tea, strawberries, grapes, tulips and even cut flowers. Its impact could be more severe in years to come once the Codex Alimentarius Commission, the UN agency vested with the power to set global foodstandards, completes the codification of food standards for international food trade.

Concluding Remarks

In the light of the above discussion it can be concluded that India's export performance in the EU in the agro-based items will eventually depend on how the producers and exporters would respond to the new incentive structure, on the one hand, and the emerging challenges in the EU market, on the other. The exporters would gain if they target non- traditional markets within the EU market and export non-traditional and newer items like vegetables, fruits and flowers, in addition to traditional ones. Continuous upgradation of technology to adhere high technical and health standards will be key to export growth.

The success of India's efforts would, however, depend upon the extent to which the infrastructural bottlenecks, which are looming large in the economy, are overcome. Our interactions with the selected exporters have revealed that most exporters have frustrating experience regarding all modes of transportation from road to sea to air. Inadequate and unreliable power supply, long delays due to operational hassles in getting credit and procedural complexity[16] are experienced as the other major hindrances to their export operations.

It is widely felt that the authorities are always suspicious about the honesty and integrity of an exporter; which results in a much longer time in various pre- and post-shipment clearances. What is worse, the wide divergence between the policy intentions and their actual implementation seems to be one single factor, which has hurt the export growth most. It is undoubtedly true that the Government with its quick response to exporters' needs has proved to be export-friendly though not to the same extent at the operational level.

The export dynamism of Indian exporters would be dependent on: how fast they equip themselves with the required information base and technology backup which can provide adequate and timely feedbacks regarding the European consumer's choice and preferences and changes in the EU trading environment. In this regard, even the mind-set of the exporters, that have grown from the fact of operating for long under a protective shelter, needs to be radically changed.

The present incentive structure encouraging large exporting houses ignores one fundamental aspect of the structure of the Indian agricultural economy: the bulk of Indian agro-exports are, in fact, produced by smaller entrepreneurs and farmers. Such smaller units suffer from shortage of funds for technological upgradation and modernisation, essential to enhance productivity gains and thus competitive strength. Suitable institutional support for such unit would be, thus, essential so that they can produce agro-items of international standards.

NOTES

1. This is part of a bigger study: Atul Sarma, Gerrit Faber and Pradeep Kumar Mehta : *"Meeting the Challenges of the European Union: The Prospects of Indian Export"*, Sage Publishers (in print), sponsored by Indian Council of Social Science Research, New Delhi and Institute of Social Science Research in Developing Countries, the Hague, under the Indo-Dutch Programme on Alternatives in Development, June 1995.
2. This phase of economic reforms and structural adjustment became inescapable because of the policies of liberalisation pursued since mid 1985. These resulted in mounting fiscal and external deficits by 1990. The fiscal deficit became around 8.5% of GDP and the foreign exchange reserves touched the rock bottom at $1.1 billion, which were barely adequate to meet three weeks' import requirement. For details regarding the liberalisation process, see, Dutta R. (1987), *India's New Economic Policy,* S. Chand & Co., New Delhi.
3. For various policy changes, see, P.L. Sanjeev Reddy and V. Vithal Babu (1996): *India Trade and Investment Guide,* Vol. I of the three volume series, Economy & Trade, New Delhi.
4. In this liberal environment, the number of foreign collaboration approvals shot up from 703 in 1990 to 1854 in 1994 and 915 in the first five months of 1995. Even the number of technical collaborations increased from 502 to 800 between 1990 and 1994. The total technology payments rose Rs. six billion in 1990-91 to Rs. 14.2 billion in 1994-95. See, Ramchandran, R. (1995): "The Truth about Technology Imports", *The Economic Times,* New Delhi, Oct. 12.
5. The weighted average tariff has been brought down to 32 per cent. It is expected that this will be further reduced to 20 per cent by 1996-97, as indicated by the Commerce Minister while addressing the World Economic Forum on December 5, 1995 in New Delhi
6. The SSTH status was granted to those exporters with export turnover of Rs. 7.5 billion during the preceding three licensing years or Rs. 10 billion in the preceding year.
7. The cumbersome and lengthy procedures were considered to be a serious impediment to export growth as these resulted in considerable delay in exports in addition to breeding corruption and bribe. For evidence, see, Nair R.M. & P. Kaul (1995): "Looking for the Easy Way Out", *The Economic Times,* May 1.
8. For example, the WTO agreements proposed that the US should reduce subsidies by 25 per cent of the concurrent rate of $50 per tonne in six years. Such cut in subsidy can be expected to provide price competitiveness, though by a thin margin, to Indian wheat exports.
9. As many as nearly 36 per cent of the exporters contacted were hopeful of achieving 20 per cent or more export growth and another 26 per cent expected an annual growth of I5-20 per cent. Broadly speaking, the majority of the big exporters were expecting faster export growth. A number of medium

and large exports were of the opinion that the new economic environment would enable them to become export giants in the medium to the long run.

10. Currently, there are 15 members in the EU as on January 1, 1995 with three European nations *viz.* Austria, Finland and Sweden joining the union as its member nations.
11. The sectors most widely hit by anti-dumping measures are chemicals, textiles, base metals and metal semi-manufactures and machinery.
12. For the methodology used in this paper, see, Atul Sarma *et al.* (1996), op. cit., Annexure 4.1
13. The main thing, in this regard, according to Indian Commerce Secretary, is to get out of the cycle of production, consumption and local marketing of vegetable products. See, *The Economic Times,* May 9, 1995.
14. In 1995-96, India is expected to emerge as top producer of fruits overtaking Brazil which has always held the top spot. This would become possible because of almost 42-fold increase in the fund allocation for horticulture to Rs. 10 billion in the Eighth Plan from only Rs. 240 million in the Seventh Plan..
15. As a matter of fact, a recent study by the Ministry of Commerce has identified as many as 10 types of non-tariff barriers which are severely hampering the growth of Indian exports including primary exports like fish products, fruits and vegetables, cereals, tobacco, flowers and milk products etc., See, *The Economic Times*, March 21, 1996.
16. A recent study by FIEO has shown that at any time exporters have to complete and process nearly 40 documents from the time of initiation of an export order to the realisation of export proceed. As published in the *Hindustan Times*, 27 November 1996.

6

TRANSNATIONAL COMPANIES AND INDIAN INDUSTRY

Arun Kumar

INTRODUCTION

The Indian economy started its recent process of opening up to the rest of the world in June 1991, in the face of crisis.[1] Problems were encountered on several fronts, like, the BOP, budgetary deficit, unemployment and inflation. Most critically, the country was about to default on its international payments obligation (due to a loss of confidence by the international financial community). This was not only due to the adverse trade scenario but also because of the actions of NRIs and Indian businessmen. Indian capital has used NRIs as fronts to park funds siphoned out of the economy through under and over invoicing of trade and parallel banking channels, like, Havala. In 1990-91 Indian capital at home and abroad speculated on the value of the Rupee and magnified the extent of the crisis (See Kumar, 1991b:6).

Globalization implies allowing two way flow of capital and goods. Proponents argue that foreign capital is essential to upgrade technology and make the economy efficient. Opening up forces the adjustment of the economy to the external environment. The size and influence of global capital can be gauged from the estimated daily transactions of $500 billion in early nineties (133% of the South Asian GDP). This sum dwarfs the national economies so that in today's context, opening up forces the adjustment of national economies to the interest of global capital.

Ownership of global capital is dominated by the TNCs and 90 per cent of them originate in the advanced nations (Table 6.1). Consequently, these countries further the interest of the TNC[2] which require (amongst other things) increased access to markets for accelerated growth. The WTO, the IMF and the World Bank,

Table 6.1 : Number of Parent TNC's and Foreign Affiliates, Early 1990s

Area/Economy	*Parent Corp. Based in Country*	*Foreign Affiliates Located in Country*	*Year*
Developed Countries	33,500	81,800	
Germany (FRG)	6,984	11,821	1990
Japan	3,529	3,150	1992
USA	3,000	14,900	1990
Developing Economies	2,700	71,300	
Brazil	566	7,100	1992
China	379	15,966	1989
India	187	926	1991
S. Korea	1,049	3,671	1991
World	36,600	1,74,900	

Source: World Investment Report 1993, An Executive Summary, pp. 2-3.

dominated by the advanced nations represent the interest of global capital. The advice tendered by these agencies to nations facing BOP problems and seeking their assistance is to open up, whether or not this is in the interest of the country being advised. This is the context of India's opening up—under pressure from global capital.

A country going for globalisation of the IMF and the World Bank variety is required to modify its economic policies so as to facilitate the functioning of international capital. WTO has carried this process a step further. In India since TNCs have been operating for a long time (perhaps East India Company was the first of them) and by 1990 over 900 of them were present in various forms (Table 6.1), a base for global capital has existed. With NEP changing the policy regime, a new chapter has opened up for the functioning of TNCs.

Capital is not just an abstraction or a number but carries with it social, political and economic relations. It brings with it a paradigm of consumerism and development. It effects fashions, art and culture. It has a profound effect on family, environment and individual's nations of success and so on. While this may represent greater interaction across nations which is not bad, one way influence is not desirable. With few exceptions, this is what is happening in much of the Third World.

Globalization has strengthened international capital and TNCs since it is forcing the Third World Nations to compete with each other to obtain a share of the considerable global capital.[3] The carrot dangling before each nation is that even a small fraction of it flowing in its direction can change the investment climate of that country. Consequently, TNCs are obtaining concessions not even available to local capital so that the terms of trade are shifting in favour of the advanced nations. The working of the WTO has further aided this process by enabling a tighter grip over technology. How does all this impact Indian industry?

The industrial sector is affected not just by policies specific to it but also by fiscal policies, trade policies, labour legislation and other such policies. In other words, the New Economic Policies (NEP) as a whole effect the industrial sector. The impact of TNCs on Indian industry is also going to be multifarious; through competition, access to finance and technology, impact on labour markets, income differential and uncertainty, etc. As such, to understand what is in store for Indian industries it is necessary to analyze both the specific new industrial policies and NEP as a whole.

To facilitate TNCs, FERA has been diluted and restrictions on repatriation of dividends and the requirements of indigenisation (PMP) almost eliminated. To promote marketization planning has been downgraded while licensing has been ended. Checks on the growth of monopolies are now non-existent. A variety of tax concessions have been offered to the corporate sector, the upper income groups and to investments in the share market. Foreign investments are being given special concessions over and above those offered to Indian capital. Customs duties have been reduced drastically and the borrowings by the government and the public sector reduced so as to make more funds available to the private sector. To discipline labour, an Exit Policy is sought to be introduced along with golden handshake and VRS. (See Kumar, 1994). ,

Industry has never had it so good. Yet, all this has produced an uncertain result. The rate of industrial growth slumped in the period 1991-94 (lowest after 1979-80) then it rose sharply for two years[4] (to historically highest level) and again fell after 1996-97 (See Table 6.2 and for monthly data for 1985-95 see Kumar (1996). This uncertain growth in a period of massive concessions to industry needs analysis.

The structure of Indian industry is complex. It consists of an organised and an unorganised sector. The organised sector consists of the Public and the Private sectors. The private organised sector itself is made up of the TNCs and the Indian companies. Using scale as the basis, Indian companies can be classified as large, medium or small. The unorganized sector consists of the small-scale sector and cottage

Table 6.2 : Growth in Industrial Production

Year/Plan Industry	*Plan 7th*	*Plan 8th*	*91-92*	*92-93*	*93-94*	*94-95*	*95-96*	*96-97*	*97-98*
Manufacture	7.7	9.2	0.6	4.2	8.4	11.9	14	7.4	3.6
Industry	7.5	8.0	-0.8	4.2	6.6	10.4	12.5	6.4	4.2

Source : Economic Survey 1997-98, pp 3-5 and CSO.
Note : Figures for 1995-96 to 1997-98 are provisional.

and village industries. NEP affect the fortunes of each of these components in different ways this needs to be understood to resolve the paradox.

To understand what NEP is attempting to achieve and whether it will succeed in doing so, it is necessary to analyze the performance of Indian industries in the period before NEP were launched. Though doubts about the quality of data exist, the average rate of growth of Indian industry at constant prices was close to 6.6 per cent between 1980-81 and 1990-91. Yet, dissatisfaction was expressed with this performance since the East Asian Tigers, Japan and China were doing much better in terms of growth, exporters, technological dynamism and avoiding the kind of BOP pressures India faced[5].

Proponents of NEP suggest that India's slow growth is a consequence of the shackles placed on Indian industry, export pessimism, inefficiency of Indian labour and the low level of prevailing technology. Government intervention is seen as the villain of the peace. The solution proposed under NEP was a reduced role of the state and incentives to industry (listed above). Projectionist tariffs and quotas are supposed to have made Indian industry flabby and MRTP and FERA had reined in those who were apparently rearing to grow. However, why did the private sector not expand in the international markets which are supposed to be free considering that there were not only few restrictions on exports, a variety of incentives were available?

If Indian big business and TNCs operating from India were indeed dynamic and only reined in by MRTP and FERA, they could have expanded abroad. In India itself, they expanded into most areas, directly or through other means. Their average rate of growth was higher than that of industry as a whole (Kumar, 1993a). If they had exported more, they could have grown even faster. It is argued that they were too comfortable in the domestic market and, therefore, did not make the effort abroad. In other words, they were not dynamic enough. Yet, NEP puts a great deal of faith in these entities. Would globalization make them dynamic?

EFFICIENCY AND LABOUR

'Efficiency' is the new buzz word. There can be no quarrel with making India more efficient. But it is not clear what is meant by this term or whether say, an `Exit Policy' would help achieve it. It can mean different things to different people and, therefore, used out of context or for political purposes.

One way of defining efficiency would be that with the smallest possible resource cost to society the maximum be produced for the welfare of all (not just a minority). This requires a redistribution of incomes in society and overall planning for the optimum utilization of the resources. A prerequisite for all this is a bureaucracy and an industry, which will deliver what is desired by policy. These are conspicuous by their absence.

The proponents of NEP do not accept the above definition. They argue that one has to accept the income distribution as it exists and allow individuals to maximize their welfare. For them the only policy should be to end policy and to let the markets as defined by the current distribution of wealth and political power operate. It is suggested that such markets, freed from government intervention, would be the 'most efficient' in the sense of improving the welfare of individuals as they themselves perceive it. This is a prescription for *status quo*[6].

If the theoretical argument for opening the economy under any circumstance was valid, the G-7 nations should do this good to themselves before recommending it to others. Clearly, they do not believe in it but use the argument to get other nation's markets opened. The US in violation of the then existing GATT rules used to threaten its trade partners with action under 301 (Special and Super). It has not unilaterally opened its markets and used them to force others to comply with its conditions.

It is argued that one reason for inefficiency in Indian industry is labour indiscipline due to protection and manifests itself in high wages and over employment. Whereas the latter is certainly the case to varying degrees, the former is not. In fact, in spite of the latter, the Indian wage cost per unit of output is usually less than that of most other countries in the world. It is then unlikely that Indian labour costs are the reason for India's inability to compete globally or an indication of inefficiency. The share of wages, salary and bonus in the total cost has declined since the early Seventies (Sharma, 1991).

In India, the wage indexation to inflation is incomplete even for those who are the best organised the Government employees. In all the recent pay revisions, the indexation has been partial. Data are often quoted from the public sector showing that the average emoluments of PSU workers have risen faster than the cost of living index (Economic Survey).

This is misleading. It is argued in Kumar (1989) that employment in the Public sector has changed in favour of the managerial cadres and of skilled employees. It is unclear what has happened to the age and the seniority structure but very likely, the increased skills of those employed should lead to a rise in the average emoluments. Finally, the product mix of the Public sector has changed in favour of more sophisticated products requiring more skilled workers. Thus, raw time series data on emoluments are not suitable to argue that real wages have risen or that inflation indexation exists or that labour is inefficient.

Ajit (1992) shows that in organised manufacturing, capital labour ratio went up during the Seventies and the Eighties, productivity of labour rose but that of capital declined. It may be argued that labour productivity should have risen more and over employment needs to be eliminated but given the cost structure, reduction in employment will hardly lower costs; something else needs to be done. The black economy needs to be brought under check and management practices changed. In effect, inefficiency in Indian industry may have more to do with capital than with labour. While capital has indulged in malpractices, labour has responded through indiscipline, etc.

TNCs, GLOBALIZATION AND INDIAN INDUSTRIES

TNCs In India: Possible Benefits

Under NEP, great store is set by globalization of the Indian economy to end many of the perceived ills of Indian industries. It is believed that TNCs would make available advanced technology and to introduce better management practices to upgrade Indian industry and enhance its productivity. They are expected to play a crucial role in introducing new products, promoting competition and greater choice for the consumers at lower prices. Great store is laid on the possible role in promoting exports and helping stabilise the BOP.

TNCs can be expected to do what is in their best interest but is it in their interest to promote Indian industry? Given the size of Indian capital and its technological backwardness why would TNCs help Indian capital, specially when they are being given easy access to the Indian markets. Some argue that since they are unfamiliar with the Indian markets they need Indian capital. Perhaps, but thus would only be a temporary phase and cannot be a reason for TNCs to enable Indian capital to acquire any, degree of independence or autonomy. With the marginalization of the PSUs and Indian Private Sector lacking the capability to absorb and develop technology (with few exceptions) autonomy is unlikely even if access is allowed to technology. Maruti after 15 years still designs cars in Japan and does not manufacture gear boxes. TELCO has not been able to develop an indigenous truck in over thirty years.

TNCs may introduce modern business practices or advertising, etc., but lead to reduced employment, consumerism, inequity and cultural effects. The increased choice of products is only for the well off sections since TNCs mostly produce premium products. This is true even items of daily use like, cosmetics, detergents, soaps, etc. Soft drinks, Macdonalds and KFC may be for the common man in the advanced nations but in India only the well off can afford them. The white goods sector and automobiles are clearly only for the well off. The high-pressured advertising that accompanies products manufactured by TNCs trying to establish a toehold in India is promoting greater consumerism with attendant problems.

It is unclear that there would be greater competition in the Indian market leading to reduced prices for the consumer. As argued above the premium products introduced by the TNCs tend to be higher priced ones. Thus, for the bulk of the population there is no reduction in prices. Anyway, internationally, TNCs tend to have managed competition and they are likely to practice the same in India. Pre-1991, this was the prevalent situation in India with a large number of firms operating in most products but managing competition amongst themselves. Thus, nothing much is likely to change on this front, except the names may be different.

Negligible Global Weight

Globalization would ideally have meant that while India opens itself to foreign influences it would be able to influence policies in other countries to its advantage. It has been argued by some that Indian economy has matured and can face international competition. But, India's weight in global GDP, Investment, S&T, Exports and Imports is negligible (Table 6.3). It can hardly affect international events (specially economic) so that once the only card it had, namely, access to its market, is given away for free, none need concede anything to it. There is no bargain left, only a one way impact on India is likely.

Table 6.3 : India and the World Economy in 1995 : A Comparison

	India	*World*	*Japan*	*USA*	*S.Korea*	*China*
1. GDP (Billion $)	324	27,846	5,109	6,952	455	698
2. Exports (Billion $)	31	5,145	443	585	125	149
3. Imports (Billion $)	35	5,246	336	771	135	129
4. Inv/GDP (%)	25	23	29	16	37	40
5. Pvt Cons/GDP *(%)*	68	63	60	65	54	46
Share in Total Household Consumption (%) in 1990						
6. Food	52		16	13	35	61
7. Consumer Durables	3		6	7	5	

Source : World Development Report, 1997 and 1990.

In the reckoning of the advanced nations, in economic terms, India counts for little. India would have to globalise on their terms. Capitalism has tended to increase concentration and centralization; amongst nations, within nations and within groups. International experience is consistent with this. Most of the Third World countries which came into the orbit of international capital in the Seventies and the Eighties have had to pay a heavy price.[7] Economic drain from the Third World is going on apace (UNCTAD, UNICEF and ILO have documented this). They have had to give in to more and more demands from the advanced nations and the TNCs. Globalization has drawn India also into this web.

NEP are based on the logic that economic agents do the best for themselves if left free by governments and this through the invisible hand leads to the betterment of society. If this is accepted then surely the TNCs and the G7 would also do what is best for them. Why would they not act on it? They know India is weak and willing to make concessions. Why would they be interested in a positive sum game *vis-a-vis* India when they could get more in today's situation? Since they do not constitute a whole with India, what is best (getting the maximum) for them is not the best for India but at a cost (Kumar, 1991b). Exports illustrate this.

Export Possibilities

Developing India as an export base would require significant increase in exports in certain sectors. This would mean increased international competition. Who would promote exports, TNCs or Indian capital? Table 6.4 shows that since 1991, only 8 per cent of Investment proposals are for Exports and the foreign equity involved is 12 per cent. In other words, exports from India are hardly a priority for capital—Indian or foreign.

Table 6.4 : Industrial Investment (Aug. 1991 to Oct. 1996)

Category	*Number*		*Proposed Inv. (Rs. Cr)*		*Employment*
	Total	*Foreign*	*Total*	*Foreign Equity*	
IEMS	27,743		5,37,926		49,53,916
LOIs	2,714		88,907		6,17,976
IEM+LOI	30,457	4,391	6,26,833	71,743	55,71,892
EOUs	2,810	956	50,224	6,248	4,91,176
GDR		36		10,196	
TOTAL	33,267	5,383	6,77,057	88,188	60,63,068

Source : SIA STATISTICS, Vol. II, No. 8, Dec. 1996. Min of Industries; GOI, p. 2.

Note : 1. Data reveals that upto March 1998, IEMs increased to 32,918 involving an investment of Rs. 6,09,184 crore and employment of 56,51,000. LOIs were 3127 with an investment of Rs. 1,01,774 crore and employment of 7,34,000 (Economic Survey 1997-98 : 101), 1995 was the peak year.

2. IEM - Industrial Entrepreneur Memoranda.
LOI - Letter of Intent.
EOU - 100 per cent Exports Oriented Units.
GDR - Global Depository Receipts.

The TNCs interest is in the Indian market and in promoting the interest of their parent companies in the world markets but not in increased *net* exports from India. The strategy of the TNCs, controlled by the parent companies, would be to maximize their global profits and not only that of a subsidiary. For this, export from India need not be a priority. Opening up of markets leads to access to local markets and increased profits. Increased net exports from India do not ensure larger profits specially if world trade is growing slowly. Can this happen as a result of strategic tie up with TNCs? For this India would have to become a part of the global production structure of some TNCs. This is a complex matter and would take a while given the state of Indian politics and of infrastructure. It has not yet happened in the last seven years.

TNCs are also supposed to be afraid of loss of control over their technology if they do not have control over the firm. Hence they may prefer imports or assembly of goods to manufacture. Would 100 per cent equity change this since then the TNCs would get the entire profit for themselves and would have no fear of loss of control over technology? Even then the argument for exploiting the Indian market would stand as a better option than increasing net exports.

Indian big business cannot export more unless they get access to foreign markets. In today's world this is also dependent on the TNCs. If Indian businesses are unable to face competition from TNCs in their own preferred home markets it is unlikely they would be able to do so in the international markets. It is worth noting that in most foreign collaboration agreements (whether equity or technical or financial collaboration) in India, there are restrictions on exports. Post 1991, conditions of collaboration have become more adverse since TNCs have gained the upper hand *vis-a-vis* Indian partners (Table 6.5).

Table 6.5 : Conditions of Foreign Collaboration: A Comparison

Years *Category*	*1988-90*	*1991-93*
1. By Duration		
a. Ten years and more	11%	36%
b. No duration	15.6%	0.4%
2. By Royalty Rate		
a. 5% and above	24.8%	46.5%
b. 3% and less	61%	49.4%
3. By Export Clauses in Technology Agreements		
a. Differential royalty	15%	22.3%
b. 100% exports	15.12%	11.04%
c. Buyback	4.7%	1.02%
d. Export Oriented	36.2%	16.9%
e. More than 40% financial equity	4.8%	30.9%

Source : Subrahmanian (1996)

Table 6.5 shows that India is not gaining access to markets due to the restrictive conditions in collaboration agreements. Clearly, for the maximization of their global profits TNCs prefer to sell in the Indian markets. After all, a stage of Indian goods manufactured with cheap labour constitutes a threat to their global profits. Indian businessmen have got access to some intermediate level technology which will enable them to compete better with other Third World countries. Table 6.6 shows that 90 per cent of FDI is concentrated in 9 industries which represent intermediate technology or sectors, like, Telecom and services which are not involved in exports. If significant exports take place from the remaining sectors, this can only lead to the deterioration of India's and its competitor's terms of trade vis-a-vis the advance nations. Hence, even if Indian industry (not TNCs) export more, it may only be under adverse conditions.

Table 6. 6 : Sector-wise Approvals of Foreign Investments and Collaborations

Name of Industry	*Total No.*			*Amount of FDI*	*% of Total*
	Tot	*Tech*	*Fin*	*(Rs. Cr.)*	*Approvals*
Metallurgical	385	229	156	5198	5.89
Fuels	261	107	154	17327	19.65
Electrical	1701	772	929	5326	6.04
Telecommunication	289	76	213	20016	22.70
Transportation	497	274	223	5760	6.53
Chemicals	1020	580	440	5561	6.31
Food Processing	542	119	423	5671	6.43
Service Sector	363	11	352	7780	8.82
Hotel and Tourism	187	65	122	2224	2.52
Grand Total (All)	9761	4378	5383	88188	

Source : SIA NEWSLETTER, Nov. 1996. Min. of Industries, GOI, pp 7-9.

Export Led Growth and Agriculture

Under NEP, increasing *net* exports has become critical to reduce the current account deficit and the country's dependence on foreign borrowings. That would also enable the country to repay its debt and the interest on it. Increase in net exports will also enable the Indian economy to recover from recession; they constitute additional demand. This is termed as 'Export led growth'.

As already argued, exports depend to a large extent on TNCs who dominate the world markets and on other countries allowing access to their markets. For instance, there could be greater trade with our neighbours—SAARC countries and China—due to advantages in transport costs. But each member of SAARC denies access to its markets to other countries of the region. Similarly, there could be greater trade with China but again, access to each other's market is limited. In brief, the prospects of export led growth are not bright because (a) TNCs may not be interested in promoting Indian exports, (b) market access elsewhere is difficult, (c) Indian costs are high in spite of cheap labour, (d) under NEP subsidies are disallowed, and (e) quality is indifferent due to technological reasons.

What about increasing exports of traditional goods, like, agriculture and allied goods (20% share). Under NU, with fewer restrictions on exports of agricultural produce and devaluation, agricultural exports should have spurted. However, international trade in these commodities is controlled by a few TNCs. According to Korten (1995) these companies dominate the US markets as well (p. 224). Even if food processing sector grows and tries to export, the market is controlled by TNCs. Table 6.6 shows that this is not a priority area for TNC investment (6.43%) so that it is unlikely to boost exports, India would have to give more concessions to the TNCs to make it attractive for them to market Indian products and disturb their currently existing arrangements[8].

Indian success in agricultural exports would cause an adverse shift in the terms of trade for its competitors, as has been the case with tea, coffee, sugar, cashewnuts, etc. In effect, the Indian farmers may benefit little since on the one hand the international prices are likely to drop and on the other hand, they would have to concede a bulk of the reduced profits to the TNCs. Two consequences would follow from such exports. First, Indian agriculture would be subject to the pattern of international demand and secondly, adversely affect India's food security. Indian farmers may divert the best land towards plantation crops for exports and reduce land under basic foodgrains required by the local population.Under NEP, changes in land legislation enable large plantations to come up is being envisaged. This will have adverse consequences for the rural poor and for industrialization.

It is not that the country should not try to increase exports but it should not only depend on this. There are two other problems with this strategy (Kumar, 1991b). First, all the nations in the world cannot achieve an export surplus simultaneously. Some have to have a deficit for others to have a surplus. The country should certainly try to have a surplus but with all the Third World nations simultaneously trying to have a surplus, prices of their exports would drop. The terms of trade would shift against the Third World, then current account would not improve and make repayments of debt more difficult.

Finally, it needs to be clarified that the old distinction between traditional and manufactured goods is not a good one in the modern context. India's exports are now largely of manufactured goods. The distinction should be made between goods produced with advanced technology or using intermediate and low technology. As technology changes, a former high technology goods may become one of low technology. For instance, earlier technology differentiated between manufactured goods and raw materials but now the divide is between manufactured goods produced by the advanced nations and the rest. Technology and the new regime of intellectual property rights have become critical in this context.

WTO and Access to Technology

World Trade Organization (WTO) is a reality. It has not only redefined the international trade regime but even national laws to suit TNCs. It puts most Third World Nations on par with the advanced nations in matters of trade, like, market access and national treatment to foreign capital and has strengthened the control of TNCs on technology. If India had free access to international technology, it could be a threat to TNCs domination in the world markets. Today, high technology is closely held and not available. WTO governs the regime of intermediate technology and strengthens the control of TNCs over it (See Kumar, 1993b).

For Indian exports not to lower the global profits of the TNCs which give either the technology or access to markets or both, the terms on which technology (intermediate level) is to be made available to Indian businesses have to be stiffer (as Table 6.5 shows). Not only do TNCs profits rise, outgo of foreign exchange from the country in the form of repatriated profits and fees of various kinds also rise. Additional outflow of foreign exchange occurs since foreign collaborators insist on their own consultancy and supply of plant and equipment. Finally, the mechanism of transfer pricing is used to siphon out undeclared profits and constitute further drain of foreign exchange. Indian businessmen's interest in stashing profits abroad makes them collude with the TNCs[9].

The advanced nations have typically not allowed access to high technology. The recent experience with advanced computers, cryogenic rockets and earlier with nuclear technology point to this. The history of the Uruguay Round of GATT negotiations reveal the real intentions of G-7 to retain monopoly over technology while talking of free trade to obtain access to other markets.

Among the most harmful effects of the new regime of intellectual property rights on the Third World would be the set back to their R & D. This would prevent them from catching up with the advanced nations and make them permanently dependent. As it is, investment in advanced technology is lumpy and so high that most Third World Nations cannot go it alone and even if they make a limited effort, the only object can be that as these technologies mature, they, can position themselves to exploit them.

For instance, even though India is way behind the front runners in rocketry or nuclear or aerospace or electronics or plasma fusion or generalised software or bio-technology, it is capable of posing challenges (not catching up) by investing in R & D. Even this may become a thing of the past under the new Intellectual Property Rights regime. Different processes cannot be used to arrive at a given product or concept. Laggards in development will have to produce some other product so it may not even worth researching—R & D will receive a setback.

International Division of Labour and Environment

One of the aspects of globalization is an international division of labour and specialization based on 'comparative advantage'. A comparison of Tables 6.6 and 6.7 with Table 6.8 indicate that the pattern of investments is changing drastically compared to what existed before 1991. Sixty five per cent of all investment proposals are for 5 sectors namely, Chemicals, Metallurgical, Textiles, Cement and Gypsum and Paper and pulp. Most of these are highly polluting industries.

In the case of the Third World it has been argued that they should not be sensitive to pollution since development is more important. Further, because of its cheap and unskilled labour, it is supposed to have an advantage in agriculture and low and intermediate technology products. These assumptions imply that India should concentrate effort on agriculture, intermediate technology and for polluting industries.

Pollution imposes hidden costs on society which people have to

Table 6.7 : Industrial Investment Proposals (Selected Industries) Percentage Break Up for Aug. 1991 to Nov. 1996.

Total Proposals			*IEMs*		*LOIs*	
Sch. No.	*Ind. Group*	*No*	*Inv%*	*Empl%*	*Inv%*	*Empl%*
19	Cbemicals	5,223	20.4	12.7	33	8.1
1	Metallurgical	4,901	17.1	19.1	0.6	1.5
23	Textiles	4,786	15.5	19.9	4.5	19.7
35	Cement & Gypsum	702	7.8	3.4	0.8	0.7
24	Paper & Pulp	1,208	5.3	3.9	3.6	4.0
5	Elect. Equip.	1,784	4.3	5.3	0.6	3.0
6	Telecomm	964	2.4	3.0	0.8	3.0
7	Transport	459	2.5	2.8	5.3	4.8
8	Indus Mach	681	1.9	1.6	0.2	0.6
22	Drugs & Pharm	1,179	0.6	1.2	5.2	10.4
25	Sugar	326	0.3	0.3	10.0	23.5
TOTAL (ACTUAL)		**30,802**	**5,40,987 (Rs. Cr.)**	**49,92,196**	**90,999 (Rs Cr.)**	**6,32,113**

Source : Same as for Table 6.4, p. 9.

bear. Mr. Larry Summers the then Economic Adviser to the World Bank presented this logic sharply by arguing that polluting industries should be relocated in the Third World since it is optimal that people there die of disease than in the advanced countries (Reported in *The Economist* in February 1992). As pointed out, under the garb of technology and capital inflow, India may be becoming host for heavily polluting industries relocating from the advanced countries to India (like, chemicals and metals). India needs to guard against likely disasters in its headlong drive towards inviting foreign capital and technology.

Further, if such technologies and production relocate in the Third World and advanced technology and clean products in the advanced countries, competition amongst the Third World can be used to keep the prices of these goods low for the advanced countries while the prices of advanced product can be kept high through monopoly over technology. Terms of trade would shift against the Third World and lead to a drain from these economies.

In India, even before TNCs have entered in a big way, there is a race to export at any cost. To attract foreign investment, environmental standards are being lowered (Kumar, 1994) and agricultural exports

Table 6.8 : Principal Characteristics by Major Industry Group (1991-92) Arranged in Descending Order of NVA

Code	*Industry*	*Factor-ies(%)*	*Inv K (%)*	*Employ (%)*	*Output (%)*		*Per Employee*	
					Gross	*NVA*	*FC (Rs.)*	*NVA (Rs.)*
35-36	Mach (not tpt)	11.4	8.7	10.4	11.8	15.1	98007	97386
40	Electricity	0.2	28.1	10.4	9.2	13.3	680198	85254
30	Chemicals	6.5	11.9	7.0	13.2	12.9	299093	122744
20-21	Food Products	17.6	7.4	13.4	14.5	8.2	58808	40769
33	Basic Metals	5.43	16.3	7.3	12.0	7.5	435662	68554
37	Transport	3.3	4.1	6.0	5.3	6.7	100572	75221
32	Non-Metal Min	8.8	4.3	5.5	4.1	6.0	150483	72204
34	Metal Prod.	6.1	1.4	2.7	2.2	2.4	67435	59801
39	Repair, K Goods	1.6	0.3	2.3	0.5	1.3	16303	37598
38	Other Manf	1.6	0.8	1.2	0.9	1.2	78547	71055
97	Repair Serv	1.5	0.1	0.8	0.2	0.4	19348	38354
TOTAL (ALL)		112 ('000)	221234 (Rs. Cr.)	8194 ('000)	299196 (Rs. Cr.)	54827	185392	66915

Source : Summary from Annual Survey of Industries.
Note : FC : Fixed Capital, *NVA :* Net Value Added.

encouraged. If successful, cropping pattern of Indian agriculture would then be geared to the demands of the advanced nations and not the Indians. A decline in the nutritional standards of the poor is likely. Only the rich farmers and agri-businesses may benefit from this.

TNC Led Industrial Restructuring

TNCs when they enter a Third World nation try to capture markets both by eliminating competition and establishing their hold. Existing products need to be displaced to establish their products. This requires establishing their brand names, buying out existing local brands or even whole companies producing those goods. Even the biggest Indian companies are too small to match the financial and technological clout of TNCs. They are unequal in scale of production or advertising.

Kumar (1994) argues, the penetration of the Indian market is taking place through establishing of TNC brand names and control over managements of companies in which they are interested. Thus, Lehar-Pepsi has become Pepsi. Coca-Cola bought out the Indian market leader's (Parle held 60 per cent of the market) brand names. In the soap market, Godrej after initial collaboration with Proctor & Gamble is now fighting them and TOMCO has been bought out by

Hindustan Lever. In joint venture companies like, DCM Daewoo, Kinetic Honda and Maruti Suzuki, the Indian partners have had to relinquish control. Pressure is building up on other companies as well.

India, historically, before independence, was an open economy with low tariffs. This caused several Indian industries to be wiped out in the nineteenth century. Only during the two World Wars when the British rulers needed Indian industries, they were allowed to grow. Also, in some cases, like sugar industry, when tariffs were imposed, the industry grew rapidly. As an open economy, Indian industry and the economy stagnated under British rule during the first half of the twentieth century. Even though times have changed, it is a hardly reassuring history and throws doubt on the model of unquestioning globalization.

The lowering of tariffs and removal of quantity restrictions since 1991 has led to dumping by foreign companies of goods, like, ball bearings, chemicals and drugs, DAP fertilisers and capital goods. In contrast, it is interesting that where tied aid is provided, goods are sold at higher prices. NTPC was reportedly being forced to buy at 30 per cent higher prices from the Japanese who had offered project aid. BHEL's order book has suffered since it is unable to match the credit offered. It is a classic case capturing the market and then raising prices.

TNCs and Privatization

Privatization consists of two activities—disinvestment of PSU equity and private provision of public services. The first is a policy issue, which is based on the notion that states should retreat from economic activities to enable the markets to expand. The second consists of response of individuals to breakdown of public services like, drinking water, electricity, health and education. TNCs have interest in both.

Public sector in India is seen to be a drag on the economy. The fiscal deficit is taken to be a result of their dissaving. It is argued, disinvestment of PSU shares will promote efficiency and solve the problem of budgetary deficit. However, disinvestment has been slower than desired since (a) there has been political opposition to it, (b) (more importantly) the stock markets have faced repeated crisis and (c) Indian capital is not large enough to absorb the huge assets involved.

TNCs have eyed the purchase of profitable PSUs. For instance, it has been reported that Siemens and ABB were interested in BHEL, one of the best run Indian companies. In fact, privatization has the potential of turning PSUs into subsidiaries of the TNCs. When the first round of privatization occurred in 1992, it was widely reported that forward trading took place on behalf of the TNCs and their agents.

In fact, if even 49 per cent of the equity of the biggest of the Indian public sector companies, like, BHEL, Indian Oil, ONGC and SAIL are sold at their replacement value. the Indian capital market would not be able to absorb it except at throwaway prices. Only the TNCs have the capital to buy these companies equity at prices close to the replacement value. There was talk of a debt equity swap as attempted in Chile, Brazil and Maxico. In fact, this was due to pressures from the IMF and the World Bank even though it was clearly unnecessary.

Further, the TNCs or the Indian capitalists are unlikely to invest in the PSUs unless they get management control. This is feasible even with say, 5 per cent of the equity as long as the government, usually the largest shareholder, agrees. If management control is not available to the private sector (Indian or TNC) they are unlikely to invest large sums and privatization will not work. After all, the logic of privatization is a change of style of management, otherwise nothing would have changed. In India, businessmen do not invest only for book profits. That is why they do not even relinquish control over loss making units.

It may be argued that if a TNC purchases a public sector concern, it would run it well, bring in technology, etc. However, this does not logically follow. To maximize its global profits, it could use the firm to expand its own sales in the Indian markets. This could be through shutting down the Indian company to eliminate competition or running the plant such that it sells its own products with a minimal of value addition in India. Over a period, it could even claim that the plant needs to be shut down since it is not profitable or that Indian labour is not productive, etc. In any case, it may result in an increased outflow of foreign exchange under a variety of pretext as already pointed out[10]. The indigenous technological capability would be adversely affected given that a bulk of it has been associated with the Public Sector.

Further, most of the so called sick PSUs are not necessarily sick considering their asset base. If revaluation of the assets of the public sector units is resorted to and a part of the loans from the government converted to equity, given its responsibility for creating the mess in the first place, these units will turn the corner.

Financial restructuring along with revaluation of assets should be resorted to even if privatization is thought to be desirable since then government can obtain a higher price for its assets, and, therefore, the budgetary support would be higher. Such a privatization will also give a fighting chance to many of the presently sick PSUs to turn the corner. With a higher asset base, they would be able to raise more funds in the market for working capital and revival. Unfortunately, the NEP has not addressed these problems. The haphazard privatization of the public sector imposes a heavy cost on the nation. Tandon (1997) analysing international experience of privatization finds that it has not been very successful since by itself it is no panacea. He believes, market conditions are critical (p. 3210).

Clearly, neither Indian capital nor the government have a clear line of thinking on the PSUs. Disinvestment is sought to be attempted while to increase demand in the economy, the size of the Plan is sought to be enhanced. PSUs are beset with many problems, which need to be resolved but they are the whipping boys in the existing ideological climate. Indian capital does not even realise (or is helpless) that it is axing its own feet under pressure from international capital.

Globalization and Financial Sector

One of the corollaries of opening the economy to inflow of foreign capital is financial opening up of the economy—its closer integration into the world financial markets. Foreign capital would not like to be tied to the Indian economy since it is looking for global profit maximization; it likes to enter and exit when it suits it. It would also like Indian financial markets to be free and more closely integrated so that it could exploit opportunities as they arise. It pushes for financial deregulation—internally and externally.

For instance, if foreign capital invests in industry it may wish to raise additional funds in the stock markets and want the price of its stocks to rise. This would be facilitated by inflow of foreign capital. Investors would also want to take money out of the country when the opportunity or the need arises. In other words, flows of FDI and FII are linked up. Further, many of the TNCs are also active investors in various international financial markets to make a profit, to cover risks of fluctuations in currencies, stock prices, etc. (See Korten, 1995:199) Hence they, prefer opening up of all the financial markets. Consequently, India introduced capital account convertibility for foreign capital even though Indian capital does not have such a facility.

However, such a situation results not only in the flows of FDI but also of hot money which have the potential of destabilising the markets, as has been seen in SE Asia since 1997 (and in India since 1995). Today the SE Asian, the Japanese and the S. Korean economies are portrayed as financially unsound due to the so called existence of 'crony capitalism'. However, this is a false argument since links between banks and industry have always existed even in Europe and the USA. Further, if the economy faces a crisis, the portfolio of non-performing assets (NPA) increases as has happened recently in Asia. The real problem is that unstable markets lend themselves to speculative activities and discourage long term investments. They also tend to make policies in effective and reduce governments capacity to give direction to the economy and solve its problems. (See Kumar, 1996 and 1997).

Slow Response of Foreign Capital

In spite of the many concessions already offered to foreign capital, FDI into India is small (Table 6.9). The ratio of actual inflow to approvals has been small (21 per cent) since 1991. The higher figure for 1991 reflects the pre-1991 situation. There is no doubt that a time lag problem exists but in comparison to China (the ratio is around 40 per cent) India lags far behind. Something other than a time lag is

Table 6.9 : Foreign Collaborations

Item	*1991*	*1992*	*1993*	*1994*	*1995*	*Total upto Oct.96*
No. approved	950	1520	1476	1854	2337	10077
Tech Collab	661	828	691	792	982	4607
Foreign Inv.	289	692	785	1062	1355	5470
Amt. of Foreign Invest (Rs. Cr.)	530	3890	8860	14190	32070	88290
Actual Inflow	351	675	1787	2982	6370	18479
(FDI+NRI)	(66.2)	(17.4)	(20.2)	(21.0)	(19.9)	(20.9)

Source : SIA NEWSLETTER, Nov 1996, Min. of Industries, GOI, p. 2 and p. 10.

Note : 1. Figures in brackets are per cent of Actual to Approvals.

2. Actuals/Approvals for 1996 were 21.4%, upto Nov 1997 it was 20.9% and for the total upto Nov 1997 it was 20.1% (Economic Survey 1997 98:87). In terms of dollars, approvals declined in 1996 but rose in 1997 while the actual continued to rise through the period.

important. Growth rate in approvals has slowed down since 1996 so that the ratio may temporarily rise but it does not augur well for inflow of FDI in the long run.

Foreign companies are being offered favourable terms like lower taxes, sovereign guarantees, higher debt-equity ratios and freedom from social obligations. In the case of the power sector they were offered 16 per cent post tax rate of returns in dollar terms. FII is given 10 per cent concession in income and capital gains taxation. Foreign banks have few restrictions on computerization or little obligation to set up rural branches. Table 6.10 shows that investment (65%) is tending to concentrate in the 6 advanced states. UP and Haryana probably refer to areas in the proximity of Delhi and should be read as Delhi. Regional disparities can only worsen.

Table 6.10 : Industrial Investment Proposals (state-wise) Percentage break up for August 1991 to November 1996

Total Proposals	*IEMs*			*LOIs*	
States	*No. %*	*Inv. %*	*Empl %*	*Inv %*	*Empl %*
Maharashtra	17.9	18.2	17.3	12.2	16.5
Gujarat	14.8	20.2	14.5	19.9	8.5
UP	9.9	9.7	9.7	9.0	13.3
TN	9.8	6.0	8.4	9.8	14.5
AP	6.8	7.8	6.4	9.7	9.4
Haryana	6.5	3.5	6.0	4.1	6.4
TOTAL (Actual)	30802	5,40,987 (Rs. Cr.)	49,92,196	90,999 (Rs. Cr.)	6,32,113

Source : Same as for Table 6.4, p. 8.

The uncertainty in the economic scenario represented by the fluctuations in economic variables (Kumar, 1996) is being compounded by the prevailing social and political uncertainty. TNCs react to this by delaying their investments. The economy suffers because TNCs are a cause of the uncertainty and because their response to concessions is muted.

In a nutshell, indiscriminate opening up to attract FDI from TNCs is not justified either by the experience of the recent successful industrialisers or India's own historical experience or by the prevailing world circumstances or India's own stage of development. If TNCs enter India in a big way, it will pose problems but if they do not then too under NEP there would be problems (perhaps even greater).

SIZE OF MARKET AND THE MIDDLE CLASS

One of the inducements held out to the TNCs is the supposedly large middle class market. It has been variously estimated to be around 250 million individuals, about 27 per cent of the Indian population, and to be larger than most world economies. The argument is erroneous since even if it is true that the Indian middle class is numerically large, its purchasing power is not.[11] The Indian economy is about 1 per cent of the world GDP. Even if the Indian middle classes earn the bulk of this income, they are small in absolute purchasing power (See Table 6.3 and Kumar, 1994).

In fact, a bulk of the Indian middle and upper middle class is below the poverty line of most of the 20 high income countries. Certainly the Indian middle class aspires to have the standard of the Western middle class but cannot purchase most of the goods that the latter takes for granted. The Indian middle class market is potentially large but that is not the reality of today.

In 1995, there were around 10 million colour televisions and automated two wheelers in the country. Even if the ownership of these items is a criterion for belonging to the middle class, there would be no more than 10 million middle class families out of a total of about 180 million, that is, about 6 per cent of the total. However, TNCs interested in selling their premium products are looking to those families which spend freely. These are the owners of personalised four wheeled vehicles.

Families owning cars and jeeps may not number more than 2 million if one nets out taxis, multiple ownership of cars and jeeps, etc. There would be some families (specially in rural areas) who could afford to keep a personalized four wheeled vehicle but do not. They would perhaps have a colour television or a two wheeler. Assume that one-third of the owners of CTVs and two wheelers belong to this group, then the Indian middle class of the kind in which the TNCs are interested is no more than 5.3 million families or 3 per cent of the population or 27 million individuals.

Even this group will have an average annual family income (inclusive of black incomes) of less than Rs 10 lakh or $ 25,000. Since this class invests a major portion of its wealth in real estate, its consumption of consumer durables still does not match that of the average middle class family in the rich nations. The rest of the middle class of say 200 million may provide a largish market for detergents and soaps, tooth paste, cheap audio systems, processed foods, tea, plastic goods etc. but not for premium products.

In the Eighties, the country made the mistake of believing that there was a large market for consumer durables and this could provide the engine of growth. Mrs Indira Gandhi first in 1982 and Rajiv Gandhi more so after 1985 tried to boost the demand for consumer durables. After an initial burst of demand, met by imports and import intensive production, the markets saturated after 1989. Growth started petering out and the country simply faced a balance of payments difficulty.

Globalisers do not distinguish between essentials and inessentials and suggest that imports be freely allowed – a clear signal to the rich to import what they wish to. There is implicit faith in the market's self-corrective mechanism. It is argued that a rise in net imports would lead to a devaluation of the rupee and an increase in the price of imports, and, therefore, a fall in the demand for imports. Among other things this ignores the fact that demand for luxuries from the rich is inelastic since they are hardly price sensitive. The squeeze would take place on the import of essentials as their domestic prices rise.[12] But, this would make the rate of inflation go up and real wages would fall. The consumption of the rich would be at the expense of the poor.[13]

Amongst the factors, fuelling the growth of the Eighties was demand created by rising fiscal deficit. The reduction in the primary fiscal deficits by the government since 1991 and little rise in aggregate private investments resulted in the industrial recession of 1991-94 and the slow down in the last two years. This effect could have been more severe but for the reduction in the current account deficit and the difficulties faced (due to pressure from TUs) in retrenching staff and closing down plants and offices.

Suppose that NEP are successful in attracting foreign capital and technology to India, it will mean that capital intensity of production will rise and aggravate unemployment. The top 20 TNCs in the Fortune 500 list produced in 1990 an output 6 times larger than India's GDP but their work force was only 7 per cent of India's (Kumar 1994). Not that India is about to be taken over, it points to the prospect that increases in output can be achieved without generating additional employment. [See Korten (1995) for the US context and Kumar (1993a) for Indian experience].

If high technology is to produce for the local market, it would displace local production and cause a rise in unemployment.[14] When displacement is from Indian small and medium scale, loss of employment is large and goes unreported. In the case of Indian large scale sector the displacement would be less but has been reported in many instances and resisted by the TUs.[15] In some instances, TNCs may farm out work to small and medium scale businesses but these would be mostly in high technology areas with low employment potential and not in the traditional small scale sector. Capital intensity would rise even if small and medium scale sectors expand.

Some have argued for allowing FDI into relatively low technology areas rather than in others since that would generate employment. These analysts make the wrong comparison. They forget that TNCs will displace Indian producers in the low technology areas by far more capital intensive technology and thereby make additional employment generation difficult. The issue is not to protect either high or low technology areas but both sectors need protection for different non-comparable reasons. (Kumar, 1994 discusses this in greater detail).

Under the proposed 'Exit Policy', millions from the middle and lower middle classes would lose jobs. This would reduce demand and deepen recession[16]. The government has been unable to push this policy aggressively due to political opposition. In a nutshell, if labour market component of NEP were to be implemented, recession would deepen further.

In brief, the *net* effect of entry of TNCs with their capital intensive technology and the pressure it puts on Indian industry to also go in for similar technology has been a decline in employment rather than an increase[17] in spite of some growth in small and medium sectors. This effect coupled with the earlier mentioned reduced market for Indian organised sector due to imports and the reduction in demand from the government sector is keeping the base of economic growth narrow.

What would happen to the 8 million who enter the work force every year? Who would give employment to those who are retrenched due to closures and Exit policies? Indian industry facing loss of markets, unable to compete globally and facing an uncertain investment climate in India has increasingly turned to trading and speculative activity in the share market (as explained below). If this trend persists, there would be deindustrialisation and greater unemployment.

UNCERTAIN INDUSTRIAL CLIMATE

Growing Uncertainty

Due to the stagflationary tendencies in the economy, as shown by the negligible growth in the industrial sector in the last two years and the potentially high inflation in spite of its low rate just now, it is unlikely that total investment in the economy is going to increase. With excess capacity in several sectors, inflow of foreign capital may slow down in the coming years. This is the dilemma of investment in and growth of the Indian economy.

Other than the government and the TNCs, the source of investments is the Indian private sector. It has raised large amounts of capital since 1991. What has this meant for investments and is this trend likely to continue? Indeed, the market has displayed highly unstable behaviour since 1991 so that the large amount of capital raised in the markets has not helped raise the level of real investment in the economy. Reports suggest that upto 1995, money was diverted for speculation in the secondary market itself or into the real estate market managements have been buying their own scripts to prevent hostile takeover bids.

NEP have introduced uncertainty for Indian businesses in four ways. First, the threat of takeover and loss of control over management. Secondly, the risk of technology since they do not have access and cannot develop the latest technology. Thirdly, threat of entry of new players and finally, inability to influence policy the way TNCs are able to. With all this, Indian capital is tending to take a short term view by moving into trading and speculation (for immediate gains).

Indian businesses are familiar with this since speculation and trading have been the most profitable investments due to the link with the black economy. Due to the increased uncertainty, this picture is unlikely to change in spite of concessions to capital. The Indian private sector is then unlikely to increase its levels of investment, and, therefore, fail to boost the growth rate of the economy.

The expected increase in the rate of growth of the economy then depends on the actions of foreign capital—Foreign Direct Investments (FDI). The dilemma for the Indian economy is that if it comes, it creates uncertainty for Indian capital and if it does not come, given other factors, the economy will tend to stagnate.

Concessions to Investment

In a market driven reform process, policy cannot directly be used to generate demand to end recession. Only concessions to investment can be given in the hope that higher profitability will result in higher levels of investment. This is what has been attempted since 1991 but without success. The reason is that the reform process also simultaneously raises the degree of uncertainty and, therefore, the higher expected profitability is discounted by businessmen.

Take the case of incentives to exports. Since January 1991 the Rupee has devalued substantially *vis-a-vis* the dollar and raised the profitability of exports. Inflation and withdrawal of export concessions have eroded only a part of this gain. Yet, exports have not shown a sustained surge. Leaving it to the markets has not worked Exporters have repeatedly sought state intervention.

It is argued that investments are better than loans. In the present context, with low interest rates internationally and the high profits being earned by a majority of TNCs in India, this argument is weak. Foreign investments have to be serviced even if with a time lag (in many cases, this lag is small). This calculation ignores the costs associated with use by TNCs of transfer pricing, etc. But, the biggest costs are indirect, like, budgetary concessions, increased uncertainty and stagnation in investment, loss of policy control and inability to fulfil national goals.

In sum, opening up to global influences creates uncertainty. Individual businessmen find this difficult to cope with and require help from the state. The Indian state (and businessmen) has realised this but slowly and perhaps too late. It is TNCs with their more advanced technology, brand names, marketing skills and financial clout which is ideally situated to take advantage of the concessions to investment. Indian capital has lost markets and its share of profits despite the concessions obtained by them.

Investment in R & D

Absorption and development of technology will be critical for sustained long term growth of the Indian economy. TNCs are unlikely to develop technology in India, they will simply import it where needed. Indian capital facing growing uncertainties is unlikely to compound them by trying to develop its own technology. R&D is known to be the riskiest of all investments specially when competitors already have more advanced technology. The public sector facing a resource crunch and under attack on grounds of poor profitability is unlikely to risk more investment in R&D.

Yet, all successful industrialisers have been technologically dynamic while the trend in India seems to be in the opposite direction. The Japanese resorted to the famous 1:4 formula which stipulated that for every Yen of technology imported four Yen be spent on its absorption. Indian (private) industry did not even spend a fraction of the funds needed to absorb technology and resorted to repeated imports of technology. The National laboratories and CSIR have by and large not been able to perform the task they were required to because of other reasons. NEP do not correct these deficiencies and now the sword of TRIPS and TRIMS is hanging on Indian research. In brief, globalization will adversely affect whatever little indigenous R&D was taking place and make Indian industry even less dynamic than it has been.

CONCLUSION

NEP hit at the very root of the indigenous strengths of the Indian economy, developed since Independence. Temporary phases of good growth cannot hide the overall trends. It is not a question of 'there must be some good in NEP'. It is a package which must be viewed as a whole and not in bits and pieces. Its negative effects on the economy and specially the poor relate to its totality (Sėe Kumar. 1991b). Here it is argued that the few positive aspects are much more than negated by others.

Globalization under NEP spell trouble for Indian industry. The public sector is being dismantled/gifted to the private sector. The organized private sector is unable to withstand the competition from the TNCs. Hence sickness and recession can be expected to deepen. The traditional small and the medium scale sector faces a crisis due to shrinking markets. A few success stories apart, the country may deindustrialize. Indian capital confronts increased uncertainty and may move into trading and speculation and as a junior partner of the TNCs. This fits well with the past practices based on the black economy.

Technological backwardness will grow and threaten the country's independence. There are serious social costs associated with the increased presence of TNCs and their implication for the environment, for inequity, for food security, for regional differentiation and social strife. With opening up, the economy has become far more unstable than earlier and this will affect the already marginalised in society. (See Kumar, 1996).

Can TNCs be expected to act in India's best interest? Unlikely since they mostly originate in advanced countries whose interest they advance. Even for themselves, they look for global profit maximization and not just what they may be able to generate in India so that they may not have a long term interest in the economy. Competition in the economy is unlikely to increase in general since the TNCs are likely to cater to the demand from the upper income groups (3 per cent of the households) and are likely to collude with each other as they do in the international markets.

TNCs would not be interested in developing technology in India but only in selling their intermediate and low technology at a price. WTO would help in this by strengthening control over technology. TNCs would encourage exports only of certain items (based on agriculture and polluting technology) under their own control. This would enable them to corner the profits and also keep the international prices of these goods low. In effect, income terms of trade would turn adverse for the Third World as a whole.

A nation's competitiveness or its comparative advantage are far more complex than simply a matter of entry of a few firms, be they TNCs. Since TNCs are typically interested in premium products, neither will prices decline nor will choice increase for the common man. Given the small size of Indian markets for the products of TNCs and the possibility of their further contraction due to decline in the size of the middle class with retrenchment in organized industry and the likely recession, TNCs by themselves cannot take India to a new growth path. Investments by TNCs are small compared to the total but have tremendous potential for destabilization. At least in principle, Indian industry may act in India's best interest but that cannot be expected from TNCs since that is not their interest. There can be no blanket preference for TNCs in all areas as globalizers would like. The question has to be globalization for what? It has to be based on the interest of the majority of Indians.

NOTES

1. Earlier phases when the Indian economy was opened up are the pre-independence period and parting with the Asiad in 1982 and accelerating

with the Rajiv Gandhi period. However, these phases of openness differ substantially from what has been initiated in 1991. There is a paradigm shift both nationally and internationally,

2. It is often argued that today capital respects no boundaries so that it is not tied to nation states. This argument is incorrect since TNCs or mutual funds originate in specific countries and their governments represent their interests in world fora, like, the W TO or when they face problems like when Enron was in trouble, the US government intervened with the Indian government Korten (1995) quotes US Treasury officials as saying 'that for every $1 the US Government contributes to the World Bank, more than $2 comes back to the US. (p. 167).
3. Not only the nations are competing, in India even the State governments are vying with each other to offer greater concessions to attract foreign capital. This has globally weakened labour vis-a-vis capital.
4. There has been much attempts to present a brighter picture of performance of the economy and data have been repeatedly changed (See Kumar, 1994). Data change within the same document as in the Economic Survey, 1997-98 between pages 3 and 5. A higher growth of the industrial sector may be a result of the reporting of the previously unreported output by the private sector in order to dress up their balance sheets.
5. Problems have appeared in these countries in the last two years but it cannot be denied that they did considerably better than India in the Eighties and the first part of the nineties.
6. Can Globalization and entry of TNCs be called *status quoist*? The *status quo* referred to here is between the propertied and the non-propertied. If amongst the set of the propertied, new actors like, TNCS become dominant at the expense of Indian capital this does not make policy less *status quoists*. It implies that Indian capital has been short sighted.
7. The success of the NICs since the Seventies needs to be viewed in the context, of the fight of capitalism against communism. Without belittling their achievements, it needs to be stressed that access to technology and markets was allowed to these countries. Capitalism for its own needs allows certain regions to grow. Further, some of these countries noted in their own best interest and refused to succumb to outside Pressures.
8. Perhaps this is the reason that Pepsi, when it entered India in 1988 promised increased agricultural exports from India but did not deliver on its promise. Post-1991, it requested that it should not be forced to export since Coca-Cola was not required to.
9. In the case of Maruti, a prime cause of the dispute between the government and Suzuki was the over pricing of capital goods to be imported from Suzuki for purposes of expansion. This was also a ploy by Suzuki to take over the company by forcing a larger expansion of the equity base.
10. The Maruti episode proves that TNC is not even happy with equal (50%) partnership and wants control. However, control is a matter of the larger partner conceding control and this is feasible in many cases as has been the case with the Indian private sector since before 1991.

11. Various market surveys show that even those who have small income own consumer durables. Such data are used to argue for the existence of a large Indian middle class. Typically such data are unreliable since most Indians do not correctly report their incomes. The NCAER income survey in 1976 gave a total for national income, which was 45 per cent less than that given by the National Accounts Survey. Thus people not only did not declare the black incomes but they did not report the white incomes correctly, It is quite likely that those reporting small incomes and owning consumer durables are hiding a bulk of their incomes and those with genuinely small incomes will not be purchasing such goods.
12. This argument differs from that in Korten (1995). He assumes that the poor do not consume imported goods (p. 168) but in India typically, edible oil, pulses, fertilisers, petro goods, etc., are imported and enter the consumption bundle of the poor.
13. Even if markets are flexible and self correcting, history is not since time is unidirectional. Human misery takes its toll. Children who may have to suffer malnutrition or go without education or girls who have to go without medical treatment would pay a price even if markets recover. This is no consolation.
14. Korten (1995) reports that Fortune 500 industrial firms shed 4.4 million jobs between 1980 and 1993. During this period, their sales increased 1.4 times and assets by 2.3 times. The average salary of the CEOs increased 6.1 times. (p. 218).
15. Firms, like, TOMCO and PAL which were either taken over or went for collaboration with TNCs tried to fire a large part of the work force and faced long strikes.
16. Any impact this may have on increased investment would take time so that immediately excess capacity would manifest itself and that would dissuade investments. Demand has become a problem without large scale retrenchments pointing to what could have happened.
17. A comparison of Tables 6.4 and 6.8 indicates that while in 1991-92, Fixed Capital per employee was Rs. 1.85 lakh, the proposed investment is Rs. 10 lakh per worker. As Tables 6.6 and 6.7 show, investment approvals are tending to be for the capital intensive sectors.

REFERENCES

Ajit, D. (1992). Industrial Growth and Employment: An Analysis of Labour Absorption in Manufacturing Sector in India. RBI Staff Studies, December.

Government of India, Ministry of Finance (1988). *Economic Survey 1997-98.*

Gupta, D. (1992a). Employment, Output and Productivity Trends in India's Small Scale Industry. RBI Staff Studies. August.

Gupta, D. (1992b). Industrial Sickness—Issues and Options. RBI Staff Studies. November

Korten, D.C. (1995). *When Corporations Rule the World.* West Hartford: Kumarian Press.

Kumar, A. (1989). Unemployment, Technological Dynamism and the Need for Government Intervention: A Closer Look at 1989-90 Budget. *Economic & Political Weekly*. August 5.

Kumar, A. (1991a). Liberalization : The Return of the Sahab Bahadur, *Mainstream*. Annual Number.

Kumar, A. (1991b). Structural Adjustment Policies: Loss of Sovereignty and Alternatives. *Lokayan Bulletin*. November-December.

Kumar, A. (1991c). The Present Economic Crisis and the Black Economy, *Competition and Success Review*. December.

Kumar, A. (1993a). New Economic Policies: Prospects for the Industrial Sector. *Economic Growth and Social Change*. September.

Kumar, A. (1993b). Uruguay Round and the Third World: Grim Prospects. *Mainstream*. December 25.

Kumar, A. (1994). Proposals for a Citizens Union Budget for the Nation for *1994-95 : An Alternative to the Fund-Bank Dictated Budget*. Union Budget for 1994-95. Mimeo. Preparatory Committee for Alternative Economic Policies, New Delhi.

Kumar, A. (1996). New Economic Policies, Instability and Policy Ineffectiveness; *Economic & Political Weekly*. November 23.

Kumar, A. (1997). S E Asia: Trapped in the Financial Crisis. *The Economic Times*. December 17.

Sharma, K.C. (1991). Investment and Financial Behaviour of Public Limited Companies. *Reserve Bank of India Occasional Papers*. June.

Subrahmanian, K.K., *et al.* (1996). *Foreign Collaboration under Liberalization Policy Pattern of FDI and Technology-transfer in Indian Industry since 1991*. Reserve Bank of India.

Tandon, P. (1997) Efficiency of Privatized Firms: Evidence and Implications. *Economic & Political Weekly*. December 13.

World Bank (1997). *World Development Report*. New York: OUP

7

FOREIGN DIRECT INVESTMENT IN SOUTH ASIA

Need for Harmonising A Common Investment Area

Indra Nath Mukherji

ROLE OF FOREIGN DIRECT INVESTMENT IN SOUTH ASIA

All South Asian Countries (SAC) have been attempting to woo Foreign Direct Investment (FDI). A number of factors have contributed to this trend. All SAC are capital deficit. External resources have played an important role in bridging their saving investment and export-import gaps. The earlier emphasis on relying primarily on official external assistance for bridging the foreign exchange and savings gaps is giving way to attracting more private capital flows, primarily in the form of equity. This is not only because of diminishing availability of external assistance, (partly a reflection of recession in the capital surplus countries), but also a growing awareness of greater possibilities of combining the advantages of greater capital availability with the acquisition of know-how and marketing skills of the investor. In recent years the possibility of using FDI to enhance exporting capabilities is also being recognised. Further, in the context of current currency crisis in East and South East Asian countries, FDI is being considered as more stable and secure source of domestic investment in comparison to short term and more volatile private financial institutional flows.

RECENT TRENDS IN FOREIGN DIRECT INVESTMENT

FDI in SAC has been increasing steadily in recent years. Table 7.1 shows this trend.

FDI in South Asian Countries (SAC) has increased from less than half a billion US dollars in 1990 to 2.6 billion dollars in 1996. During the same period the developing countries (DC) attracted US dollars 24.5 billion in 1990 which increased to US dollars 109.5 billion in

Table 7.1 : Foreign Direct Investment in Developing Regions (value in US $ millions)

Countries/Regions	*1990*	*1991*	*1992*	*1993*	*1994*	*1995*	*1996*
South Asia	**464.0**	**456.0**	**624.0**	**841.0**	**1231.0**	**1791.0**	**2632.0**
Bangladesh	3.0	1.0	4.0	14.0	11.0	2.0	15.0
India	162.0	141.0	151.0	273.0	620.0	1300.0	2300.0
Maldives	6..0	7.0	7.0	7.0	8.0	9.0	10.0
Nepal	6.0	2.0	4..0	6.0	7.0	8.0	7.0
Pakistan	244.0	257.0	335.0	346.0	419.0	409.0	200.0
All DCs	**24500**	**33500**	**43600**	**67200**	**83700**	**95500**	**109500**
Sub-Saharan Africa	900	1600	800	1600	3100	2200	2600
East Asia & Pacific	10200	12700	20900	38100	44100	51800	61100
Europe & Central Asia	2100	4400	6300	8400	8100	17200	15000
Latin Am & Caribbean	8100	12500	12700	14100	24200	22900	25900
Middle East & North Africa	2800	1800	2200	4200	3000	300	2200

Source : World Bank Debtor Reporting System Presented in Pigato (1997).

1996. Thus the share of SAC in total inflows of FDI increased marginally from 1.9 per cent in 1990 to 2.4 per cent in 1996. It will be apparent that in spite of considerable increase in FDI flows to SAC during the nineties, its share remains a minuscule of total flows of all DC.

Among SAC India received the maximum FDI, its value increasing consistently from a mere 162 million US dollars in 1990 to 2.3 billion US dollars in 1996. Pakistan came next in importance in attracting FDI from US dollars 244 million in 1990 to US dollars 200 million in 1996. The value of FDI in Pakistan having increased to US dollars 419 million in 1994, declined to US dollars 200 million in 1996. The other SAC have been attracting much less FDI and no consistent increase in the trend may be noticed. In a marked contrast to SAC, some regions, particularly East Asia and Pacific have succeeded in attracting much more FDI than South Asia.

Sectoral Patterns

In Bangladesh the two Export Processing Zones (EPZ) (in Chittagong and Dhaka) have been the main channel for FDI inflows in manufacturing. Since its inception in 1981, 106 projects have been approved in the Chittagong Zone by October 1995, with a cumulative total of $ 56 million. The Dhaka Zone has been in operation since 1993, and has approved $ 110 million for 36 projects. Among the sectors attracting FDI in the EPZs, textile (including knit and leather) account for the bulk of foreign investment, followed by electric and electronic parts and metal products. Recent increases in FDI inflows went to the service sector, notably in Telecommunications.

In India the sectoral pattern of FDI flows has changed considerably. The share of the manufacturing sector, while being predominant, has nevertheless declined from 85 per cent in 1990 to 59 per cent by 1995, following the opening up of infrastructure and services to FDI. Within manufacturing, FDI flows appears to have shifted from heavy capital goods to other industries. The top four-fuel (with 28 per cent share), chemicals, services and metals account for more than 50 per cent of all FDI approved since 1991. With the approval of FDI in Cellular Mobile Telephones, FDI investment in Telecommunications jumped to 25 per cent in 1996. Unlike in China, FDI in India has been directed mainly to the domestic market.

In Pakistan as in case of India, FDI has been directed mainly to the domestic market (with the exception of textiles and agro-business). Approved projects in the Karachi Export Processing Zone have totalled less than $ 100 million since its inception in early eighties. More recently, an increasing amount of FDI has gone to service sectors, including Privatisation programmes (for example banks) and infrastructure. At the end of 1993, manufacturing accounted for about 60 per cent of total $ 650 million, while the rest went primarily to the service sector with little going to agriculture and mining.

In Sri Lanka about 55 per cent of FDI flows since 1993 have gone to manufacturing sectors, which is slightly lower than their share of 60 per cent in cumulative FDI between 1978-93. Within manufacturing, the share of textile (clothing and leather goods) has steadily declined, although it remains the single largest sector attracting FDI (accounting for 30 per cent of all inflows). In contrast, agricultural products and beverage sectors and non-metal mineral products have taken an increasing share.

Source of FDI

FDI in Bangladesh originates mainly from Asia. In 1994-95 India,

Korea, Japan, Malaysia and Singapore were the leading sources, accounting for more than 70 per cent of the total. The United States and the United Kingdom were the only significant investors from industrial countries.

The US continued to be the largest source of FDI for India in the period following liberalisation, accounting for 30.3 per cent of the total flows (up to 1995), up from 25.5 per cent in the 1980s. Other major sources are UK (7.5 per cent), Japan (5 per cent), Switzerland (4.6 per cent), and Germany (3.2 per cent). In recent years the share of FDI from East Asia showed remarkable increase. According to data for 1996, Korea was the leading source of FDI in India, second only to the US.

In Pakistan nearly half of FDI inflows since mid sixties came from the US, mostly for oil exploration. In 1995 however, the US share of FDI inflows to Pakistan declined to less than a third, while FDI from Japan and Asian NIEs (notably Hong Kong) has increased significantly. By contrast, UK, once the dominant FDI investor in the country, has been disinvesting in recent years.

In Sri Lanka, Asian countries have been the major foreign investors. Based on approval figures (for end 1995), Singapore led as the major source for FDI. Korea was the second leading investor followed by Japan, Hong Kong, and the US.

FDI REGULATORY POLICIES

With the establishment of Board of Investment (BOI) in 1989, and the liberalisation of industrial policy in 1991, Bangladesh significantly improved the regulatory environment including allowing wholly foreign owned joint ventures and abolishing performance requirements. New sectors have been progressively opened to foreign investment as for instance, the telecommunication sector in 1996. Most sectors with the exception of a few are (such as arms, nuclear energy, forestry, railroad) are now available for direct foreign participation.

In India the investment regime has been significantly liberalised during the 1990s. Of particular importance was the decision to eliminate discriminatory treatment of enterprises with more than 40 per cent equity and open a number of sectors to domestic and foreign private investors such as power (March 1992), mining (March 1993), coal (March 1994), telecommunication (May 1994), and pharmaceuticals (September 1994). Prior government approval in decisions concerning expansion, diversification, merger and acquisition was eliminated. Entry barriers were reduced to only a selected group of sectors. The corporate tax rates were reduced for foreign as well as domestic companies.

In Pakistan facilitation and promotion of FDI has been encouraged since the 1990s. The Pakistan Investment Board was established in 1991. The removal of government clearance requirement (except for certain sectors), relaxation of foreign ownership requirements, liberalisation of foreign exchange regulations (such as holding of foreign currency accounts) etc. were some of the elements of Pakistan's liberalisation of FDI policies.

Sri Lanka has adopted the most open foreign investment regime. It introduced a one-stop shop on foreign investment matters. In November 1995, the government strengthened preferential treatment for export oriented, hightech and high value added sectors as well as large infrastructure projects.

Barriers to Entry

All SAC maintain some barriers to entry of FDI in areas they deem necessary from the point of view of national interest. In Bangladesh defence equipment, International Air Transportation, Railway transport, Security printing, Forestry and Nuclear energy are excluded. In India defence products, Atomic energy, Coal and Lignite, Mineral oils, Railway transport, and Radioactive materials have been excluded. In Nepal Small Scale Industries (except in cases where foreign investors do not require repatriation of income or investment—in such cases 100 per cent equity is permitted). In Pakistan Arms and Ammunition, Security printing, High explosives, and Radioactive materials is excluded. In Sri Lanka 15 sectors including Fishing, Professional services and Mining are restricted.

Scope for Full Ownership

In Bangladesh, Sri Lanka and Pakistan full ownership is permitted, subject to government approval in all other sectors. In India full ownership in 35 priority, Large scale export-oriented and Power enterprises with government approval is permitted. In Nepal 100 per cent equity is permitted in Large-scale industries only.

Performance Requirements

In Pakistan, Sri Lanka and in Bangladesh no performance requirements apply. In India no local content requirements are required on new projects. In Nepal Nepalese workers must be employed after a grace period of seven years.

Transfer of Profits and Convertibility

In India, Pakistan, Sri Lanka, Bangladesh and Nepal restrictions apply on transfer of profits and convertibility. In India foreign exchange balancing mandate is required for consumer goods sector. In Pakistan State Bank approval is needed in banking, Insurance, Airline and Shipping sectors. In Bangladesh provision of transfer is subject to control of BOI and Central Bank. In Nepal repatriation instalments is fixed by HMG. In Sri Lanka no restrictions apply.

Incentives

All SAC have developed Export Processing Zones. India provides tax concessions for Oil, Power, Shipping and Air transport sectors. In Pakistan tax holidays, credits and rebates for exporters are available in certain sectors and designated regions. In Sri Lanka tax concessions are available for more than 90 per cent exporters, agriculture and training facility sectors. Grants are available to electronic exporters. In Bangladesh interest on foreign loans is tax exempt. Tax exemption is further provided on royalties, technical know-how fees. In Nepal five-year tax holiday, upto eleven years, is provided. Tax concessions are also available to exporters who export more than 90 per cent of their output.

SAARC INITIATIVES IN INVESTMENT HARMONISATION

It is now well accepted that there is considerable linkage between trade and investment. While trade could follow investment, quite often it could become a precursor to trade. Studies have established that while trade complimentarities between SAARC Member States is limited, considerable production complimentarities exist between the Member States. This points to the potential for setting up joint ventures among SAARC Member States.

It is also being recognized that the provision of mere fiscal concessions on a competitive basis for favouring FDI is not the answer to attracting more FDI. In this process the states are merely likely to lose revenue without necessarily attracting much FDI. FDI is more influenced by Stable macroeconomic Environment; Stable political regimes, Transparent FDI regulations permitting simplification of procedures and approval process, extended market, and adequate infrastructural facilities.

In this context the SAARC bodies have been laying emphasis on initiating measures for harmonizing policies for promotion of investments and their protection in the region.

The First SAARC Economic Co-operation Conference (SECC) organized by the SAARC Chamber of Commerce and Industry (SCCI) on 19-21 November 1996, established a number of Working Groups to examine various issues like trade, investment, tourism, etc. The Working Group on Investment made a number of useful recommendations relating to mobilization of investment, foreign direct investment, and intra-regional investment opportunities.

The SECC suggested that to the extent feasible, economic reforms relating FDI should be harmonized so as to ensure some consistency and predictability. In this context Member Countries could set up a Centre for gathering information, analytical work and monitoring of investment activities and potential. Member countries could formulate a proper framework of incentives, institutions and information networks in order to attract FDI on a large scale.

The Group further explored the possibilities of raising funds through regional and Multilateral Financial Institutions such as South Asian Development Fund, a proposed South Asian Development Bank, the World Bank, etc.

The Group suggested that possibilities of free investment among stock markets in the region and for setting up a common stock exchange within the region needed to be explored.

The Group identified a number of sectors for joint ventures. It identified infrastructure including those of transport and tourism, energy and hydropower resources, telecommunication, agri-business including biotechnology and small and medium enterprises.

While acknowledging the competitive environment emerging from the WTO proposal on Multilateral Investment Agreement (MIA), the Group expressed concerns pertaining to MIA in a number of areas. It held that national priorities on development could not be compromised and investment decisions could not be looked at in isolation from flows of other factors of production particularly labour and technology.

The Committee on Economic Cooperation (CEC) at its Sixth Meeting held in New Delhi from 16-17 November, deliberated on the subject of promotion of intra-regional investment and establishment of joint venture catering to national, regional, and international markets. For this purpose the Committee felt it necessary to have all relevant information from the Member States, including their policies and regulations concerning direct foreign investment, capital market investments, investment protection measures, etc.

At the Eighth SAARC Summit, it had been decided to establish "a three-window South Asian Development Fund (SADF). With the merger of SAARC Fund for Regional Projects and the SAARC Regional Fund and a third window for social development and infrastructure development".

At the Seventh Meeting of the CEC held in New Delhi from 28-29, October, 1996, the Committee agreed that common Agreements may be evolved by the SAARC Member States for investment promotion, protection of investments, avoidance of double taxation and share market and portfolio investment. Pakistan offered to host a Meeting regarding avoidance of double taxation.

At the Eighth Meeting of CEC held in New Delhi from 21-22 April, 1997, the delegation of India informed the Committee that the meeting on Promotion of and Protection of Investment would be held in New Delhi in September/ October 1997. The delegation of Pakistan informed that it would soon announce the dates for hosting the Meeting on Avoidance of Double Taxation.

In pursuance of above, the First SAARC Meeting on Promotion and Protection of Investment was held in New Delhi from 29-30 September 1997. The Meeting noted all earlier deliberations held by CEC and Ninth SAARC Summit declaration on the subject as also the recommendations of the Working Group on investment set up under SECC. The Meeting pointed to a number of essential features of policies for promotion and protection of investments as well as procedure for settlement of disputes.

ELEMENTS OF INVESTMENT HARMONISATION

Fair and Equitable Treatment to Investments

This provision is to ensure that investments made by investors of other countries and returns on such investments are accorded fair and equitable treatment at all times.

National and Most Favoured Nation Treatment

Under the principle of national treatment the host country assures foreign investors of a treatment no less favourable than the treatment extended to its own investors in respect of operation, management, maintenance, use and enjoyment of investments. The MFN principle implies extending to investments and investors a treatment no less favourable than that accorded to investments or investors of any other country.

Free Repatriability of Returns

Under this principle investments and returns on investments are guaranteed full and free repatriability. Transfers are permitted in freely converted currencies at the choice of the investor to be made at the prevailing market rate of exchange on the date of transfer.

Protection Against Expropriation

Under this principle the host country extends the assurances that investments made by foreign investors shall be expropriated or nationalized only for a public purpose in accordance with law on a non-discriminatory basis and against payment of fair and equitable compensation.

Even in case where an investor suffers losses on account of war or other armed conflict, a state of emergency or civil disturbances, he has to be assured that he would be compensated for the losses in a manner similar to domestic investors or other foreign investors.

Limited Current Account Convertibility

The SAARC Member States may consider adopting limited current account convertibility for the purpose of liberalizing cross border capital flows, as has been the practice between India and Nepal.

Avoidance of Double Taxation Agreement

Pakistan may be requested to set firm dates for holding a Meeting on Avoidance of Double Taxation Agreement. Currently India has such Agreements with 51 countries. These could form models for adoption as well as harmonization.

Procedure for Settlement of Disputes

A mutually acceptable mechanism for dispute resolution provides a high level of comfort to foreign investors. A foreign investor should be free to approach the local legal administrative bodies or domestic law court for judicial relief. He should further be permitted to take recourse to the domestic arbitration facilities and arbitral bodies. In this regard a foreign investor should receive the same treatment as a domestic investor.

The investor may, if parties to the dispute agree, opt for international conciliation such as the one under the Conciliation Rules of the United Nations Commission on International Trade Laws (UNCITRAL).

If appropriate intra-regional venue for arbitration is agreed upon among SAARC Member States, it would considerably reduce the cost and time spent in arbitration proceedings and thereby instil investor confidence.

ASEAN EXPERIENCE

The Agreement by ASEAN Members for the Promotion and Protection of Investments is an initiative at foreign investment harmonization, which could provide valuable experience for SAARC Member States. The ASEAN Investment Area seeks joint investment promotion for ASEAN, attempts to harmonize and simplify investment rules and facilitation measures, and provide for cross listing of ASEAN stocks. In order to provide for transparency and predictability each Contracting party has to ensure the provision of up-to-date information on all laws and regulations pertaining to foreign investment. Regarding dispute settlement, the provisions of ASEAN Dispute Settlement Mechanism apply to the settlement of disputes under the Agreement. SAARC too could do well to set up a SAARC Dispute Settlement Mechanism.

REFERENCES

Pigato Maria *et al.* (1997) *South Asia's Integration into the World Economy*, The World Bank.

SAARC (1997). *First Meeting on Promotion and Protection of Investment*, New Delhi 29-30 September, 1997.

8

EXTERNAL SECTOR REFORMS IN INDIA
An Evaluation

K.S. Dhindsa and Anju Sharma

India's inward looking industrialization policy adopted after independence stemmed from the pursuit of self reliance and a strong belief in export pessimism. Although export pessimism dominated the economic policies of many developing countries but in the face of growing evidence to the contrary, it gave way to more realistic assessment of trade prospects in the late 1960s and 1970s. As many developing countries shifted to outward oriented policies to exploit the growing trade opportunities, Indian policy makers on the other hand persisted with the same import substitution[1] policy till the end of 1980s. Export pessimism[2] became for india a self fulfilling prophecy as its share in the world exports fell steadily from 2.0 per cent in 1950-51 to 0.4 per cent in 1989-90. So keeping in view the poor export performance of India, a slow but steady process of domestic deregulation was started in the mid 1980s and India began its opening to foreign trade investment. Although the liberalization process started in the 1980s[3] but the scope of economic reforms was made wider and deeper in the 1990s. It was realized that the permanent solution to the balance of payment problems lies in the liberalization and globalization of international trade, capital flows and market determined exchange rate.[4] The aim of these reforms was to generate a market orientation for the previously highly regulated domestic economy. Yet the liberalization of trade and foreign investments policies could be effective only if combined with appropriate reforms in the industrial policy and maintenance of macro economic stability. In the present study an attempt has been made to :

(a) discuss reforms in trade and foreign investment sector in India, and

(b) evaluate the impact of these external sector reforms on the Indian economy.

Tabular analysis has been used in this study. Data has been collected from various sources namely World Development Indicators, Reserve Bank of India, Merchandise Trade Data Set, Economic Surveys, Indian Custom Tariffs, World Bank Estimates, Handbook of Statistics on the Indian Economy. Directorate General of Commercial Intelligence and Statistics, Ministry of Finance, Government of India.

Reforms in the Trade Sector

Until 1991, India maintained a trade and investment regime characterized by heavy quantitative restrictions and high tariffs on imports, a complex system of export subsidies, an overvalued exchange rate and various restrictions on foreign investment. Although the reforms of 1991 caused a sea change in each of these components of the policy, but even yet much remains to be done before the Indian economy is completely integrated with the rest of the world. In the present section an attempt has been made to highlight various reforms which took place in the trade sector.

Import Licensing Policy

Before 1991, India adopted a policy of quantitative restrictions through import licensing regime which restricted the import of consumer goods, raw materials, intermediate goods and capital equipments. Import of certain items was allowed keeping in view the essentiality and non-availability of these items in the domestic market. Only essential mass consumption goods like foodgrains, edible oils, sugar and kerosene oil could be imported and that is also through official agencies, just to eliminate domestic shortages.

During the 1980s, attempts were made to simplify the licensing system in order to provide easier access to the imports of intermediate goods by placing many such items on the readily importable Open General License (OGL) list. Some import of capital goods were also eased through the flexibility of the discretionary licensing regime in order to encourage technological upgradation, particularly in export oriented industries. The number of capital goods included in the OGL list increased from 79 in 1976 to 1107 in 1987 and 1329 in 1990.

Another source of liberalization was the decline in the share of canalized imports.

After the reforms in 1991, several changes were made in the import licensing policy. Different import items were classified into 26 lists, each list having a different approval procedure. For most of the goods other than final consumer goods, the reforms in the very first year removed quantitative restrictions on imports. In April 1992 a single negative list (comprising some intermediate goods, a few capital goods and most consumer goods) was introduced which replaced the import licensing, thereby eliminating the scope for discretionary decisions, bureaucratic delays and inefficiencies over a wide range of items. Liberalisation of consumer goods started in 1992 when large exporters received special import license as an incentive, allowing them to import certain consumer goods specified in positive list. The positive list has been expanded further and recently the special import license route has been opened to a wide range of fabrics. Government is also committed to make the trade of consumer goods free within a short period subject to the requirement of environment, safety and security.

The Tariff Structure

Before 1991, a complicated tariff structure with high and differentiated rates across various industries supplemented quantitative controls on imports. During the 1980s, though some items were shifted from the restricted list to the Open General License (OGL) list, but higher tariffs were imposed on the import of these goods. In the 1980s, tariff levels in India were among the highest in the world. In June 1991, the maximum level of import duties reached as high as 250 per cent on several items even after excluding goods such as liquor with much higher rates. The import weighted custom tariff was 117 per cent on intermediate goods and 97 per cent on capital goods. For the economy as a whole the import weighed tariff rate was 87.

In order to dismantle systematically the high cost inward looking Industrial regime and make Indian Industry globally competitive, there were two options namely : (a) to reduce the tariff rates as well as their dispersion and, (b) to make the Indian capital goods sector efficient and facilitate its technological revival. A phased reduction in the tariffs thus became an important component of the reforms and tariff rates were reduced in all budgets presented from 1991 onwards.

The Tax Reform Committee (1992) recommended that by 1997-98, the tariff structure should have custom duties of 20 per cent on capital goods, 25 per cent to 30 per cent on intermediate goods and 50 per cent on consumer goods. The government accepted these recommendations and import duties on capital goods, far out of line with international norms and having a cascading effect on the cost structure of Indian industry were reduced substantially. The composite duty rate on import of various capital goods needed to set up new projects fell to 25 per cent from 85 per cent. The duty on import of machinery for electricity generation, petroleum refinery and coal mining came down to 20 per cent and that for fertilizer dropped to zero. The earlier facility of duty free imports of capital goods by firms registered under the 100 per cent Export Oriented Units (EOUs) scheme and those in Export Processing Zones (EPZs) remained intact. The Export Promotion Capital Goods (EPCG) scheme was introduced under which any actual user can import capital goods with a 15 per cent duty by undertaking to export four times the value of the machines over a period of 5 years. Intermediate goods such as metal and chemicals also obtained substantial trariff reduction.

Export Promotion Incentives

Before the introduction of economic reforms, high levels of protection through import licensing and tariffs created a strong bias against export-oriented industries. Due to prevailing high prices in the import competing industries through higher levels of protection, resources like capital and labour had the tendency to shift more towards import competing industries and less towards export-oriented industries. Inefficiency in the import competing industries could be passed on in the form of higher domestic prices without any fear of competition from imports. This raised the general cost structure of Industry and exports suffered from negative effective protection.

The authorities decided to offset the anti export biases in trade policy with incentives and subsidies. These included the schemes for providing cash assistance to offset the burden of indirect taxes at earlier stages of production and to provide an element of subsidy to cover various hidden costs, duty drawbacks to refund custom duties paid on imported inputs and to enable exporters to obtain duty free imported inputs through advance licensing. The value of these incentives net of taxes increased from 2.3 per cent of the value of exports in 1960-61 to 11.1 per cent in 1989-90. Since the late 1980s, income earned from exports has been exempted from paying tax. All these incentives, however, imposed a growing burden on the budget but did not fully offset the disadvantages of high cost structure. At the best they removed the impact of negative effective protection[5] on exports.

Some special schemes also encouraged the export promotion activities. A number of Export Processing Zones provided facilities for 100 per cent export oriented units located in the zones to obtain the import of raw materials, intermediate goods and capital goods free of import licensing at zero duty. With the removal of quantitative restrictions and a shift to a new competitive exchange rate, a large part of export subsidy regime was abolished. Cash compensatory support ended very early when the rupee was devalued by 24 per cent in July 1991. The major export incentives which still continue included duty drawbacks and the advance licensing schemes to large exporters to import the inputs they need duty free.

In order to promote exports, various types of tax concessions are allowed to the exporters. Tax holiday schemes are the extensions of the provisions which exempt certain incomes from the purview of income tax. Tax holiday was given to the newly established industrial undertaking in Free Trade Zones, Electronic Hardware Technology Parks, Software Technology Parks or Special Economic Zones. This scheme provides for complete tax exemption in respect of the profits and gains of an industrial undertaking set up in any of these Free Trade Zones. Complete tax exemption can be claimed in respect of any five consecutive assessment years falling within a time frame of 8 years beginning from the year in which the industrial undertaking starts its production.

Foreign Investment

Investment in a country by individuals and organizations from other countries is an important aspect of international finance. This flow of international finance may take the form of portfolio investment (acquisition of securities) or direct investment (creation of productive activities). Prior to reforms, India retained a very restrictive and highly selective policy towards foreign investment. Important areas of the economy were kept close to the private investment. Even in areas open to private investment, foreign direct investment was allowed only selectively with a preference to areas involving technology transfers while foreign investment in the secondary capital market was not allowed at all. In the second half of the 1980s, government began to seek foreign investment.

In order to eliminate dependence on short term debt[6], restrictions on both foreign direct investment and portfolio investment were eased considerably. In 1991, government allowed Foreign Direct Investment in almost every sector of the economy. Now the foreign equity proposals need not to be accompanied by technological transfers as required earlier. New policy encouraged foreign equity upto 100 per cent in Export Oriented Units, the power sector, electronic and software technology parks. Approvals for foreign investment come either through automatic routes or through Foreign Investment Promotion Board (FIPB). The Foreign Exchange Regulation Act (FERA) has undergone substantial amendments to remove restrictive provisions on the operation of companies with foreign equity of 40 per cent or more. India has joined the Multilateral Investment Guarantee Agency (MIGA) for protecting investment against risks such as wars, civil disturbance and expropriation. Bilateral Investment Protection Agreements have also been concluded with many countries.

These economic reforms brought liberalisation of trade in service sector like banking, insurance and telecommunications. Foreign direct investment upto 74 per cent in the private banks is permitted under the automatic route. According to the 1997 WTO Financial Service Agreement, India committed to permit 12 foreign banks branches annually. Foreign direct investment upto 100 per cent in permitted in e-commerce. Automatic approval is available for equity in electronics and softwares. These units can be set under several schemes including Export Processing Zones, Export Oriented Units, Special Economic Zones, and Software Technology Parks etc. Joint Ventures are now permitted in both exploration and development of oils and refineries. The telecommunication sector is also opened up for foreign investment. Air transport, until recently a public sector monopoly, has been opened up to the private sector. Private toll roads have also been commissioned.

As far as portfolio investment is concerned, in 1992 the government announced a policy encouraging portfolio investment in Indian industry. The Indian capital markets are thus opened to foreign institutional investors such as pension funds and broad based mutual funds subject to the regulation by the Securities and Exchange Board of India. Indian companies also gained access to capital markets abroad through mechanisms such as Global Depository Receipts or Euro investment. Favourable tax treatment via capital gains tax of only 10 per cent and taxation of dividends at 20 per cent applies to both types of investment. Portfolio investment flows routed through Mauritius have an additional advantage of zero taxation on capital gains.

Exchange Rate Structure

Till 1991, various foreign exchange transactions were tightly controlled by the government and the RBI. After reforms these controls have been removed to a large extent and further liberalization is still continuing. India switched over to a market determined exchange rate system on March 1,1993. In February 1992, a dual exchange rate system was introduced which allowed the exporters to sell 60 per cent of their foreign exchange in the free market and 40 per cent to the government at the lower official exchange rate. In 1993, the official exchange rate was unified with free market exchange rate. In 1994 many current account transactions including education, medical expenses, foreign travel and all current business transactions were permitted at the market exchange rate. Now the exchange rate is flexible and allowed to depreciate as necessary to maintain competitiveness. In 1993 rupee was made fully convertible on trade account. This measure contributed significantly to boost India's exports. At present, there is almost full convertibility on the current account and partial convertibility on the capital account. The Committee on Capital Account Convertibility which submitted its report in 1997 highlighted the benefits of a more open capital account but at the same time cautioned that capital account convertibility could pose tremendous pressures on the financial system. Justifiably, the Indian government has been very cautious in this regard, particularly after the disastrous experience of some east Asian countries. It is true that globalization has led to financial integration in world markets and presently large amounts of capital move freely across countries.

Foreign Exchange Reserves

The gradual liberalization of restrictions on various external transactions has resulted in the enlargement of foreign exchange market. The foreign exchange reserves of India include foreign currency assets held by the Reserve Bank of India, gold holdings of the Reserve Bank and SDRs. Foreign exchange reserves in India have increased from US $ 1.1 billion in july 1991 to U.S.$ 41.12 million in January 2001, which is sufficient for meeting the payments of 8 months of imports. These reserves came not only from export earnings but also from various forms of borrowings including NRIs deposits. Realising that the Foreign Exchange Regulation Act (FERA) passed by the government in 1973 was not in tune with the economic reforms started since 1991, the government replaced it with a new legislation called Foreign Exchange Management Act (FEMA) which came into effect from June 2000. Under FEMA, foreign exchange law violations are treated to civil rather than criminals.

Evaluation of External Sector Reforms

The policy makers observed a wave of export pessimism during the 1950s. Economists were of the view that India's exports are supply constrained and they are not responsive to price changes. However Ghosh's (1991) research[7] showed that exports of manufactured goods are responsive to relative price changes. In July 1991, quantitative restrictions on some import items were removed, few items were decanalised, implying that these items can be exported by individuals rather than by the government agency. Later on some consumer goods were placed under the freely importable category. In some infrastructure activities, 100 per cent equity was allowed.

In the Indian equity market, portfolio investment by Foreign Institutional Investors (FII) was allowed. It was thought that all foreign equity had to be only routed through foreign institutional investors registered both with the Securities Exchange Board of India (SEBI) and Reserve Bank of India. Both primary and secondary market investments upto 24 per cent of the total liquidity of any company were allowed. In case of equity funds, an equity debt ratio 70 : 30 was allowed. Long term capital gains tax and dividend tax were reduced to 10 per cent and 20 per cent respectively. In order to raise foreign equity funds, the Global Depository Receipt (GDR) was allowed. For reducing short term external debt and for its proper management, the External Debt Management Unit (EDMU) was set up. The move towards market-determined exchange rate was considered essential because this will automatically bring equilibrium in its balance of payments.

In this section we study the impact of reforms on India's exports and imports.

Exports increased from US$ 17,865 million in 1991-92 to US $ 44,560 million in 2000-01 and imports increased from US$ 19411 million to US$ 50,537 during the same period (Table 8.1). It is to be noted that growth rate of exports and imports have shown fluctuations during 1991-92 to 2000-01. The growth rate of exports became negative in the year 1998-99 and this is largely due to recession witnessed in US and European Union countries. Export-import ratio ranged between 73and 94 during 1990s. The share of India's exports in world exports increased from 0.52 per cent in 1990-91 to 0.67 per cent in 1999-2000 and the share of India's imports in world imports increased from 0.67 per cent to 0.75 per cent during the same period. India also experienced higher export growth rate than world export growth rate during the 1990s (Table 8.2). India's ranking in Export growth has improved by 6 points during 1990s as against 1980s.

Trade deficit which stood at 3.2 per cent of GDP during 1980-90, declined to 3.1 per cent of GDP during the period 1992-2000. The current account deficit decreased from 1.8 per cent of GDP to 1.1 per cent of GDP during the same period (Table 8.3). Although the current account was in deficit throughout the years, but invisibles (export services) were in surplus during this period. Invisible accounts of the current balance of payments have remained more than 48 per cent of,

Table 8.1 : India's Foreign Trade during 1990-91 to 2000-2001

(U.S $ million)

Year	*Export*	*Imports*	*Trade balance*	*Growth rate (per cent)*		*Export-Import Ratio*
				Export	*Import*	
1991-92	17,865	19,411	-1,545	-	-	92.0
1992-93	18,537	21,822	-3,345	3.8	12.7	84.7
1993-94	32,238	23,306	-1,068	20.0	6.5	94.2
1994-95	26,331	38,654	-2,324	18.4	22.9	91.9
1995-96	31,795	36,675	-4,880	20.8	28.0	86.7
1996-97	33,470	39,132	-5,662	5.3	6.7	85.5
1997-98	35,006	41,484	-6,478	4.6	6.0	84.4
1998-99	33,219	42,389	-9,370	-5.1	2.2	78.4
1999-2000	36,822	49,671	-12,848	10.8	17.1	73.8
2000-2001	44,560	50,537	-5,976	21.0	1.7	88.2

Source : RBI, Hand Book of Statistics, RBI Bulletin.

Table 8.2 : India's Ranking of Exports and Imports at World Level

Indicators	*1990-91*	*1999-2000*
Share of India's Exports in World Exports (per cent)	0.52	0.67
Share of India's import in World Imports (per cent)	0.67	0.75
India's Export Growth (per cent)	7.7	8.9
World Export Growth (per cent)	5.4	6.3
India's Ranking in Export Growth (Worldwide)	52	46
India's Rank in World Exports (Share-wise)	33	32
India's Rank in World Imports (Share-wise)	29	26

Source : World Development Indicators, WTO Merchandise Trade data set.

trade balance during 1993-94 and 2000-2001. The foreign exchange earned through the non-factor services (which include transportation, insurance and travel) increased from US$ 535 million in 1993-94 to US$ 2478 million in 2000-2001 (Table 8.4).

The balance on investment income component was negative during the period 1992-93 to 2000-2001, whereas earnings from private transfers increased from US$ 5265 during 1993-94 to US$ 12798 million during 2000-2001. Borrowings from official transfers ranged between US$ 307 million to US$ 416 million during 1992-93 to 2000- 2001 (Table 8.4).

The dual exchange rate was introduced in February 1992 under which exporters will surrender 30 per cent of their foreign exchange earnings at the official exchange rate and the remaining 70 per cent of foreign exchange earnings can be sold at free market rate. In 1993-94 budget, the Finance Ministry decided to opt for integrated free market exchange rate and government abolished the official exchange rate. In order to strengthen the free market exchange rate system, import of gold was liberalized Under 'Hawala' or illegal (unofficial) market, the agents operating in Western Europe used to buy foreign workers remittances and they used to sell foreign exchange earnings to smugglers of gold. As a result of liberalizing gold import the difference between the official exchange rate and unofficial exchange rate decreased considerably. Due to this, the non-resident

Table 8.3 : Major Indicators of Trade Sector in India (as % of GDP at Current Market Prices)

Indicators	*Pre-crisis period 1980-90*	*Post-crisis period 1992-2000*
Fiscal Deficit as % of GDP (centre)	6.6	5.2
Fiscal deficit as % of GDP (Centre & States)	7.2	7.4
Current Account deficit	1.8	1.1
Trade deficit	3.2	3.1
Exports (F.O.B)	4.7	8.5
Import (C.I.F.)	7.9	11.6
Export/Import ratio	0.63	0.86
Foreign Exchange Reserves	-0.2	1.1
Manufactured Exports	2.8	6.3
Capital Inflows	1.6	2.2
Ratio of Net Imports of Manufactured goods to Manufacturing GDP	8.4	2.5
Invisibles (net)	1.4	2.0
Non-factor services	0.4	0.4
Official Transfer	0.2	0.1
Private transfer	1.1	2.5
NRI Deposits (net)	0.4	0.4
Commercial Borrowing	0.4	0.5

Source : Directorate General of Commercial Intelligence and Statistics (DGCIS), RBI Hand Book of Statistics on Indian Economy.

Table 8.4 : Invisible Receipts (US. $ million)

Year	*Non-factor Services*	*Investment Income*	*Private Transfer*	*Official Transfer*	*Total*
1993-94	535	-3270	5265	368	2898
1994-95	602	-3431	8093	416	5680
199596	-197	-3205	8506	345	5449
1996-97	726	-3307	12367	410	10,196
1997-98	1319	-3521	11830	379	10,007
1998-99	2165	-3544	10280	307	9208
1999-2000	4064	-3559	12256	382	13,143
2000-01	2478	-3821	12798	336	11,791

Source : RBI Hand Book Statistics in Indian Economy RBI, RBI Bulletin.

Indians (NRIs) started sending their remittances through official channels and this in turn strengthened the free market exchange rate system. Custom duty on gold was further reduced to 15 per cent.[8] Earlier the returning Indians were allowed to import gold upto 5 kg at a duty of Rs. 220 per 10 grams. After some time, exporters and selected banks were allowed to import gold at low custom duties. Thus the government could maximize revenue collection from import of gold by putting gold under unrestricted Open General License list.

In 1994 the government made rupee freely convertible on the current account and the people were allowed to buy foreign currency for travel, medical and study purposes. In 1999-2000 a law regarding current account convertibility was passed. The real effective exchange rate showed no depreciation during the post reform period after depreciating by an average of 2 per cent per annum during 1980s, while nominal effective exchange rate showed depreciation of 4.6 per cent during 1990s as against 3 per cent during 1980s. RBI credit to the government decreased from 20 per cent in 1980s to 5.6 per cent in 1990s. Inflation also fell from 7.2 per cent to 6.7 per cent during the same period (Table 8.5). There was an annual average foreign exchange reserves accumulation of 1.1 per cent of the GDP in the post reform period as compared to annual draw down of 0.2 per cent of the GDP

Table 8.5 : Growth Rates of Main Economic Indicators (per cent)

Indicators	*Pre-crisis 1980-90*	*Post-crisis 1992-2000*
Nominal Effective Exchange Rate	-3.0	-4.6
Real Effective Exchange Rate	-2.0	20.0
Inflation*	7.2	6.7
RBI credit to Govt.	20.0	5.6
Bank credit (net)	18.5	14.0

* Inflation is measured in terms of wholesale prices

Source : RBI Hand Book of Statistics on the Indian Economy.
WTO World Merchandise Trade data.

during eighties Table (8.3). External debt as percentage of GDP declined from 28.7 per cent in 1990-91 to 21.9 per cent in 1999-2000. Another interesting point to be noted is that the short-term loan as percentage of total external debt declined from 10.2 per cent to 4.0 per cent during the same period. Commercial borrowings as a percentage of GDP also declined from 0.7 in 1990-91 to 0.1 in 1990-2000 (Table 8.6).

Table 8.6 : India's External Debt during 1990-91 and 1999-2000

Indicators	*1990-91*	*1999-2000*
External Debt in US $ (million)	83801	98436
External Debt as % of GDP	28.7	21.9
Short term debt Loan as % of Total debt	10.2	4.0
Commercial Borrowing as % of GDP	0.7	0.1

Source : Hand Book of Statistics of Indian Economy.

Although the fiscal deficit of the centre decreased from 6.6 per cent of GDP in 1980-90 to 5.2 per cent of GDP in 1992-2000, but the combined fiscal deficit of the Centre and States increased marginally from 7.2 per cent to 7.4 per cent during the same period (Table 8.3). Adoption of managed floating exchange rate reduced the external spill overs effect of the fiscal deficit on the current account deficit, whereas the removal of import barriers has reduced the effect of fiscal deficits on inflation. This is so because the shortage of goods in the domestic market is removed by increasing the supply of goods through higher level of imports. If external shock occurs and lasts for a longer period, it is recommended that the country should resort to depreciation of the currency and if external shock appears to be short lived then external borrowing is a better policy option.

Total foreign investment increased from US$ 559 million in 1992-93 to US$ 5099 in 2000-2001. Portfolio investment is very volatile and undependable and it became negative (US$ 61 million) during 1998-99 as against US$ 3312 million in 1996-97 (Table 8.7). Foreign investment is desirable and it should be more in the form of direct investment. Presently the share of portfolio investment in total foreign investment is high and this needs to be reversed. Direct foreign investment in India ranged between US$ 315 million and US$ 3557 million during 1992-93 and 2000-2001. It needs to be noticed that the gap between approval of foreign investment and actual flow is too large and therefore remedial actions to enhance the actual utilization of foreign investments needs to be undertaken. The average annual growth rate in the services sector increased from 6.9 per cent in 1981-91 to 8.1 per cent during 1991-2001, but average annual growth rate in the industrial sector declined marginally from 6.8 per cent to 6.4 per cent during the same period. This slow down in the industrial activity could be attributed to harsh labour laws, reservation of small scale industries and power shortage and perhaps because of these reasons large scale firms are still unwilling to make big investments in the industrial sector. If a large part of GDP originates in industry, then India will be able to expand exports and imports. Because of slow growth in industrial sector, imports have simply failed to absorb the foreign exchange generated by remittances and foreign investment flows.

Table 8.7 : Foreign Investment in India (US $ million)

Years	*Direct Investment*	*Portfolio Investment*	*Foreign Investment*
1992-93	315	244	559
1993-94	586	3567	4153
1994-95	1314	3824	5138
1995-96	2144	2748	4892
1996-97	2821	3312	6133
1997-98	3557	1828	5385
1998-99	2462	-61	2401
1999-2000	2155	3026	5181
2000-01	2339	2760	5099

Source: RBI Hand Book of Statistics on Indian. Economy RBI Bulletin.

Despite these good effects of economic reforms, the post reform period is marked by jobless growth. According to NSS data on employment as against the growth of employment at rate of 2.04 per cent per annum during 1983-94, employment growth rate fell to 0.98 per cent per annum during 1994-2000. Growth rate of employment in agricultural sector fell from 1.60 per cent per annum in 1983-94 to – 0.34 per cent per annum during 1994-2000 (Table 8.8).

Table 8.8 : Annual Growth Rate of Employment in Various Sectors

(Per Cent)

Sector	*1983-94*	*1994-2000*
Agriculture	1.60	-0.34
Manufacturing	2.14	2.05
Services	3.53	2.42
Total	2.04	0.98

Source : Planning Commission Report of Task Force on Employment Opportunities and Economic Surveys.

Employment in the organized sector decreased slightly from 7.9

per cent of total employment in 1983 to 7.1 per cent in 1999-2000. The percentage of employment in unorganized sector to total employment has remained almost stagnant at 92 per cent (Table 8.9). The growth rate of employment in the organized sector decreased from 1.20 per cent in 1983-94 to 0.53 per cent in 1994-2000, while the growth rate of employment in unorganized sector fell from 2.01 per cent to 1.3 per cent in the same period (Table 8.9).

Table 8.9 : Employment in Organized and Unorganized Sector in India

(Per cent)

Year	*Organised sector*	*Unorganised sector*	*Total Employment Percent*
1983	7.9	92.1	100.00
1994	7.3	92.7	100.00
1999-2000	7.1	92.9	100.00
Growth Rate of - Employment			
1993-94	1.20	2.01	2.04
1994-2000	0.53	1.3	0.98

Source : Computed from Planning Commission Report of the Task Force on Employment Opportunities.

Conclusions

As a result of external sector reforms in India there was an improvement in the overall balance of payments situation and the real effective exchange rate did not show any depreciation. The decrease in fiscal deficit is reflected in lowering the current account deficit. Foreign exchange reserves increased by 1.1 per cent in the post-reform period as compared to annual draw down of – 0.2 per cent in reserves during the pre reform period. Foreign investment has also gone up considerably after reforms.

In order to increase foreign exchange earnings from foreign tourists, better transport services between various tourist sites, provision of more entertainment facilities and better hospitality towards tourists need to be provided. The movement in the exchange rate is found to be a powerful instrument in bringing adjustment in the current account deficit. So far as the impact of these economic reforms on employment is concerned, it is found that the growth rate of employment is much lower in the post-reform period as compared to pre-reform period. The growth rate of employment in the agricultural sector was negative during 1994-2000. Thus the post-reform period is marked by the jobless growth. The combined deficit of the centre and states is still very high and this must be brought down to a lower level. The efforts to reduce fiscal deficit ought to be done both on revenue and expenditure side. Other unfinished reform agenda includes institutional reforms, amendments in labour laws and further reduction in custom duties.

NOTES

1. Though import substitution policy was desirable for setting up heavy industries, but in the late 1970s it was realized that since the import substitution policy has caused greater misallocation of resources and hence it has kept growth rate at around 3 per cent, commonly known as "Hindu Rate of Growth', export promotion policy based on comparative cost advantage needs to be pursued.
2. Many studies including Manmohan Singh, Deepak Nayyar and K.S. Dhindsa brought out the fact that India's poor export performance from 1950 to 1970 is due largely to internal supply factors rather than slow growth of demand of traditional export commodities. All these people were of the view that since India's share in world exports of major traditional commodities has declined, therefore increase in domestic production and increase in profitability of foreign sales vis-a-vis home sales through devaluation was needed to enhance India's export performance.
3. See Ishar Judge Ahluwalia (1991), 'Productivity and Growth in Indian Manufacturing,' Oxford University Press, Oxford. She pointed out that liberalisation started during 1980s, though on a mild scale. Her study also reveals that productivity growth in manufacturing sector during 1980s was higher than the productivity growth experienced during the 1960s and 1970s.
4. It is argued that a dual exchange policy needs to be followed for capital goods, intermediate goods, workers remittances and technology transfer. Under this exchange rate system the exporters would surrender 30 per cent of total export earnings at official exchange rate and the remaining 70 per cent can be sold at market exchange rate.
5. Negative effective protection occurs when the import duty on imported inputs is higher than the import duty on finished product.
6. Short term debt rather than portfolio equity investment is believed to cause balance of payments problems. Capital inflows through portfolio investment was thought not to be the cause of balance of payment problem.
7. See Ghosh, Arun (1991): Eighth Plan: Challenges and Possibilities in Balance of Payment: *EPW*, Vol. XXV, No 6, February 9. Earlier studies revealed that Indian exports were not very responsive to relative price changes. However, the above study by Ghosh brings out that price elasticities of demand for manufactured exports are high. It was, therefore thought that the depreciation of Indian rupee would increase the demand for India's manufactured goods abroad. Thus keeping in view the finding of this and other studies done by the Planning Commission, the Indian rupee was devalued in 1991.

8. Fifteen per cent import duty on gold was imposed. The implication of keeping fifteen per cent import duty on gold and thus not making import of gold free is that the authority did not want to eliminate illegal/or Hawala exchange market altogether.

REFERENCES

Ahluwalia, Ishar Judge (1991). *Productivity and Growth in Indian Manufacturing*, Oxford University Press, Oxford.

Bhagwati, Jagdish and T.N. Srinivasan, (1975). *Foreign Trade Regime and Economic Development : India*, National Bureau of Economic Research, New York, Columbia University Press.

Dhindsa, K.S. (1981), *India's Export Performance :Some Policy Implications*, Intellectual Publishing House, New Delhi.

Ghosh, Arun (1991). *Eighth Plan : Challenges and Possibilities in Balance of Payments. EPW*, Vol. XXVI, No. 6. February 9.

Lal, Deepak (1972), *When is Foreign Borrowing Desirable ?* Bulletin of the Oxford University, Institute of Statistics.

Myrdal, Gunnar (1968). *Asian Drama : An Inquiry into the Poverty of Nations*. Periodical Service Company.

Nayyar, Deepak (1976). *Indian's Export and Export Policies in the Sixties*, Cambridge University Press, Cambridge.

Reddy, Y.V (2002). India's Foreign Exchange Reserves : Policy, Status and Issues, Special Lecture at National Council, New Delhi, May 10.

Reserve Bank of India (2002). *Report on the Currency and Finance*, 2000-01, RBI, Mumbai.

Singh, Manmohan (1964). *India's Export Trends and the Prospects for Self Sustained Growth*, Oxford, Clarendon Press.

Virmani, Arvind (1991). 'Demand and Supply Factors in India's Trade', *Economic and Political Weekly*, Vol. XXXVI, No 6, February 9.

Section-II

EMPLOYMENT, POVERTY AND REGIONAL DISPARITIES

9

NEO-LIBERALISM OF NEW ECONOMIC POLICY, GLOBALISATION AND UNEMPLOYMENT IN INDIA

Sri Prakash

HISTORICAL PERSPECTIVE

New economic policy (NEP), adopted by the Government of India in 1991, is also known as the policy of macro stabilisation and structural adjustment programme. This was the planned initiative to rapidly complete the twin processes of liberalisation and globalisation of the Indian economy, though there exists a sceptic view that the policy had been adopted under duress due to the pressures exerted by the IMF-World Bank combines, which granted loans to overcome the foreign exchange difficulties that the comity faced at that point in time. The policy arose from the compulsion of the economic expediency of crisis proportions rather than being dictated by the force of conviction or the shifts in the ideological paradigms. It is also postulated, therefore, that the relative lack or success of the failure of the policy to make positive impact on growth, inflation balance of trade, fiscal deficit and employment is accounted by the half-hearted and halting manner of its implementation. But some adverse effects of the policy are quite visible and disturbing. Its impact on employment is one such visible area of the failure of NEP.

The current phase of globalisation is neither new nor are the objectives and the forms of globalisation different from those of the earlier phases. The current process of globalisation is, in fact, the third phase of the processes of the annexation, integration and synthesisation of the less developed economies into the production and marketing arrangements and programmes of the developed West, though the nature and degree of integration and synthesization varied from phase to phase. The first phase of globalisation was initiated during the Mercantilist era. During this phase, the objective of the developed world was to accumulate maximum bullion through commodity exports. The game plan was simple and straightforward to find the export markets, to expand the existing markets, to expand the range and the size of the export baskets by the inclusion of new products in it, and to bring the commodity markets of the importing countries under the fold and some sort of control of the exporters. Naturally, the first phase of globalisation was extremely narrow in concept, loose in form and limited in scope.

Search for the colonies as the export markets for the goods produced on centralised large scale during the first phase of first industrial revolution was an extended but modified form of the initial Mercantilist approach to globalisation (Nayyar, 1996). The second phase of globalisation was started sometime during the seventh-eighth decades of the nineteenth century. International trade was firmly established as the 'engine of growth' during this phase due mainly to the centralised large scale specialised production, based on international division of labour. Since the European countries succeeded in forging ahead of the Asian and African countries in industrial development, they had acquired a comparative advantage in manufactures. Therefore, international division of labour, and hence, production and free trade, according to the theory and policy of comparative advantage was hypothesized to benefit all the countries of the world. However, the exports of finance, capital and human resources through international migration on a relatively large scale also entered into the export baskets along with the commodities. Large scale exodus of the Europeans to America, Australia, New Zealand, Asia and Africa was a special facet of this phase of globalisation, though the theory of comparative advantage assumed complete mobility of the goods and relative immobility of labour and capital between the national frontiers. However, contrary to the assumption of immobility of capital and labour, both these items along with the general goods emerged in the centre stage of international trade.

The process of globalisation was imparted an impetus by the rapid growth of new and faster means of transportation and communication. Knies maintains that the growth of trade and improvement in the means of communication and transportation facilitated the simultaneous development of various countries of the world (quoted in Marshall,

1961, Appendix A, p. 623). However, Marshall himself opined that the discovery of India and America by Vasco da Gama and Columbus raised the "commercial questions from a secondary to a dominating position among the nations of Western Europe." It not only transformed international trade into the pivot of social, economic and political activities but it also pushed world-wide large scale migration of human resources into the centre stage of the development process (Marshall, 1961, Appendix B, p. 625). The growth of trade led to the emergence of the process of integration of not only the commodity markets but also generated the processes of integration and unification of the financial, capital and technology markets of the world.

GLOBALISATION : THE CONCEPT

Globalisation may be defined as the operationalisation of the following processes: (a) expansion of the commodity and factor markets; (b) intensification and the deepening of the interdependencies among the national economies through the exploitation of their complementarities in production structures; and (c) ultimately, the internationalisation of all national markets, including those for services, through the integration and synthesisation of national economies into the intricate networking of the world economy (Prakash and Dutta, 1996). But the market orientation, on the one hand, and the highest degree of openness of the national economies, on the other, are the necessary conditions of the success of globalisation. It implies the minimum role of the state in the economy and the least policy interventions by the government in the autonomous functioning of the market (Prakash, 1994). Thus, the new economic policy is based on the premises of uninterrupted growth of foreign trade and the initiation of the twin processes of liberalisation through the dismantling of the control regimes of licensing and permits and the globalisation of the national into an essential component of the world economy not only through trade but also through the acceptance and absorption of foreign capital investment, finance, technology, and goods and services in the national economies. In other words, the closeness has to be replaced by openness of the economic systems. Such policies have been in operation in other developing countries for more than two decades. But India is a new entrant in the current game. However, the Indian economy had remained tied to the British economy for nearly two centuries. Obviously, India had faced the onslaught of the earlier phases of the globalisation also.

EMPLOYMENT AND ECONOMIC ANALYSIS

Employment has not unfortunately been in the centre stage of economic analysis. It has always been kept at the margins of the economic theory. This is so even in the case of Keynes' *General Theory of Money, Interest and Employment.* Notwithstanding the fact that employment occupies third spot in the title of Keynes' book, employment generation sneaks into analysis only as the tool for demand mobilisation in order to stabilise the economy in the downward phase of the cycles.

Classical Theoretical Paradigm

Classical theory is based on the assumption of the effectiveness of the market mechanism and the efficacy of its operationality. It naturally ascribes the minimalist role to the state and the government in the economy, since the theory has been based on the complete and unflinching faith in the efficacy of the autonomously operating forces of demand and supply in maintaining the market in stable equilibrium. Whenever the equilibrium is disturbed, such powerful forces come automatically into operation as to restore the market back to its equilibrium. Disequilibrium is, thus, self-effacing, endowing equilibrium with the attributes of stability, self-correction and adjustment.

The classical theory postulates wages to be perfectly flexible to operate as an instrument of equilibration. It is, therefore, assumed that the wage fluctuations will force the demand to adjust to the changes in supply or vice-versa in order to maintain the labour market in equilibrium. Thus, wages like other commodity prices are treated as totally flexible in this theoretical framework. It is also assumed that, just as all other prices are determined by the long run cost of production, wages, the price of labour, converge towards the long run subsistence cost of labour. But the cost of subsistence depends upon the customs and traditions. Demand for and supply of labour are equalised at the equilibrium wage rate, which equals the long run cost of subsistence. Population growth or decline in its size determines labour supply, while the demand for labour is derived from the commodity production schedules and programmes of the producers. Consequently, actual wages may differ from the equilibrium wage rate only in the short run. Fluctuations in the market wage rate around the equilibrium wage rate restore parity between demand and supply of labour, just as the fluctuations of the market prices around the normal or equilibrium price of other goods and services restore parity between their demand and supply.

Two implications of the above analysis are obvious: (i) wage theory is just a parody of the classical price theory, validating our thesis of employment having been kept in the margins of economic analysis, and (ii) unemployment is only a short run, and hence, temporary phenomenon. Economy, in fact, tends to be in full employment stable long run equilibrium. Thus, the classical theory does not even admit the need for the development of analytically critical concepts of employment/unemployment, tools and methods of measuring employment and/or unemployment, and the evolution of the theoretical framework for analysing the causes and consequences of unemployment. The faith in the efficacy and effectiveness of the market to maintain itself in stable equilibrium was further reinforced by the Say's law of the markets that supply creates its own demand. Naturally, there is hardly any possibility of general over-production of either labour or commodities, and hence, the probabilities of unemployment and unsold stocks of goods were assumed to be zero, provided that the wages and prices remained flexible. Normally, unemployment does not exist as a problem either at macro or micro theoretical levels.

Depression and Emergence of Keynesian Revolution

The depression of the late twenties and early thirties invalidated the classical postulates and their premises. The paradox of the received theory being at variance with the observed facts and the prevailing reality having no theoretical paradigms to explain it confronted the analysts with the empty boxes of theory to explain the reality, while the emptier boxes of facts stared the received theory in its eye. The widespread unemployment and the consequent poverty and immigration of the masses placed employment in the centre stage of both theory and policy. The *General Theory of Money, Interest and Employment* attempted to bridge the gaps between the practice and precept and the theory and facts. The general theory of Keynes postulates that (i) the economy can be in equilibrium at less than full employment level, (ii) deficiency of effective demand causes unemployment, and (iii) the deficiency of demand may be covered by public expenditure. The theory was widely acclaimed and accepted both by the analysts and policy makers. Consequently; the growth of public expenditure and government interventions in the economy, were recognised as the effective tools of macro stabilisation. Keynesian theory and its policy implications have remained in the centre stage of economic analysis and policy and programmes of macro stabilisation upto the sixties.

The period of twenty years of the fifties and sixties witnessed the rapid reconstruction and dynamic growth of the war ravaged and damaged economies of Japan and Western Europe, on the one hand, and the initiation and the nurturing of industrialisation based development of the Eastern Europe and the Third World, whose development had been stultified and delayed for centuries by the colonial exploitation, on the other. The consequence of the rapid growth was such rapid expansion of demand for human capital as to force even the developed US, Britain, West Germany and France to import high and middle level manpower from the Third World.

Impact of Oil Crisis

The emergence of the oil crisis in early seventies, however, altered the course of the world economy. The members of OPEC raised the oil prices four-fold in 1973. The oil prices were again doubled in 1979. Thus, the oil prices rose roughly eight times during a short period of about 5 years. The distressing consequence of this development was (i) the slowing down of the growth of both the developed and the developing countries, (ii) resultant sluggishness and stagnation of demand, and (iii) ignition of the cost-push inflation. The inflation rate depends upon the employment rate and the behaviour of demand. But given the inflationary conditions, no specific behaviour of total demand will generate fall employment and price stability, though Philips associates the concept of demand pull inflation with the rate of wage increase that would be expected at the given unemployment rate. But what Philips designates as demand pull inflation is really (i) the observed dependence of the wage changes on average unemployment rate. Unemployment rate constrains and constricts the wage hikes by wage setting groups in anticipation of productivity gains and inflation, social norms and government intervention. But when wage cost accounts for the substantial proportion of production cost, annual wage hikes granted through negotiations between the powerful trade unions and employers pushes up the production costs first, and hence, cost push inflation even before the demand pull can come into operation, since the wage increase becomes a part of the increased costs immediately after its grant; (ii) wage hikes can generate demand pull inflation only if the wage hikes exceed the actual rise in inflation and productivity, anticipated by the unions and employers during the wage negotiations; and (iii) there is a time lag between the accrual of increased wage incomes and expenditure. Thus, both in principle and practice this phenomenon should be interpreted as the process of cost push inflation (Culbertson, 1968; Prakash and Goel, 1987).

The paradoxical existence of the demand recession in the midst of inflation has been the regular feature of the modern economies since the seventies. The chief reason of this malady is that the markets for industrial goods are only monopolistically or oligopolistically competitive rather than being perfectly competitive. In such markets, cost based fix-prices prevail (Prakash, 1979 and 1986; Prakash *et al.*, 1995; Mathur and Prakash, 1981). Fix-prices are generally determined on the principle of cost plus pricing. Excess or deficient demand has no impact on fix prices Hence, these prices do not rise or fall with the rise or fall in demand (Hicks, 1965 and 1975). Invariance of prices even in the face of deficient demand accounts for the presence of recession in the presence of inflation.

The presence of powerful trade unions and the welfare and minimum wage regulations of the state tend to make wages behave as Fix-prices. Wages, in fact, are highly upward flexible but almost totally downward rigid. Consequently, relatively less employment is provided at higher wages. But the distribution of unemployment is asymmetrical among the social groups. Unemployment affects the unskilled or less skilled and uneducated or less educated poor workers more than the affluent sections of the work-force. Upgradation of qualifications and/or skill requirements is only one among many methods used by the entrenched groups to protect their own interests at the cost of the weak, poor and unemployed.

Emergence of New Theoretical Paradigms

Emergence of neo-classical or supply-side economies has been helped by many factors. The basic political philosophy of Reagonomics and Thatcheromics have nurtured the supply-side economics. Besides, under the benign but shadowing patronage of such developed economies as the US, Germany, France, Japan and Britain international agencies like World Bank, IMF and World Trade Organisation have been imposing the neo-classical ideology and its policy prescriptions upon an ever increasing number of developing countries under the grab of the comditionalities associated with the loans granted by these agencies to overcome the short-run problems of management of the economies of the Third World.

The slackening of growth of the developed countries has greatly accentuated unemployment not only in the developed but also in the developing world. The developed countries in order to overcome slowing growth, high wages, increasing unemployment at home and unprecedentedly intensifying competition for the foreign markets have opted for the development and commercial exploitation of ever newer technologies, having ever rising knowledge and capital intensity and even greater degree of labour displacing capability. The minimal scales of new technologies are ever so high and consistently rising as to make the domestic markets of the home countries of such technologies too small to operate. This induces the search for foreign markets to facilitate the exploitation of the economies of scale to make their technologies economically viable. This prompts the multinational corporations (MNCs) to compel for the third country markets.

Interests of the developed West will be served only if the policy prescriptions of the supply-side economics are accepted and implemented by the Third World so as to leave their commodity, service, capital, finance and technology markets free for the monopolistic or oligopolistic MNCs to operate unhampered by state regulations and controls. It does not matter if the domestic industries of the developing countries are eliminated from their own markets under the onslaught of unequal competition. So the pressure to push through the neo-classical thought and its policy packages is continuously rising for averting the consequences of (i) the slowing of the growth of the developed world, and (ii) the resultant rise in unemployment to unacceptable levels.

When the German, French and Japanese economies were registering growth at exceptionally high rates during the fifties and sixties, only nominal unemployment due to structural frictions prevailed. In fact, the West European economies were importing manpower from the outside world. West Germany alone absorbed more than 60,000 Indian nurses in the early sixties to overcome the shortages of paramedical personnel. This is just an illustration of one sector's labour scarcities of one occupational category which; in fact, reflects the general shortages of manpower in the booming labour markets. But now the ever rising unemployment has raised the unemployment rates 3 to 6 times their levels in the early seventies. The fixity of prices in the presence of recession in some sectors in the midst of inflation in other sectors of the economy lowers the sectoral and hence, the overall growth of the economy, resulting in rising unemployment. Then, the labour displacement by new technology also transforms employment into unemployment. Institutional rigidities make the wages behave as the fix-price even in the presence of demand recession. This generates demand recession in the labour markets also. Downward rigidity but the upward flexibility of wages in anticipation of rise in productivity and prices transforms into cost push inflation which, in its turn, leads to sectoral demand recession, on the one hand, and subsequently, to demand pull inflation, on the other. Despite this, the developed countries are not ready to introduce reforms in their labour market operations, since any lowering of the wages will lower the standard of living, which they are not ready to compromise, though they exert pressure on the developing countries to reform their labour markets by abolishing child labour and the observance of international labour standards. They also advocate eco-friendly measures. All these provide excuses to the developed West to indulge in discrimination against the imports from the Third World. Though they exert pressures on developing countries to leave all their markets free to operate according to the laws of the game, called competition, yet they impose restrictions not only on immigrants from the Third World to prevent their own labour markets to operate according to the laws of demand and supply but also restrict the commodity exports of the developing world.

In order to deny the need for labour market reforms, some economists have questioned the concept of unemployment itself, while others are dissatisfied with the method of its measurement. Knowledge and capital intensive modern technology not only displaces labour but the rapidity of technological development has also substantially reduced the average life of technology itself. Consequently, technology-centric economic growth results in growth without employment, while the substitution of new for existing technology at shorter intervals deepens unemployment, in the process of economic growth. Besides, the high cost and highly priced current and new goods are produced on much larger scales than the prevailing ones. Thus, the need for manifold expansion of the market size is embodied in R&D design itself. The need for the exploitation of the Third World markets is inevitably linked to these facets of growth. But the economic policies, pursued by the Third World since the fifties, act as the bottlenecks and hurdles in this search for the markets. Therefore, the international agencies are used to get the policies of stabilisation and structural reforms implemented by the Third World in order to keep the real objectives of the developed West under wraps. However, the implementation of structural reforms has adversely affected most of the Third World countries. Adverse effects on growth, unemployment and inflation have been relatively more pronounced (for empirical evidence, see Mathur, 1991).

Defence and Critique of Supply-Side Economics

One branch of neo-classical analysis uses the classical concept of natural employment rate. An implication is that there corresponds some natural unemployment rate to the natural employment rate. Hence, unemployment shall be a problem only if it crosses the natural rate. Another implication may be that the institutional wage rigidities account for full and partial unemployment. These rigidities make it difficult to generate employment without accelerating inflation (Friedman, 1968). It also implies that the developing economies should have the 'exit' policy in operation and the employers should have the right to 'hire and fire'. It may, however, be noted that unemployment has persisted in the developed world despite the fact that they have had the exit and hire and fire policies in operation. If such policies are operationalised in the Indian economy, the dimension of the adverse consequences may be gauged from the fact that 4.1 lakh persons are employed in 58 sick public sector undertakings, whereas 4.5 lakh persons are employed in sick private large industrial units and 36 lakh persons are employed in sick small industrial units. Thus, the employment of as many as 44.6 lakh persons shall be endangered by such policies. In the developing economies, like the Indian one, where neither the state provides unemployment allowance, nor there is an insurance cover against the risk of unemployment, the impact of exit and hire and fire policies shall be disastrous.

The neo-classicals use the concepts of natural rates of employment and unemployment to convince the general public, analysts and policy makers that either the prevailing high unemployment rates are natural, or these are an inseparable and inevitable component of the short run cyclical fluctuations. This transitory phenomenon will inevitably disappear in the long run. It may, however, be noted that such short run cyclical fluctuations now occur at such short intervals with methodical regularity as to make these almost a regular feature of the operations of the market economies. Thus, the short run phenomenon tends to converge towards the long run facet of the economy. It is also argued that a large proportion of current unemployment is voluntary which signifies the substitution of leisure for work (Eltonji, 1982). It may partly be true in the case of the developed countries. But the thesis is invalid for the developing world. A recent household survey by NCAER has revealed that nearly 57 per cent Indian households earn an annual income of Rs. 25,000 or less. For slum households of Delhi and Bombay, it has also been established that the inadequacy of adult male earnings at such low earnings as mentioned above forces the female participation in employment (Prakash and Dutta, 1996), on the one hand, and the substitution of employment for the education of the children, on the other (Prakash and Dutta, 1995 and 1996). There is no question of substitution of leisure for work for the vast majority of these poor Indians.

Some economists treat unemployment as the 'period of job search and waiting for employment' (Keifer and Neumann, 1979). At the individual level, search and waiting period may last from few days to few weeks. Unemployment, therefore, is not a problem at the macro level. Not only this, expenses incurred on the 'job search' and the opportunity cost of waiting for employment may be treated as investment. Investment in job search and waiting enhances the probability of access to better and higher income yielding jobs, which also raises the efficiency of resource allocation. Thus, investment in job search and waiting enhances rather than diminishes social welfare. Again, the job-search and waiting in India ranges from few days to some years, depending upon the levels and types of skills and education possessed by the unemployed, Even if at the micro level, the period of job search and waiting is extremely short, the problem cannot be dismissed as of negligible dimension at the macro level. The ever rising backlog of unemployment at the end of each Indian Five Year Plan is a testimony to this. If the incidence of unemployment is allowed to become unbearable, it may lead to social unrest and even insurgency. Unrest in Kashmir, Punjab and Assam arose mainly due to high incidence of unemployment among the educated youth.

Clark and Summers (1990) have also mobilised empirical evidence against the above thesis. They have collected evidence to show that those engaged in job search and waiting for employment remain largely unemployed. It may also be surmised that the longer the duration of waiting and job search, the higher will be its cost and the greater shall be the depression and disillusionment of the job seekers. The prolonged job search may lead to deskilling and/or forgetting whatever has been learnt. Thus will reduce not only the probability of employment but also the probability of employability of the job-seekers. Thus will make such persons accept whatever jobs at howsoever low wages come their way, making the investment in job search and waiting infructuous. This phenomenon explains largely the mismatches between the level and the type of education received and the occupation and sector of employment in India, especially in the case of educated manpower.

The consequences of such tendencies in market oriented liberalisation in the developing economies reflect the mismatches between education and training received and the low income employment in occupations needing no or low education and training. It leads to the suboptimal utilisation of the human capital, and hence, the loss of growth potential.

Several economists have challenged the neo-classical propositions (Davidson, 1991). Pisarydes (1989) propounds the thesis that the deficiency of demand and the structural factors cause unemployment. Index of trade unionism and unemployment have been found to be positively related, while unemployment insurance, social security measures and the size of the labour force have also been empirically found to be directly related. But the first two variables are inversely related to the number of persons going out of the labour force. Thus, the institutional factors and inflexibility of wages are held responsible for unemployment, though the fact is that the modern technology promotes employmentless growth. Under such circumstances, the responsibility of the state to generate employment with or without growth is further increased. It may also be suggested that the need for the maintenance of the aggregate demand at high levels warrants an increase rather than a decrease in the roles and functions of the government and the state in economic affairs (Blankard and Summers, 1990).

The above analysis establishes that the concept, measurement and the causes of unemployment have still not been settled either at the theoretical or practical level. Therefore, the effects of NEP on employment or unemployment in India must be analyzed with reference to the above mentioned theoretical and practical limitations.

EMPIRICAL EVIDENCE

The International Experience

Growth of income and trade have declined substantially during last twenty years. Income of several countries has been rising consistently at relatively low rates, while there has been a consistent rise in inflation rates. During 1975 and 1982, international trade has recorded negative growth, resulting in an increase in unemployment.

The new economic policy and structural adjustment programmes have been implemented in several countries during this period. South Korea, Singapore, Hongkong, Taiwan and to a certain extent, China have been quite successful in accelerating growth and containing the balance of payments problem in check under new policy regimes. But unemployment and inflation have increased sharply, while the pattern of distribution of income and wealth has been altered in favour of the rich and against the poor. Economic conditions of the poor and the labouring classes have been adversely affected. Latin America, taken as a whole, has recorded a decline of 9.5 per cent in employment during the period from 1980 to 1984, whereas unemployment in Chile and Venezuela has increased by 7 to11 per cent. Overall unemployment has, in fact, increased by 50 to 100 per cent, while unemployment rates have touched the level of 14 to 20 per cent (Hoevan, 1987). Rise in unemployment and inflation in Latin America has led to a decline of 10 to 20 per cent in real wages, while the decline in real wages in Africa has ranged from 30 to 40 per cent. These data relate only to the large organised sectors of these economies. Real wages in unorganised and informal sectors has declined even more rapidly (Hoevan,1987). The decline in real wages at such high rates invalidates the thesis that unemployment is caused by inflexibility of wages and institutional rigidities. So far as growth is concerned, real per capita incomes of Columbia, Chile and Venezuela in the late eighties have been reduced to the levels of the late fifties and early sixties under the new policy regimes. The experiences of other developing countries have not been much different from the experience of Latin America and Africa. The international experiences of the adverse effects of NEP on growth, employment and inflation does not inspire much confidence and hope regarding the impact of NEP on the Indian economy.

The Indian Experience

Unemployment, partial unemployment and low wage employment are the main factors of poverty in India. Employment and partial employment at extremely low wage rates make poverty highly complex and intricate. The Planning Commission has estimated the number of those living below the poverty line to be 36 per cent of the total population. All these poor people are directly related to the twin phenomena of unemployment, low wage employment and partial employment.

Eradication of poverty by 2002 has been accepted as an important goal of planned development (Economic Survey, 1993-94, p. 156). The Eighth Five Year Plan (1991-96) estimated 170 and 60 lakh persons to be openly or partially unemployed. The size of labour force was estimated to increase by 350 lakh persons. These estimates warranted employment to rise at an annual rate of 2.6-2.8 per cent. The realisation of this goal required gross national product to rise by 5.6 per cent per annum. It is, thus, implied that the employment elasticity of output is 0.46. We have estimated employment elasticity of income from the observed facts in order to test the relevance and reliability of above estimates (see Table 9.1). It may be noted that employment refers to the persons employed in units employing ten or more persons, though the gross domestic output relates to all the sectors and units operating within them. It is also observed that the employment intensity of production in the unorganised and informal sectors is much higher than the employment intensity of output of the organised and large sectors of the Indian economy. It is also known that the Indian unorganised and informal sectors generate substantial proportion of total employment opportunities. Our estimates of employment elasticity of income are, therefore, underestimates of the true values of these elasticities since the values in the numerator are consistently underestimated, while the denominator has approximately correct values. All the same, we may be able to discover the short and long run trends of the elasticities and the nature of changes in the interrelations between income and employment.

Table 9.1 : Sector-wise Growth Rates of GDP, Employment and Elasticity

Year/Sector	*Public*	*Private*	*Total*	*GDP*	*Elasticity*
1981-82	2.98	2.06	2.68	5.8	0.46
1982-83	3.20	0.07	2.20	2.6	0.85
1983-84	2.50	2.72	0.86	7 9	0.11
1984-85	2.38	-0.50	1.50	3.8	0.39
1985-86	2.40	-0.89	1.95	4.1	0.48
1986-87	1.92	0.14	1.32	4.0	0.33
1987-88	1.64	-0.38	1.28	4.1	0.31
1988-89	0.69	0.83	0.73	10.2	0.07
1989-90	1.71	1.73	1.71	6.9	0.25
1990-91	1.58	1.25	1.48	5.2	0.28
1991-92	0.80	2.61	1.20	0.5	2.40
1992-93	0.60	0.06	0.45	5.2	0.09
1993-94	0.62	1.01	0.73	6.0	0.12
1994-95	0.11	1.63	0.71	6.9	0.12

Five Yearly Averages of Employment Elasticities

1981-85	*1986-90*	*1991-95*
0.38	0.24	0.17

Source : Economic Survey (Various years)

A perusal of Table 9.1 leads to the following important inferences :

(i) Public rather than private sector has been the main generator of employment opportunities in the Indian economy. It might have been partly the result of the dominance of economic structure by public sector and partly due to the employment policies pursued by the private and public sectors.

(ii) Employment in public sector has increased consistently, whereas employment in private sector has declined in 3 years despite the positive growth of income. Employment in private sector in the other 2 years has remained almost invariant. It implies that the growth of output of the private sector need not necessarily lead to the growth of employment. Private sector, specially the organised large sector, may have employmentless growth.

(iii) The growth of employment has declined both in the public and private sectors, though the deceleration of employment growth has been much more rapid in public rather than private sector. The deceleration of employment growth has been much more marked since 1991, that is, after the adoption and implementation of NEP.

(iv) As against the declining growth of employment, the growth of income has been accelerated moderately. It implies that the rapid or sluggish growth of income is no guarantee for employment growth. The coefficient of rank correlation between employment growth and growth of income is -0.37. The negatively significant coefficient signifies an inverse relationship between the growth of income and growth of employment.

(v) During a period of 15 years, employment in public sector has increased more rapidly than the growth of employment in private sector in all the years except 1991-92.

(vi) Employment has grown consistently at much lower rates than the rates of growth of GDP. Consequently income is not only employment inelastic, but the employment elasticity of income has almost negligible values. Low employment elasticities of income imply statistical invariance of employment irrespective of rapid or slower growth of income. Employment may, therefore, depend less on the growth of income than on other factors.

(vii) The employment elasticity of income has been declining consistently through time during the five yearly periods from 1981-85,1986-90 and 1991-95. The rates of decline in the elasticity have been so high as to reduce the value of the elasticity in the last five years to half of its initial value. The absolute value itself is practically zero. The period of 15 years, covered by the study, has been chosen to coincide with the two distinct phases of liberalisation under Rajiv Gandhi and Narasimha Rao.

(viii) Only in 4 out of 15 years covered by the study, the absolute value of the employment elasticity of income has been equal to or more than 0.46, the value used by the Planning Commission for fixing the target date for the realisation of the objective of full employment. These 4 years might have coincided with the years in which the bunched-up vacancies have been filled up. It may imply the tendency of the vacancies to bunch up before these are actually filled up. The time lags involved in the occurrence of the vacancies and their filling up may either be due to the procedural delays or due to sheer inertia in filling up the vacant posts, or due to the policy of keeping the posts vacant for prolonged periods. This may specially be the case in public sector undertakings and the government. The conjecture is supported by the fact that, except for 1992 when employment grew more rapidly in private than public sector, in all other years, employment has grown mainly in the public sector.

(ix) Employment elasticity has depicted great deal of temporal variability. It has varied between 0.07 and 2.4. But the five yearly mean values of the annual elasticities, averages having been calculated to smoothen the series, highlight the rapidly declining trend through time. Upgradation of the technological base of production and the consequent rise in productivity lead to the rapid declines in employment per unit of output, and hence, a decrease in the employment intensity of output. It implies acceleration of growth of income with the deceleration of growth of employment. This supports our thesis that the modern technology is not only capital and knowledge intensive but labour displacing also. Negativity of the significant coefficient of rank correlation between growth of employment and income growth also supports this thesis.

These results suggest that the objective of full employment, planned to be realised by the year 2002, warrants the complete reversal of the trends in operation. The trend reversal will, however, require the development of labour and knowledge intensive techniques of production rather than to import foreign technologies or to invite MNCs to establish their production facilities, based on modern technologies, in India. The trend reversal cannot be effected under the NEP regimes of globalisation, liberalisation and privatisation of the Indian economy. The above results also validate our thesis that the Indian economy under NEP has recorded *employmentless growth* which has further casualised, marginalised and immigrating the poor. Public sector has been constructed and constrained under NEP, while the private sector has failed to generate requisite employment opportunities despite all the incentives furnished by the government for propping it up and its growth.

The other possibility is that more employment opportunities have been generated in the unorganised small and informal sectors of the economy. But employment in these sectors is provided at extremely low wages and, more often, under conditions of casualisation, marginalisation and immigration of the workers. In pre-independent India, unemployment of surplus labour was usually disguised in agriculture. This role of disguising unemployment of the surplus labour is now being played by the tertiary and the urban informal sectors of the Indian economy.

During the current phase of liberalisation and globalisation, industrial output has grown at much lower rate than the expected rates. This may be accounted partly by lower than warranted inflows of foreign direct investment (FDI) and partly by the failure of the domestic industrialists to come out of their inertia. A large proportion of inflows of foreign funds is accounted by 'hot money' and investment in stocks rather than in production facilities. The growth of income during this period has largely been the result of autonomous agricultural development. Fortunately, agricultural sector has been left alone by the new policy regime, except the partial or full withdrawal of fertiliser, power and water subsidies, enjoyed till then by agriculture. The gaps left in public investment in agriculture due to these policy measures must have been filled up by farmers own private farm investment. However, the process of urbanisation has gathered greater degree of momentum, resulting in large scale casualisation and marginalisation of employment in urban sectors of the economy. Casualisation and marginalisation are generally the characteristic features of self-employment in the informal sector. This proposition can be tested empirically.

The data furnished by the midterm appraisal of the Eighth Plan show employment in industries to have increased annually by 2 per cent. But the growth of industrial employment is accounted mainly by the modern and traditional decentralised small scale industries. In fact, employment in the medium and large industries has declined by 1.5 per cent. Whereas growth of employment in the decentralised small scale enterprises has ranged from 2.6 to 3.1 per cent per amum. Besides, the casual, transitory and incidental employment in rural and urban sectors increased from 31.2 in 1987-88 to 33.5 per cent of the total employment in 1993-94. It may imply that almost all those living below the poverty line are absorbed in the informal sector. The above facts lend support and credibility to our propositions. The empirical evidence garnered for this study also shows that the triple processes of globalisation, liberalisation and structural reforms have adversely affected employment in the Indian economy. It is, in fact, difficult to mitigate mutually interrelated unemployment, partial unemployment, low wage employment and poverty in a labour abundant economy like the Indian one through investment by MNCs in industries. Organised industries account for an extremely low proportion of output and employment. The accelerated development of agriculture, irrigation and small scale industries, using labour intensive techniques of production can alone mitigate the twin problems of poverty and employment.

REFERENCES

Blankard, Oliver and Lawrence M. Summers (1990), "Histeresis and the European Employment Problem", in Summers, Lawrence M. (ed.) *Understanding Unemployment,* The MIT Press, Cambridge, Massachusetts.

Chikan, Attila (ed.)(1981), *Economics and Management of Inventories*, Elseviere.

Clark, Kim and Lawrence M. Summers, (1990), "Labour Market Dynamics and Unemployment : A Reconsideration", in Summers, (ed.) (1990).

Culbertson, John, M. (1968), *Macroeconomic Theory and Stabilisation Policy*, McGraw Hill Book Co.

Davidson, Paul (1991), *Controversies in Keynesian Economics*, Edward Elgar Publishing Co. Ltd., Cheltenham Glos.

Eltonji, J. (1982), "The International Substitution Model of Labour Market Fluctuations", *Review of Economic Studies,* Vol. 31, pp. 491.

Friedman, Milton (1968), "The Role of Monetary Policy", *American Economic Review*, Vol. 58.

Hicks, J.R. (1965), *Capital and Growth*, Basil Blackwell, Oxford.

——, (1975), *Essays on Crisis in Keynesian Economics*, Basil Blackwell, Oxford.

Hoevan, R.V D (1987), "External Shocks and Stabilisation Policies : Spreading the Load", *International Labour Review,* Vol. 126.

Johri, B.M. (ed.) (1996), *Economic Liberalisation and Globalisation,* Commonwealth Publishers, New Delhi.

Keifer, N. and Neumann, G. (1979), "An Empirical Job Search Model with a Test of the Constant Reservation Wage Hypothesis," *Journal of Political Economy,* Vol. 87, February.

Marshall, A. (1961), *Principles of Economics*, (Reprint), Macmillan, London.

Mathur, P. N. (1991), *Why Developing Countries Fail to Develop?*, Macmillan, London.

——, and Prakash, S. (1981), "Inventory Behaviour of Indian Agriculture and its Effects on General Price Level", in Chikan (ed.) (1981).

Nayyar, Deepak (1996), "Globalisation : The Past in Our Present Export Led Growth in Developing Countries : 1960-80", *Indian Economic Journal,* Vol. 43.

Pisarydes, Krestopher A. (1989), "Unemployment and Macro Economics", *Economica,* Vol. 53.

Prakash, S. (1979), "Flexprices in Indian Economy : A Study of Determinants of Foodgrain Prices", University College of Wales, Aberystwyth (Mimeo).

——, (1981), "Cost Based Prices in Indian Economy". *Malayan Economic Review,* Vol. XXVI.

——, (1986), "Industrial Wages and Prices of Foodgrains : A Study of Lead-Lag Structure in Indian Economy", *The Economy Journal of Nepal*, Vol. IX No 1.

——, (1994), "Liberalisation of Indian Economy and Relevance of Nehru-Mahalanobis Strategy of Growth", in Sinha (ed.) (1994).

——, and Dutta, R. (1995), *Male Earnings, Female and Child Participation in Labour Force and Education : A Study of Delhi and Bombay Slums*, National Institute of Educational Policy and Planning, New Delhi.

——, (1996), "New Economic Policy Analysts of Actual and Perceived Impact on Indian Economy" in B.M. Johri, (ed.) *Economic Liberalisation* and *Globalisation*, Commonwealth Publishers, New Delhi.

——, and Goel, V (1987), "Price and Output Movements of Agro-Based Industries in Indian Economy, 1951-80," in V.S. Mahajan, (ed.) *Studies in Industrial Economy of India,* Vol . II, Deep and Deep, New Delhi.

——, and Goel, V. (1987), "Marketed Surplus, Prices and Traders' Stocks of Foodgrains in India—A Study of Wheat in Patiala Mandis", in Attila Chikan (ed.), *New Results in Inventory Research*, Part A, Elseviere.

——, Sengupta, K. and Chowdhury, S. (1995), "Input Output Modelling of Costs, Margins and Fixprices in Indian Economy", Paper Presented at the XI *International Conference on Input Output Techniques*, New Delhi.

Sinha, A.K. (ed.) (1994), *New Economic Policy of India*, Deep and Deep, New Delhi.

10

RECENT TRENDS IN NON-FARM EMPLOYMENT EXPANSION FOR RURAL HOUSEHOLDS IN INDIA

G.K. Chadha

INTRODUCTION

Significance of Non-farm Employment

For a number of reasons, big peasant economies, typically characterised by population pressures, an ever-declining land-man ratio, small and fragmented holdings, highly unequal land distribution structures etc., cannot rely for too long on agriculture alone as a source of employment to their rural households. Guided by the development experiences all over the world, it is plainly true that the ultimate solution for rural and under-employment does not lie in agriculture alone. While the continuing importance of agriculture as a source of employment and income to rural households cannot be disputed, the moot point that needs to be underlined is that limits to expansion of 'productive employment' in agriculture are reached sooner than later, and consequently, transfer of working population out of agriculture has to be an inescapable long-term outcome of all development effort. This is all the more essential in the developing countries including India, where the age-composition of the population is skewed more in favour of the younger members while the level of fertility is not showing much diminution which further exasperates the problem of land scarcity.

On the other hand, it is extremely doubtful if the preconditions for effectuating enhanced labour absorption in agriculture could be fulfilled, especially those connected with the creation of egalitarian land distribution structure (Islam, 1987, p. 2). Not only that, the overall effect of technological change in agriculture has been seen to be labour-saving and capital-augmenting, rather than the other way round, so that the labour absorptive capacity of agriculture steadily shrinks, *inter alia,* under the increasing weight of new and changing farm production technologies. The consistently declining employment elasticity with respect to aggregate agricultural output from 0.54 during 1972-73/1977-78 to 0.49 during 1977-78/1983, and further down to 0.36 during1983/1987-88 readily testifies this tendency for the Indian case (Bhalla, 1994, p.131).

Apart from the employment consideration, the advocates of agriculture-led growth theories also visualise important roles for the rural non-farm sector in stimulating agricultural growth through inter-sectoral linkages. A modern agriculture is based on strong forward and backward linkages with industry and other non-agricultural sectors some of which may partly be available in the rural areas themselves.

Finally, in the face of growing social and economic problems associated with urban expansion, it is increasingly realised that the network of rural non-farm activities could play an important role in containing large-scale rural to urban migration. Thus, through localising employment in the rural areas themselves, the rural non-farm activities would contribute in easing urban congestion and reducing the pressures on scarce urban infrastructural facilities (e.g. housing, transport, education, etc.). Undoubtedly, labour exodus from rural areas, which is the main breeding-ground for urban slums and a host of socio-economic problems, would get intercepted (Islam, 1987, p. 2).

Luckily, a growing realisation on the need to diversify the economic base of rural India was seen during the 1970s and 1980s. In particular, some bold policy initiatives were mounted to strengthen the industrial sector of the rural economy. These initiatives did show some positive effects. Today, the rural areas have a fairly big share of 'modern' small-scale industrial enterprises. There is no doubt that over years, industrial dispersal into the countryside has picked up. As an adjunct to the general phenomenon of higher industrial growth during the eighties, many small-scale and tiny industrial units got located in rural areas under the pressure of push and pull factors, varying significantly from state to state. Quite normally, ancillarization has been growing in many industrial lines, with rural industries chipping off a part of its benefits.

Besides the expanding rural industrial sector, other non-agricultural activities such as construction, trade and transport, services, etc. also started growing in rural India. The total effect of these non-farm expansions was a considerable restructuring of the rural work-force. This process worked well during the seventies and eighties and its beneficial impact on rural poverty was clearly discernible.

But then, a depressing trend ensued since the late eighties. The growth rate of non-farm employment for rural workers fell sizeably between 1987-88 and 1993-94. The fall was rather precipitous for rural female workers. It has naturally caused a great disappointment both to the policy analysts and development administrators who have been watching, with satisfaction, the steady pace of non-farm expansion in the earlier two decades or so. Many explanations for the slower pace of non-farm growth have starting coming in, some firmly grounded in hard empirical facts and figures while others are yet in the form of conjectures. And, the debate is going on.

DATA AND CONCEPTS

This chapter joins the on going debate. It puts together comparable NSS data, from as many rounds as possible, to build some sort of a farm and non-farm employment profile and try to see the relative rural/urban and male/female gaps, in diverse aspects of non-farm employment. We base our analysis only on NSS data primarily because, for delineating temporal changes, this source is the best to draw upon. It is in the fitness of things to take note of the diverse insights that NSS data provide and the limitations that they impose on an inquiry of the kind we have undertaken.

First, the NSS data are such that we are obliged to make all inferences through employment estimates only, nothing can be said about incomes. Second, the time profile cannot go too far back because temporally comparable data started pouring in only since 1972-73. Specific to our requirement, NSS data on farm and non-farm components of employment are available for five points of time: 27th round (covering October 1972- September 1973), 32nd round (July 1977- June 1978), 38th round (January-December 1983), 43rd round (July 1987-June 1988) and 50th round (July 1993- June 1994). The 1993-94 NSS report does throw a few hints about the rural/urban and male/female employment effects of the new economic policies introduced in July 1991, we catch on such hints rather boldly. Thirdly, our analysis is based on the usual (Principal or Principal+subsidiary) status data only; current weekly and current daily status data/trends are not looked into, primarily for paucity of space. Finally, while the N.S.S. data do show what percentage of rural work-force is engaged in different gainful activities or what is the share of rural workers in total work-force under each production sector, they provide no straight clue on whether a particular source of employment is in rural, semi-urban or urban areas. The employment estimates for the rural households are thus free of locational specificities. Accordingly, all references to 'rural non-farm employment' imply such employment for rural workers/households, not necessarily rural-located.

Table 10.1 : Annual Compound Growth Rate of Employment for Usual (Principal+Subsidiary) Status Workers by Workers' Sex, Residence and Broad Sectors of Employment

	Rural Male		*Urban Male*		*Rural Female*		*Urban Female*	
Production Sector	*77-78 to 87-88*	*87-88 to 93-94*	*77-78 to 87-88*	*87-88 to 93-94*	*77-78 to 87-88*	*87-88 to 93-94*	*77-78 to 87-88*	*87-88 to 93-94*
1	2	3	4	5	6	7	8	9
Agriculture	0.30	1.37	1.59	3.46	3.41	1.49	6.45	0.36
Mining & Quarrying	4.18	1.46	6.44	3.65	9.51	1.20	7.76	-1.54
Manufacturing	2.78	0.53	2.02	2.12	4.91	1.48	4.12	1.36
Utilities	5.55	1.47	5.04	3.65	-	-	8.76	10.50
Construction	0.19	-1.00	6.16	6.70	18.06	-15.74	8.63	5.08
Trade	3.50	2.74	2.65	3.97	3.00	1.21	4.83	3.65
Transport and Communication	5.98	3.09	2.48	3.65	14.60	1.20	2.11	9.84
Finance, Real Estate, etc.	8.43	1.45	4.44	5.08	-	-	9.95	11.53
Community and Personal Services	2.30	3.66	2.78	4.36	1.47	2.83	3.44	7.13
Total Non-Agriculture	3.83	1.52	2.74	3.75	5.17	0.17	4.88	4.54
All Sectors	1.48	1.92	2.70	3.72	3.65	1.24	5.31	3.39

Source : 1. For 1977-78/1987-88 growth rates, Chadha G.K., *Indian Journal of Labour Economics. July-September,* 1993, p. 302.

2. Growth rates for 1987-88/1993-94 are computed from data in Government of India, *NSS Report No. 406, June 1996,* pp. 52-56, 82-86.

NON-FARM EMPLOYMENT GROWTH FOR RURAL WORKFORCE

We begin to look at the growth rates of employment for male and female workers, both in rural and urban areas, to delineate their respective areas of fast expanding employment. Table 10.1 throws up clear contrasts between growth rates upto 1987-88 and those in the subsequent years. The decelerating pace of employment expansion spread over a wide range of production and service activities needs to be underlined for the post-1987/88 years. First, the pre-1987/88 growth profile.

Fast Pace of Employment Expansion: 1977-78/1987-88

For rural male workers, the areas of fast employment growth have been construction, transport-communication-storage, finance-real estates, mining- quarrying, and so on, and areas of slow employment growth have been agriculture especially livestock (showing negative growth). In other activities, employment grew fairly modestly. For rural female workers, construction, transport-communication-storage and mining-quarrying have been areas of very high employment growth; in their case, manufacturing too has shown a fairly impressive growth momentum. In total terms, the growth of non-farm employment for rural male and female workers compares very well with that for their urban counterparts. This is as well true for manufacturing employment and many other non-farm sectors. Particular attention once again goes to the remarkably higher employment growth for both categories of rural workers over their urban counterparts, under construction and transport-communication-storage sectors. Perhaps, a lot of new activities during the decade 1977-78/1987-88 under these sectors came up in rural areas themselves, more readily improving the employment access of rural workers than would have been the case otherwise. In brief, the decade 1977-78/1987-88 reflects a relatively better performance for the rural workers in total terms as well as in terms of individual non-farm components. This does not, however, obliterate the fact that the share of rural workers was (and is) still a small fraction for certain types of non-farm activities.

Decelerating Pace of Employment Expansion: 1987-88/1993-94

But then, the position changed dramatically during the period

1987-88/1993-94. Except for community and personal services among the non-farm activities, and agriculture, the employment growth slackened in every branch of economic activity, as far as rural male workers are concerned. In construction, employment grew negatively. The growth deceleration was far more serious in the case of rural female workers. For example, against a compound growth rate of employment of 14.66 per cent per annum during 1977-78/87-88, the employment for female workers grew just by 1.20 per cent per annum during 1987-88/93-94 in transport-communication-storage sector; in construction, it was a near catastrophy, a swing from +18.06 per cent during 1977-78/1987-88 to –15.74 per cent during 1987-88/93-94, and so on. Female employment suffered in agriculture too. In brief, the growth of employment suffered practically everywhere, among the rural females more than that among their male counterparts and among urban females more than their male counterparts. Even between the urban and rural females, the latter suffered more serious reverses in many sectors of the Indian economy. To put it more openly, the years 1987-88/1993-94 did not auger well for rural workers, especially the female workers among them. For rural females, the non-farm employment as a whole hardly witnessed any growth; total employment grew the slowest (a mere 1.24 per cent per annum), and for some sectors, the setbacks were astonishingly big. The male-female differentials widened in the rural areas, while in the urban areas, the female workers improved their employment growth record by impressive margins. The sagging performance for the rural female workers in recent years is thus a cause of worry.

The contrast between the pre- and post-1987-88 experiences need to be pursued in more detail. As a matter of fact, looking back into the 1970s, we readily discover that the 1980s had ushered in a big quantitative improvement in the employment situation for the rural work-force in general and female workers in particular, compared with the 1970s. Table 10.2 presents employment data in a more telling manner. For each of the four sub-periods, viz. 1972-78, 1978-83, 1983-88 and 1987-94, the increments to work-force under each major production sector have been given for workers of both sexes, separately for rural and urban areas. The temporal profile is nearly complete in some sense and can, therefore, yield more authentic changes since 1972-73.

Table 10.2 : Industrial Distribution of Increments to Work-force between 1972-73 and 1993-94 by Industry Division. Rural-Urban Residence and Workers' Sex

Industry Division	*Male*				*Female*			
	1972-78	*1978-83*	*1983-87*	*1987-94*	*1972-78*	*1978-83*	*1983-87*	*1987-94*
1	2	3	4	5	6	7	8	9
Rural India								
1. Agriculture	55.1	48.2	21.7	70.2	75.8	85.0	-18.8	104.4
2. Manufacturing	12.7	12.9	14.4	2.6	15.6	9.4	25.3	8.2
3. Construction	3.2	7.8	27.8	-2.3	-2.6	1.3	70.3	-23.0
4. Trade-Hotelling	13.3	7.7	17.4	9.8	5.9	1.7	7.2	3.0
5. Transport - Communication	3.5	6.4	7.1	4.4	0.1	0.1	1.4	0.1
6. Community and Personal Services	9.9	14.8	7.7	15.4	4.6	1.4	7.8	7.3
7. Other Services	2.3	2.2	3.9	10.8	0.6	1.1	6.8	– 3.3
Urban India								
1. Agriculture	9.8	10.9	0.2	8.1	29.2	29.4	20.0	3.8
2. Manufacturing	30.6	23.9	19.7	10.2	40.4	13.1	29.3	10.6
3. Construction	3.9	8.7	10.2	9.8	-0.2	7.5	6.3	4.8
4. Trade-Hotelling	28.1	15.8	28.7	23.6	6.6	13.3	11.4	10.9
5. Transport - Communication	13.3	10.9	8.1	9.7	1.1	4.3	-2.2	3.2
6. Community and Personal Services	11.1	26.3	29.1	26.3	22.7	30.4	33.4	63.4
7. Other Services	3.2	3.5	4.0	12.3	0.0	2.0	1.8	3.3

(Contd.).

(Contd.)

1	2	3	4	5	6	7	8	9
Total India								
1. Agriculture	40.2	33.0	11.7	59.7	64.7	76.1	0.3	78.4
2. Mining-Quarrying	1.1	1.6	2.5	0.8	0.5	1.1	2.1	0.5
3. Manufacturing	18.6	17.4	16.9	11.3	21.5	10.0	27.3	9.3
4. Utilities	1.5	1.0	1.6	2.6	neg.	0.1	1.7	0.0
5. Construction	3.4	8.2	19.6	4.1	-2.1	2.3	38.7	2.8
6. Trade-Hotelling	18.2	11.0	22.6	8.6	6.1	3.6	9.3	3.0
7. Transport - Communication	6.7	8.3	7.5	3.7	0.4	0.8	-0.4	0.2
8 Services	10.3	19.5	17.6	9.2	8.9	6.0	21.0	5.8

Source : 1. For 1972-78, 1978-83 and 1983-88 figures, Visaria-Minhas, *op. cit.* 1991 (p. 978).
2. For 1987-94 figures, (1) Sarvekshana, Special No., September, 1990,. S 218-247, and (2) NSS Report No. 409, March 1997, pp A163-176.

During 1972-77, 55.0 per cent of the incremental male workers and 76.0 per cent of female workers were assigned to agriculture alone. During the next five years, it was only 48.0 per cent for male workers but a high figure of 85.0 per cent for female workers. The decisive break came during 1983-88 when only 21.7 per cent of the addition to the rural male work-force was absorbed by agriculture, and the remaining about 78.0 per cent went over to non-agrochemical jobs. The qualitative improvement for the female workforce was far more decisive in this sub-period when the absolute number of workers assigned to agriculture actually declined, and non-farm employment received a big boost. As noted earlier, construction, trade and manufacturing activities for female workers received very high shares of incremental workforce during those crucial years. Most interestingly, manufacturing activities have been absorbing a fairly good proportion of the incremental workforce, during each of the first three sub-periods, in respect of workers of both sexes. In net terms, the close of the eighties reflects a much better qualitative outcome compared with the position in the beginning of the seventies.

In contrast, there are no sudden breaks for the urban areas which have had their steadily expanding sectors in manufacturing, trade and services during the first three sub-periods. In comparative terms, the rural India has been doing better till about the late eighties in that in addition to shedding its over-weight of agricultural employment, it steadily improved its labour absorptive capacity in non-agricultural sectors some among which seem to have shown remarkably high expansion since the mid-eighties. In overall terms, the eighties have augured a much better employment-restructuring phase in rural India compared with urban India, as also compared with itself during the 1970s.

But then, significant reversals set in for rural workers during the period 1987-88/1993-94. As much as 70.0 per cent of the incremental jobs coming up for rural male workers during these years were in agriculture alone; services had a share of 15.3 per cent and trade hotelling of 10.0 per cent. Very few additional workplaces were thus available to rural male workers in each of the remaining sectors; in fact, a small proportion of them seems to have been dislodged from construction activities let alone the availability of fresh jobs to them. The situation was far more serious with rural female workers. A very big percentage of them, engaged in construction activities in 1987-88, were dislodged from there, and thrown back to agriculture. Only about

7.0-8.0 per cent of additional workplaces were available in 1993-94 compared with 1987-88, in manufacturing and services. Clearly, agriculture absorbed most of the new female workers besides providing 'refuge' to others dislodged from construction (or any other) sector during the post-1987-88 years.

The relatively bigger setbacks for female workers are discernible on two counts. They suffered because rural areas in general lost their restructuring verve of the 1980s, just when we entered the 1990s. They also suffered because in terms of male-female inter-sectoral job adjustments, they would be called upon to 'go back to agriculture' and let their male counterparts straddle the squeezing market for rural non-farm jobs. To some extent, their own weak educational and skill background works against them, especially when secondary sector jobs, more particularly those in the 'modern' manufacturing activities, become more and more skill selective. To some extent, withdrawal of child labour from the labour market, presumably because 'economic conditions are getting better' and 'children have started going to schools' may be another explanation for the squeezing tendencies witnessed during the period 1987-88/1993-94.

The post-1987/88 picture throws up sharp contrasts for urban male and female workers, compared with their rural counterparts. First, there is no 'absolute decline,' either for urban male or female workers, in any of the sectors, as was the case for rural workers, especially the females, under the construction sector. In fact, 12.0 per cent of the additional urban male workplaces and 6.0 per cent of those for their female counterparts, found their way in this sector, during 1987-88/1993-94. Either the sources of employment under this sector have been dwindling in the rural areas, possibly because the pace of public (and private) investment has been facing a slack during the post-1987/88 years, or some of these sources dried up, in certain parts of rural India soon after the 'relief-against-1987-drought' schemes were withdrawn, or the locale of some of the construction activities shifted to urban areas. Second, the dwindling proportion of additional workplaces in the manufacturing sector, most noticeably for urban females, points to the fact that employment aspirations of the increasing army of labour force are not met by this sector. Additional workplaces would have to be located in other sectors. Perhaps, this is the reason that the urban female workers found 65.0 per cent of additional jobs in the services sector against only 11.0 per cent of them in the manufacturing sector, during the post-1987/88 years.

Lastly, the post-1987/88 sectoral deployment of the incremental workforce suggests a more stable pattern for urban compared with rural workers; the inter-sector stability is lacking all the more from rural female workers, compared with their urban counterparts. The *ad hocism,* discernible most conspicuously for rural females, points to many of their infirmities, as formal job seekers, not only in competition with rural males but also with their own urban sisters, particularly for non-agricultural jobs needing higher educational and skill standards.

The highly disappointing pattern of non-farm employment growth for the rural, especially female workers during the post-1987/88 years, is a cause for worry. It looks nearly conspiratorial that during 1987-88/1993-94, a no-entry signal was displayed to them in all non-farm sectors except community and personal services. Going by the semi-aggregative sector-level estimates in Table 10.2, it is clear that the magnitude of reversal differed sharply from one non-farm sector to the other. To fix precise ideas about the real sources of reversal, or the production/service activities which, in a broad sense, are 'refusing' to take on rural workers, we must see the inside realities of each sector. Luckily, the 1987-88 and 1993-94 NSS data enable us to peep into each production sector, at 2- or (from the view point of rural-urban contrasts, at a less than complete) 3-digit level of industrial classification. Table 10.3 is the outcome of this attempt. We have stayed at the 2-digit level of classification primarily because within each description all this level, individual 3-digit level items, being too many and reflecting an embarrassingly disparate picture on the number of workers involved, would blur rather than capture the real changes more expressly from the viewpoint of rural workers. Again, to assimilate the degree of distress the rural workers have been undergoing in the recent past, and the likely employment stringency they may face in the years ahead, all changes are described both in absolute numbers as well in percentage terms. Table 10.3 has many things to say.

First, the most disquieting fact is the decline in the absolute number of rural workers, in a wide range of production/service activities. The most glaring cases are manufacture of cotton textiles, textile products (except footwear), wood and wood products including furniture and fixtures, leather and fur products, basic metal and alloy industries, etc. under manufacturing; construction/maintenance of buildings, roads and water reservoirs, etc. under Construction; public administration

Table 10.3 : Distribution of Incremental Workers (Principal+Subsidiary Status) by Major Production Sectors, Workers' Sex and Place of Residence : 1987-88/1993-94

(Absolute Change in '00 Workers)

Sector/ Sub-Sector	*Rural Male*		*Rural Female*		*Urban Male*		*Urban Female*	
	Absolute Change	*% Change*	*Absolute Change*	*% Change*	*Absolute Change*	*% Change*	*Absolute Change*	*% Change*
1	2	3	4	5	6	7	8	9
Agriculture								
1. Field Crop Production	+1,01,105	+9.8	+73,583	+12.1	+5,579	+18.7	+405	+1.7
2. Plantations	+4,168	+15.2	+1,023	+7.4	+1,466	+86.0	+1,077	102.3
3. Livestock	-14,958	-27.3	-5,494	-5.4	+69	+1.5	-157	-1.8
4. Agri. Services	2,220	+36.4	3,915	+150.5	+631	+148.1	+50	+21.4
5. Forestry	-1,108	-18.2	-5,010	-64.2	+103	+24.2	-326	-70.0
6. Fishing	+2,360	+30.9	+995	+114.8	+409	+24.0	-92	-39.3
7. Total (1 to 6)	+93,788	+8.5	+69,012	+9.3	+8,257	+22.7	+957	+2.0
Manufacturing								
8. Food Products	+4,580	+33.4	+2,309	+38.0	+1,825	+18.6	+485	+16.6
9. Beverages, etc.	+696	+9.1	+4,746	+34.2	+290	+8.5	+1,237	+19.2
10. Cotton Textiles	-3,739	-17.2	-2,090	-21.9	-203	-1.6	+577	+12.3
11. Wool, Syn. Fib.	+1,942	+63.7	+1,839	+192.8	+2,507	+65.3	+576	+82.1
12. Jute, Mesta Txt.	139	+9.1	+908	+95.2	-239	-7.0	+334	+142.7
13. Text. Products	-8,453	-50.0	-3,021	-31.7	-3,596	-26.4	-2,062	-27.1
14. Wood Prodts.	-1,519	-7.7	+1,442	+20.8	+1,314	+17.1	+393	+33.6
15. Paper Prodts.	+139	+9.1	N.I.	-	+172	+3.4	-175	-15.0

(Contd..)

(Contd..)

1	2	3	4	5	6	7	8	9
16. Leather Prodts.	-1,385	-45.4	N.I.	-	+716	+24.0	+359	+102.3
17. Rubber Prodts.	+1,803	+118.2	N.I.**	-	+4,843	+189.4	+1,662	+355.1
18. Chem. Prodts.	+139	+9.1	N.I.*	-	-886	-17.3	-1,161	-62.1
19. Non-metallic Mineral Prodts.	+1,252	+9.0	-484	-8.0	+171	+3.3	-217	-13.3
20. Basic Metal Ind.	-1,385	-45.4	N.I.	-	-903	-12.4	-67	-19.1
21. Metal Products	+417	+9.1	N.I.	-	+1,211	+16.7	+50	+21.4
22. Machine Tools	+279	+9.0	N.I.**	-	+699	+13.7	+25	+21.4
23. Elect. Machinery	+139	+9.1	N.I.	-	+496	+11.6	+267	+45.6
24. Transport Eqpt.	N.I.*	-	N.I.	-	-886	-17.3	+25	+21.4
25. Other Mfg.	+2,081	+33.3	+128	+7.4	+2,490	+41.7	-8	-0.6
26. Total Mfg.	-4,402	-3.8	+6,836	+11.9	+10,448	+9.5	+2,652	+8.4
Agro-based (8 to 16)	-7,601	-9.4	+6,133	+12.8	+2,786	+4.5	+1,958	+7.8
Others (17 to 25)	+3,199	+9.1	+703	+7.4	+7,662	+16.2	+694	+10.6
27. Utilities	+418	+9.1	N.I.	-	+1,228	+24.0	+192	+82.1
28. Construction	-6,497	-11.5	-15.962	-68.2	+10,079	+45.5	+1,212	+28.0
29. Trade	+13,750	+17.7	+1,342	+7.4	+24,119	+26.3	+274	+23.9
(1) Wholesale								
a. Food	+1,943	+63.7	N.I.**	-	+2,285	+44.7	+217	+61.8
b. Textiles								
c. Total Wholesale	+5,409	+118.3	N.I.**	-	+7,742	+75.7	+785	+223.7

(Contd..)

(Contd..)

1	2	3	4	5	6	7	8	9
(2) Retail								
a. Food Articles	+2,650	+5.6	-36	0.0	+5,630	+15.4	+577	+8.7
b. Textiles	+418	+9.1	N.I.	-	+2,252	+24.0	+384	+82.1
c. Hotel+ Restaurant	+835	+9.0	+192	+7.4	+1,912	+15.1	0	0.0
d. Total Retail	+8,341	+11.4	+411	+2.3	+16,377	+20.1	+1,956	+17.6
30. Transport, Storage and Communication								
a. Transport	+5,832	+21.3	N.I.**	-	+8,682	+22.6	+459	+56.0
b. Storage and Warehousing	N.I.	-	N.I.	-	+103	+24.2	N.I.**	-
c. Communication	+139	+9.1	N.I.	-	+614	+24.0	+192	+82.1
d. Total	+6,112	+20.0	+64	+7.4	9.928	+24.0	+793	75.3
31. Finance, Insurance and Real Estate	+556	+9.1	N.I.**	-	+5,168	+34.6	+1,295	+92.3
32. Community, Social and Personal Services								
a. Pub. Admn. & Defence Services	- 2,215	-7.1	+192	+7.4	+4,626	+10.6	+1,939	+33.8
b. Education, Scientific & Research Services	3,333	+18.3	+1,378	+22.7	+3,615	+33.9	+3,677	+43.1

(Contd..)

(Contd..)

1	2	3	4	5	6	7	8	9
c. Personal	+11,652	+64.0	+3,751	+28.8	+11,323	+94.9	+9,535	+84.1
d. Total	+21,378	+24.2	+4,710	+18.1	+26,966	+29.2	+15,903	+51.1
33. All Sectors	+1,39,102	+9.1	+63,893	+7.4	+1,02,347	+24.0	+25,083	+21.5
Agriculture	+93,788	+8.5	+69,012	+9.3	+8,257	+22.7	+957	+2.0
Non-Agriculture	+45,314	+11.9	-5,119	-4.1	+94,090	+24.9	+24,126	+29.7

Note : N.I.= Not included because of negligible employment figures either in 1987-88 or 1993-94 or in both.
N.I.* Implies a marginal loss while N. I.** means a marginal gain, between 1987-88 and 1993-94.

Source: 1. For 1987-88 figures, *Sarvekshana, Special Number,* September 1990, pp. S218-S247.
2. For 1993-94 figures, *NSS Report No.* 409, March 1997, pp. A163-A176.

and defence services under Community, Social and Personal Services, and so on. Even under Agriculture, livestock and forestry-logging suffered serious job shrinkages, as far as rural workers are concerned. In addition to the above shrinkages, suffered commonly by rural males and females, the latter lost some workplaces in the manufacture of chemicals and chemical products and transport services as well. And to complete the story for the rural females, they have had, both in 1987-88 and 1993-94, a negligible employment base in many other branches of manufacturing (e.g. manufacture of paper, leather, rubber, chemicals and their products, basic metal and alloy industries, basic metal products, machinery and machine tools, electrical machinery, apparatus and appliances, transport equipment and parts). In total terms, the post-1987/88 years have brought no cheers to rural workers.

Second, under manufacturing, rural females are losing their ground to their male counterparts while no such tendency seems to be working among the urban female workers. For example, in 1987-88, there was very litle employment in high skill-intensive and technology-intensive jobs in a wide range of industries (e.g. paper, leather, rubber, chemicals, basic metals, metal products, machine tools, electrical machinery, transport equipment, etc.); undoubtedly, their educational, training and skill deficiencies stood in their way. In 1993-94 too, their entry into these branches of manufacturing did not witness any noticeable improvement. On the contrary, even under the (loosely defined) set of agro-based industries, usually characterised by less education-intensive and skill-intensive requirements, their gains are confined to a select few, namely the manufacture of food and food products; beverages, tobacco and tobacco products; wool, silk and synthetic fibres, and, wood and wood products (including furnitures and fixtures). It seems the rural female workers are being pushed out of their traditional manufacturing activities (textiles and textile products) presumably because the highly competitive international market cannot be effectively catered to by their unskilled labour and low product quality, and so on. The pressure of highly demanding quality standards is confirmed through a substantial decline of jobs for rural males as well. In plain terms, the rural female workers are getting dislodged from 'formal' to 'informal', family-based sources of manufacturing employment. This is a disturbing development of the early nineties especially because the rural workers in general and rural females in particular generally look out for industrial sector jobs, in the rural located manufacturing enterprises. For rural females, the constraints for moving to urban industrial jobs are formidable indeed, no less from educational and skill point of view as from the social point of view.

Third, the most devastating squeeze is discernible in respect of construction sector jobs; a precipitous 68.0 per cent decline for rural females and a 12.0 per cent decline for rural males against a 46.0 per cent and 28.0 per cent gain for urban males and females, respectively. It is preposterous that as many as 22,00,000 rural construction workers (or 16,00,000 females among them) lost their jobs between 1987-88 and 1993-94 while as many as 11,00,000 additional jobs became available in their very sector to their urban counterparts. For the Indian economy as a whole (rural-urban combined), the net loss on such a colossal scale is impossible to imagine, for 6-7 post -1987/88 years. This astonishing development has attracted diverse interpretations to some of which we briefly return later in this chapter.

Lastly, trade too has a pro-urban bias. Once again, the worst-placed are rural females even in respect of retail trade, not only compared with urban or rural males but with their urban sisters as well. Summarily, the same fate awaited the rural female workers in the remaining non-farm sectors, most ostensibly transport-storage-communication and finance-insurance-real estate sectors; their presence is hardly noticeable.

In brief, the recent years provide a disappointing employment scenario for the rural workers in general, and rural female workers in particular. Whatever additional employment came their way was largely confined to agricultural sector; the construction activities which lent them a highly flourishing phase of employment expansion during 1983-88, are now working against them; perhaps the locale of such jobs is shifting from rural to urban areas or the slackening pace of public (and private) investment in rural areas is squeezing the total size of this sector, or whatever new jobs are coming up in this sector are qualitatively superior for which the big mass of 'unskilled' or 'uneducated' female workers are not qualified. For all that one can anticipate under the changing regimes of globalization and competitiveness, the future job markets in the non-agricultural sectors are sure to pose more and more difficulties for the rural workers, especially the future job-aspirants among the rural females.

Table 10.4 looks at the post-1987/88 non-farm job expansions/ contractions in a more telling manner. First, the steady shift from agriculture to non-agriculture, so vividly discernible for the

Table 10.4 : Rural Workers' Share in Incremental Workplaces by Major Production/Service Sectors and Workers' Sex : 1987-88 and 1993-94

Sector/ Sub-sector	*Rural Workers' Share in Employment*						*Rural Workers' Share in Incremental/ Decremental Employment during 1987-88/ 1993-94*	
	1987-88			*1993-94*				
	Male	*Female*	*Total*	*Male*	*Female*	*Total*	*Incremental*	*Decremental*
1	2	3	4	5	6	7	8	9
Agriculture								
1. Field Crop Production	61.0	35.8	96.8	60.6	36.3	96.9	96.7	0.0
2. Plantations	62.3	31.5	93.8	61.0	28.8	89.8	67.1	0.0
3. Livestock	32.2	63.0	92.2	26.7	64.6	91.3	0.0	99.2
4. Agricultural Services	65.2	27.8	93.0	51.4	40.3	91.7	90.0	0.0
5. Forestry-Logging	41.2	52.7	93.9	59.0	33.0	92.0	0.0	94.9
6. Fishing	73.1	8.3	81.4	70.8	13.2	84.0	89.1	0.0
7. Total Agriculture (1 to 6)	58.5	37.8	96.3	58.2	37.9	96.1	94.6	0.0
Manufacturing								
8. Food & Food Products	42.2	18.7	60.9	43.9	20.1	64.0	75.0	0.0
9. Beverages, Tobacco, etc.	24.3	44.3	68.6	21.7	48.6	70.3	78.0	0.0
10. Cotton Textiles	34.1	23.7	57.8	28.7	21.4	50.1	0.0	96.6
11. Wool & Synthetic Fibres	35.7	11.2	46.9	32.4	18.1	50.5	55.1	0.0
12. Jute, Mesta Textiles	24.9	15.6	40.5	22.9	25.6	48.5	75.8	0.0
13. Textile Products	35.3	20.1	55.4	27.3	21.4	28.7	0.0	67.0
14. Wood & Wood Products	55.7	19.5	75.2	49.2	22.5	71.7	45.8	100.0
15. Paper & Paper Products	19.5	0.0	19.5	20.9	0.0	20.9	44.7	0.0

(Contd..)

(Contd..)

1	2	3	4	5	6	7	8	9
16. Leather Products	47.8	0.0	47.8	27.4	0.0	27.4	0.0	100.0
17. Rubber Products	33.5	0.0	33.5	22.6	12.6	35.2	21.7	0.0
18. Chemical Products*	14.9	16.9	31.8	25.2	0.0	25.2	100.0	0.0
19. Non-metal Mineral Products	51.7	22.9	74.6	54.9	20.5	75.4	88.0	69.0
20. Basic Metal Products	28.6	0.0	28.6	20.1	0.0	20.1	0.0	58.8
21. Metal Products	37.9	0.0	37.9	36.3	0.0	36.3	24.9	0.0
22. Machine Tools	36.8	0.0	36.8	32.6	9.1	41.7	27.8	0.0
23. Electrical Machinery	23.9	0.0	23.9	22.9	0.0	22.9	15.4	0.0
24. Transport Equipment	22.6	0.0	22.6	0.0	0.0	0.0	0.0	0.0
25. Other Manufacturing	33.7	12.8	46.5	36.5	10.2	46.7	47.0	0.0
26. Total Manufacturing	36.9	18.3	55.2	33.8	19.5	53.3	34.3	100.0
Agro-based Manufacturing (8 to 16)	37.4	22.2	59.6	33.4	24.6	58.0	56.4	100.0
Other Manufacturing (17 to 25)	35.6	9.7	45.3	34.6	9.2	43.8	31.8	0.0
27. Utilities	46.1	0.0	46.1	42.4	0.0	42.4	22.7	0.0
28. Construction	53.1	22.0	75.1	52.5	7.8	60.3	0.0	100.0
29. Trade	39.1	9.1	48.2	38.0	8.1	46.1	36.0	0.0
(1) Whole Sale Trade								
a. Food Articles	35.8	0.0	35.8	35.9	6.7	42.6	43.7	0.0
b. Total	30.2	0.0	30.2	33.3	3.1	36.4	38.8	0.0
(2) Retail Trade								
a. Food Articles	46.0	11.8	57.8	44.7	10.8	55.5	29.9	100.0
b. Textiles	31.7	0.0	31.7	28.6	0.0	28.6	13.7	0.0

(Contd.)

(Contd..)

1	2	3	4	5	6	7	8	9
c. Hotel-Restaurant	35.1	10.9	45.1	34.4	9.6	44.0	35.0	0.0
d. Total	39.8	9.9	49.7	38.6	8.8	47.4	32.3	0.0
30. Transport, Storage and Communication								
a. Transport	40.7	1.3	42.0	40.8	0.0	40.8	39.0	0.0
b. Storage**	0.0	0.0	0.0	0.0	0.0	0.0	0.0	0.0
c. Communication	35.3	0.0	35.3	31.6	0.0	31.6	14.8	0.0
d. Total	41.3	1.2	42.5	40.4	1.0	41.4	36.6	0.0
31. Finance, Insurance and Real Estate	27.2	0.0	27.2	21.9	3.1	25.0	7.9	0.0
32. Community, Social and Personal Services								
a. Public Adınn. & Defence Services	37.1	3.2	40.3	32.6	3.2	35.8	2.8	100.0
b. Edn., Scientific and Research	42.0	13.9	55. 9	38.9	13.4	52.3	39.2	0.0
c. Personal Services	33.5	23.8	57.3	33.0	18.4	51.4	42.5	0.0
d. Total	37.2	10.9	48.1	35.8	10.0	45.8	37.8	0.0
33. All Sectors	52.0	29.5	81.5	51.0	28.5	79.5	61.4	0.0
Agriculture	**58.5**	**37.8**	**98.3**	**58.2**	**37.9**	**96.1**	**94.6**	**0.0**
Non-Agriculture	**39.4**	**13.0**	**52.4**	**36.9**	**11.1**	**48.0**	**27.7**	**100.0**

Note : 1.* In chemical industries, the additional workplaces coming up during 1987-88/1993-94 were very few (about 14,000; see Table 10.3 above), mostly going over to rural males. On the other hand, the substantial (nearly 2,04,700) contraction of jobs in respect of both urban males and females, indicates a kind of general 'ailment' of the industry.

2. ** In storage and warehousing, very few rural workers were involved, both in 1987-88 and 1993-94; hence, their estimates are not included (see Table 10.3 above)

Source :1. For Columns 2 to 7, see Govt. of India, *Sarvekshana,* Special No., September 1990, pp. S218-S247, and Govt. of India, NSS Report No. 409, March 1997, pp. A163-A176.

2. Columns 8 and 9 are derived on the basis of information in Table 10.3.

pre-1987-88 years, seems to be totally halted since 1987-88. For agriculture as a whole, there is hardly any change in the percentage of rural male or rural female workers. In other words, agriculture has again surfaced, as a refuge of the last resort when rural workers are either thrown out of non-farm jobs, or additional jobs are not forthcoming there to accommodate all job-aspirants, or the competition for non-farm jobs is becoming more and more intense.

Second, for a wide range of manufacturing sectors, the percentage share of rural workers in general, and rural female workers in particular, has declined during 1987-88 and 1993-94. The decline for cotton textiles, textile products, leather products, chemical products, basic metal products, transport equipment, etc. needs to be underlined in particular. In plain terms, the rural workers, especially the females among them, have started losing their ground to urban job-claimants, in education, training-and skill-intensive manufacturing jobs, since the latter are far better off in meeting the new pre-requisites for such jobs.

Third, the rural workers are losing their ground in most of the other non-farm sectors as well. As pointed out earlier, construction sector has done them the utmost damage. Their declining share in public administration and defence services; education, scientific and research services; and personal services under Community, Social and Personal Services Sector is as much conspicuous as in transport and communications under Transport, Storage and Communication, and, in retail trade especially in textiles, under Trade.

Fourth, rural workers' share in job losses occurring during 1987-88/1993-94, unambiguously throws their bare weak position and disadvantage. In a number of sectors/sub-sectors, the axe fell almost exclusively on the rural workers (Col. 9, Table 10.4), in some cases, expressly on rural female workers (Col. 4, Table 10.3). For example, in manufacturing as a whole, it is the rural workers alone who suffered job losses; under individual sub-sectors, cotton textiles, wood and wood products, and, leather and leather products revealed the same one-sided pattern of job contractions. In textile products, non-metallic mineral products and basic metal products, a very big proportion (60-70 per cent) of job losses belonged to the rural workers. The catastrophe in respect of construction sector jobs gets reconfirmed through a zero per cent share of the loss accruing to rural workers. Again, the sufferance of public administration and defence services jobs exclusively on the rural workers' account is another disturbing feature of recent years.

Fifth, the rural workers fared no less poorly in respect of additional jobs coming up between 1987-88 and 1993-94 (Col. 8, Table 10.4). For example, in the manufacturing sector, only about a third of such additional jobs came to their share (against all losses being exclusively borne by them). Even in their traditional stronghold of agro-based manufacturing, they gained just about one-half of the additional jobs. In certain manufacturing areas, their gain was nil, while in some others, it was very low ranging from 15.0 to 30.0 per cent of the additional jobs, and so on. In many other non-farm sectors/sub-sectors too, their vulnerable position is equally discernible. Their extremely low share of additional jobs (e.g. 0.0 per cent in construction, 2-3 per cent in public administration and defence services under Community, Social and Personal Services. 7-8 per cent in Finance, Insurance and Real Estate, 14-15 per cent in communications under Transport, Storage and Communication, 13-14 per cent in retail trade in textiles or 30-32 per cent in Retail Trade as a whole, etc., signals two unfavourable possibilities for the rural workers. On the one hand, it indicates the increasing incapability of rural workers to compete with their urban counterparts, and, on the other hand, it hints at a slackening pace of rural industrial intensification. This is partly reinforced by the fact that a fairly sizeable chunk (75-80 per cent) of additional jobs in food and food products and beverages, tobacco and tobacco products under agro-based sub-sector fell to their share. It is clear, once again, that the rural workers are finding it difficult to gain a foothold in education-, skill-, and technology-intensive industrial sector jobs, and are consequently taking refuge both in agriculture and in agriculture-related manufacturing activities. For rural workers, the structural retrogression on the employment front is clearly at work. In all likelihood, this retrogression will intensify itself in the years ahead.

EXPLANATIONS FOR THE POST-1987-88 REVERSES

The post-1987-88 reverses in employment diversification for the rural workforce have been interpreted differently by different analysts. Most of these interpretations are yet to be tested and validated through rigorous empirical studies. Let us, however, run through these interpretations and develop some idea about the vulnerable position of rural workers in the emerging labour market scenario.

One view is that rural child workers, including the females among them, are withdrawing from the labour market and going 'back to school'. On the basis of the available data, including the peeping window that the 1993-94 NSS report provides, one is tempted to lend a nodding approval to this hypothesis (Chadha, 1997, p. 191). A small absolute improvement of this kind cannot, however, hide the highly inferior position of the rural *vis-a-vis* urban children.

The fiscal compression exercised during the early years since the July 1991 economic reforms, *viz.* 1991-92 and 1992-93, was bound to make its own impact on employment compression. The non-agricultural activities receiving big jolts under fiscal compression are summarily the very same where employment for the rural workers, more seriously for the female workers, suffered the most. Construction is the most typical example of this kind. The significance of public expenditure for fostering rural development in general, and specific nonagricultural activities in particular, thus needs to be rehabilitated (Sen, 1997).

According to another interpretation under the drought conditions of 1987-88, the level of non-farm employment was 'artificially' buoyed up through a series of short-term relief programmes. The expansion of non-farm employment during 1977-78/1987-88 or 1983/1987-88 might have been much less faster had the drought relief programmes not intervened (Parthasarathy, 1997, pp. 12-15). But then, the 1993-94 level of non-farm employment was a normal marketdriven outcome. This interpretation, therefore, advises that too much need not be read from the 1987-88 'high' levels of non-farm employment. There is some truth in this view. But as a general explanation for all parts of rural India, it is much too hard to be accepted. Indeed, the ferocity of the 1987-88 drought was very high in Gujarat and Rajasthan where non-farm employment 'expanded' sizeably for rural males from 20.1 and 21.7 per cent, respectively in 1983 to 31.4 and 34.7 per cent in 1987-88 (Chadha, 1997, p. 198). But then, the interpretation might better rest with these two states only, no big expansion of non-farm employment was discernible in 1987-88 over 1983 for most other states. In fact, the trajectory of non-farm employment growth runs smoothly from 1972-73 to 1987-88, for most of the states other than Gujarat and Rajasthan. And then, the halting or slackening pace sets in during the post-1987 years, for many states including Gujarat and Rajasthan. The drought hypothesis has thus no universal appeal.

Another explanation associates the sluggish or halting pace of non-farm employment expansion during 1987-88/1993-94 to the poor performance of agriculture during the very first two-three post-1991 reform years. The poor performance is strikingly discernible for the poorer regions, where production of coarse cereals or total cereals or total foodgrains suffered severe setbacks during 1991-92 and 1992-93, and in some states, during 1993-94 as well (Govt. of India, 1997A, pp. S19-S21). Many reasons are given for the poor showing of agriculture but the most convincing explanation is the dwindling pace of investment in agriculture, especially of public investment, since mid-1980s (Govt. of India, 1997A, p. 155). In any case, for the lower strata of the rural society, such production setbacks entailed severe income and purchasing-power setbacks. In addition, food prices were hiked up rather sharply soon after the economic reforms came in July 1991. The sum total effect of all these developments was a squeeze in the demand for non-agricultural goods and services. To put the record straight, a major portion of the demand for rural non-farm items comes from the lower strata of the rural households. In brief, the fortune of the rural non-farm sector in India cannot, and must not, be seen independent of the rural farm sector, most significantly because even today, nearly two-third of rural workers are still engaged in agriculture, and their demand for non-agricultural goods and services counts for much in the growth of the rural non-farm sector.

Yet another explanation holds the slackening pace of urbanisation responsible for the poor showing of non-farm growth in recent years. "In Korea and Taiwan, it is the pace or urbanisation that has contributed to rapid growth of non-agriculture. In India, the growth of urbanisation has been slow. In 1980s, there was a further slackening of urbanisation" (Parthasarathy, 1997, p. 16).

Many more explanations can be thought of. And it has also to be agreed that the growth of non-farm sector depends on a whole host of factors, some originating in rural areas themselves and some coming in from outside, some emanating from short-term exigencies and some arising out of long-term structural changes taking place in the normal course of economic development. The last set of factors are of fundamental importance and must, therefore, be spelt out, both conceptually and empirically. For example, in India, when agricultural growth picked up well during the 1980s, especially in the lagging eastern states, non-farm activities too grew fast. The initial spurt of non-farm expansion was in the nature of *ad hoc* response to rising demands from agriculture, partly for production and partly for consumption purposes. The hard yardsticks of price efficiency, product quality, rural-urban competitiveness, etc. did not immediately intervene. But then, by the close of the 1980s, market considerations started overtaking the *ad hoc* adjustments. This tendency, so is believed by this theory, got more intensified after economic reforms came in July 1991. Under the new dispensation, some non-farm activities must, therefore, decline; some must grow especially those linked up with modern production sectors, and some others would persist on just because they are a part of village economic and social existence. The relationship between a maturing economy and the future of rural non-farm sector is thus an extremely valuable area of policy research.

In the mean time, it is in order to take stock of the supply side of the rural labour market. In this context, the best would be to understand what is in the offing in the industrial sector, especially its most important constituent of manufacturing. For rural workers, employment in the manufacturing sector is a vexatious issue. This is especially so for the female workers who have indeed to contend with numerous social, cultural and economic constraints. Joining a job in a 'modern' manufacturing enterprise is not that easy, most pronouncedly because of lack of education and skills. Perhaps, the structure of industries in the rural areas, or in the nearby semi-urban locations, has been undergoing a 'silent transformation' towards better production technologies and extended market linkages. While job opportunities in such enterprises are becoming scarcer for the wide mass of illiterate and lowly educated rural workers, most unmistakably the females among them, the household industrial enterprises are also losing their grip in the employment market. Whatever way one may look at the impending impact of economic reforms, including the urge to gain industrial competitiveness in the global context, it is for sure that the rural workforce in India is not yet ripe enough to take up more specialised and skill-oriented industrial jobs. The urge for decentralizing more of modern industrial activity into and around the countryside would thus bring limited and highly differentiated employment gains to rural labour force. For rural females, this seems to have been the most certain stumbling block in occupational upgradation in recent years.

If one looks into the educational status of the present generation of rural workers, one is certain to discover that to the present lot of illiterate and unskilled rural workers; especially the females among them, the future may not promise much. But then, what is likely to happen to the future generations of rural workers? Is the present generation of rural people, particularly the young girls, getting prepared for education-and skill-intensive jobs, which they may wish to join in the foreseeable future. Among other aspects, the likely educational attainments of the present generation of rural boys and girls, say, after 5, 10 or 15 years, would clearly indicate if they are preparing themselves to face the impending labour market realities. Let us first look at educational capabilities of the people who are already in the rural workforce.

EDUCATIONAL BACKGROUND OF RURAL WORKERS: PRESENT GENERATION

Table 10.5 gives educational background of the present lot of rural workers. A few striking differences between male and female workers. Firstly, both in agriculture and non-agriculture, the proportion of workers goes on declining as we move towards higher levels of educational attainments; this is happening more steeply and decisively in respect of female workers. In particular, the big bulk of illiterate workers, both in agriculture and non-agriculture, need to be specially underlined for male and female workers. It is extremely distressing to note that even after 45 years of India's planned economic development, nearly 83.0 per cent of female agricultural workers and 62.0 per cent of female non-agricultural workers are still illiterate. By all reckoning, female education does not seem to have witnessed a big improvement in Independent India since the present generation of workers does largely comprise those born after Independence.

Secondly, it also seems pretty clear that the proportion of illiterate workers in non-agriculture is much less than those in agriculture; in particular, the proportion of workers with higher educational attainments (say, secondary level schooling and above) is much too big, for both sexes, in non-agriculture compared with agriculture. *It is thus abundantly clear that educational attainment is a highly facilitating support for a shift from agriculture to non-agriculture.* The point has deep significance for the future generations of workers in that in times ahead, the technical and managerial requirements of non-farm jobs are bound to increase further and if concrete improvements for rural educational system do not occur apace, the rural labour force is bound to suffer further in the market for non-farm jobs.

Table 10.5 : Educational Background of Principal Status of Rural Workers engaged in Agricultural and Non-Agricultural Activities by Mode of Employment and Workers' Sex : 1987-88/1993-94

(Percentage)

Level of Education (Schooling)	*Year*	*Percentage of Workers Engaged in*										*All Rural Workers*
		Agriculture					*Non-Agriculture*					
		S.E.	*Wage Labour*			*Total Agr.*	*S.E.*	*Wage Labour*			*Total Non-Agr.*	
			RS.	*CL.*	*Tot.*			*RS.*	*CL.*	*Tot.*		
1	2	3	4	5	6	7	8	9	10	11	12	13
						Rural Male						
Not	87-88	45.8	71.2	68.0	68.3	54.4	35.2	13.9	53.2	32.7	33.9	49.0
Literate	93-94	43.0	65.6	62.7	62.9	51.0	30.9	11.1	43.0	23.9	27.9	44.6
Upto	87-88	31.1	22.8	24.8	24.6	28.6	38.1	25.0	32.1	28.4	32.9	29.7
Primary	93-94	30.3	21.9	26.4	26.0	28.7	35.1	19.9	35.9	26.3	31.1	29.4
Middle	87-88	13.4	3.2	5.3	5.0	10.2	15.1	17.6	10.5	14.2	14.6	11.4
Level	93-94	14.5	6.8	7.8	7.6	11.7	17.8	17.9	14.3	16.4	17.0	13.2
Secondary Level	87-88	9.7	2.8	1.9	2.0	6.8	11.6	43.5	4.2	24.7	18.6	9.9
and Above	93-94	12.2	5.7	3.3	3.5	8.6	16.2	51.1	6.8	33.4	24.0	12.8
						Rural Female						
Not	87-88	81.5	90.0	90.8	90.7	85.0	73.8	42.4	83.5	71.6	72.1	83.0
Literate	93-94	80.0	85.7	86.5	86.2	83.1	65.5	32.2	74.8	57.3	61.6	79.9
Upto	87-88	13.3	7.8	7.8	7.8	11.3	19.4	13.9	13.0	13.2	16.4	12.0
Primary	93-94	14.8	9.3	10.9	10.7	12.9	23.3	15.6	18.5	17.3	20.5	14.0

(Contd.)

(Contd..)

1	2	3	4	5	6	7	8	9	10	11	12	13
Middle	87-88	3.6	1.4	1.1	1.1	2.6	5.3	11.5	2.7	5.3	5.3	3.1
Level	93-94	3.8	3.9	2.1	2.4	3.0	6.9	11.6	4.9	7.6	7.2	3.6
Secondary Level	87-88	1.6	0.8	0.3	0.4	1.1	2.5	32.2	0.8	9.9	6.2	1.9
and Above	93-94	1.4	1.1	0.6	0.7	1.0	4.3	40.6	1.8	17.8	10.7	2.5

Note : 1. S.E. Self-Employed; R.S.=Regular Salaried Jobs; C.L. = Casual Labour.
2. The 1987-88 figures relate to persons of age 15 years and above, while for 1993-94, those with age 5 years and above are included. The margin of discrepancy is, however, negligible.

Source : 1. For 1987-88, *Sarvekshana*, Special Number, Sept. 1990, pp.S-94-S95.
2. For 1993-94, Govt. of India, NSS Report No. 406, June 1996, pp. 70-71.

Thirdly, there is a striking difference between agriculture and non-agriculture as regards the educational background of self-employed contrasted to the wage paid workers. In agriculture, 63.0 per cent of wage paid male workers (86.0 per cent among females) are illiterate against only 43.0 per cent of their self-employing counterparts (80.0 per cent among females); on the other hand, in non-agriculture, 24.0 per cent of wage-paid male and 57.0 per cent of wage-paid female workers are illiterate while the corresponding percentages for self-employing male and female workers were 31.0 and 65.5; respectively. More important is to see the glaring differences between agriculture and non-agriculture as we move towards higher levels of educational background of wage-paid workers. As high as 51.0 per cent of male and 40.6 per cent of female workers in salaried jobs in non-agriculture had at least secondary level schooling to their credit; the corresponding percentages in similar jobs in agriculture were merely 5.7 and 1.1 per cent, respectively.

Finally, as the level of education improves, the incidence of casual labour employment declines steeply both in agriculture and non-agriculture; about 90.0 per cent of male casual labourers in agriculture and about 80.0 per cent of their brethren in non-agriculture are either illiterate or educated upto primary level only; these percentages for female casual labourers are 97.0 and 93.0 respectively.

In brief, the present generation of rural workers, especially the female workers, are greatly handicapped in terms of their educational background and technical capabilities. Since the possibility of educational and skill upgradation for most of them seems rather remote, their employability in alternative, better paid and skill-intensive non-farm jobs, is a big question mark. In all likelihood, a preponderant majority among them, especially those in their mid-thirties and beyond would never be able to catch up with the changing job requirements, and would summarily end up with the jobs they have in hand. Naturally, therefore. we have to cast our hopes on the new generation of workers.

Expected Educational Achievements of the Future Labour Force

In this context, the most important question is: will rural India throw up a better educated and technically trained labour force, say, after 10 or 15 years? Will the future job claimants be better equipped to face the more rigorous job requirements, especially in the expanding export-linked non-farm production and services sectors? Ready-made answers are not available. Nonetheless, on the basis of the available data, some tentative (although not very pleasing) answers can be framed. Table 10.6 throws up a few such answers.

Firstly, in each age-group, the proportion of rural people not attending any educational institution is much higher than that of their urban counterparts. Even as late as in 1993-94, nearly 40 per cent of rural children (age-group 5-9 years) do not go to school while for the corresponding urban children, the absenteeism does not touch more than 18 per cent of them. That nearly one-third of the rural children (age group 10-14 years) do not go to school is a highly disconcerting feature inasmuch as this is the age at which they should ordinarily be pursuing at least middle level of schooling; a big majority of urban children in this age-group is indeed doing so.

Again, more than two-thirds of the rural children in the age-group 15-19 years do not attend any educational institution; some of them never ever went to school while others dropped out at one stage or the other. In total terms, the rural people are way behind their urban counterparts in terms of current status on attending educational institutions.

Secondly, the rural children, compared with their urban counterparts, in each age-group, are late in reaching a given level of schooling. For example, in the age group 5-9 years, 58 per cent of urban children reach primary level of schooling against 45 per cent among the rural children; in the age-group 10-14 years, 44 per cent of urban against 29 per cent of rural children reach middle level of schooling; the differences manifest themselves most conspicuously in respect of technical degrees/diplomas. especially when the adolescence is crossed over.

Thirdly, the worst placed are the rural females, in terms of attending school or acquiring varying level of education, in each age group. It is a clear proof of their social handicap that nearly 80 per cent of the rural females (against 50 per cent of their urban sisters) have done up with education by the time they enter the age-group 15-19 years; the handicap encompasses nearly the whole lot of rural females as soon as they move beyond their teens. The worst for them is in respect of technical degrees/diplomas. Just about 2.5 per cent of rural females (age-group 15-19 years) are engaged in such professional studies against as many as 13 per cent of the corresponding urban females. In the next age-group (20-24 years), their relative position is far worse, for the simple reason that most parents, especially those in

Table 10.6 : Distribution of Persons (Age 5 Years and above) by Status of Current Attendance in Educational Institutions for Different Age Groups in Rural and Urban India : 1993-94

Age-Group (Years)	*Current Status on Attending Educational Institutions*	*Rural Areas*			*Urban Areas*		
		Male	*Famale*	*Persons*	*Male*	*Female*	*Persons*
1	2	3	4	5	6	7	8
5-9	Not Attending	33.5	44.0	38.5	16.2	20.3	18.1
	Pre-Primary Schooling	15. 4	12 .6	14 .0	22. 0	19. 0	20. 7
	Primary Schooling	48.4	41.2	45.0	58.0	56.9	57.5
	Middle & Higher Levels	2.6	2.2	2.4	3.6	3.8	3.7
10-14	Not Attending	24.0	44.2	33.2	13.2	18.4	15.6
	Pre-Primary to Primary	34.0	25.6	30.2	28.6	24.7	25.7
	Middle Level Schooling	33 .9	23 .9	29. 3	44 .5	43. 2	43 .9
	Secondary & Higher Levels	8.2	6.2	7.3	13.8	13.5	13.7
15-19	Not Attending	58.7	79.2	68.0	43.0	50.2	46.3
	Pre-Middle to Middle to Level	9.4	5.2	7.5	7.6	5.7	6.7
	Secondary to Higher Secondary Level	26 .3	13 .1	20. 3	34.5	30. 9	32. 8
	Technical Degree and Diploma	5.6	2.5	4.4	14.8	13 .2	14.1
20-24	Not Attending	89.2	97.1	93.2	77.3	86.6	81.8
	Pre-Secondary to Higher Secondary	4.1	1.4	2.8	4.6	2.5	3.6
	Technical Degree	4.8	1.1	2.9	11.7	7.3	9.6
	Technical Diploma	1.8	0.4	1.1	6.2	3.5	4.9

Source : Govt. of India, *N.S.S. Report No. 409, March 1997*, pp. A79-A84.

rural areas, would like their daughters to be married off, latest in their early twenties. To complete the story, technical qualifications for the rural females, confined as they are to a microscopic minority among them, do not go beyond diploma in (village) crafts. The rural lasses may better be trained in tailoring, weaving, embroidery, steno-typing, or still better, trained in 'good cooking' and 'child rearing'.

Finally, to comprehend the future realities in a different (and somewhat unconventional but telling manner), we look at the educational attainment of the *present-day children, adolescents* and the *adults/youth* among rural/urban males/females. Table 10.7 gives us adequate material to reiterate some of our earlier conclusions. First, the proportion of children, adolescents and the youth who are below the (notionally) expected level of educational attainment is uniformly the highest among the rural females, followed by rural males, urban females and urban males. While a substantial gap exists between the males and females in rural India, the male-female gaps are indeed very small in urban India. The male-female gap in rural India (better interpreted as discrimination against females) sets in right when the child reaches the school-going age (5-9 years), and keeps on widening itself as we go upto senior-aged children, adolescents and adults, and so on. By comparison, the proportion of urban females below the (notionally) expected level of educational attainment, is only a shade higher than that of their urban counterparts, in each age-group. Happily, the gap shows no tendency to increase as we move up on the age group ladder. In one word, by and large, the urban girls and women are doggedly striving to stay close to urban boys and men, for all levels of education.

Secondly, the obverse side brings more distressing comparisons. The proportion of children, adolescents and the youth falling within the (notionally) expected range of educational attainment is the lowest for the rural females, next higher for rural males, followed upwards for urban females and urban males, for each age-group or each range of educational attainment. It is rather frightening to see that just about 11 per cent of rural females in the age-group 20-24 years are within the expected range of educational attainment (secondary level schooling and above), against 29 per cent among rural males, 40 per cent among urban females and 50 per cent among urban males. The rural females' attainment of professional degrees makes a shameful reading. In brief, the relative 'neglect' of rural areas, and within those areas, of females compared with the males, is so apparent.

Table 10.7 : Distribution of Persons by Level of Educational Attainment for Different Age-Groups Separately for Rural and Urban Males/Females : 1993-94

Catagory of Persons	*Age-Groups (Years)*	*Notional Range of expected Level of Educational Attainment Specific to the Age-Group*	*%Distribution of Persons in Terms of Actual Educational Attainment*			*% Persons Falling in Each Age-Group*
			Below the Notionally Expected Range	*Amidst the Notionally Expected Range*	*Above the Notionally Expected Range*	
1	2	3	4	5	6	7
Rural	5-9	Pre-Primary to Primary	40(40.0)	60	-	15
Male	10-14	Primary to Middle	53 (18.1)	47	-	14
	15-19	Middle to Secondary	51 (23.4)	45	4	12
	20-24	Secondary & Above	71 (28.0)	29	-	9
	25-29	Professional Degree	94 (35.9)	6	-	9
Rural	5-9	Pre-Primary to Primary	50(50.0)	50	-	14
Female	10-14	Primary to Middle	64 (35.5)	36	-	12
	15-19	Middle to Secondary	70 (45.6)	28	2	10
	20-24	Secondary & Above	89 (59.3)	11	-	10
	25-29	Professional Degree	99 (67.2)	1	-	10
Urban	5-9	Pre-Primary to primary	23 (23.0)	77	-	13
Male	10-14	Primary to Middle	37 (7.4)	62	1	13
	15-19	Middle to Secondary	33 (10.7)	55	12	13
	20-24	Secondary & Above	50 (11.4)	50	-	11
	25-29	Professional Degree	82 (15.2)	18	-	9

(Contd...)

(Contd..)

1	2	3	4	5	6	7
Urban Female	5-9	Pre- Primary to Primary	26 (26.0)	74	-	12
	10-14	Primary to Middle	37 (11.4)	62	1	13
	15-19	Middle to Secondary	36 (15.9)	50	14	12
	20-24	Secondary & Above	60 (25.2)	40	-	1
	25-29	Professional Degree	87 (31.4)	13	-	10

Note :
1. Pre-Primary Comprises literates through NFEC/AEC, TLC and others as well as children in school not yet reaching the primary standard.
2. Education above secondary level (refer age-group 20-24 years in the table) include higher secondary, graduates and post-graduates in agriculture, engineering/technology, medicine.
3. Professional degree (against age-group 25-29 in the table) means graduates and post-graduates in agriculture, engineering/technology, medicine, etc.
4. In Column 4, the figure in parentheses is the percentage of totally illiterate persons in the specified age-group.

Source : Govt. of India, *NSS Report No. 409, March 1997*, pp. A46-A50.

Thirdly, and finally, the 'neglect' becomes all the more apparent if we look at the proportion of totally illiterate persons in each age-group (figures in parentheses under Col. 4, Table 10.7). In spite of the 'national effort', spanning over the past five decades, towards providing *universal primary education*, in 1993-94, nearly 50 per cent of rural females and 40 per cent of rural males, in the age-group 5-9 years, are totally illiterate. These are the people who will swell the ranks of labour market after about 10 years. We are bound to witness the rural females, and to a lesser extent rural males, waging a losing battle in the then non-farm employment market largely because they would have no 'educational attainment' to support their case. Again, nearly 36 per cent of rural females and 18 per cent of rural males in the next higher age-group 10-14 years, have remained totally illiterate, against 11 per cent among ubran females and 7 per cent among urban males. These people would join the labour market after about 5 years, making matters worse not only for themselves but also for those of their senior but illiterate and unskilled fellow job-aspirants. Yet again, about 46 per cent of rural females in the most determinative age-group 15-19 years are bereft of any educational attainment against 23 per cent among rural males, 16 per cent among urban females and 11 per cent among urban males. This is the age-group which must have released, by now, job-aspirants into urban and rural labour markets.

The foregoing analysis delineates the *relatively* stronger and weaker partners in the future labour market unquestionably, the rural females seem to be getting highly marginalized in the matter of education, training and skill formation. Compared with all other categories of prospective job-seekers, their *relative* inferiority 10, 15 or 20 years hence, in competing for education- and skill-intensive jobs, is transparent besides the usual social and cultural infirmities that they will continue to suffer from. Their Achilles heel is no more a secret. In total terms, it is clear enough that unless public policy intervenes effectively to break the educational barriers of the groups neglected so far, the segmentation would get more and more solidified, marginalization of an increasing proportion of population would increase, social tensions most notoriously those bred by the past policy regimes would further spread over the Indian society, and so on. No right thinking Indian would like this to happen.

REFERENCES

Bhalla, Sheila, 1994, "Globalization, Growth and Employment", in G.S. Bhalla and Manmohan Agarwal (eds.) *World Economy in Transition—An Indian Perspective,* Har-Anand Publication, New Delhi.

Chadha, G.K., 1993, "Non-Farm Employment for Rural Households in India : Evidence and Prognosis", *Indian Journal of Labour Economic,* No. 3, July-September.

——,1993A, "*Non-farm Sector in India's Rural Economy; Policy, Performance and Growth Prospects,* VRF Series No. 220, Institute of Developing Economy, Tokyo, October.

——, 1994, *Employment, Earnings and Poverty : A Study of Rural India* and *Indonesia,* Sage Publications, New Delhi.

——, 1996, *The Industrialization Strategy and the Growth of Rural Industry in India,* ILO/SAAT Working Paper, New Delhi, June.

——, 1997, "Access of Rural Households to Non-Farm Employment : Trends, Constraints and Possibilities", in *Growth, Employment and Proverty : Change and Continuity in Rural India,* eds. G.K. Chadha and Alakh N. Sharma, Vikas Publishing House Pvt. Ltd.

Government of India, 1980, *Sarvekshana,* III/3, NSSO; January.

——, 1981, *Sarvekshana,* V/1&2, NSSO; July-August.

——, 1990, *Sarvekshana,* Special No., NSSO; September

——, 1996, *Key Results on Employment and Unemployment : NSS 50th Round (July 1993-June 1994), NSS Report No.* 406, NSSO, Ministry of Planning, Department of Statistics.

Government of India, 1997, *Employment and Unemployment in India. 1993-94, NSS Report No. 409,* NSSO, Ministry of Planning, Department of Statistics.

——, 1997A, *Economic Survey of India,* 1997, Ministry of Finance.

Islam, Rizwanul, 1987, *Rural Industrialization and Employment in Asia,* ILO/ ARTEP, New Delhi.

Parthasarathy G., *et al.,* 1997, "Share of Non-Agricultural Labour Force on All-India and States : Prospects of Sustained Increase", (mimeo.), February.

Sen, Abhijit, 1997, "Structural Adjustment and Rural Poverty : Variables that Really Matter", in *Growth, Employment and Poverty : Change and Continuity in Rural India,* eds. G.K. Chadha and Alakh N. Sharma, Vikas Publishing House Pvt. Ltd, New Delhi.

Vaidyanathan, A., 1986, "Labour Use in Rural India : A Study of Spatial and Temporal Variations", *Economic and Political Weekly,* No. 52, December 27.

Visaria Pravin & Minhas, B.S., 1991, "Evolving an Employment Policy for the 1990s: What do the Data Tell Us?", *Economic and Political Weekly,* No. 15, April 13.

11

NEW ECONOMIC POLICY AND ITS IMPACT ON EMPLOYMENT AND POVERTY OF THE SCHEDULED CASTES

Some Observations

Sukhadeo K. Thorat

Introduction

This Chapter intends to assess the impact of the far reaching economic reforms initiated by the government in response to a major economic crisis in early 1991 on economic situations of Scheduled Castes in India. This is done by looking at the trends in few important aspects namely, (a) employment/ unemployment, (b) poverty, (c) employment under the reservation, and (d) by examining some of the theoretical issues underlining the new economic policy in as much as they relate to the specific social and economic situation of Scheduled Castes in India.

The new economic measures were initiated in July 1991. An attempt to measure the impact of on-going economic reforms is faced with difficulty as only a few years have passed since reform has been initiated. The assessment has become more difficult in the case of Scheduled Castes as the relevant data on the employment, poverty and other indicators are not available for the years under reforms. The employment and consumption statistics (on the basis of which poverty ratios are estimated) and information on the incidence of wage labour and other aspects for Scheduled Castes are available upto 1987-88. Therefore, impact of new economic measures on the economic situation of Scheduled Castes can at best be understood indirectly, by looking at trends in some variables and directly in the case of only few variables.

Why New Economic Policy (NEP)

The NEP comprising of *"Stabilization"* and *"Structural Adjustment"*, programmes was initiated at least initially as a response to overcome the crisis in two areas, (a) external debt crisis, and (b) Fiscal deficits (public debt crisis).

The external debt crisis which surfaced in early 1991 brought India closer to default in meeting its international payment obligations. The balance of payment crisis (which roughly means that receipts from foreigners were less than payment to foreigners) was the result of policy of liberalisation of trade regime beginning with the mid 1970s and 1980s which encouraged imports disproportionately in relation to export earnings, the gap being met from finance by borrowing from abroad, ultimately leading to a debt trap. The current account deficit doubled from an annual average of $ 2.3 billion (1.3% of GDP) in the first half of the 1980s to an annual average of $ 5.5 billion (2.2 per cent of GDP) in the second half of 1980s.

This was sustained by continuous increase in external debt which increased by more than two and a half times in a decade from $ 23.8 billion at the end of 1980-81 to 62.3 billion at the end of year 1990-91. The debt service burden also rose from 15 per cent of export earnings in 1980-81 to 30 per cent of export earnings in 1990-91. What is more important is that the external resources were used mainly for consumption and much less for investment purpose. Due to the end of any further external support by early 1991 the foreign reserves dropped to a level that would not have paid for import even for a fortnight.

The fiscal deficit or crisis (the gap between government spending and receipts) was also in making for a while and it was also accumulated through the 1980s. The fiscal deficit was met by borrowing at home and it mounted steadily leading to accumulation of internal debt. The fiscal deficit grew as the internal debt of government rose from Rs. 485 billion (35 per cent of GDP) at the end of 1980-81 to Rs. 2830 billion (54 per cent of GDP) at the end of 1990-91 and interest payment on debt almost doubled from 10 per cent to 19 per cent. Like the external borrowing, the public borrowing was also mainly used for consumption purpose and less for investment purpose and the latter did not earn a rate of return which was not high enough to finance interest payment on entire borrowing.

The external and internal debt reached the unsustainable level.

By mid-1990s the room for manoeuvre to live either on borrowed money or on borrowed time had been completely used. (Bhaduri and Nayyer, 1996).

Crisis Management Response

In tune with theoretical framework of IMF and World Bank, the government introduced programmes of (a) Stabilisation, and (b) Structural adjustment.

The"Stabilization Programme" (SP) has a main objective of correcting balance of payment crisis at least in short-run by reducing deficit on current account and to curb inflation, but the issues relating to employment and poverty received passing attention. The main instruments for "Stabilization" are fiscal policy and monetary policy, both are applied in a manner so as to reduce the level of aggregate demand. In addition, the devaluation of domestic currency is used to improve balance of payments (by making the country's goods cheaper relative to foreign goods). This package of policies was used under which there was a sharp reduction in fiscal deficit of government, a tight money policy and substantial devaluation of the rupee in two instalments in July 1991.

The "Stabilization Programme" (SP) was accompanied by "Structural Adjustment Programme" (SAP). The essence of Stabilization is to compress demand and it was hoped that the reduced demand will mostly reduce the prices rather than output and employment. The SAP on the other hand is recommended for promoting supply (assuming that demand squeeze will not have adverse effect on supply response).

The main elements of SAP are to shift resources :

(i) from non-traded goods to traded goods sector and within latter form import substituting activities to export activities; and

(ii) away from Government Sector to private sector.

Apart from such reallocation of resources, the SAP seeks to improve resource utilisation by:

(a) increasing the degree of openness of economy, and

(b) changing the structure of incentives and institutions in favour of private initiative and against state.

The general economic philosophy is to rely more on market forces, dismantle controls, as far as possible by relying more on prices and reduce the public sector in the hope that the vacuum will be filled by the private sector. The underlying assumption is that industrialization based on state intervention leads to inefficient allocation and utilisation of economic resources. In tune with this theoretical presumption the Government of India had initiated several structural policy changes in July 1991 which include, (i) the industrial sector, (ii) the trade regime; (iii) foreign investment; (iv) foreign technology; (v) the public sector; and (vi) financial sector.

Theoretical Foundation of NEP and its Limitations

The theoretical foundation of the "SP and SAP" is based on the economic proposition relating to what economists called "Price adjustment or mechanism". The argument runs like this, a reduction in the Government deficit would correspondingly reduce the trade deficit by making the Indian goods more price competitive in world market. That is reduction in the government expenditure along with tight money policy will reduce the aggregate demand and thus the domestic prices relative to foreign price. And this is supposed to promote export (or reduce import) and thereby reduce trade deficit. Thus reduction in fiscal deficit is supposed to reduce the trade deficit through lowering prices of exportable goods.

But there is an alternative proposition based on "quantities or output and incomes rather than prices." The alternative proposition is that as the general expenditure is reduced through decline in government expenditures and tight money policy, the purchasing power in the economy falls (leading to reduction in the aggregate demand) to begin with directly in the government sector and then indirectly in private sector for producers and workers who supply to meet the demand from the government. It is argued that the decline in the purchasing power could be something like three times the original reduction in the government deficit. This fall in purchasing power and shrinking of market at home for selling goods typically brings a loss of income and employment all round and increase in poverty. It is thus falling income and purchasing power which reduce imports until the trade deficit is, reduced again to match the reduced government deficit.

This is the "Income Adjustment Proposition" and plausibility of it has been established in many countries. Evidence is now irrefutable that substantial reduction in the government deficit reduces the trade deficit very significantly through a reduction in the level of economic activities *i.e.* employment and output rather than simply reducing the rate of inflation in the country attempting stabilisation. It may reduce the trade deficit only at a great social cost by reducing output and employment drastically (Bhaduri and Nayyer, 1996). It is this line of evidence we seek to present in the following analysis in the Indian context.

NEP and its Impact on Employment

The wage labourers (both in agriculture and non-agriculture) constitute the large segment of poor in the country. Their income and consumption level is thus determined by the level of employment and the wage rate, and any change in these variables also brings a change in their income level. The contraction in public expenditure, consequent upon the reduction in aggregate demand will bring the reduction in employment level and increase in unemployment rates. The statistics on unemployment rates during pre- and post-reform period support this observation.

(a) The usual status data show that there has been a declining trend in unemployment rate between 1977-78 and 1990-91 for male and female both in rural and urban areas (the only exception being the drought year of 1987-88) (Table 11.1). For instance the unemployment rate for mäle based on usual and weekly status increased from 1.3 per cent and 2.2 per cent in 1990-1991 to 2.0 per cent and 3.1 per cent in 1993-94. Similarly for female the rates increased from 0.4 and 2.1 per cent in 1990-1991 to 1.30 per cent and 2.9 per cent respectively in 1993-94. There was also all round increase in unemployment of male and female in urban areas. This increase in unemployment rate in post-reform period (*i.e.* between 1990-91—1993-94) should be understood against the trend of decline between 1972-73 and 1990-91.

(b) The decline in employment rate occurred mainly in secondary and tertiary employment in the rural sector. The percentage of male worker in secondary and tertiary sector has declined between 1990-91 and 1993-94. This has reversed the steady increasing trend observed right from

Table 11.1 : Unemployment Rates

	Rural				*Urban*			
	Male		*Female*		*Male*		*Female*	
	Usual Status	*Weekly Status*	*Usual Status*	*Weekly Status*	*Usual Status*	*Weekly Status*	*Usual Status*	*Weekly Status*
	1	2	3	4	5	6	7	8
1977-78	2.2	3.6	5.5	4.1	6.5	7.1	7.8	10.9
1983	2.1	3.7	1.4	4.3	5.9	6.7	6.9	7.5
1987-88	2.8	4.2	3.5	4.4	6.1	6.6	8.5	9.2
1989-90	1.6	2.6	0.8	2.1	4.4	4.5	3.9	4.0
1990-91	1.3	2.2	0.4	2.1	4.5	5.1	5.4	5.3
1992	1.6	2.2	1.2	1.2	4.6	4.6	6.7	6.2
1993-94	2.0	3.1	1.3	2.9	5.4	5.2	8.3	7.9

Source : *a.* S.P. Gupta, *EPW,* June 3, 1995.
Consumer Expenditure and Employment Survey, NSS, 1992.
b. NSSO, 5th Quinquennial Survey, 50th Round. (July 1993, June 1994).

1977-78 to 1990-91 both in secondary and tertiary sector. In the case of female workers the ratio declined between 1990-91 and 1991-92 in secondary sector but showed some recovery in 1993-94. Yet it was much below the level achieved in 1987-88 and (10.00 per cent) and 1989-90 (12.4 per cent). In the case of tertiary sector the decline in post-reform period was quite clear. *i.e.* a decline from 7.00 per cent in 1990-91 to 5.6 per cent in 1993-94 (Table 11.2).

(c) Thus the impact of new economic measures was mainly on rural-non-farm sector and urban sector. Obviously there was a reverse movement of workers from rural-non-farm sector to agriculture. This very well reflected in the increase in the percentage of male worker in agriculture from 71.10 per cent in 1990-91 to 74.1 per cent in 1993-94 and 84.9 per cent to 86.2 per cent for female. This declining trend in secondary and tertiary sector, however, comes under check between 1992 and 1993-94 due to reversal of cut in public expenditure in rural areas.

(d) The rate of growth of employment in the organised sector of the economy (public and private taken together) dropped from more than 1.7 per cent per annum in late 1980s to 1.2 per cent in 1991-92 and 0.6 per cent in 1992-93.

(e) Within the organized industrial sector in the post-reform period the employment in private sector either remained stagnant or increased marginally but the same has declined in public sector enterprises from 2.2 per cent per annum in pre-reform period, (*i.e.,* 1981-1990) to 1.2 per cent in post-reform period (*i.e.* 1990-1992).

Table 11.2 : Percentage Distribution of Usually Working by Broad Group of Industry : Rural

Year	*Male*				*Female*			
	Primary All	*Secondary All*	*Tertiary All*	*Casual Labour Principal Status*	*Primary All*	*Secondary All*	*Tertiary All*	*Casual Labour Principal Status*
1977-78	80.6	8.8	10.5	27.0	88.1	6.7	5.1	40.0
1983	77.5	10.0	12.2	29.9	87.5	7.4	4.8	42.2
1987-88	74.5	12.1	13.4	32.1	84.7	10.0	5.3	40.2
1989-90	71.7	12.1	16.2	30.9	81.4	12.4	6.1	39.9
1990-91	71.0	12.1	16.9	31.7	84.9	8.1	7.0	41.0
1992	75.7	10.4	13.9	31.4	86.2	7.8	6.0	41.6
1993-94	74.1	11.2	14.7		86.2	8.3	5.6	

Source : a. S.P. Gupta, *EPW,* June 3, 1995.
Consumer Expenditure and Employment Survey, NSS, 1992.
b. NSSO, 5th Quinquennial Survey, 50th Round (July 1993, June 1994).

This discussion clearly indicates that it is the rural non-agricultural and urban informal employment which has suffered the most. It is well-known that growing public expenditure was in the past mainly responsible for rapid employment growth in rural non-agricultural sector in the 1980s. The reduction in public expenditure and the consequent reduction in aggregate demand could not but adversely affect employment in rural non-farm sector and urban-informal sector. It may be noted that the rural non-farm employment in India has been growing at much faster rate between 1977-78 and 1987-88 than the agricultural employment. The percentage share of rural non-farm employment in total employment increased from around 14 per cent to 17 per cent and in rural employment from 17 to 22 per cent between 1977-78 and 1987-88. And this has been a major factor for reducing poverty between 1977-78 and 1987-88.

The recent statistics on employment by NSS for the year 1993-94 confirmed the above observations (Table 11.3).

Table 11.3 : Annual Compound Growth Rate of Employment for Usual (Principal+Subsidiary) Status Workers by Workers' Sex, Residence and Broad Sectors of Production :1977-78/1993-94

Production Sector	Rural Male		Urban Male		Rural Female		Urban Female	
	77-78 to 87-88	87-88 to 93-94	77-78 to 87-68	87-88 to 93-94	77-78 to 87-88	87-88 to 93-94	77-78 to 87-88	87-88 to 93-94
1	2	3	4	5	6	7	8	9
1. Agriculture	0 .30	1.37	1. 59	3. 46	3. 41	1.49	6.45	0.36
2. Mining & Quarrying	4.18	1.46	6.44	3.65	9.51	1.20	7.76	1.54
3. Manufacturing	2.78	0.53	2.02	2.12	4.91	1.48	4.12	1.36
4. Utilities	5.55	1.47	5.04	3.65	—	—	8.76	10.40
5. Construction	0.19	1.00	6.16	6.70	18.00	15.74	8.63	5.08
6. Trade	3.50	2.74	2.65	3.97	3.00	1.21	4.83	3.05
7. Transport Communication etc.	5.98	3.09	2.48	3.65	14.60	1.20	2.11	9.84
8. Finance, Real Estate, etc.	8.43	1.45	4.44	5.08	—	—	9.95	11.53
9. Community and Personal Services	2.30	3.66	2.78	4.36	1.47	2.83	3.44	7.3
10. Total Non-Agriculture	3.83	1.52	2.74	3.75	5.17	0.17	4.88	4.54
11. All Sectors	1.48	1.92	2.70	3.72	3.65	1.24	5.31	3.19

Source : 1. For 1977-78/1987-88 growth rates, Chaddha, G.K., *Indian Journal of Labour Economics,* July-September, 1993, p. 302.
2. For 1987-88/1993-94 Growth Rates, Government of India, *NSS Report No.* 405, *June* 1966, pp. 52-56, 82-86.

(a) The annual (compound) growth rate of employment for usual (principal + subsidiary) in non-agriculture sector reduced from 3.83 per cent per annum during 1977-78/ 87-88 to 1.52 per cent per annum for male and from 5.17 per cent per annum to 0.17 per cent per annum for female in rural areas.

(b) This has occurred due to decline in several non-farm activities for male which include mining and quarrying, manufacturing, utilities trade, transport, finance and construction. The most severe downfall was in construction where the growth rate was negative (– 1 per cent per annum).

(c) In the case of rural female a major decline occurred in the same sectors. But there was a sharp fall in employment in construction sector (– 15.74 per cent per annum).

(d) In agriculture sector there has been an increase in the employment of rural male worker.

(e) In urban areas the major decline has occurred for female workers in mining and quarrying, manufacturing, construction and agriculture.

Unemployment Situation of Scheduled Castes

The Scheduled Castes constitute a significant section of the poors in India. A look at some of the variables of economic level of living brings out this fact quite clearly.

In 1991, of the total rural workers about 82.00 per cent were engaged in farm activities and the remaining 18.00 per cent in non-farm activities. This division for Non-SC/ST was 75.00 per cent and 25 per cent respectively. In other words, the occupational pattern of SCs was much less diversified as compared to Non-SC/ST. Further within agriculture, the percentage of wage labour among SCs was nearly 50 per cent. Only 33 per cent of them were cultivators. Reverse was, however, true for non-SC/ST as much as 55 per cent worked as cultivators and only 20 per cent worked as wage labour in agriculture.

In fact the Scheduled castes agricultural labour constitutes 33 per cent of the total male agricultural labour in the country, although their share in total male population was only 18.50 per cent (Table 11.4).

Table 11.4 : Percentage of Workers by Industrial Categories : Rural (Male) 1991

Category	*Scheduled Caste*				*Sheduled Tribe*				*Others*			
	1961	*1971*	*1981*	*1991*	*1961*	*1971*	*1981*	*1991*	*1961*	*1971*	*1981*	*1991*
1. Cultivator	42.90	34.94	36.70	33.11	68.46	63.63	62.52	61.28	63.74	59.27	58.44	54.74
2. Agriculture-Labour	32.83	50.24	46.82	49.27	19.57	28.48	26.72	27.89	12.12	19.19	18.30	20.14
3. Agriculture	75.73	85.18	83.52	82.39	88.03	92.11	89.24	89.19	75.86	79.26	76.74	74.88
4. Non-Agriculture	24.27	14.82	16.48	17.61	11.99	7.89	10.76	10.81	24.14	20.74	23.26	25.12

Source : NSS Employment Survey, CSO, various years.

Thus a small proportion of SC households own or cultivate some land. Among them also as many as 73 per cent were marginal farmers with average of less than 2.50 acres of land. Another 13 per cent were landless households. So nearly 86 per cent of SC households in 1991 were landless and near landless households (Table 11.5).

Table 11.5 : Size Distribution of Ownership Holding by Size Class

	Scheduled Caste		*Scheduled Tribe*		*Others*		*All*	
Category	*1982*	*1992*	*1982*	*1992*	*1982*	*1992*	*1982*	*1992*
Landless	12.61	13.34	17.11	11.50	10.18	9.85	11.33	11.25
Marginal	72.41	72.91	43.26	54.90	52.2	53.95	55.32	60.63
Small	8.4	7.85	17.36	17.54	16.09	13.58	14.7	13.42
Semi-medium	4.52	3.86	14.27	11.39	12.05	10.08	10.78	9.28
Medium	1.8	1.83	7.07	4.02	7.66	11.48	6.45	4.54
Large	0.26	0.21	0.93	0.65	1.82	1.06	1.42	0.88
Total	100	100	100	100	100	100	100	100

Source : NSS, Landholding Survey, CSO, Delhi.

The high incidence of landlessness and near landlessness among SC population creates an enormously high proportion of wage labour among them. The information generated by successive Rural Labour Enquiries throw additional light on the incidence of wage labour among SCs in rural areas (Table 11.6). In 1987-88 (the latest Rural Labour Enquiry Survey), of the total SC rural households as high as 63.14 per cent were wage labour households. This proportion was quite high compared to 31.16 per cent among others. Further nearly 63.14 per cent of wage labour households among SCs owned some land and the remaining 24.2 per cent were without any land. Thus a substantial section of land owning households among the Scheduled Castes also resort to wage employment due to the smallness of the land that they owned. In fact it was observed that nearly 75 per cent of wage labour households with land belong to the marginal farmers owning land less than 1.49 acres.

This discussion indicates that nearly 63 per cent of SC households has to resort to wage employment to earn major part of their income. Obviously the economic well-being of them would depend on the employment opportunities both in farm and rural non-farm sector under the new economic regime.

Table11.6 : Some Features of Rural Labour Households of Scheduled Castes in India

Category & Years	Percentage of Rural Labour Household	Percentage of Rural Labour Household with Land	Percentage of Rural Labour Household without Land	Total
1. Scheduled Caste				
1964-65	—	42.3	57.7	100
1974-75	57.41	44.4	55.6	100
1977-78	63.18	42.6	57.4	100
1983	62.55	37.77	62.23	100
1987-88	63.14	75.54	24.46	100
2. Scheduled Tribe				
1964-65	—	46.2	53.8	100
1974 -75	31.03	51.3	48.7	100
1977-78	43.11	52.7	47.3	100
1983	44.05	50.04	49.96	100
1987-88	49.60	83.09	16.91	100
3. Non SC/ST				
1964-65	—	44.30	55.70	100
1974-75	26.65	52.27	47.73	100
1977-78	28.88	53.17	46.83	100
1983	29.14	46.33	53.67	100
1987-88	31.16	80.92	19.08	100

Source : Rural Labour Enquiry Report. NSSO, Delhi

Table 11.7 presents the unemployment rates for SC and others for the year 1977-78, 1983-84 and 1987-88 (the latest year for which the data are available). We observed some important features concerning the unemployment situation of SC *vis-a-vis* the other. In the case of unemployment rate based on usual status there is no significant difference in the unemployment rate between the SCs and others. In fact the unemployment rate of SCs is slightly lower than that of others. This has been the case in earlier years as well. This is not suprising as the NSS treat a person to be usually employed if he or she works for more than 180 days in a year. Since SC workers have limited alternative other than wage employment their participation in the work around the year would be certainly higher than others. However, no sooner we move on to the unemployment rate based on current weekly status and current daily status, the picture changes completely. The unemployment rate for SCs turn out to be much higher than the other group. For instance in 1977-78 and 1983-84 the unemployment rate (based on daily status) of SC male workers was 6.73 per cent and 7.16 per cent respectively. These rates were

Table 11.7 : Unemployment Rate Percentage of Unemployment (age 5 years and above) according to Usual, Current Weekly and Daily Status : Rural

Category	Year	Male				Female			
		Usual Principal Status	Usual Status	Current Weekly	Current Daily	Usual Principal Status	Usual Status	Current Weekly	Current Daily
Scheduled Caste	1987-88	1.30	0.09	—	—	1.40	1.10	—	—
	1983	1.14	0.76	3.22	7.16	0.50	0.23	2.16	4.23
	1977-78	1.23	—	2.93	6.73	2.58	—	1.90	4.09
Scheduled Tribe	1987-88	0.80	0.40	—	—	0.80	0.60	—	—
	1983	0.49	0.34	1.47	3.29	0.18	0.80	1.21	2.57
	1977-78	0.52	—	1.57	3.31	1.22	—	1.23	2.37
Others	1987-88	1.70	1.10	—	—	0.48	0.70	—	—
Non SC/ST	1983	1.49	1.03	2.15	4.03	0.43	0.29	0.91	1.72
	1977-78	1.57	—	2.15	3.90	1.53	—	0.97	0.97

Source : Employment Survey, NSS.

significantly higher compared with 3.90 per cent and 4.03 per cent for others respectively. Similar gap exists for female labour too. The same must be true for the year 1987-88 (NSS does not provide the data in weekly and daily status after 1983-84).

Table11.8 : Employment in Rural Non-Farm Sector : Percentage of Rural Non-Farm Workers to total Rural Workers

Category	*1977-78*	*1983*	*1987-88*	*1990-91*	*1992-93*	*1987-88/ 1992-93*
General						
Male	19.3	22.20	25.5	29.00	24.30	– 4.70%
Female	11.80	12.20	15.30	15.10	13.80	– 9.80%
Secheduled Caste						
Male	—	—	24.56	—	23.40	—
Female	—	—	17.37	—	15.66	—

Note : Figures for 1992-93 are based on interpolation.
Source : Employment Survey, NSS.

There are other features which need to be emphasised. First the unemployment rate (based on usual status) was higher in the age group of 15-29 years (5.50 per cent) followed by those in age group of 10-14 years (3.67 per cent) (Table 11.9). Secondly, besides the persons in productive age group (*i.e.* 15-29 years and 30-49 years) the children of age less than 14 years and the aged persons above 60 years also participate in the work due to economic compulsion. The participation rate was 16.30 per cent and 42.15 per cent for persons in the age group 10-14 years and above 60 years respectively. Third feature is that little less than one-fourth (*i.e.* 23 per cent) of workers were engaged in rural non-farm activities (Table 11.8). And fourthly the SCs account for about 22 per cent of total unemployed in the country. This share varies between 31 per cent to 36 per cent for persons in the age group above 30 years. The share was obviously much higher than their share in total population (Table 11.9).

This factual account of unemployment situation of the Scheduled Castes upto 1987-88 does not help us to estimate the direct impact of NEP on their employment. But it certainly tells a story that since there has been a decline in the growth rate of employment in rural-non-farm sector (particularly for female workers), urban informal sector, in public sector and near stagnation in the growth rate of employment in organised private sector, it must have affected more severely the employment of Scheduled Castes as they mainly depend on wage paid employment. Close to a quarter of them are engaged in rural-non-farm activities. And any fall in that sector must have severely affected their employment and income particularly of the workers in the age group of 15-19 years and 45-59 years where the ratio of employment in rural non-farm sector is higher than the average for SCs.

Table 11.9 : Age-wise Distribution of Scheduled Caste Workers, 1987

Status	*5-9*	*10-14*	*15-29*	*30-44*	*45-59*	*60 and above*	*All*
Employed in ('000)							
Agriculture	76.7	1648.9	12104.4	10406.1	6680.2	2179.8	33091.4
Non-Agriculture	15.3	327.2	3653.8	3215.6	1767.5	449.9	9429.6
Total	92.0	1976.2	15758.3	13616.9	8450.8	2636.1	42537.5
Unemployed in ('000)	0	75.5	918.9	299.5	136.16	38.0	1468.81
Percentage share in total unemployed	0	27.61	18.96	30.35	35.0	35.88	21.91
Labour force in ('000)	92.0	2051.7	166.77	13923.4	8586.9	2674.1	44005.6
% in Agriculture	83.37	83.43	76.81	87.38	79.05	82.69	77.79
% in Non-Agriculture	16.63	16.53	23.19	23.62	20.09	17.31	22.21
Unemployment rate	0.00	3.67	5.50	2.15	1.58	1.42	3.36
Participation rate	0.06	16.30	61.89	76.95	73.80	42.15	41.44
Total Unemployed worker (General) in ('000)	0	272.8	4946.5	986.7	388.1	105.9	6699.94

Source : Employment Survey, NSSO. 1987-88.

We do not have the actual statistics on non-farm employment of SC for post-reform period *i.e.* after 1990-91. However, we can work out in a somewhat crude way the magnitude of decline by using the rate of decline observed for general population. The percentage of general non-farm male workers declined from 25.5 per cent in 1987-88 to 24.30 per cent in 1992 and for female from 15.30 per cent to 13.80 per cent respectively. The ratio declined by 4.70 per cent in five years period for male and by 9.80 per cent for females (This has certainly reversed a strong increasing trend observed during pre-reform period). In 1987-88 about 25 per cent of SC male and 17.39 per cent of SC female were engaged in rural non-farm activities. At this rate of decline the percentage of SC male and female worker in rural non-farm must have declined to 23.40 per cent and 15.66 per cent respectively in 1992-93.

The decline in employment in rural non-farm and urban informal sector was obviously the outcome of curtailment in the government expenditure. It is well known that growing public expenditure was in part mainly responsible for rapid employment growth in the rural non-farm sector in 1980s.

This evidence in favour of decline in employment in rural non-farm sector is indirect as it is based on the trends in general population. But there is more direct evidence which clearly supports decline in the absolute as well as ratio of Scheduled Caste employees in public sector i.e. recruitment in government services and public sector undertakings. The banking sector where the process of reform has been slower than the government and public sector undertakings, the decline was not yet visible.

Impact on Employment under Reservation

Due to privatisation in some sectors and cut in government expenditure and also slowing down of public sector of the employment of SCs and STs has been reduced after 1991. (Table 11.10) presents the relevant data on employment of Scheduled Castes in public sector. The data, in fact, support this assumption at least for trends in employment of SCs in government services and public sector undertakings after 1990. It is observed that during the pre-reform period *i.e.* between 1956 and 1990 there has been a steady increase in the employment of SCs in government services. The absolute number as well as the percentage of SCs/STs in government jobs and services improved until 1990.

After July 1990, the new measures have led to decline in employment of SCs in government services and jobs. The absolute number of SC employees has gone down from 6.28 lakh in 1991 to 6.04 lakh in 1992. There was also decline in the percentage share of SC employees between 1991 and 1992.

Identical trend is observed in employment of SCs in public sector undertakings. Since the beginning of the reservation in this sector there has been a considerable improvement both in absolute numbers and percentage share between 1970 and 1990. However, the representation varied across types of services. The representation of SC was much below the required quota in grade 'A' and 'B' services. There was a concentration in Grade 'C' and 'D' jobs. As a result of the new measures, however, the recruitment of SCs has gone down substantially. The absolute number of Scheduled Caste employees in public sector undertakings has declined from 4.32 lakh in 1990 to 3.69 lakh in 1992 (Table 11.11). Their percentage share has also

Table 11.10 : Representation of Secheduled Castes in Government Jobs

Year	*No. of SCs*	*Percentage*	*Percentage Change*
1956	212754	14.98	—
1957	253308	13.87	– 17.30
1958	215940	12.38	17.30
1959	223124	12.12	3.22
1960	228497	12.42	2.35
1961	235968	12.40	3.17
1962	267001	12.62	11.76
1963	283208	12.83	5.58
1964	298369	13.17	5.08
1965	311425	13.28	4.19
1966	316073	13.38	1.47
1967	334744	13.39	5.58
1968	341010	13.18	1.84
1969	359943	13.62	5.26
1970	291874	13.09	– 23.32
1971	360042	13.34	18.93
1972	370584	13.48	– 2.84
1973	340938	13.99	– 8.70
1974	395453	13.67	13.79
1975	408879	13.84	3.13
1976	421685	14.18	4.69
1977	441463	14.61	1.64
1978	448713	14.81	4.23
1979	467712	15.12	4.89
1980	490592	15.64	– 0.08
1981	490194	15.19	6.27
1982	520994	16.67	2.90
1983	536037	16.35	– 1.21
1984	529573	16.03	7.13
1985	567356	16.32	– 2.85
1986	551161	15.95	– 0.78
1987	555471	16.18	– 2.08
1988	543905	16.30	4.54
1989	568600	16.41	3.78
1990	590108	16.97	6.54
1991	628709	17.20	3.87
1992	604347	17.12	– 2.91

Source : SC/ST Commission Report, Delhi, Various Years.

declined from 19.54 in 1990 to 17.74 per cent in 1992. This decline has occurred more prominently in 'B', 'C' and 'D' grade jobs. Thus the burden of the fallen employment has fallen on the relatively poor among the scheduled castes.

In public sector banks, the negative trend in employment of SCs has not yet set in.

The analysis indicates that the reservation policy has helped the SCs in getting access to jobs in government services, public sector undertakings and public sector banks. At least at the aggregate level their recruitment has been in proportion to their share in population. But after 1990, *i.e.* after the introduction of the new economic measures which are aimed at privatisation and reduction in the role of government, the employment of SCs has declined both in absolute numbers and in proportion. The new measures, thus, have reversed the positive trends set in since 1956.

Impact on Poverty

Poverty ratio as estimated by Expert Group Method shows that generally rural poverty has steadily declined during pre-reform period, from 56.4 per cent in 1973-74 to 34.4 per cent in 1989-90, but after 1990-91 poverty level increased sharply during the first 18 months of the reform period from 35.0 per cent in 1990-91 to 44.00 per cent in 1992-93. This upward trend was reversed as poverty declined marginally to 37.5 per cent in 1993-94. Thus the post-reform trends in rural poverty do not suggest any improvement, the initial impact of stabilisation / structural adjustment package was adverse particularly in rural areas.

Two different explanations are offered for increase in rural poverty during post-reform period. Tendulkar and Jain (and others) do not attribute sharp increase in rural poverty between 1990-91 and 1992-93 to reform *per se* but to fall in agricultural output by 2 per cent between 1990-91 to 1991-92, which in turn is due to bad monsoon and higher post-reforms inflation. Sen (1996), however, differs with Tendulkar and Jain. Sen argued that the decline in poverty till during 1980s (upto 1987) was mainly due to significant improvement in rural-non-farm employment (as agricultural employment growth has been quite sluggish) which drove real wages up and caused poverty to decline. The non-agricultural growth led to a betterment in the condition of labourers during the 1980s. And in turn, this was largely due to increase in government expenditure and due to the availability of government cheap credit to the small scale industries. The onset of stabilisation and structural adjustment programme has led to large decline in rural non-farm employment pushing millions of self-employed and casual rural non-agricultural workers to agriculture, thus reducing per worker income in agriculture. Thus, Sen believes that the massive increase in rural poverty by over 60 million people in the first 18 months of reform was to a very large extent a direct result of stabilisation structural adjustment policies. The decline in rural poverty between 1992-93 and 1993-94 supports this assumption as there was a restoration of public cuts and with the result a rise in rural non-farm employment—both of male and female (Only exception being share of female in tertiary sector).

Where do the Scheduled Castes stand in this situation? The poverty ratios are available for SCs only for the year 1983 and 1987-88 and, therefore, like employment/unemployment we cannot know the trends after 1987-88.

Table 11.11 : Representation of Scheduled Castes in Public Sector Undertakings

Year	*No. of SCs*	*Percentage*	*Percentage Change*
1970	40640	7.24	—
1971	59108	9.26	45.44
1972	103416	12.70	74.96
1973	198273	16.89	91.72
1974	218142	16.39	10.02
1975	236810	17.25	8.56
1976	275362	17.47	16.28
1977	283248	16.85	2.86
1978	300405	17.29	6.06
1979	317401	17.44	5.66
1980	318204	17.08	0.25
1981	335441	17.23	5.42
1982	338347	17.25	0.87
1983	267043	18.08	8.48
1984	371625	18.10	1.25
1985	395622	18.94	6.46
1986	399382	18.86	0.95
1987	414539	19.42	3.80
1988	423879	19.50	2.25
1989	428491	19.57	1.09
1990	432890	19.54	1.03
1991	365421	16.98	- 15.59
1992	369834	17.74	1.21
1993	371022	17.88	
1994	364252	18.02	

Source : SC&ST Commission Report, Various Years, Delhi

Table 11.12 presents the poverty ratios, total and by household types for rural and urban areas for the SCs and others. In 1987-88 half of the SC population was below poverty.The ratio was as high as

Table 11.12 : Percentage of Persons below Poverty Line by Household Type for each Social Group, 1987-88

Category	*Self Employed Agriculture*	*Self Employed in Non-Agriculture*	*Agriculture Labour*	*Non-Agriculture Labour*	*Others*	*All*
Rural						
SC	41.26	41.6	59.77	46.49	29.98	50.05
ST	52.51	47.22	68.28	59.02	23.41	51.32
N-Buddhist	37.51	29.56	65.63	43.33	38.31	55.12
Others	27.68	31.42	53.3	34.45	19.26	34.37
All	31.59	36.58	57.51	43.62	21.87	39.06

Category	*Self Employed*	*Regular Wage Earner/ Service*	*Casual Labour*	*Others*		*All*
Urban						
SC	61.48	43.69	73.45	56.84		56.98
ST	47.29	43.09	76.81	49.49		51.51
N-Buddhist	36.06	45.08	87.77	33.61		53.92
Others	43.14	25.26	70.11	32.21		37.21
All	44.34	28.25	71.49	37.96		40.12

Source : Employment Survey, NSSO, 1987-88.

55.12 per cent for the neo-Buddhists. The poverty level was indeed high compared to 39.06 per cent among the other group (*i.e.* non-SC/ST). The incidence was 60 per cent in the case of agricultural labour followed by 50 per cent in non-agricultural labour. The ratio was relatively lower for persons engaged as self-employed in agriculture and self-employed in non-agriculture sector (about 41per cent each). However this was much higher than the other groups.

In urban areas the poverty ratio among SCs was higher than their counterpart in rural areas (57 per cent). By comparison this was much higher compared to other group (*i.e.* 37.21 per cent). The incidence was quite high among the casual labour in urban areas (73.45 per cent). The incidence was also particularly high among the casual labour of neo-Buddhists group (87.23 per cent).

In 1987-88 around a quarter of the poor people in the country belongs to Scheduled Castes. The absolute number works out approximately to 49.41 million persons, out of the total of 213.10 million poor persons in the country in 1987-88. In 1993-94 there were about 244.86 million poor persons in rural areas. If we assume that the poverty ratio of SC did not change much or if at all changed it may have declined only marginally. Under this assumption then the 25 per cent of 244.86 million work out to about 55.15 million persons. This means there was an addition of about 57 to 60 lakh poor people in rural areas among SCs in a period of five years *i.e.* between 1987-88 and 1993-94.

Besides, there is an addition to urban poor as well. In 1987-88 the urban poor belonging to SC constitutes about 16 per cent of the total poors in the country which comes to a total of about 11.16 million persons. Assuming that the urban poverty among SC also remained constant or declined only marginally, the absolute figures of urban poors belong to Scheduled Castes and neo-Buddhists roughly comes out to be 12 to 13 millions. Thus in 1993 the tentative number of total poors among the Scheduled Castes could be somewhere between 65 to 68 million persons.

Privatisation, Market and Caste Based Discrimination

One of the important aspects of NEP is a move towards privatisation. The general economic philosophy is to depend more on the market forces, thus minimise the public sector and fill the vacuum by private sector. The underlying presumption is that economic organisation based on state intervention leads to inefficient allocation and utilisation of economic resources. There is a whole lot of discussion regarding state failure versus market failure with regard to their economic role. The problem is posed in terms of choice between state failure and market failure, or in terms of complementary role of the state and the market rather than as a substitute.

In the context of mega move towards privatisation (not only in area of production, infrastructure, but also in large number of social services such as education, power, communication etc.) and their channelisation through market, the issue of market failure became important. In the shift towards marketisation the economists talk about market failure referring to the economic situations such as presence of monopoly/oligopoly or what is called "imperfect market", externalities, public goods and merit goods. They also refer to what is called "information failure" of the market. There are other perhaps even more important market failures. For example, reliance on market often generates inflation, unemployment and poverty and income inequality (Bhaduri and Nayyer 1996).

While these market failures are discussed, not much is being talked about the market failures that specifically relate to the scheduled castes. The Scheduled Castes not only suffer from the various market failures referred above and quite surely more extensively than others, additionally they suffer from the market failures which arise out of the caste and untouchability based discrimination (and hence from the lack of access) in factor and product market. The economists have barely began to talk about this, but perhaps not realising the serious implications for the scheduled castes, in the context of privatisation and withdrawal of the state as well as the planning process under the NEP.

But before we discuss the nature of market failure associated with caste based discrimination, let us try to understand the imperfection observed in factor market in general. We take an example of labour market as it is important for the Scheduled Castes. Does the recruitments in the private organised sector indicate efficient and equitable working of labour market?

Discussing about the working of labour market institution in India, Papola (1992) made some important observations. Discussing the role of Employment Exchange (EE) (which increased from only 75 in 1947 to 850 in 1991), Papola observed that the "EE has been responsible for bringing about some change in the system of recruitment in the organised sector: from chaotic and highly personalized, unfair system towards, with a degree of orderliness, impersonal methods and fairness". The effectiveness of EE has been rather limited in total industrial employment as notification of vacancies by employees through EE declined to 70 per cent from 83 per cent between 1947-53 to 55 per cent in 1980s.

Thus, not all vacancies are notified through EE and thus the recruitments through the informal channels are common. Predominance of the informal or particularistic modes of recruitment are found to be common in Indian factories. Studies on Pune, Bombay, Ahmedabad and Coimbatore clearly bring out that "contact and influence dominate the scene".

The important results of these studies are as follows :

(a) In over two-third cases, the workers got information about availability of the jobs from friends, relatives and neighbours. Employment Exchanges were the sources for 1.5 per cent persons in Bombay, 10.6 per cent in Coimbatore, 20 per cent Ahmedabad, and 25 per cent in Pune who had registered with employment exchanges. Newspaper advertisements provide information about their jobs to 1.5 per cent in Bombay, 2.2 per cent in Pune, and 10.6 per cent in Coimbatore.

(b) Jobs were secured on the basis of recommendation or introduction by friends, relatives and persons of the same region and caste, (generally employee of the same factory), 67 per cent of cases in Pune, 61 per cent in Ahmedabad, Bombay and Coimbatore. Placement through EE accounted for 2 per cent of jobs in Pune and Ahmedabad.

This reveals that informal channel are predominantly used in about the 60 per cent of the cases because they turn out to be efficient from the point of view of employer but are highly iniquitous from the point of employees.

Where do the scheduled castes stand in this situation? The access to employment market to the scheduled caste persons in the private organised sector is likely to be much lower. Given the high level of recruitment in this sector through "informal channels" and given the inadequate access to the network of opportunities for the scheduled castes due to powerlessness, the discrimination in their case on general count might be of a high order. However, besides the high probability of general discrimination, the scheduled castes suffered in the private employment market specifically due to discrimination based on the caste and untouchability.

There is likely to be very little disagreement in pointing out the role of caste and untouchability as one of the most important sources of discrimination and segmentation. Caste-untouchability based discrimination is the most obvious form, which is used as strategy of exclusion from certain labour markets and jobs.

That discrimination leads to segmentation has been amply proved by the nature of their occupation. There are limited number of studies which tried to examine the caste-untouchability based discrimination in the labour market. But very few attempts were made which examine the caste-untouchability based discrimination in other factor market such as land market (in purchase and leasing of land), capital market, information trade, and inaccess to social services such as housing, education, sanitation etc.

The statistics on land ownership, employment, unemployment, wages, credit do provide some evidence in favour of caste-based discrimination and segmentation in private sector. The official statistics presented in the earlier section do indicate that the incidence of landlessness is higher among the SCs as compared to non-SC/ST. Similarly the proportion of agricultural labourers in 1991 was 50 per cent among SCs and only 20 per cent among non SC/ST. The percentage of cultivator among them was 33 per cent but 55 per cent among Non-SC/ST. The magnitude of marginal farmers among them was 73 per cent. This was quite high compared to 50 per cent among others. Due to high landlessness and near landlessness the incidence of wage labour household among them was nearly 63 per cent but only 31 per cent among others. So segmentation in employment in the case of SC workers was quite clear as large section of them are concentrated in unskill-manual labour in rural areas.

The statistics on wage rate from Rural Labour Enquiry revealed the possible presence of discrimination in the payment of wages. The daily wage paid to SC labour in agriculture was relatively lower compared to other labour in 8 states in 1964-65 and 1973-74, in 4 states in 1983-84 and in 9 states in 1987-88. Similarly the wage paid to SC labour was lower in rural non-farm activities in 8 states in 1964-65, in 12 states in 1973-74, in 15 states in 1983 and in 7 states in 1987-88. (Das, Minakshi, 1996).

The discrimination in employment is reflected in higher unemployment rate among them. The unemployment rate (based on current daily status) in 1977-78 and 1983-84 of SC male works out to 6.73 per cent and 7.16 per cent compared to only 3.90 per cent and 4.03 per cent for others respectively. Similar gap has been observed in the case of access to social amenities (Kundu 1994).

Caste-based Discrimination: Implication for Growth and Discrimination

The caste based discrimination in so far as it excludes or reduces the access of scheduled caste persons to various factor market *i.e.* labour, land, capital, information and social service sector it has implications on the earning capacity, employment and income of the Scheduled Castes. In that sense it is inhibitive to economic growth and income distribution. (Kaman 1994). It is inhibitive of the objective of distribution because discrimination and segmentation exclude people in having access to employment and other income earning assets. This leads to exclusion from opportunities for maximization of income and economic welfare in private sector.

This is in fact is the base for reservation policy for scheduled caste/scheduled tribe in India in only one segment of organised sector *i.e.* public sector jobs. This constitutes, however, only around 3 per cent of total employment. The move for privatisation on large scale will reduce even this small component in future and will further expose the Scheduled Castes to the discrimination in private sector.

The growth implication of discrimination in labour market and other factor markets are not as easily appreciated a argument based on distribution. (Kannan 1994). The policies aimed at economic growth could be adversely affected by discrimination and segmentation mainly (a) by reducing effective demand in the economy due to lack of purchasing power with discriminated group (and hence generate stimulant for output growth); and (b) by *lack of qualitatively better human resources with good education and skill due to pre-market, discrimination particularly in access to education.* This would affect the productivity and production as only limited number of human resources are available for production purposes. In so far as affirmative action provides opportunities to discriminated group (although on a limited scale) to develop capabilities and skill it helps the productivity in the country to raise further.

Thus the caste based discrimination and segmentation in factor markets in organised private sector are incompatible with the objective of growth and distribution which are pursued under large scale privatisation as part of NEP.

Role of the State

Given this type of market failure what is indeed required is more state intervention and not less to make the access to labour, land, capital markets and access to various social services more open to the discriminated groups. In fact the economic role of the state has to be redefined in the view of the known situation of market failure and state failure. There is a view which contradict the position that government should not participate in economic organisation because (a) the government has no money, and (b) the public sector organisations generally use resources inefficiently.

Bhaduri and Nayyer argued that large scale government spending is in fact essential and such spending either by way of borrowing or deficit financing will be non-inflationary and sustainable as long as (a) the real rate of growth of the economy (or investment money) is greater than real rate of interest at which government borrows, (b) government spending is directed to economic and social infrastructure facilities, (c) government not only spends effectively but also mobilises resources effectively.

They argued that the rate of growth of economy in real form will be higher than real rate of interest if (a) government spendings are shifted from consumption to investment, (b) government's public investment should be used in the creation and development of physical infrastructure particularly power, transport, communication, irrigation and also in social consumption, such as education, health, etc.

The increase in productivity of public expenditure, therefore, requires a meaningful restructuring of public sector to raise its efficiency and productivity. It is argued that there is no unique relationship between ownership and performance. The efficiency of an enterprise is determined more by compilation in the market structure and competence in the management than by nature of its ownership. Thus it is essential to expose public sector firms to compilation in the market. Similarly it is crucial to provide the management of public sector enterprises with an autonomy and follow it up with an accountability.

REFERENCES

Bhaduri, Amit and Nayar Deepak (1995), *Intelligent Persons Guide to Liberalization,* Penguin.

Papola, T.S., "Labour institutions and economic development in India (1992)".

12

ECONOMIC REFORMS AND POOR IN RURAL PUNJAB

Sucha Singh Gill and Jaswinder Singh Brar

India has adopted vigorous economic reforms under the structural adjustment programme since July 1991. The economic policy has witnessed a quantitative and qualitative shift both in the micro and macro contexts. The role of the state in the economic sphere has substantially been curtailed. The state-oriented economic regime, constructed over the last four decades, has been transformed into the market oriented one. To ensure growth and efficiency, the market forces have become the prime movers in resource allocation. The new economic policy has increasingly been designed and toned up in such a manner so as to facilitate the integration of Indian economy into the world economy. The process of privatisation, liberalisation and globalisation has touched every type of economic activity because of the structural interdependence of the production, distribution and consumption channels. The policy has far reaching implications for the agricultural and rural sector of the economy. More than a half of the decade has passed since the introduction of the economic reforms, time is appropriate to assess the impact of reforms on the living standards of the people. The present study is an attempt in that direction. It deals with the impact of economic reforms on the rural poor in the Punjab. For this purpose this chapter has been organised into six parts. The first part deals with the economic reform measures. The second part specified the general approach, data base and methodology of the study. The third part is concerned with the employment status and earnings of the various sections of the rural poor. The changes in consumption pattern have been analysed in part four . In the fifth part the role of public safety nets have been discussed. While the last section sums up the major observations.

I

Economic Reform Measures and Rural Economy

Economic reforms have differential impact on the various sections of the society. When the process of economic reforms gained considerable momentum, there were conflicting reports about the net impact of the adjustment process on the extent of poverty, both in the rural and urban areas (Sen, 1996). The economic policy measures are ultimately translated into price and income changes. The efficacy of market based reforms is doubted amidst the skewed distribution of income, substantial poverty and unemployment of the labour force. Apprehensions have been expressed in various studies about the social costs of economic reforms (Singh, 1993). The benefits of market reforms to an individual person or household or any other economic unit, whatsoever may be, depends upon the extent of the one's participation in the market. If the income does not move with corresponding changes in the general prices then it affects the consumption standards adversely. The burden of marketisation is more felt by weaker and vulnerable sections of the society.

Agriculture works as the hub of the rural economy. Agriculture being a state subject it was not directly touched by policy changes. Most of the state governments avoided changes in land legislation, tenancy and ceiling laws etc. But the macro policy changes have a very broad sweep leading to changes in some critical areas which have direct implications for the agricultural sector and its bearing on rural population. The rural poverty, employment opportunities, supply and market prices of foodgrains and agricultural production are deeply interconnected (Tendulkar, 1995). The economic reforms have considerable direct and indirect, positive and negative impacts on rural areas. The measures like reduction of industrial protection both tariff and non-tariff, devaluation, fertilizers subsidy reduction, fall in the public investment in agriculture, increase in the issue price of public distribution system and decline in allocations for anti-poverty central schemes have far reaching implications for rural areas (Dev, 1995).

The rural economy of the agriculturally advanced states like Punjab is highly commercialised. The agriculture of the state has observed a very high growth rate after the introduction of new production technology and experienced green revolution in mid sixties. The human and animal power based agricultural operations have been replaced by the machines operated with electricity and fuels (Kahlon, 1976 and Chadha, 1986). The power operated machines speeded up the agricultural operations and resulted in the double and even triple cropped area. The cropping intensity stood at 180.9 in 1993-94. The development process in agriculture progressively replaced the family labour by hired labour. The proportion of agricultural labourers in the total workforce is around 40 per cent. A large number of labourers migrate into the state from East U.P. and Bihar seasonally. Majority of agricultural labourers work as casual labourers and only a small proportion of them are employed on yearly contract basis. A large number of agricultural labourers work as casual labourers on non-farm activities within and outside the rural areas in the lean period in agriculture. The annual contract basis labourers negotiate advance receipt of the yearly wages and also get interest free loans to meet their day-to-day requirements. The casual labourers work on piece rate basis both in cash and kind and sometimes on daily cash wage rates. The whole system of production has been changed from traditional *(Jajmani)* to modern one, establishing relationship between cultivators and labourers as those between employer and employee.

From the last few years it has been reported that the agriculture of the state has reached a plateau. Near saturation in agricultural production along with rising production costs have severely affected the profitability in agriculture. The prices of various inputs like fertilizers, insecticides, weedicides, agricultural machinery and diesel have increased at the fast rate. The adverse terms of trade of agricultural sector *vis-a-vis* the non-agricultural sector have further suppressed the income of the agriculturists. The agricultural operations require a very high amount of working capital. The commercialisation and mechanisation of agriculture has established a linkage between the commodity market, credit market and labour market with cultivator as the central and linking factor (Gill, 1996). The amount of loans available from the organised sector for the working capital requirements of the agricultural operations are not enough. So the farmers resort to borrowing from the informal sources at exorbitant rates of interest. Thus the economic reforms, which have affected the input or output prices, immediately affect the agricultural production, rural income and employment, consequently the agricultural labourers and artisans also. The state being agriculturally most advanced in the country and production operations being mechanised and commercialised the impact of policy changes is expected to be more pronounced. The effect of the reforms are to be reflected in terms of days of employment and wage rates for agricultural labourers and artisans and their consumption pattern (Gupta, 1995).

II

General Approach and Methodology

In order to decipher the impact of economic reforms on the poor a survey has been conducted in the rural area. The study covers the two districts of the state named Patiala and Fatehgarh Sahib, purposely selected. These two districts represent the wheat-paddy cropping pattern which is the dominant cropping pattern of the state. The study covers the five years of the post-reform period from 1991 to 1995. There are 9 developmental blocks in Patiala district and 4 developmental blocks in Fatehgarh Sahib district. Out of these 3 blocks, the data have been collected from 10 blocks. Out of the 10 blocks, 7 blocks in Patiala and 3 in Fatehgarh Sahib were identified. Further, one village in each block was selected. The selection of the village was guided by the living connections of the investigating team with the village. The general information about the village in terms of the infrastructure, basic health and educational services was collected. Attempts have been made to understand the dynamics of the village economy as a unit. Information from the elected village chief have been collected about the type of facilities being provided by the government during the study period.

The survey was carried out during the months of February and first week of March 1996. The method of group as well as individual interviews have been used. The individual interviews were semistructured and a questionnaire was used for the purpose. The information reported in this chapter forms actually the part of a wider study conducted to assess the impact of economic reforms on the agriculture sector as such and rural land, labour and credit markets. This chapter focuses on the impact of economic reform exclusively on the agricultural labour and artisans, *i.e.* the landless section of the village community. The results have been reported for 67 agricultural labourers and 21 artisans. Out of 67 agricultural labourers, 47 were casual agricultural labourers and 20 as regular/ contractual agricultural labourers working on yearly basis with fixed annual cash as mode of payments. The term artisans have been used in a broad sense including the vendors, petty shopkeepers, weavers, carpenters, iron smith, scavengers, rickshaw pullers and shoe-makers etc. Due to short time span of the study it was not possible to make an indepth analysis of the extent of quantitative change in the consumption pattern. But the attempt was made to capture the direction of change. The results are indicative in nature.

III

Employment and Earnings

The employment data is collected in terms of the actual number of working days in a year during the study period. From Table 12.1, it is evident that out of 47 casual agricultural labourers, 37 (78.72 per cent) reported no change in thc days of their employment. But 6 casual labourers reported increase, whereas 4 casual labourers have reported somewhat decrease in the days of employment. However the employment of 20 regular agricultural labourers have remained the same during the study period. This emerges from the nature of their employment. The case of artisans is not different from that of the casual labourers. As many as 16 (76.19 per cent) out of 21 artisans reported no change in their days of employment, 3 artisans reported some increase in their employment, while 2 artisans reported some decline in the number of working days. Thus, it can be concluded that there is no change in the quantum of employment. The situation of no change in employment can be explained by two factors. First, the time period is short to capture any change. Secondly, in dynamism of the fast growing economy of Punjab it is difficult to capture employment changes in one sector. Any decline in employment is likely to attract low number of migrant labourers without changing employment of the locals. At the same time many labourers go on shifting their place (within rural urban setting) and nature of work (agricultural and non-agricultural).

Table 12.1 : Number of Respondents Reported Change in Employment : 1991-1995

Employment Status	*Increase in employment*	*Decrease in employment*	*No Change in employment*	*Total no. of respondents*
1. Casual Labourers	6	4	37	47
2. Regular Labourers	-	-	20	20
3. Artisans	3	2	16	21
Total	9	6	73	88

From Table 12.2, it is clear that the average annual earnings of agricultural labourers/artisans have been growing every year at current prices. The level of average annual earnings of regular labourers has remained higher than those of casual labourers, but remained below than that of the artisans. But in order to get the real earnings, the current price earnings have been deflated by the cost of living index of agricultural labourers/artisans with base at 1991. From Table 12.3, it becomes clear that the average annual earnings in real terms in case of regular labourers have been rising since 1991. But in case of casual labourers there was a sudden spurt upward in the year 1992 over 1991, when the earnings increased from Rs. 5500 in 1991 to Rs. 6105 in 1992 and subsequently declined continuously end reached to Rs. 5720 in 1995. Thus increase in annual earnings negotiated by casual labourers has not been enough to compensate the cost of living. On the contrary the regularly employed labourers have been able to negotiate real rise in their earnings. Hence, the two size classes of agricultural labourers experienced opposite changes in real earnings. The average annual earnings of regular labourers have been higher than the casual labourers by 43.57 per cent in 1995. The average

Table 12.2 : Average Annual Earnings of Agricultural Labourers/Artisans (in current prices, rupees)

Year	*1991*	*1992*	*1993*	*1994*	*1995*	*No. of labourers*
Category						
a. Regular Labourers	6900	7350	7700	9509	11035	20
b. Casual Labourers	5500	6851	7020	7404	7686	47
c. Artisans	9310	9680	9548	10943	12049	21
d. Weighted Average of (a+b)	5903	6994	7215	8009	8650	–

Table 12.3 : Average Annual Earnings of Agricultural Labourers/Artisans (in constant prices, rupees)

Year	*1991*	*1992*	*1993*	*1994*	*1995*
a. Regular Labourers	6900	6550	6622	7566	8212
b. Casual Labourers	5500	6105	6037	5891	5720
c. Artisans	9310	8626	8212	8707	8966
d. Weighted Average of (a+b)	5903	6332	6205	6372	6437

earnings of both the casual and regular labourers in real terms increased from Rs. 5903 in 1991 to Rs. 6437 in 1995. However, the position of rural artisans, who work as agricultural labourer in peak season in agriculture, is better compared to both of the casual and regular labourers in absolute terms. From the table, it is evident that at current prices the earnings of artisans increased from Rs. 9310 in 1991 to Rs. 12049 in 1995. But in real terms, their earnings declined from Rs. 9310 in 1991 to Rs. 8966 in 1995. No doubt, during the last two years of study, *i.e.* 1994 and 1995, their earnings recovered slightly, but remained lower by 3.69 per cent of 1991's level. The fate of casual labourers and artisans is similar, because of the similarity in their employment. If we exclude the regularly employed agriculture labour who in the total sample of 88 constituted around 22.72 per cent, then the casual labourers and artisans have been facing a decline in their level of income in the wake of reforms.

IV

Consumption Pattern

The impact of economic reforms on the consumption pattern of the various groups of respondents have been measured in terms of the exclusive disappearance of some items from the consumption basket, disappearance of some items and reduction in the use of some other items, simply reduction in the use of some items and no change in the normal consumption. From Table 12.4, it emerges that as many as 33 labourers (*i.e.* 49.25 per cent) have reported that no change occurred in their general daily consumption pattern during the study period. The change in consumption pattern in the form of exclusive disappearance of some items, disappearance of some items accompanied by reduction in the use of some other items and simply reduction of consumption of some items without inclusion or exclusion of others is felt by 34 labour households *i.e.* 50.75 per cent of the total. But the table reveals that 6 households of agricultural labourers *i.e.* 8.96 per cent, have dropped certain items from their consumption. While 7 labour households (10.45 per cent) have partly reduced the consumption of some items and completely dropped others from their consumption basket. As many as 21 households (31.34 per cent) have reduced the consumption of some items during the study period.

Table 12.4 : Change in Consumption Pattern of Agricultural Labourers/Artisans

Category of Change	*Number of Labourers*	*Number of Artisans*
1. Some items disappeared	6 (8.96)	5 (23.81)
2. Some items disappeared, consumption of others reduced	7 (10.45)	1 (4.76)
3. Reduction in consumption of some items	21 (34.34)	5(23.81)
4. No change	33 (49.25)	10 (47.62)
Total	67 (100)	21 (100)

Note : Figures in parentheses are percentages of the total.

So far as the artisan households are concerned, majority of them have experienced a negative change in the consumption. The number of such households is 11 (*i.e.* 52.38 per cent) against the 10 households (47.62 per cent) experiencing no change during the study period. The 5 households (23.81 per cent) have experienced a decline in the consumption of some items. Whereas one household (*i.e.* 4.76 per cent) has experienced disappearance of some items accompanied by the decline in the consumption of others. But 5 households (*i.e.* 23.81 per cent) have experienced the disappearance of some items from the consumption basket.

The items disappeared from the consumption basket are pulses, sugar, butter oil, meat and liquor. The sugar has been replaced by gur. The items of reduced consumption are pulses, vegetables, edible oils, butter oil, and in few cases of milk, clothes and sugar also.

The general feeling among the respondents was that these items have become very costlier because of steep increase in their prices in recent years. Pulses are fast becoming beyond the reach of agricultural labourers and artisans. It must be emphasised that pulses are the only source of protein in the diet of common man. In no case reduction of foodgrains in consumption was experienced during the study period. The change in consumption pattern towards decline indicate that the bottom sections of rural society *i.e.* agricultural labourers and artisans have been put in tight condition. These may be termed as victims of recent policy changes, having adverse impact on the rural area of Punjab.

V

Public Safety Nets

For the protection and upliftment of the poor, the government has started a number of schemes, both at the central and state levels. Some schemes are specifically rural poor oriented while some others are for the overall infrastructural development of the rural economy. The schemes like Unnat Gram, Mid Day Meal in schools, Public Distribution System (PDS), Mahila Mandal, Community Bio-gas Plants and Integrated Child Development Scheme (ICDS) are for the entire village community. The rural poor can avail of these facilities as the part of the rural society. The programmes like Jawahar Rozgar Yojna (JRY), Indira Awas Yojna (IAY) and Integrated Rural Development Programme (IRDP) are specially for the weaker sections. Under the IAY, a lump sum grant is given to the landless poor for the construction of the houses in the rural areas. The IRDP is specifically the rural poor oriented scheme. Under this, the yellow card holders have been provided concessional loans and other facilities to start the productive activities. The programme essentially is aimed at the assets generation on the part of the poor so that they could be provided with long term sources of income.

From the survey, it emerged that the above mentioned schemes are not running in proper manner. *Ad hocism,* irregularities of grant sanction and lack of general awareness have reduced the effectiveness of the schemes. In one district, no grant under the JRY and IAY has been provided in the last year of the study. Further, from the survey it becomes clear that the formulation of various schemes from the top are not consistent with the ground realities. The inter-state differences in terms of level of development, wage rates, per capita incomes, consumption patterns and general socio-cultural set-ups must be taken care of while deciding the various parameters of the developmental schemes. In case of JRY, the approved rate of wages was exactly half of the prevailing market wage rates. It poses a great difficulty in running the schemes. This requires the manipulation of accounts. A worker actually employed for one day, in papers has to be shown employed for two days. Moreover, in majority of the cases, a contractor is employed in the construction of streets or drains who brings his own labourers both local and migrant and are shown to be employed under the JRY. Thus, the actual number of mandays generated would be significantly lower than that of reported in the papers.

The mid-day meal for school children have been started only in two out of nine developmental blocks in Patiala district. But it has not been started in the other district yet. Ironically the mid-day meal scheme has been totally diverted from its actual objectives. Students did not get the prepared meal in the premises of the school. Instead, they have been provided the grain as such which they brought at home and is shared by the whole family. One of the objectives of the mid day meal scheme was that it would work as catalyst for the increase in enrolment rate or reduction in the drop-out rates. The lack or absence of requisite infrastructure such as crockery and cooking staff is the major problem in providing the prepared meal in the school. In the case of PDS, the subsidized sugar and kerosene oil is indiscriminately available to the whole of the village inhabitants. However, during the study period the food subsidy especially for the poor has not been made available.

Even if there is no leakage of funds under the target oriented schemes for the rural poor, the possession of yellow card is compulsory. This scheme was introduced in early 80s. From Table 12.5, it is evident that among the sampled households only 43.28 per cent of the agricultural labourers and 33.33 per cent of artisans were having yellow cards. In fact the yellow cards have been issued in a partisan manner because of the peculiarities of the village power structure. Besides, some of the poor have lost their cards while families which came into existence at later years could not avail of this facility. It must be noted that the actual operation of the safety nets programme is much below the desired level. The IRDP has been availed of by 20 per cent of agricultural labourers and 24 per cent of the artisans. The mid-day meal programmes in schools has been availed of by 4 per cent of agricultural labourers and 14 per cent of artisans. JRY has helped only 3 per cent of the agricultural labourers and 10 per cent of the

Table 12.5 : Number of Rural Poor who availed of the Schemes

S.No.	*Name of the Scheme*	*Agricultural Labourers*	*Artisans*
1.	PDS*	63 (94)	21 (100)
2	IRDP	13 (20)	5 (24)
3.	Mid Day Meal	3 (4)	3 (14)
4.	JRY	2 (3)	—
5.	IAY	3 (4)	2 (10)
6.	Flood Relief	2 (3)	1 (5)
7.	Mahila Mandal	—	1
8.	ICDS	—	—
9.	Yellow Card	29 (43.28)	7 (33.33)

* Sugar and Kerosene only.

Note : Figures to parentheses are rounded and are percentages of the total of each category of beneficiaries.

artisans. Flood relief has benefited to small proportion of agricultural labourers and artisans. The respondents reported almost nil benefits from Mahila Mandals. None in the sample benefited from ICDS. In this way, it becomes clear that the role of public safety nets in the rural areas has been peripheral and it does not cover a vast section of the rural poor.

VI

Concluding Observations

From the above discussion of economic reforms and its impact on rural poor certain observations can be made. The marketisation of hitherto state-oriented economic activities has created a difficult situation for the larger sections of masses. The impact of the reform process on employment of agricultural labourers and artisans is neutral. It may be due to the past faster growth momentum of the economy of the state. The workers got almost similar number of days of employment. But the impact of reforms on consumption standards is adverse. The workers both casual and regular in agriculture and artisans have reduced the consumption of certain items, and even they had stopped the use of some items altogether. The decline in consumption standards need urgent attention because the quality of work force is the real determinant of the growth of a nation. The public safety nets programmes have been initiated to avoid or minimise the social costs of reforms. But the performance of public safety nets is very dismal and much below the desired level. It has been observed that they have been totally digressed from their intended targets and have bypassed the majority of the target groups. The *ad hocism,* uncertainty, lack of awareness, laxity on the part of administration and virtual absence of voluntary associations in rural areas have reduced the effectiveness of the different schemes. The public safety nets programmes designed on the basis of all India averages are of no use for advanced states like Punjab. The rural poor expect a greater and better role from the government in the public safety nets.

REFERENCES

Chadha, G.K. (1986), *The State and Rural Economic Transformation :* The case of Punjab 1950-1985, Sage Publications, New Delhi.

Dev, S.M (1995), "Economic Reformıs and Rural Poor", *Economic and Political Weekly*. Vol. XXX, No. 33, August 19, pp. 2085-2088.

Gill, Anita (1996). Interlinked Agrarian Credit Markets in Punjab : Exploitative Yet Growing, *Economic and Political Weekly,* Vol. XXXI, No. 10, March 9, pp. 586-588.

Gill, S.S (1990), *Migrant Labour in Punjab* (Miemo), Department of Economics, Punjabi University, Patiala.

——, (1994), *Economic Development and Structural Change in Punjab : Some Policy Issues,* Principal Iqbal Singh Memorial Trust. Ludhiana.

—— (1996). *Unionisation* of *Agricultural Labour* : *Punjab Experience*, Mimeo, Department of Economics, Punjabi University, Patiala.

Gupta, S.P. (1995), Economic Reforms and its Impact on Poor, *Economic and Political Weekly*, Vol. XXX, No. 22, June 3, pp. 1295-1313.

Kahlon, A.S. (1976). Impact of Mechanisation on Punjab Agriculture with special reference to Tractorization, *Indian Journal of Agricultural Economics*, Vol. 21, October-December.

Sen, A. (1996), Economic Reforms, Employment and Poverty : Trends and Options, *Economic and Political Weekly*, Vol. XXXI, No. 35-37, Sept., Special Number, pp. 2459-2477.

Sidhu, H.S. (1991), *Agricultural Development and Rural Labour* : *A Case Study of Punjab and Haryana,* Concept Publishing House. New Delhi.

Singh, A.K. (1993), Social Consequences of New Economic Policies with Particular Reference to Levels of Living of Working Class, *Economic and Political Weekly,* Vol. XXVIII, No. 7, Feb, 13, pp. 279-285.

Singh, Manjit (1995), *Uneven Development in Agriculture and Labour Migration* (A case study of Bihar and Punjab), Indian Institute of Advanced Studies, Shimla.

Tendulkar, S.D. and L.R. Jain, (1995), Economic Reforms and Poverty, *Economic and Political Weekly,* Vol. XXX, No. 23, June 10, pp. 1373-1377.

13

REGIONAL DEVELOPMENT DISPARITIES AND ECONOMIC REFORMS IN INDIA

Ashok Mathur

Introductory Background

When India became independent in 1947, it inherited from its colonial masters an economic legacy which had many negative features. But it was not completely devoid of certain positive assets, particularly when compared to a number of other third world countries which in the years to follow emerged from foreign rule. Among the latter one could include the inheritance of an efficient administrative and legal system, some basic, components of infrastructure like railways and road system, a rudimentary public health system which had been able to bring under control the periodic visitation of major epidemics, at least a neucleus of some factory industry like the Jute and Cotton Textiles and a few other lines of industrial production. On the other side of the balance sheet was the very meagre impact of these positive developments in relation to the total size and population of India. Agriculture, which was the mainstay of the bulk, had been grossly neglected. Consequently, apart from a very low level of average per capita income, the economic structure of the country was highly lop-sided in two directions. First, as is well known, it was highly tilted towards the primary sector, with only a small proportion of the income, and even more so employment, being contributed by the secondary and tertiary sectors. And the primary sector—mainly agriculture—had abysmally low levels of productivity.

Secondly, whatever limited changes in the positive direction which had taken place during the British period were not evenly distributed among different parts of India. The chief beneficiaries of the port oriented railway network were the three port centres—namely

Table 13.1 : State Per-Capita Income and their Ranks

State	1950-51 at 60-61 prices NCAER	1960-61 at 60-61 prices NCAER	1970-71 at 70-71 prices SSB	1980-81 at 70-71 prices SSB	1989-90 at 80-81 prices SSB
(1)	(2)	(3)	(4)	(5)	(6)
Andhra Pradesh	258	289	585	647	1770
Rank	11	13	10	8	10
Assam	335	428	535	558	1650
Rank	6	7	13	12	12
Bihar	181	222	402	441	981
Rank	17	17	17	17	17
Gujarat	381	403	829	904	2629
Rank	3	4	3	4	4
Haryana	364	396	877	1060	3193
Rank	5	5	2	2	3
Himachal Pradesh	270	283	651	711	2098
Rank	10	10	6	6	6
Jammu & Kashmir	227	248	548	642	1954
Rank	16	16	12	10	8
Karnataka	287	313	641	687	2109
Rank	8	9	8	7	5
Kerala	304	326	594	621	1560
Rank	7	8	9	9	14
Madhya Pradesh	236	293	484	517	1909
Rank	15	11	16	15	16
Maharashtra	373	480	783	957	3281
Rank	4	2	4	3	2

(Contd..)

(Contd...)

(1)		(2)	(3)	(4)	(5)	(6)
Orissa		252	268	485	477	1557
	Rank	13	15	15	16	15
Punjab		444	485	1070	1354	3658
	Rank	2	1	1	1	1
Rajasthan		256	272	645	337	1705
	Rank	12	14	7	13	11
Tamil Nadu		245	344	581	584	1864
	Rank	14	6	11	11	9
Uttar Pradesh		271	292	486	519	1512
	Rank	9	12	14	14	13
West Bengal		471	462	722	793	1958
	Rank	1	3	5	5	7

Note : Estimates of per capita income of Himachal Pradesh, Jammu & Kashmir, Haryana and Punjab for 1950-51 and 1960-61 have been derived by assuming that the same relative distance related between them in 1950-51 and 1960-61 as in 1970-71. Admittedly, estimates for these states for the first two periods are less reliable. Assumptions had to be made for estimating figures for 1989-90 in respect of Madhya Pradesh, for which data are available only at 1970-71 prices, and for four states for which 1988-89 data were available.

Calcutta, Bombay and Madras—and some of the urban centres lying along the main arterial routes. The bulk of hinterland in fact suffered the backwash effect and deindustrialisation through decline of the old centres of well-established traditional handicraft industries which had to face the onslaught of unhindered inflow of imported manufactured goods. The impact of substantial amount of foreign (British) capital which was invested in the plantation sector, was again regionally confined to the north-eastern part of India. The canal colonies of the Punjab made a visible impact on foodgrain output, but only in northern India. Spread of industries to some of the newer centres of manufacturing in South India during the earlier part of present century was again confined primarily to a few centres like Coimbatore and Madurai.

Thus, on the eve of independence, India had not only an economically backward economy, but one that was highly differentiated regionally with a patchwork of some islands of development around nodal points of growth in port towns or a few other commercial and administrative centres having linkages with the metropolitan economy in Britain (See B. Chattopadhya & Moonis Raza, 1975). The focus of this chapter is on the course of developments on the regional front during the post-independence phase in India. At first stage this chapter examines as to what extent the era of planned development has been able to rectify distortions in some of the important dimensions of regional development. At the second stage it explores the likely regional impact of changes in the main contours of economic policy during the era of economic reforms.

Trend of Regional Incomes

Trends in the levels of regional development measured in terms of per capita State Domestic Product (SDP) have been investigated by a number of scholars, including the present writer. Two main points emerge from these researches :

(1) If one compares ranking of the major states in terms of their per-capita S.D.P. at the beginning of the planning era (1950-51) and in the contemporary phase, the top four of five states and the lowest four or five ranking states have remained roughly the same, though with some minor changes of ranks within each category. This is evident from

Table 13.1, based on an earlier paper of the present author (1994) covering the period 1950-1990 and Table 13.2, based on AK. Singh's paper (1997) which portrays the position up to 1994. As may be observed between 1950-1990, Punjab, Maharashtra and Gujarat continue to be among the top four. The only visible change is the sliding down of West Bengal out of the top four category and moving in of Haryana into the top four category. This new composition of the top four states is the same in 1994.

Table 13.2 : Per-capita SDP of 1991-94 at 1980-81 Prices

State	*Triennium Average*	*Rank*
A.P.	1777	XII
Assam	2030	IX
Bihar	1135	XVII
Gujarat	2489	VI
Haryana	3454	III
Himachal Pradesh	2126	VII
J & K	1775	XIII
Karnataka	2288	V
Kerala	1955	X
Madhya Pradesh	1666	XIV
Maharashtra	3679	II
Orissa	1567	XVI
Rajasthan	1804	XI
Tamil Nadu	2275	VI
Uttar Pradesh	1600	XV
West Bengal	2081	VIII

Source : A paper by Ajit Kumar Singh (1997)

The category of 'lowest four' has continued to contain within it Bihar and Madhya Pradesh. The distinct movement out of this category has been that of J&K, which moved up from 16th to 8th rank by 1990, but thereafter has slid back to 13th rank by 1994 (Table 13.2), presumably reflecting the impact of disturbances in the State. Orissa remained in this category till 1989-90; but 1991-94 estimates for this state show it to have moved up to 10th rank. In the overall scenario, these rank changes do not add up to very much.

(2) Rank changes, however, are not a very sensitive indicator of the direction of change in the regional development

scenario. For a more precise portrayal, one can either make a recourse to inter-regional indices of per-capita SDP or some measure of inter regional disparity in per capita SDP. Here we consider the weighted co-efficient of variation of per capita SDP of the major states. For the period up to mid-sixties, interpretation of the trend is not identical among different authors. This partly reflects the greater degree of data problems during the earlier years. The present author, among other scholars, found some evidence of a decline in regional income disparity in this earlier phase of development after the initiation of development (See Ashok Mathur, 1983). However this trend did not continue subsequently and after mid nineteen-sixties almost all scholars have found evidence of an increase in regional income disparity This is quite evident from Table 13.3, which has been reproduced from author's earlier paper (1994), except the last entry for 1993-94,

Table 13.3 : Spatial Variability of Inter-State Per Capita Incomes (SDP) : Estimates of Weighted Co-efficient of Variation (C.V)

Year	*C.V. at 1960-61 Prices(1)*		*C.V. at 1970-71 Prices (2)*	*C.V. at 1980-81 Prices (3)*
1950-51	26.7	NCAER data	-	-
1955-56	23.5	NCAER data	-	-
1960-61	24.2	NCAER data	-	-
1964-65	19.6	CSO data	-	-
1965-66	24.6	SSB data	-	-
1970-71	24.7	SSB data	-	-
1975-76	27.2	SSB data	28.23	-
1980-81	30.2	SSB data	31.35	29.52
1985-86	29.4	SSB data	30.52	30.21
1986-87	30.3	SSB data	31.43	-
1988-89	32.5	SSB data	-	31.72
1989-90	27.9	SSB data	-	27.31
1993-94	—	SSB data	-	35.03

Source : Mathur (1994) and A.K. Singh (1997) for last row.

Note : It may be noted that in the first column all the estimates of co-efficient of variation are not at 60-61 prices, since data at 60-61 prices are not available right through up to 1989-90. What has been done is to adjust the actual 1980-81 to 1986-87 estimates at 70-71 prices in the same ratio as that between 1975-76 C. V. estimates at 60-61 and 70-71 prices. A similar approach was used to estimate 1988-89 and 1989-90 C.V. figures at 1960-61 prices on the basis of data at 1980-81 prices.

which is based on A.K. Singh's paper (1997). Although there are fluctuations, the rising overall trend of regional income disparity is unambiguous.

A.K. Singh has also estimated the ratio of maximum-minimum gap over the years. This simple but very expressive measure brings out the magnitude of rising disparity, the ratio having moved up almost continuously from 1.90 in 1960-61 to 3.61 in 1993-94.

Sectoral Disparities

Among single indicator measures of regional development, per capita SDP is perhaps the best. But it is not adequate by itself. Special disparity in terms of its sectoral components may not all be moving in the same direction. Therefore, we may next examine the behaviour of regional disparities in primary, secondary and tertiary sectors. Estimates of sectoral SDP per capita are given in Table 13.4, which is based on author's earlier work (1994). There are two main points which emerge from these trends.

Table 13.4 : Inter-Temporal Trend of Sectoral Co-efficients of Variation of Per Capita SDP

Year	*Primary Sector*	*Secondary Sector*	*Tertiary Sector*	*Base Year*
1961	17.23	57.05	38.70	at 60-61 prices
1966	19.07	52.90	38.93	at 60-61 prices
1971	25.55	52.80	38.58	at 70-71 prices
1976	24.64	53.17	50.01	at 70-71 prices
1981	29.20	53.36	41.62	at 70-71prices
1986	35.77	48.74	40.34	at 70-71 prices
1981	52.70	69.18	53.59	at 80-81 prices
	(29.20)	(53.36)	(41.62)	adjusted to match 70-71 prices data at 80-81 prices
1986	62.81	77.04	66.18	adjusted to match 70-71 prices data at
	(34.80)	(59.42)	(51.40)	80-81 prices
1989	50.72	63.73	53.32	adjusted to match 70-71 prices
	(28.10)	(49.16)	(41.41)	data at 80-81 prices
1990	47.70	55.72	51.16	adjusted to match 70-71 prices data at 80-81 prices

Source: Estimated from State Statistical Bureaus (SSB) data published by CSO in annual volumes of Estimates of State Domestic Product and Capital Formation. State Population for respective years as estimated in these publications, are used as weights for deriving weighted C. V.

(1) First, within the primary sector, which primarily reflects the agricultural scenario, the regional disparities have been on rise since mid-sixties This is essentially a consequence of the regionally differentiated impact of the seed-fertiliser technology which was more successful in those areas which were already agriculturally better off. They had resources to meet the more demanding needs of the new agricultural technology in terms of irrigation and credit requirements. There is some evidence that this tendency might have got reversed after mid-eighties. Estimates of co-efficient variation have been prepared by the author only up to 1990. The last row in Table 13.4 shows a decline of co-efficient of variation for 1990 compared to 1976. If one places this evidence together with state-wise rates of agricultural growth during 1983-95 (Table 13.5), which are based on G.S. Bhalla's research work (1997), this trend appears to have continued into the nineteen-nineties. Rajasthan and West Bengal, which were previously agriculturally poor performers reveal a visible upward movement in their agricultural growth performance, attaining the first and second rank respectively during the decade upto 1992-94. Hopefully, this phase may mark a turning point in the regional agricultural income disparities from an upward towards a downward movement. In fact co-efficient of variation of agricultural growth across states, according to G.S. Bhalla's research project emerged to have declined to 45 per cent during 1983-95 from 85-86 per cent during the two previous decades. If this is sustained, it would play a significant role in helping to bring about a decline in overall regional income disparities in the country.

(2) The second main point which emerges from Table 13.4 is that regional disparities in the secondary sector, which means primarily the industrial sector have shown some indication of a decline since sixties. Although this trend has not been consistent on a year to year basis, and all commentators about the scene may not be unanimous in their interpretation, this broad declining trend appears to the author to be quite evident. In the initial phase inter-state distribution of public sector investment in industries played an important role in bringing about this trend since some

Table 13.5 : Regional Agricultural Growth Rates : 1983-95

State	*Agr. Growth Rate p.a. (%)*	*Rank*
1. Andhra Pradesh	3.08	VIII
2. Assam	2.15	XIII
3. Bihar	2.08	XIV
4. Gujarat	1.90	XV
5. Haryana	4.71	III
6. Himachal Pradesh	2.20	XII
7. J &K	0.33	XVII
8. Karnataka	3.92	VI
9. Kerala	2.24	XI
10. Madhya Pradesh	4.71	IV
11. Maharashtra	2.87	IX
12. Orissa	1.15	XVI
13. Punjab	3.87	VII
14. Rajasthan	5.02	II
15. Tamil Nadu	4.59	V
16. Uttar Pradesh	2.83	X
17. West Bengal	5.39	I
(C. V. %)1983-95	45	—
(C. V. %)1973-83	86	—
(C.V. %)1965-73	85	—

Source : G.S. Bhalla, 1997.

of the major industrial projects in the core sector were located in industrially backward states like Orissa, Bihar, Madhya Pradesh and Andhra Pradesh. Beyond seventies, the character of Public sector investments shifted towards petroleum and chemical based industries. These could better flourish in areas where infrastructure and supporting industries already existed. Consequently, even the public sector investment tended to shift towards more developed states. This reduced the impact of Public sector investment on the decline of regional industrial disparities (see V.K. Seth, 1987). However, the spread of small and tiny scale industrial units has been regionally more diversified. Consequently, spatial diversification of the overall industrial sector appears to exhibit a positive trend during much of the nineteen-eighties. This is despite the fact that large Private industrial investment, as revealed by Industrial Licensing data, and industrial credit provided by Financial Institutions like IDBI, IFC, have been regionally distributed in a regressive manner, a larger share going to the more developed states. Whether the changes in current economic policy scenario shall tend to promote or retard this trend is an issue to which we shall turn shortly.

Trends in Regional Poverty Scenario

At this stage, let us see the impact which the above regional disparity trends and various target-oriented programmes of the government have been able to exercise in influencing the well-being of that chunk of population which survives near or below the subsistence level. The poverty alleviation programmes of the government, despite various limitations which have often been pointed out, have no doubt helped to bring about a decline in the proportion of population surviving below the poverty line—both in rural and urban areas. This would be true irrespective of whatever methodology is used to estimate poverty, as long as the same methodology is applied to successive rounds of NSS data. Although the proportion of rural population afflicted by poverty has been higher in rural areas than in urban areas between 1973-74 and 1987-88, the decline had been sharper in the rural areas (from 56.44 per cent to 39.06 per cent) than in urban areas (from 49.23 per cent to 40.12 per cent). Consequently, over the country as a whole, rural-urban disparity in terms of the incidence of poverty shows a tendency towards decline up to 1987-88. However, during 1987-94, the urban poverty declined at a faster rate as compared to rural poverty rate, having declined to 37.27 per cent in rural areas and 32.36 per cent in urban areas by 1993-94 (Press Information Bureau, 1997).

However, when we look at the incidence of poverty across the regions whether within the rural or within the urban segment—the story is not rosy. As argued quite forcefully by A.C. Julka and P.K. Sharma in their paper (1991) a few years back, it is the better off states with superior implementation capacity, which have been able to achieve higher rates of decline of poverty than the less developed states. Consequently, over the years, the co-efficient of variation of poverty ratios across the states has widened both in rural and urban areas. According to estimates given in S.R. Hashim's paper (1996) which in turn are based on the Report of the "Expert Group" of the Planning Commission, this regional co-efficient of variation increased from 22.85 per cent to 40.37 per cent in the rural segment, and from 26.52 per cent to 46.78 per cent in the urban segment during 1973-1988.

Regional Disparities in Infrastructure Development

Per capita SDP and poverty ratios look at the level of well-being and its broad distribution among two groups—the 'poor' and 'non-poor'. However, in order to better comprehend the scenario of overall disparities in regional development, it is imperative to examine the trends in growth of infrastructure, since it plays a key role in promoting the process of regional development. It is to this dimension that we now turn. The attention is focused here on three basic components of infrastructure, namely irrigation, power and road transport. The analysis of this section is based on results presented in an earlier paper of the present author (1994).

Table 13.6 gives the absolute as well as rank position of each state in terms of these components of infrastructure at two points of time, 1961 and 1989. The influence exercised by these on the level of regional development measured in terms of per capita income may be gauged from the rank correlation between these infrastructure variables and per capita income given below for two points of time :

		Correlation Co-efficient	
		1961	*1989*
1.	SDP per capita and irrigation	+ 0.19	+ 0.28
2.	SDP per capita and installed generating capacity	+ 0.72	+ 0.68
3.	SDP per capita and power generation	+ 0.66	+ 0.63
4	SDP per capita and road length	+ 0 30	+ 0.19

As may be seen, the strongest influence among the infrastructure variables considered here is exercised by power availability. Irrigation and road length are correlated to per capita income to a much lesser extent.

The extent of regional disparity in case of these infrastructure variables and whether their behaviour over time follows a pattern similar to that of per capita income disparity is brought out by Table 13.7, which gives a co-efficients of spatial variation in these variables. As may be observed, disparity among the states is much higher in case of road infrastructure compared to that in case of the other variables. It is higher in case of power generation compared to installed power capacity which is a reflection of sub-optimal usage of the installed capacity in many states. We return to this point shortly.

Table 13.6 : State-wise Infrastructural Development

State	1961 Area Irrigated (%)	1961 Installed capacity per lakh person	1961 Power Generation per lakh person	1961 Road length per 100 sq. km.	1989 Area Irrigated (%)	1989 Installed Capacity per lakh person	1989 Power Generation per lakh person	1989 Road length per 100 sq. km.
Andhra Pradesh	29.38	0.7	2.8	19.90	35.84	6.2	2.2	43.55
Rank	4	13	11	11	7	6	5	10
Assam	23.63	0.2	0.3	24.02	15.07	2.1	0.4	66.33
Rank	7	17	17	9	14	17	17	4
Bihar	18.56	0.7	3.2	46.55	36.31	2.2	0.4	37.11
Rank	11	11	10	3	6	16	16	11
Gujarat	7.51	1.7	6.5	13.10	28.88	9.7	3.7	28.30
Rank	15	4	5	13	8	4	4	14
Haryana	29.20	2.7	10.9	28.06	65.66	11.0	3.8	49.51
Rank	5	1	1	8	2	2	3	7
Himachal Pradesh	15.61	0.7	0.9	5.98	17.35	3.1	1.3	34.01
Rank	12	12	15	16	13	15	13	12
Jammu & Kashmir	38.07	0.6	1.1	4.73	41.06	3.4	1.4	6.91
Rank	3	15	14	17	5	14	11	17
Karnataka	9.22	0.8	4.6	32.62	18.05	6.8	2.0	51.98
Rank	14	8	7	7	12	5	8	6
Kerala	21.83	0.8	3.8	50.27	13.92	5.1	2.1	71.06
Rank	8	7	8	2	15	9	7	1
Madhya Pradesh	5.16	0.8	2.1	8.45	13.41	5.6	2.1	16.78
Rank	17	9	12	15	16	7	6	16

(Contd....)

(Contd...)

State		1961				1989			
		Area Irrigated (%)	Installed capacity per lakh person	Power Generation per lakh person	Road length per 100 sq. km.	Area Irrigated (%)	Installed Capacity per lakh person	Power Generation per lakh person	Road length per 100 sq. km.
Maharashtra		6.48	1.9	9.1	16.58	11.98	10.9	4.2	47.76
	Rank	10	3	2	12	17	3	2	8
Orissa		18.65	0.7	3.4	20.08	23.31	4.6	1.3	67.76
	Rank	10	10	9	10	10	11	12	3
Punjab		41.1	1.4	5.2	35.64	91.00	14.5	6.3	65.06
	Rank	2	6	6	5	1	1	1	5
Rajasthan		12.49	0.3	0.5	12.04	21.29	3.5	1.3	19.46
	Rank	13	16	16	14	11	13	14	15
Tamil Nadu		44.20	1.6	7.4	35.98	47.51	5.2	1.7	98.52
	Rank	1	5	4	4	4	8	9	2
Uttar Pradesh		25.43	0.6	1.7	33.64	48.62	3.9	1.1	31.09
	Rank	6	14	13	6	3	12	15	13
West Bengal		21.51	2.1	7.8	73.82	23.92	4.9	1.4	46.36
	Rank	9	2	3	1	9	10	10	9
All India		18.34	1.1	4.4	23.93	30.43	6.8	2.4	28.31

Disparity in terms of area irrigated has tended to increase since 1961. The increasing disparity is one of the important factors behind the trend of increasing disparities in the agricultural sector, to which attention has been drawn at an earlier stage in this chapter. Irrigation is an important area where policy measures are needed to bring about greater regional spread. The picture is somewhat brighter in case of installed capacity for electric power generation. Here the disparity appears to have declined after 1961 though there has been some increase during the last decade. However, in case of actual power generation, after an initial decline during sixties, the regional disparity has subsequently been on the rise. And for purposes of economic performance, it is actual power generation which is more important.

Table 13.7 : Regional Disparity in Infrastructure (Co-efficient of Variation in Percentage Form)

		1961	*1971*	*1981*	*1989*
1.	Area irrigated (%)	55.17	63.82	66.73	65.52
2.	Installed capacity per capita	64.68	56.15	52.81	57.93
3.	Power generation per capita	75.97	61.56	68.19	70.73
4.	Road length per 100 sq. km.	66.86	104.06	101.49	102.40

In the context of spatial disparity, it is of interest to examine the pattern of growth of infrastructure of the states. Annual growth rates of each infrastructure variable considered by us are given state-wise during the period 1961-89 in Table 13.8. At the all-India level these growth rates are given separately for each decade towards the end of the Table 13.8. Looking at the inter-state picture, one finds that states which have done very well in terms of growth of one item of infrastructure have not always done equally well in terms of others. In irrigation the best performers is that of Gujarat followed by M.P., Haryana and Punjab. In case of power the best performers are Assam followed by Himachal Pradesh and Rajasthan, which are all within the category of less developed states. At the other end of the spectrum of power growth are states like West Bengal and Gujarat, whch are well-developed states, although Bihar, a backward state, is also at the lower end of the spectrum of power growth.

Table 13.8 : Annual Growth Rates of Infrastructure (1961-89)

State	*Gross Irrigated Area*	*Installed Power Capacity*	*Power Generation*	*Road Length*
Andhra Pradesh	0.79	9.42	9.29	2.87
Rank	14	4	6	7
Assam	0.28	10.75	11.51	2.07
Rank	16	1	3	10
Bihar	2.22	5.53	2.93	0.80
Rank	11	16	17	16
Gujarat	4.89	8.21	8.39	2.96
Rank	1	7	8	6
Haryana	3.69	7.08	6.55	2.04
Rank	3	13	14	11
Himachal Pradesh	3.36	6.81	11.55	9.02
Rank	5	14	2	1
Jammu & Kashmir	1.14	8.30	11.37	0.13
Rank	13	6	4	14
Karnataka	2.61	9.48	7.19	1.67
Rank	8	3	12	13
Kerala	0.89	8.01	7.85	6.20
Rank	17	11	10	2
Madhya Pradesh	4.34	8.90	10.62	2.47
Rank	2	5	5	8
Maharashtra	2.53	8.14	7.38	3.84
Rank	9	9	11	4
Orissa	2.30	8.19	6.70	4.43
Rank	10	8	13	3
Punjab	3.40	8.00	8.58	2.17
Rank	4	12	7	9
Rajasthan	2.86	10.37	14.11	1.73
Rank	6	2	1	12
Tamil Nadu	0.00	5.58	4.52	3.66
Rank	15	15	15	5
Uttar Pradesh	2.85	8.02	8.30	0.27
Rank	7	10	9	15
West Bengal	1.20	4.65	3.90	1.61
Rank	12	17	16	17
All India	2.38	8.29	8.06	2.12
1961-71	3.28	11.35	11.05	2.11
1971-81	2.53	8.19	8.20	8.11
1981-89	1.06	4.71	4.25.	0.28

Finally, one would like to examine the extent to which growth of these three infrastructural components can be taken to explain inter-state variations in rates of growth of SDP. For this purpose the correlation of rates of growth of SDP with infrastructural rates of growth are given for the period 1961-89 in Column (1) of Table 13.9.

Table 13.9 : Growth Rates 1961-89

	1	2
Gross Irrigated area	+0.48	+0.47
Installed power capacity	+0.37	+0.55
Power Generation	+0.17	+0.57
Road Length	-0.19	-0.43

The correlations in case of power variables are less strong than what one would expect. This is a phenomenon which was discussed by the author in an earlier study (1987). It was argued there that in assessing the role of infrastructural variables one has to incorporate the initial availability ratios. One of the reasons for this is the fact that if one starts from a small base, the growth rate tends to get magnified and vice-versa. Such a distortion needs to be corrected and for this purpose adjusted growth rates of infrastructure have been estimated which magnify or compress actual growth rate of a state depending upon whether that state was high up or low down in terms of its initial availability of any particular item of infrastructure. The procedure adopted for this purpose involved three steps, the first of which was to convert the actual growth rates of infrastructure and the initial availability ratios of 1961 (as given in Table 13.6) into an index form, treating all-India growth rates and initial availability ratios of each infrastructure equal to 100. These indices were then averaged to yield a composite index of growth and initial availability for each state. The actual infrastructured growth rates were then multiplied by this composite index to obtain what may be called adjusted infrastructural growth rates. These incorporate 'initial availability effect'.

Column (2) of Table 13.9 gives correlations of growth rates of SDP with the adjusted infrastructural growth rates. As may be seen, the adjusted growth rates of power infrastructure variables show considerable improvements over the correlations of non-adjusted growth rates of power variables. The improvement is particularly evident in case of power generation. In case of irrigation, unlike the results obtained in the earlier study of author (1987) pertaining to an earlier period, the present correlation does not reveal any improvement after conversion to adjusted growth. One of the reasons responsible for this could be that irrigation has been correlated in the above analysis with overall growth rate and not growth rate of agriculture, which was done in earlier study.

In order to study the collective influence of above infrastructural variables, regressions of output growth *(g)* on the adjusted infrastructural growth rates for the period 1961-89 are given below :

$$g = 2.40 + 0.005\ IRA + 0.018^{**}\ IPCA - 0.006\ RLA$$
$$(0.89) \qquad (2.5) \qquad (1.97)$$
$$F = 5.02^{***}......,\ \bar{R}^2 = 0.43^{**}............ \quad (1)$$
$$g = 2.29 + 0.005\ IRA + 0.019^{***}\ PGA - 0.007^{***}\ RLA$$
$$(0.97) \qquad (4.01) \qquad (2.27)$$
$$F = 0.34^{***};\ \bar{R}^2 = 0.50^{***}................ \quad (2)$$

Where

IRA denotes adjusted growth rate of irrigated land
IPCA denotes adjusted growth of installed power capacity
PGA denotes adjusted growth rate of power generation
RLA denotes adjusted growth rate of road length
&* indicate significance at 0.05 and 0.01 level respectively.

The difference between equations (1) and (2) lies in the fact that whereas the former incorporates growth of installed capacity as an explanatory variable, the latter includes growth of power generation as an explanatory variable. It is the latter equation which yields better results, the regression co-efficient of power generation being significant at 0.01 level.

It may also be noted that regression co-efficient of installed power capacity is less significant than that of power generation. This could be an indication of the fact that optimum utilisation of the installed capacity is not always made. This is quite evident from Table 13.10, which gives state-wise ratios of power generation to installed capacity at four points of time. It may be seen that there is a wide variation in the ratio across the states. This ratio has been low in Assam all throughout. In Bihar, Karnataka, Orissa and West Bengal it was high to start with but has been declining. On the other hand the ratio was poor in J&K, Himachal Pradesh and Rajasthan but has improved considerably over the past three decades. For the country as a whole, there is a small, but continuous decline over the period which is not a good sign.

What is further disquieting is the picture revealed by decade-wise all India rates of growth of infrastructural facilities, which are given at the end of Table 13.8. It may be observed that both in case of irrigation as well as power growth there is a secular decline in the momentum of expansion of these key factors in growth process. Even if this partly reflects the fact that at initial stage, infrastructural growth rates tend to be high when one starts from a small base, it is a segment to which development policy needs to give particular attention.

Table 13.10 : Power capacity utilisation Ratio

States	*1961*	*1971*	*1981*	*1989*
Andhra Pradesh	37.7	48.3	40.5	36.4
Assam	16.2	20.5	22.3	19.6
Bihar	42.2	27.5	27.5	21.0
Gujarat	37.3	46.1	42.4	39.0
Haryana	39.6	36.7	42.1	34.4
Himachal Pradesh	13.2	12.2	34.0	44.6
Jammu & Kashmir	19.6	11.6	38.1	42.8
Karnataka	54.3	54.1	47.1	30.0
Kerala	42.7	39.0	54.7	41.0
Madhya Pradesh	25.2	37.9	9.9	39.0
Maharashtra	46.9	43.1	43.2	38.4
Orissa	43.9	31.3	32.6	29.8
Punjab	37.6	34.8	44.1	43.6
Rajasthan	16.7	27.9	43.8	38.6
Tamil Nadu	45.3	28.7	30.8	34.1
Uttar Pradesh	26.3	42.4	30.3	38.3
West Bengal	36.4	33.5	32.7	29.7
All India	38.8	37.8	37.7	36.4

Economic Reforms and Regional Development

It is in the background of the foregoing trends in regional disparities in development that one can now try to make an assessment of what may be the likely impact of new directions in economic policy which have emerged as a part of the economic reforms package. The reforms had their roots in the latter part of nineteen eighties although they crystallised into their present form only in 1991, As far as the author can see, there are three ways in which one can try to evaluate the possible implications of economic reforms for regional economic disparities. The first approach would be to examine the trend of spatial disparities after 1991 and see if these differ in a substantial way from the earlier trends which have been examined in the preceding portion of this chapter. Apart from the fact that the present author has not as yet made any substantial attempt to investigate the trend of regional disparities in the nineties, the main point is that available data for the nineties would not be of a sufficiently long duration to permit a firm conclusion to be reached.

In view of this, one can approach the issue from two other directions. Among these, one way would be to consider major elements of the economic reforms package and trace the channels through which they could exercise an influence on regional disparities. The third way of approach would be to see whether, on the basis of past experience of regional development, one can identify some link between the presence or absence of components of economic reforms and the earlier observed trends in disparity. The ensuing analysis is based on these two lines of approach.

The economic reforms package rests on two major planks—economic stabilisation and structural adjustment. The former aims at progressive reduction in budget deficits in order to scale down government expenditure to match its resource raising capabilities. The latter is based on the precept that continued state intervention in economic management and sheltered markets result in certain inefficiencies which can be eliminated by bringing about greater reliance upon competitive spirit of the market mechanism.

In order to assess the likely impact of these policy prescriptions on regional development, it is worthwhile to look at some of the key elements of the regional policy as it has evolved in India. Many components of the backward areas development policy were introduced in the light of the Pande Committee and Wanchoo Committee Reports after mid-sixties and during seventies. These components included policy measures like investment subsidies, concessional finance and power tariff, raw-material quotas, investment subsidies, initial tax holiday and reservation of certain lines of production for the small scale sector in the case of investments undertaken in backward areas in order to enhance the attractiveness of such areas for entrepreneurs (see also K.R.G. Nair, 1982 and 1993). It follows from the prescription of greater recourse to the market mechanism that these concessions in favour of backward areas would tend to get progressively withdrawn.

While viewing the implications of this change in the direction of policy, one needs to bear in mind two points. First, it is true that over the years many malpractices had crept into the implementation of these policies resulting in misutilisation of many of the concessions and surreptitious diversion of some of the benefits to areas which are already better developed. Some of these loopholes could be plugged through more effective policy implementation. But there is need for undertaking a comprehensive review of the various backward area incentives packages and to eliminate those which have not served the desired objectives. The second point which needs to be borne in mind is that many of these malpractices, like surreptitious diversion of raw materials to units actually located in developed locations, arise on account of the fact that backward areas do lack certain basic amenities like adequate communication channels, easy accessibility, power, medical and educational training facilities, etc., which figure prominently in entrepreneurial decision making. In fact, the essential edifice of Myrdal-Hirschman divergence hypothesis is that such features of backward areas generate the backwash and polarisation effects of development in an environment of completely unhindered operation of free market forces. It is, therefore, imperative to bear in mind that while greater reliance is placed upon the free market mechanism, economic policy cannot ignore provision of these facilities —a good many of which fall in the realm of basic infrastructure— that determines entrepreneurial attractiveness of backward areas and enhance competitive capability of such areas. Thus, while selective scaling down or elimination of some direct forms of assistance of units located in backward areas may be desirable, these need to be supplemented by steps to enhance the provision of basic infrastructural facilities in the backward regions in order to improve their inherent competitive strength. In the absence of essential infrastructure, achievement of greater productive efficiency of backward areas would be a distant dream.

It is here that implications of the other plank of economic reforms, namely stabilisation policy, becomes important. This plank often necessitates simultaneous scaling down of public investment expenditure on infrastructural facilities. This is an area where one has to be cautious. Economic policy changes which do not provide for adequate availability of power, transport and other social overheads in backward areas, in addition to withdrawal of direct forms of assistance to units in backward areas, are bound to have a twin pronged regressive impact on less developed regions. These could result in deepening of regional disparities even in segments like the industrial sector where there is evidence of progressive regional diversification. Here it is also pertinent to remember that if in the realm of infrastructure investment there is progressive shift towards private investment the private investment is not likely to be driven by the needs of backward area development, but by profitability of these investments in backward areas, where it is bound to be relatively low. Thus infrastructural investment in these areas runs the risk of diminution in the absence of an overall view of development, which generally only a state authority like the Planning Commission can take.

Foreign Investment and Backward Area Development

Another direction in which the economic reforms have ushered in policy changes is that of encouraging inflow of foreign investment to supplement domestic savings through greater openness of the economy. Success to date on this front has been limited. Moreover, portfolio investment, which can be subject to short term reverses, has tended to be more prominent than Foreign Direct Investment (See Amit Bhaduri and Deepak Nayyar, 1996). However, from the point of view of creating production capabilities and imparting growth impulses, it is FDI which is more important.

How far are foreign direct investment inflows even if it is assumed that they would pick up after a time lag likely to aid in development of backward regions? Much of private foreign investment to date has tended to get attracted to consumer goods sector where skewed income distribution in large urban centres assures quick returns. It would be difficult to expect it to gravitate towards the less developed states—particularly if basic infrastructure itself is lacking in these areas. This further reinforces the need for planned injection of infrastructural investment in backward regions, after a careful assessment of the crucial infrastructural bottlenecks in different states.

Moreover, one has to bear in mind that much of private foreign investment tends to be highly capital intensive. That is one of the channels through which it aims at achieving higher levels of efficiency and labour productivity. It follows undeniably that the impact of such investments on the labour market, and more so in the backward areas, is least expected to be in the positive direction. The objective of balanced regional development is one of the least probable outcomes of greater inflow of FDI, even if India succeeds in emulating its East Asian neighbours in attracting substantial inflows on this front.

Economic Reforms and Regional Social Development

Regional economic disparity in terms of per capita SDP, as observed in earlier part of this chapter, has tended to rise over the past three decades or so. In contrast to this, the regional picture in terms of some of the social indicators of development is more promising. A.C. Julka and P.K. Sharma (1991) estimated State-wise Composite PQLI and HDI indices, and found a declining trend in terms of regional disparity in both of these. S.R. Hashim (1996) has presented separately regional disparity coefficients for a few social indicators. His analysis reveals a mixed picture of trends. Regional disparity in terms of some social indicators like male and female literacy and crude death rate does show a tendency to decline, even though in terms of average level of these indicators India fares rather poorly in terms of international comparisons.

Much of social development responsibility devolves on the shoulders of the state. The fact that even for those indicators where overall performance is not very good by international standards, regional disparity has tended to decline, shows one of the positive benefits of state action and the pressures which are exercised in a democratic polity to generate public opinion for action on this front. (see Jean Dreze & Amartya Sen, 1995). If Economic Reforms result in gradual decline of state responsibility in this sphere, it is bound to have adverse repercussions on regional disparity in social development. That is something which policy makers should guard against.

Financial Devolution, Regional Disparity and Economic Reforms

Two major policy instruments through which interests on regional development can be taken care of in a large country with a federal set-up, and have been looked after in case of India, are the statutory awards of the Finance Commission and the Planning Commission grants for the state plans. Initially, size of population of different states used to be a major criterion governing devolution of central taxes to the states. However, over the successive five year periods, especially since the Seventh Finance Commission, formula governing financial devolution to states has been progressively tilted in favour of states having lower levels of development. Consequently, statutory financial devolution to states has been an important instrument for achieving a progressive distribution of financial resources across the country, as brought out in the research investigations of a number of scholars (see K.RG. Nair, 1982; Amaresh Bagchi, 1988; Pradhan Prasad, 1988). The situation in respect of Planning Commission grants, which in fact accounted for a larger chunk of resources transferred by the Centre to the States than that through the Finance Commission, has been somewhat different though not very widely. The Planning Commission grants have also been progressive, implying a larger proportional share to the less developed states, but not as progressive as those determined by the Finance Commission (see Ashok Mathur, 1994).

What is likely to be the impact of economic reforms on this front? If one goes by the logic of economic liberalisation, reforms process would imply that states should progressively be made to rely on their own capabilities in terms of resource generation rather than through the agency of central government intervention. Just as in the free market mechanism the precept is that each unit's fate should be determined by its competitive strength, so in the case of a federal policy, each state should get resources strictly according to its inherent resource raising strength. If one were to go by this interpretation which, one hopes, the policy planners would not accept without due modification—it would imply serious consequence for regional development in the country.

Even under the system of devolution as it has existed over the last few quinquennial, whereas resources transferred from the Centre to the states have been progressive, *i.e.* negatively related to their levels of development, the magnitude of state plan expenditure has been negatively related to the level of development of the States (see K.R.G. Nair, 1982; Sarkar, 1994). This is an outcome of the fact that the plan expenditure of a state depends upon resources transferred from the Centre as well as the States own resources generation. Whereas the former magnitude has been related to the states levels of development in a progressive manner, the latter component bears a regressive relation to level of development of the states. This is a consequence of the fact that resource raising capability, to a substantial extent, is positively related to average level of income of a state, thus creating a scenario in which the better off states are able to raise more revenue to finance their state plans than their poorer counterparts. In a situation of this type, if a new dispensation, as a part of economic reforms, were to modify the devolution formula so as to reduce the quantum of central resources which are transferred to the states on the basis of an inverse relationship to their level of development, this would hit the poorer states, developmental effort quite hard while enforcing the momentum of development in the more developed states.

This is not to argue that states' own efforts at raising resources and implementation of plan programmes should be ignored and that central government's devolution of resources should be entirely an inverse function of its development index and completely independent of state performance. In fact, in the devolution formulae devised by the Finance Commission, there already exists a certain weightage for state's efforts at own revenue generation. What can be reasonably argued is that in order to give better effect to the philosophy of economic liberalisation, an appropriate increase in this weightage is desirable. Similarly, in the modified Gadgil formula (see M. Ramalingam and K.N. Kurup, 1991), which has been broadly governing the central grants for plan expenditure of the different states, some distinct weightage should be given to different states on the basis of success in implementation of projects undertaken in preceding plan. Here the standard practice of judging success in terms of percentage of allocations actually spent needs to be modified. This does not take account of what is actually achieved by the allocated expenditure even if it is fully spent. What is needed is to devise some physical indicators of success in implementation of planned projects and to incorporate them as one of the important elements governing subsequent allocations of grants for state plans. In this form it is possible to retain progressivity of the existing devolution mechanism while incorporating some of the important elements of the economic reforms programme.

Finally, as pointed out in the earlier part of this chapter, state interventions have had some role in helping to reduce regional disparities in the social and industrial sphere. While executing a structural adjustment programme, the responsibilities of the state in social sphere and in creating conditions conducive to industrial investment in the backward areas cannot be ignored.

Note: Estimates of per capita income of Himachal Pradesh, Jammu & Kashmir, Haryana and Punjab for 1950-51 and 1960-61 have been derived by assuming that the same relative distance existed between them in 1950-51 and 1960-61, as in 1970-71. Admittedly, estimates for these states for the first two periods are less reliable. Assumptions had to be made for estimating figures for 1959-90 in respect of Madhya Pradesh, for which data are available only at 1970-71 prices and for four states for which 1989-90 data are available.

REFERENCES

Bhaduri, Amit & Deepak Nayyar, (1996), *The Intelligent Person's Guide to Liberalisation,* New Delhi, Penguin Books.

Bhalla, G.S., (1997), Ongoing Research Project on Agricultural Growth in India, Planning Commission—JNU. For a state level summary, see G.S. Bhalla, "Recent Developments in Indian Agriculture : A State-Level Analysis", *Economics & Political Weekly,* Vol . XXXII, No. 13.

Chattopadhya, B. & Moonis Raza, (1975), "Regional Development : An Analytical Framework and Indicators", *Indian Journal of Regional Science,* Vol. 7, No. 1.

Dreze, Jean & Amartya Sen, (1996), *India : Economic Development and Social Opportunity,* Delhi, Oxford University Press.

Hashim, S.R., (1996), "Regional Disparity in India", a paper presented at the School of International Studies, Jawaharlal Nehru University, New Delhi.

Julka, A.C. & P.K. Sharma, (1991) "Dynamics of Development and Inter-State Disparities in India : A Means-Ends Perspective", Paper presented at a Seminar at the Himachal Pradesh University.

Mathur, Ashok, (1983), "Regional Development and Income Disparities in India : A Sectoral Analysis", *Economic Development and Cultural Change,* April.

Mathur, Ashok, (1987), "Why Growth Rates Differ within India : An Alternative Approach", *Journal of Development Studies* Vol. 23, No. 2.

Mathur, Ashok, (1994) "Regional Economic Development and Policy in India : A *Economic Development,* New Delhi, Har-Anand Publications.

Nair, K.R.G., (1982), *Regional Experience in a Developing Economy,* New Delhi, Wiley Eastern.

Nair, K.R.G., (1993), *Regional Economics,* Research in Economics, Monograph, New Delhi, ICSSR.

Planning Commission, (1993), *Report of the Expert Group on Estimation of Proportion and Number of Poor,* GOI, New Delhi.

Press Information Bureau, (1997), "Estimates of Poverty" (mimeographed), GOI, New Delhi.

Ramalingam, M. & K.N. Kurup (1991), "Plan Transfer in States : Revised Gadgil Formula", *Economic and Political Weekly,* Vol. XXVI, Nos. 9 and 10.

Sarkar, P.C., (1994), "Regional Imbalances in Indian Economy Over Plan Periods", *Economic and Political Weekly,* March 2, 1994.

Seth, V.K., (1987), *Industrialisation in India,* New Delhi : Commonwealth Publishers.

Singh, A.K., (1997), "Inter-State Disparities in Per Capita, State Domestic Product in India : Trends and Causes", Lucknow, Giri Institute of Development Studies.

Section-III

INFRASTRUCTURAL DEVELOPMENT AND INSTITUTIONAL REFORMS

Section-III

14

ECONOMIC REFORMS, HEALTH AND ENVIRONMENT

D.N. Rao

Introduction

Health and environment issues have not been at the focus of the economic reforms in the country. They have often been seen as obstacles in the pursuit of the main goals of economic reforms. The reform process, on the other hand, has had significant impact on these two sectors which may have substantial long run effects. It is proposed to examine some of these in this chapter. The plan of the chapter is as follows. In section II we present the health profile of India which has to be kept in mind while discussing the impact of economic reforms on the health sector. In section III we discuss the key issues in health policy in the country and the salient features of the economic policy regarding environmental problems particularly from the point of view of health concerns and examine the effect of the economic reforms upon them, examine the policy options in these areas and conclude the chapter.

SECTION II

Health Profile of India

India is a signatory of the Alma Ata declaration of 1978 and is committed to attaining 'Health for All' by the year 2000. The National Health Policy which was adopted by the Parliament in 1983 reiterated India's commitment to attain the goal of "Health for All" by 2000 A.D. to ensure improved quality of life. Some of the targets set out in these policy objectives and the corresponding achievements by 1993 are shown in Table 14.1.

The Life Expectancy at birth is about 78 years in developed countries. China has attained L.E. of 68 years by 1993. India and China were at same levels in 1950 but in 1980s China had achieved the targets of HFA.

Table 14.1 : Health for All : Targets and Achievements

Indicator	*Target 2000*	*1995*
Crude death rate	9	10
Crude birth rate	21	29
Infant Mortality Rate	below 60	69
Maternal Mortality Rate (per 100,000 live births)	below 200	437
Life Expectancy at birth	64	62

Source : The World Bank Group Health, Nutrition & Population 1997 for 1995 figures.

Communicable diseases still account for a large number of deaths in India. The annual rate of infection with T.B. is nearly 1.5 per cent, nearly 50 per cent more than the global average. About 150 million cases are identified every year, nearly 3 lakh deaths are caused by this alone. Nearly one million or about one-third of the world's leprosy victims are in India. Diarrhoeal diseases take a toll of more than half a million infants annually. The World Bank and WHO have done joint exercises to compute the loss of mandays lost due to illness. Diseases were classified in 109 categories on the basis of international classification. These categories cover all possible causes of deaths and about 95 per cent of the possible causes of disabilities. The Disability Adjusted Life Years lost in 1990s were estimated at 344 per thousand population for India whereas the corresponding figures were 117 for established market economies and 178 for China (See World Bank, World Development Report, 1993. See also Rao and Bhat, 1991 and 1994). There are considerable regional variations in health status in India. A health status index calculated for different States of India (See Dev and Rao, 1992) showed a variation in the index from a low of 138 for U.P. to a high of 375 for Kerala for the year 1988.

AIDS is emerging rapidly as a serious health problem among certain sections of the population through sexual transmission, drug addiction and unsafe blood transfusion. Malaria is re-emerging. Annual incidence of malaria which had declined substantially from 6.4 million cases in 1976 to less than 2 million cases has again started showing increasing trend in some parts of the country. As fertility declines and life expectancy goes up, the age structure of population over 65 will go up and will have to face rising incidence of non-communicable diseases such as cardiovascular ailments, chronic lung diseases and cancers etc.

Degradation of the environment is reflected in its health impact in a significant manner. The impact of environmental degradation in India on urban and rural health impacts has been estimated by Brandon and Hommann in a study for the World Bank in 1996. Table 14.2 shows some of the costs of health impacts of air and water pollution.

Table 14.2 : Health Costs of Environmental Degradation in India, 1992

Problem	*Low estimate (US $mn)*	*High estimate (US$mn)*	*Average (US$mn)*
Urban air pollution	517	2102	1310
Water pollution	3076	8344	5710

Source : Brandon and Hommann, 1996.

The Brandon and Hommann study has been criticized for its omissions and hence costs could have been underestimated. Given the state of inaction and very little action on the environmental front, the health costs of environmental degradation are likely to rise sharply in the years to come.

Table 14.3 : Index of Environmental Quality in Ten Districts of India, 1988-89 to 1992-93

District	*Index of environmental quality*				
	1988-89	*1989-90*	*1990-91*	*1991-92*	*1992-93*
Jamshedpur	174.41	165.26	157.51	141.29	138.08
Ahmedabad	115.35	112.62	110. 54	108.17	106.10
Mysore	124.56	121.48	119.35	117.12	115.69
Satna	146.21	137.54	131.41	126.99	123.65
Nagpur	120.32	117 .82	115.95	114.38	113.07
Ludhiana	114.08	109.86	108.74	108.09	107.32
Agra	163.72	155.10	147.06	141.29	136.21
Kanpur	164.64	155.56	147.67	141.93	136.94
Calcutta	229.68	216.08	221.99	212.27	212.58
Delhi	102.03	100.00	105.02	103.92	104.00

Source : Purohit and Rao (1994).

An index of environmental quality constructed by the author (Purohit and Rao, 1994) shows that the index has declined sharply in almost all the cities and major towns of the country over the years. The principal determinants of the degradation in environmental quality were found to be the output of industries classified as polluting, density of and vehicles (see Table 14.3). The impact of air pollution caused by vehicular emissions has also been well documented in Slow Murder (CSE, 1997). Diseases of the respiratory tract, cancers and reproductive functions have been correlated with increasing air pollution.

SECTION III

Implication of Economic Reforms for Health Policy

Health is a state subject in the Indian Constitution. The promotive, preventive, curative and rehabilitative services are the responsibility of the state governments. Central government can only intervene to assist and it has done so in many areas such as control/eradication of major communicable and non-communicable diseases through various National Health Programmes, broad policy formulation, international health, medical and para medical education along with regulatory measures, drug control and prevention of food adulteration and family welfare (a euphemism for family planning). The expenditures incurred by the Central government are routed through the state governments under various centrally sponsored programmes. Since India is committed under the Alma Ata declaration to provide 'Health for All' through the Primary Health care approach, a huge network of Rural Health infrastructure comprising about 1,31,900 Sub-Centre, 22,156 Primary Health Centres and 2,377 Community Health Centres (as of 1995) have been set up throughout the country to provide comprehensive health care in the rural areas. The urban health care comes under the purview of local bodies. The general scenario which emerged by late eighties was as follows :

(a) The resources were spread too thin so that the PHCs etc. were inadequately provided with equipment and manpower and not enough funds for drugs etc.
(b) A large number of people were in fact consulting private medical practitioners. India in fact has recorded one of the highest levels of private spending on health care.

(c) Health care delivery system had turned iniquitous when examined when access was measured by utilization of public health facilities because access is limited to workers from the organised sector and the richer sections of the society. The poor have had to contend largely with traditional systems of medicine or self-medication or fall prey to touts etc.

Faced with the general all pervasive resource crunch the health sector has been advocating various reform measures such as :

1. Imposition of user charges in public hospitals,
2. Privatisation of health care provision,
3. Introduction of private health insurance including permission for entry of foreign health insurance companies, and
4. Removal of drug price control.

Imposition of user charges in a society with large number of poor is highly iniquitous and is against the public finance principle of ability to pay. There is a widespread misnomer about the extent of public funding of health care in India. The correct perspective has to be kept in mind before one advocates the introduction of private health insurance. The experience of developed countries with health insurance in terms of its consequences for cost of treatment and medical malpractices cannot be easily ignored particularly in the context of large scale illiteracy and poverty.

During the nineties when there was expenditure compression at the Centre, it was claimed that expenditures on health by the Central government had not been reduced. But in fact, as has been demonstrated by Tulasidhar and others, the expenditures at state level were reduced and as a result there was an overall reduction.

The environmental protection has been based on policy of command and control through the pollution control boards and a scheme of incentives for installation of population control equipment in factories. These policies have been a failure and pollution has increased enormously. An imaginative introduction of market based instruments appears to be the only way out (see Purohit and Rao 1994). Economic reforms have conclusively resulted in :

(a) Import of outdated polluting technology for manufactured goods like automobiles etc. which are being eased out of developed countries.

(b) Import of even waste of developed countries for recycling.

The social cost-benefit analysis of technology or other imports has to be much more alertly done. Considerable research as well as alertness on the part of watchdog bodies like NGOs etc. is warranted.

The menace of vehicular pollution has to be imaginatively controlled (Kumar *et al.*, 1998)

In conclusion one may say that the economic reforms process has left the health sector rudderless and some concerted policy has to be developed in this area. The social safety net which has been much talked about has to be evolved.

REFERENCES

Bardon, Carter and Hommann, Kirsten (1996). "The cost of inaction : Valuing economy-wide costs of inaction in India". Memeo, World Bank.

Centre for Science and Environment : *Slow Murder*, New Delhi, 1997.

Dev, A.K. and Rao, D.N. (1992). 'Determination of the Impact of Policy Variables on Health Status—Inter-State Study'. Memeo, Himachal Institute of Public Administration, Shimla, (Study carried out for WHO).

Kumar, K., Jain, V.K. and Rao, D.N. : A Predictive Model for Noise in Delhi, *Journal of Acoustical Society of America*, Feb. 1998.

Kumar, K., Jain, V.K. and Rao, D.N. : "A Predictive Model for Noise Pollution in Delhi". To appear in *American J. of Accoustics*, February 1998.

Purohit, M.C. and Rao, D.N. : Fiscal Intervention for Environmental Protection : A Cross-Sectional Analysis for Fiscal Prescriptions. Paper presented at the 50th Congress of the International Institute of Public Finance (IIPF), Harvard University, August 1994.

Rao, D.N. and Bhat, R.L. "Estimation of a Community Health status Index on the basis of a MIMIC Model", *The Indian Economic Review*, Vol. 26, pp. 51-65.

Rao, D.N. and Bhat, R.L.: "Health Status– An International Comparison Based on a Community Health Status Index". Proceeding of the Platinum Jubilee Conference of the Indian Economic Association, Bombay, 1994.

The World Bank Group : Health, Nutrition and Population, 1997.

World Bank : World Development Report, 1993.

15

TRANSPORT SECTOR PROBLEMS

A Critical Review of Suggested Solutions

V. Upadhyay

Indian economy is projected to grow at the rate of 6 to 7 per cent per annum in the near future. This implies a doubling of transport output every 7 to 10 years. Our transport system currently is at saturation level. To meet the heavy future transport demand, it is imperative that transport infrastructure is developed at a rapid pace otherwise it is likely to become a constraint on overall economic growth.

In this chapter we attempt to analyse the performance of the transport sector, identify the problems facing this sector and critically evaluate the suggested remedial policy measures. Our focus will be on surface transport (*i.e.* rail and road).

Overall Performance and Long Term Issues

Transport plays a very significant role in the modern economy. It is a crucial infrastructure needed for developmental process. With growing industrialisation and urbanisation, the role of transport sector in the national economy is becoming more and more significant.

There has been a massive traffic growth in our country in recent years. This growth has mainly occurred in the road sector. The share of railways in total traffic has been continuously declining. It is a development of immense significance and it has to be kept in mind while debating future policy options.

In 1980, the National Transport Policy Committee (NTPC or the Pande Committee) had predicted for the year 2000 a modal split of 72 per cent and 28 per cent for railways and roads respectively for inter-regional freight traffic. However, just the opposite seems to be happening in reality.

India was a rail dominant economy in the 1950s. It has now become a road dominant economy. Road transport is the dominant form of transport for people and goods in India. Over 80 per cent of passengers and over 60 per cent of freight move by roads. It is estimated that by the year 2000 road traffic will account for 87 and 65 per cent of passenger and goods traffic, respectively (Government of India, 1997, p. 174).

This development is a matter of concern for several reasons. Rail has many advantages over road. Road transport is energy intensive. Rail is by far the least energy intensive mode. The transport sector in India is the second largest consumer of commercial energy and is the largest consumer of petroleum based energy. In 1990, it consumed 22 per cent of total commercial energy and 43 per cent of petroleum based energy. The railways' consumption of commercial energy (coal, diesel and electricity) is only 4.3 per cent of the total whereas that of the road transport is 18 per cent (World Bank, 1995, pp. 45-46). Furthermore, road transport is exclusively dependent for its energy on petroleum products (petrol and diesel), a significant proportion of which are imported. Since rail is relatively much more energy efficient, big energy savings (as well as foreign exchange savings) can be achieved by using rail to the extent possible for freight and passenger traffic.

Transport requires burning of fossil fuels to produce energy which is a major source of environmental pollution. Road transport is much more polluting than rail transport. The criteria of safety also favours rail against roads. Roads in India have a very high fatal accident rate (about 2.65 deaths per 1000 registered vehicles per year). About 60,000 persons are killed in India every year in road accidents. Train accidents, by contrast, cause far fewer deaths : passenger fatalities due to train accidents are only 100 per year. Land requirements for expansion of capacity are much lower for rail than roads. Expansion of road transport, especially urban transport, causes more involuntary displacement of people and thereby stirs up more opposition from people. Land acquisition related problems (litigations for higher compensations, etc.) are more in case of road projects.

The existing modal shares between rail and road, therefore, do not conform to optimal shares as judged by the criteria of least economic (as well as social and environmental) cost (see Government of India, 1997, p. 171). In order to understand the underlying factors responsible for the shift in modal split in favour of road, we need to look at rail and road sectors in detail.

Rail Transport

The Indian Railways consist of an extensive network spread over 62,915 km comprising Broad Gauge (40,609 km), Metre Gauge (18,501 km) and Narrow Gauge (3,794 km). Electrified network with 12,306 km account for 19.6 per cent of the total route kilometre (Government of India, 1977, pp. 170-171). Since independence, the character of the Indian Railways operation has undergone a significant change. In the 1950s, the Indian Railways operation was freight dominant; it is a passenger dominant operation now. Traffic carried by railways in 1995-96 consisted of 273.9 BTK freight traffic and 341.9 BPK passenger traffic (See Table 15.1). Passenger traffic thus now comprises 55 per cent of rail transport output (One ton km = One passenger-km).

Table 15.1 : Traffic Carried by Railways

Category	*1980-81*	*1995-96*	*% change p.a.*
Good carried (billion ton-km.)	158.5	273.7	3.7
Passenger kilometres (billion)	208.6	341.9	3.3

Source : Economic Survey 1996-97

The Indian Railways in 1995-96 earned Rs. 6,125 crore and Rs. 15,290 crore from passenger and freight traffic, respectively (Government of India, 1997, p. 5-50). Passenger traffic which comprises 55 per cent of output accounts for only 29 per cent of revenues. Freight traffic, on the other hand, comprises 45 per cent of output and accounts for 71 per cent of revenues.

This lack of correspondence between output and revenue structures is due to the system of cross-subsidisation which is pervasive in the Indian Railways. Cross-subsidies are in fact an informal system of taxation and expenditure outside the budget. Cross-subsidies within public infrastructure services emanate from the government's desire to provide cheap food and low cost personal travel facility to common people and from considerations of regional equity. Although inspired by lofty aims, cross-subsidies quite often produce results which are undesirable and sometimes even contrary to the avowed goals.

In India, Rail passenger operation is heavily subsidised at the cost of rail freight operation. Main beneficiaries of the cross-subsidy between rail freight and passenger operations are sub-urban and inter-city rail passengers. An international comparison of freight rates and passenger fares shows that Indian freight rates (purchasing power adjusted) are about double than those of the world's other long haul freight railroads while the passenger fares are the lowest in the world (World Bank, 1995, p.16).

Subsidisation of passenger services is made possible by freight revenue surpluses which the railways generate by negotiating high tariff with the public sector units which are obliged to use rail network for transportation of their products. The net result is increase in the price of important intermediate goods such as coal, steel, mineral oil and cement which have wide economy repercussions.

As discussed above, despite being energy inefficient, polluting and unsafe mode, road transport has been registering continuous increase in its share of freight traffic over the years. If the government policy of using rail freight traffic as a source of surplus revenue generation for the purpose of subsidisation of rail passenger traffic is pursued for long, the railways will eventually lose most of their freight traffic to roads.

There are, of course, several other reasons why private shippers are increasingly preferring the energy inefficient, polluting and unsafe road transport over the railways. One important reason being that the railways are unable to provide dependable, consumer-responsive service. The railways consider their first priority to provide efficient passenger services as a result of which their freight operations suffer. The average speed of freight trains in India is only 22 km per hour and it has remained unchanged since 1970. The container transport services offered by the railways through their subsidiary CONCOR leaves a lot to be desired. All this shows that there is a plenty of room for improvement.

It in recent railway budget for 1997-98, freight rates for all goods, barring 15 essential commodities have been increased by 12 per cent. This increase in freight rates comes on top of 10 per cent increase in freight rates in July 1996. In the past one year, freight rates have thus been increased by 22 per cent. Freight rate increases of this magnitude could, quite likely, become counter productive as they tend to increase inflationary pressures in the economy.

Roads and Road Transport

India has a network of over 2 million km which makes it the third largest road network in the world. However, this network is not adequate for speedy and efficient transportation. Half of this is made up of unsurfaced roads. The National Highways which are arterial routes have currently a network of 34,298 km. Although they carry nearly 40 per cent of the goods and passenger traffic, the national highway network constitutes less than 2 per cent of the total road network (see Government of India, 1997, p. 174; and Table 15.2).

Traffic movement on the highways suffers from frequent stopovers and congestion as almost 15 per cent of National Highways and 75 per cent of State Highways are single-lane roads. Out of the total 165,000 km of National and State Highways, only 2 per cent of their length is four-lane, 34 per cent two-lane and 64 per cent single-lane. As far as National Highways are concerned, 5 per cent of their length is four-lane, 80 per cent two-lane, and 15 per cent single-lane (see Expert Group on the Commercialisation of Infrastructure Projects—The Rakesh Mohan, Committee, 1996, p. 142).

As can be seen from Table 15.2, the road network has expanded at the rate of 3.8 per cent per annum since 1951. Most of the growth however has occurred in the rural road sector (4.18% per annum), 50 per cent of village are, however, still not connected with all-weather roads. There has been very little growth of the main road network. The National and State Highways have expanded at the rate of 1.25 and 1.80 per cent per annum respectively.

Table : 15.2 Growth of Road Network (Km)

Category	*1951*	*1995*	*% change p.a.*
National Highways	19,811 (5 %)	34,000 (2%)	1.75
State Highways	60,000 (15%)	131,000 (6%)	1.80
Other Roads	318,000 (80 %)	1,935,000 (92%)	4.28
Total	**400,000 ((100%)**	**2,100,000 (100 %)**	**3.85**

Note: The figures in parentheses are in percentage of total road network.
Source : Road Development Plan 1981-2000, Indian Roads Congress quoted in the Rakesh Mohan Committee, 1996.

Table 15.3 shows growth of traffic carried by roads since 1951. Road freight and passenger traffic have both expanded at the rate of 10 per cent per annum. Eighty per cent of inter-city passenger traffic is carried by buses which make up 10 to 30 per cent of the vehicular traffic. Several factors such as flexibility, door-to-door service, reliability and tremendous growth in the number of vehicles are responsible for this significant development. Road freight and passenger traffic are expected to reach 800 BTK and 3,000 BPK, respectively by 2001.

Table 15.3 : Traffic carried by Roads

Category	*1951*	*1994*	*2001*
Freight (BTK)	6	350	800 (E)
Passenger (BPK)	23	1500	3000 (E)

E : Estimates.
BTK : Billion Ton Km.
BPK : Billion Passenger Km.

Between 1980-81 and 1993-94, the average annual growth in the number of registered motor vehicles has been above 13 per cent (See Table 15.4). During this period, the number of registered motorised two wheelers has grown at the rate of 16.22 per cent per annum. The number of registered motor vehicles is expected to reach 50 million by 2000. It is predicted that two wheelers will account for 82 per cent of the motorised vehicle fleet in 2000. This trend has been accompanied by a spectacular shift from public to private vehicular traffic. This extraordinary growth in the number of motorised vehicles, especially two wheelers with the polluting two-stroke engine, poses a serious threat to environment (ambient air quality) in urban areas. In metropolitan centres, transport is estimated to account for 75 per cent of total air emissions.

Table 15.4 : Total Registered Motor Vehicles and their Growth

	1980-81	*1993-94*	*% change p.a.*
No. of vehicles ('000)	5336	27227	13.36
No. of Two Wheelers ('000)	2599	18338	16.22
No. of Cars, Jeeps and Taxies ('000)	1147	3617	9.24

Source : Ramanathan, 1997.

The condition of both rural and urban infrastructure is highly inadequate. The United Front's Common Minimum Programme (CMP) expressed grave concern about the state of the country's infrastructure. Highways require major augmentation of capacity as well as structural upgradation. Despite the enormity of the problem, there are no significant new measures undertaken by the government for development of the infrastructure sector.

In the recent budget, the Finance Minister has increased equity contribution to the National Highway Authority of India (NHA) from Rs. 200 crore to Rs. 500 crore and levied a tax on services—from which he expects to raise Rs. 900 crore—which will go to the NHAI. However, considering the gigantic nature of the task, these measures appear too small. Funds required for improvement of National and State Highways are estimated variously between Rs. 50,000 to 90,000 crore.

The road sector has been assigned progressively low priority in successive Five Year Plans. The allocation of funds for roads constituted 6.7 per cent of the total First Five Year Plan public sector outlay. This share dropped to 5.5 per cent in the Fourth Plan, to 4.3 per cent in the Fifth Plan, to 3.5 per cent in the Sixth and Seventh Plans, and to only 3 per cent in the Eighth Plan.

Alternative Sources of Finance for Infrastructure Development

It is now widely recognised that inadequate transport infrastructure is one of the major constraints on economic growth in India. Infrastructure development requires huge funds. Building of physical infrastructure has historically been the responsibility of the state. The Indian government now, however, appears to be abdicating this responsibility. By progressively reducing budgetary support, the government is ensuring continuously diminishing role for the public sector in future infrastructure development.

At Rs. 8300 crore, the size of the railways annual plan for 1997-98 remains the same as the revised estimate for 1996-97, marking a 10 per cent decline in real terms. Budgetary allocations to the railways have been reduced from 75 per cent of the railway's outlay in the Fifth Plan to 19 per cent in the Eighth Plan.

The government is now putting greater reliance on leased resources to finance development and expansion of rail network. (Lease refers to funds raised through Indian Railway Finance Corporation and through the 'Own-Your-Wagon' and 'Build-Own Lease-Transfer' schemes). The growing recourse to lease financing is certain to increase the interest burden of the railways which could eventually lead the railways into a "debt-trap". One another aspect noteworthy in this context is that private sector does not seem to be very enthusiastic about these schemes. Economic Survey 1996-97 admits that schemes like Build Own-Lease Transfer (BOLT) and Own-Your-Wagon-Scheme (OYWS) have had only limited success in attracting private sector participations till now.

In the past, roads have generally been financed from budgetary sources and constructed by the public works departments. However, the government now admits that 'the magnitude of the task on hand and the volume of funds required for this purpose are clearly beyond the capacity of the public sector' (Government of India, 1997, p. 174). Unwilling to raise budgetary allocation to road sector, the government has amended the National Highways Act 'to enable the levy of a toll on selected improved sections of National Highways. The amendment of the National Highways Act to allow the private sector to construct and charge a fee or toll will permit the private sector to participate in construction, maintenance and operation of roads on Build-Operate-Transfer (BOT) basis. Several measures have been taken by the government to attract private sector participation. These measures encompass land acquisition, environmental clearance, simplification of procedures, tolling of 4 lanes, bypasses and bridges, equity participation in the highways sector and sharing of risks' (Government of India, 1947, p. 174).

The government has also considerably liberalised the provisions relating to foreign investment in the road sector. External assistance is being obtained for the improvement of National Highways through international agencies such as the World Bank, Asian Development Bank and Overseas Economic Cooperation of Japan.

The idea of having private toll roads in India needs to be dismissed out of hard. The experience of developed countries shows that most of these countries have supplemented the general tax revenue through toll revenue. But almost all the toll roads in these countries are publicly owned. The idea of private toll roads has not found many takers even in the rich countries including USA. The risk profile on most of the private toll road projects is 'very high given their long gestation period, long life, uncertain traffic projections, and possibility of potential interference at some time in the life of the enterprises'.

The private sector at most may be interested in small scale BOT toll operations where possibilities exist for them to enjoy monopoly position. The bridges and urban bypasses (where land has been acquired by the government) offer these opportunities to the private sector for BOT operations. Even the idea of publicly owned toll roads does not offer much hope in case of India. 'The feasibility of large scale express toll way construction depends much on the ability of government to acquire land and to relocate those dispossessed by the land acquisition process. This constraint could easily preclude large scale construction of expressways'. (World Bank, 1995, p. 36)

Access to toll roads is limited to only those who are willing to pay for their use. The existing inter-city roads allow free access to all. It is not possible to convert the existing inter-city routes into toll roads because that would deny the poor people free access to these roads and thereby deprive them of their traditional rights. If that is the case, building to toll road network would involve construction of new long routes parallel to the existing routes. The economic and social costs of this huge new construction would easily prove to be prohibitive.

There are several other ways to raise funds for infrastructure development which appear more promising in case of India. Our aggregate tax to GDP ratio is very low (about 15 per cent) not only in comparison with developed countries but also in comparison with many developing countries. There is considerable scope for raising taxes in our country. Infrastructure development could be financed from these increased taxes.

Another possibility that is suggested is to earmark road user charges to a fund that would be used exclusively for the purpose of maintenance and expansion of the road network. Fuel taxes are relatively low in India; these could be raised and earmarked for road funds. Diesel prices in India are very low by international standards (and also in comparison to petrol prices). Significant increase in revenues can be achieved by raising tax on diesel. This will also go a long way towards solving the problem of air pollution in urban areas. It is sometimes argued that expressways are necessary in order to carry high-value goods speedily over long distances. This task however, could also be accomplished by improved rail container services. What is needed in India is to consider the rail and road systems in an integrated manner. The general tendency is to treat these two systems separately while making public policy or investment decisions. This needs to be avoided.

REFERENCES

Expert Group on the Commercialisation of Infrastructure Projects (The Rakesh Mohan Committee), *(1996), The India Infrastructure Report, Sector Reports.*

Government of India, (1996-97). Ministry of Finance, Economic Division, 1997, *Economic Survey,* Vol. VIII.

Ramanathan, R., (1997). "Transport: A Crucial Infrastructure', in Parikh, K.S., *India Development Report 1997,* Oxford University Press, Delhi.

World Bank, (1995), *India Transport Sector: Long Term Issues,* (Report No. 13192-IN).

16

SOME THEORETICAL CONSIDERATIONS IN REFORM OF RURAL INSTITUTIONS IN INDIA

Sukhadeo K. Thorat

Introduction

The inefficient and inequitable functioning of institutions governing economic life in rural India has been increasingly recognised as the key constraints to broad based economic growth. This point has been particularly brought into the focus after the involvement of bureaucracy and other organizations in rural development. The late recognization about the significance of economic institutions, (as crucial as that of technological, economic and other factors) was due to the fact, the institutional framework has been taken for granted in mainstream economies and often many of the central positions are stated with a false assumption of institutional neutrality. It is only after the early 1960s that mainstream neo-classical economists have relaxed the assumption of institutional neutrality and recognised the role of economic institutions in economic growth. Since the early 1960s number of economists have addressed to this issue, and this development lead to the emergence of a whole school of neo-classical writers, who developed a well articulated endogenous theory of institutions and traced the changes in economic history to changes in institutions. In the recent literature this body of writings has been identified as what is known as "Neo-classical Institutional Economics (NIE)".[1]

It must be mentioned that Marxists have a well-known endogenous theory of institutions. The criticism by Marxists and other institutional economists in this respect have been valuable in raising the general awareness of institutions presumption in economics.

The NIE which has emerged in early 1960s highlights the shortcomings of (traditional) neo-classical paradigm and provide original insights into the evolution of economic institutions, economic functions which the institution performs, explain the new forms that institutions take and their relation with economic development. These are some of the vital questions which form the themes of NIE.

In this Chapter I intend to make a modest attempt to highlight the recent theoretical developments in the institutional economics with a purpose to identify the possible framework or starting points for reforms of rural institutions in India. The motivations behind this effort is that, in the discussion on the institutional reform in India, the policy is often articulated in a fairly loose manner without recognising the relevant underlying theoretical considerations.

What are Economic Institutions?

Institutions are usually defined as the rules of society or organizations that facilitate coordination among people by helping them from expectations which each person can reasonably hold in dealing with others. (Ruttan, 1989). They reflect the conventions that have evolved in different societies regarding the behaviour of individuals and groups relative to their own and that of others. In the area of economic relations, institutions have a crucial role in establishing expectations about the rights to use resources in economic activities and about the partitioning of income streams, resulting from such activities—institutions provide assurance respecting the action of others and give order and stability to expectations in the complex and uncertain world of economic relations[2]. Like formal organizations (such as labour unions and employers' organizations, bureaucracy), markets too, be the stock exchange, land, labour, credit, or product markets, are institutions because they embody rules and regulations, formal or informal which governs the exchange and economic relations. "Contracts", explicit or implicit, are also institutions in so far as they lay down rules which govern specified activities involving people who are parties to such contracts. Similarly cultural rules and codes of conduct, norms, values are institutions in so far as they too can constrain the relationship between different individuals or groups.

In the main stream neo-classical economics, the institutional framework is taken for granted and many of the Central propositions are sometimes framed with an unrealistic assumption of institutional neutrality. The simple laws of market supply and demand are often applied without being fully conscious of the complex institutions on which "contracts" in actual markets crucially depend. In the real world, market exchanges consume resources and property rights are costly to enforce. Thus, the institutions are not costless, but consumes resource.[3]

Economic Role of Institutions : Theoretical Perspective

In the last two decades, however, three different approaches or theories of institutions have emerged—which mainly include, *Transaction* and *Information Cost Theory, the Collective Action School, and of course the Marxian Approach.*

The Marxian School has a well known indigenous theory of institutions. In the Marxian system, the economic structure of society (which in this theory provides the foundation of its legal and political institutions) consists of property relations, and it corresponds to the level of development of productive forces (which includes all means of production and technology). The central driving force behind institutions is thus the forces of production. Changes in the forces of production particularly technological change produce over time some tension between the existing structure of property rights and productive potential of economy, and it is through class struggle that this tension is resolved in history with emergence of new institutions relating to property rights, land ownership, tenancy and labour relations. The main criticism of Marxist analysis however is that it cites some of these production relations as institutional obstacles of development in poor agrarian economy, overlooking the micro-economic rationale of the very formation of these institutions.[4] There is also a tendency or "semi-feudal" mode of production, ignoring how in the real world the same institutions (say, share cropping) adopt themselves to the development of the forces of production (with numerous cases of capitalist share—tenant farmers—as for example in Punjab or more widespread cases of cost-sharing and other forms of landlord-tenant partnership in adoption of new technology of HYV in agriculture).[5]

Within the neo-classical framework, have emerged two broad approaches to overcome the limitations of mainstream economics. It includes transaction and information costs theory on the one hand and the school of collective action on the other.

The first strand originates from a famous paper by Coarse (1960) which led to development of a whole school of neo-classical writers on property rights and transaction costs. These writers developed a well articulated indigenous theory of institutions and trace changes in economic history to changes in the institutional ground rule[6]. To begin with, the neo-classical assumption of institutional neutrality is dropped and it is asserted that real world market transactions or exchanges consume resources, enforcement of property rights and contract also cost. In the transaction cost theory, the general hypothesis is that, institutions are transaction cost minimising arrangements which may change and evolve, with changes in the nature and sources of transaction costs and means for minimising. Thus, the transaction cost[7] and the institutions that evolve to minimise these costs are the key to the efficient performance of the economies. These costs include those of information, negotiation, monitoring, coordination and enforcement of contracts. It is in the nature of transaction costs that they arise not from the production of goods but form their transfer from one to another. The key proportion in the property rights approach associated with the Coarse (1960) is that when the transaction costs are absent, the initial assignment of property rights does not matter from the efficiency, point of view because rights can be voluntarily adjusted and exchanged to promote increased production. But when transaction costs are positive and substantial the allocation of property rights is critical.

The existence of property rights and rules governing contracts helps reduce conflict and facilitates co-operation.[8] Both results in the reduction of transaction costs and thus allows the productivity gains of large-scale and improved technology to be realized.

The other strand grew out of the theory of "Imperfect Information" is particularly of Stiglitz[9]. This theory of institutions is closely related to that of transaction cost theory since information cost constitutes an important part of the former. It provides a more rigorous and sharply defined framework for analyzing institutions as a substitute for missing market in an environment of pervasive risks, incomplete markets, information asymmetry and moral hazard. Since this environment in some respects is particularly acute in developing countries, the recent literature in development economics has seen a number of attempts to model related to share-cropping and other forms of tying, credit rationing, inter-linkage between credit and land lease, labour hiring and output sale transctions and others. The "information approach" has been found quite useful in the analysis of agrarian institutions. In general, transaction and information cost approach has proved to be particularly useful for the analysis of contractual choice.

The third general approach which is distinct from transaction and information cost approach concerns collective action and the elimination of free rider problem. The theory of collective action not only provides explanations for the behaviour of individuals which can result in non-cooperation but also deal with the identification of conditions under which cooperation can be achieved. This theory has been concerned with public or collective goods not only of physical character such as pollution, highway, parks and the like but also with issues such as higher wage rates, higher price, tariff or quota, regulations, a lower tax rate or a farm policy. The main theme under this approach concerns emergence of group interests and organizations and the relationship between these interest groups and the state. It is mainly explained through the theory of rent seeking, which primarily concerned with the means that interest groups use for getting what they want.

While the two main approaches, namely, the analysis of transaction and information costs and contractual choice on the one hand and analysis of collective action and pressure groups on the other have developed separately, nevertheless many issues in these approaches are complementary. There are important similarities in the framework and axiom upon which they are based.[10] For example, as in the analysis of transaction costs, collective action is analyzed from the point of view of self-interest and bounded rationality including opportunism. Secondly, both transaction costs and collective action are affected by the same factors. Castes, ethnicity and family loyalty may affect the contractual relations among members of economic organisation by reducing transaction costs, but also may either facilitate collective action by their members by helping to solve the free-rider problems which plunge such action by increasing the transaction costs of change. Thirdly, since the role of government is emphasized in both transaction costs and collective action theories. They have to be inter-related and complementary. On the one hand, government's decisions affect the transaction and information costs of different economic agents and thereby their choice of organizational forms the type of contract (for example, tenancy laws, wage legislations and ceiling laws), on the other hand, different agents or groups have incentive to organize themselves, in such a way as to influence the government decisions in the protection of their interests. Since in this sense, collective action can be said to begin where contractual choices based on the principles of transaction costs have a lot to do with explaining institutions and changes in the process of institutional change.

Process of Institutional Change

In order to perform essential role, the institutions must be stable for an extended time period, but institutions like technology must also change if development is to occur. A clear understanding of the mechanism through which the existing institutions undergo change and how new institutions emerge has continued to elude economists.

Researchers in this area have tended to take one or the opposite view, namely, that institutional change depends on technical change or technical change depends on institutional change, the latter being governed by other independent variables. Technological determinism formed the essential base of Marxist writings. Although Marx stressed a dialectical relationship between changes in the mode of production (technical change) and in production relations (institutional change) he believed that the mode of production provides more dynamic source of change in social organisation.

Technological determinism has been a dominant theme with the work of American Institutional School as well. The institutional innovation or change has been viewed as a lagged response to the rising economic value of man and growth of productivity. In the field of development economics, primary emphasis is placed on the new income streams released by technical change as an important source of institutional change.

The other view point maintains that institutions rather than technical change is the dynamic source of economic development. *North* attributed the major western economic growth to the changes brought about by the process of population against increasing resource scarcity in the institutions which govern property rights. The neo-classical economic historians believed that the relative factor price-changes fuel the main motivate force for institutional change in history (primarily by inducing the development of property rights to the benefit of owners of more expensive factors of production). In particular, demographic change altering the relative prices of labour to land lead to the incentive for redefining property rights on land and rearrangement of labour relations. *North, Hayami* and *Ruttan* give several examples from European and Asian History suggesting that rise in the prices of land relative to labour led to more control over land, elimination of commons and a change to a system based on either owner operatorship of land by proprietor or by use of wage-labour by capitalist land owner. In other situations, when wages have increased relative to the value of land, the institutional changes occurred that gave the peasant or free holder greater control over the use of his own labour. In the situation of raising economic value of men, there has been a move from a state of slavery (or its variants in bonded or attached labour) which denied man the opportunity or incentive to invest in himself to a situation where both private and public investment in the human agent in terms of both the promotion of health and education have become institutionalized. Similarly, some argued that the new income streams released by technical change do represent an important source of institutional change. It would set in motion attempts by individuals to reallocate their personal resources and to organise and initiate collective action for the purpose of redefining property rights and production relations so as to achieve greater equity in the sharing of new income streams.

Institutional Change and Equity

In his critics, Pranab Bardhan (1989 and 1996) argued that the neo-classical institutional economists focus their attention on allocative efficiency of institutions but ignored the distributive aspects of the institutional change. The Marxists however, emphasised how institutional change depends on consideration of surplus appropriation by dominant class. The emphasis on the effect of an institutional change on control of surplus by a particular class also suggests that the question of efficiency improving institutional change cannot really be separated from that of redistributive institutional change, particularly when issues of collective action, class capacity, mobilisation and struggle are important. A shift in the focus of attention from efficiency aspects of an institution to the distributive aspects confronts with the question of "concept of power".

In this context in recent Marxist theoretical models in economics, Bardhan (1989) indentifies two distinct forms of power relation.

Roemer (1982) traces the primary focus of capitalist power in unequal distribution of property where as Bowler (1985) traces it to political structure of control and surveillance at the point of production. Both these stands of Marxist theory serve a reminder that Transaction Cost (TC) and imperfect information theories (IIT)—demonstrating constraints for efficient working in terms of T.C. and moral hazard, it underemphasized that a more democratic organization of the work process and more egalitarian distribution of assets might reduce significantly informational constraints.

Bardhan (1989) also highlighted role of ideology and the states which the NIE ignored. Marxists assign theory of ideology and state a central place in theory of History and institutional change. Although we do not have good theory of the formation, maintenance and institutionali-zation of ideology, yet we have norms, customs and enforced code of conduct shaped by different ideologies which in one case bring some order and in other situation bring conflict—in the later it is minority which suffer in the process of institutional change.

As regards the role of the states—it is either conceived as body looking on behalf of "dominant class or a passive respondent to rent seeking behaviour of various interest groups and lobbies. Bardhan draws important distinction between top political leadership (which takes general decisions) and hierarchy of agents, the bureaucracy and argued that latter may form a pressure group and mechanism to seek favours. It follows the goals that are much narrower than set by the state

Ninth Five Year Plan Approach towards Institutional Reform

Even when the state in the last five decades has spent vast sums of money in rural development, there has been a significant failure on this front. The failures (or partial success) of the states and local institutions has been in the area of land reforms, and of providing public goods like irrigation, education, health, infrastructural facilities like roads, power, credit and extension service and administration of various programmes for the poors such as IRDP and EGS. The programmes are usually administered by distant, uncoordinated bureaucracy which is insensitive to the need of the people and often little reaches the intended beneficiaries of the programmes.

The *"Approach Paper on the Ninth Five Year Plan"* recognized this problem in the following manner :

> "For realisation of intended plan objectives, the quality of design and the manner of implementation of programmes/ projects are as important as the availability of resources. Our past experience has been that many programmes fails

> to deliver the results because of failures in implementation. Time and cost over-runs in infrastructure and investment projects have been widespread and substantial. Many development programmes have also not had the desired impact on the well-being of the poors because of inadequate administrative planning and implementation. An area of priority of the Ninth Plan is to improve project implemen-tation and delivery mechanisms and to ensure that intended benefits actually reach the people. No new programmes or project should be launched without paying sufficient attention to these aspects". (Approach Paper, 1997, pp. 115)

It further observes.........

> "In view of the lessons from experience, it has become necessary to introduce the necessary correctives to reverse many of the unsustainable trends in programme/project formulation and implementation. This will be a central priority of the Ninth Plan".

On accountability it observed.........

> "Lack of accountability of the implementing agencies either to the government or to the people has been the single major cause for misappropriation of funds in development programmes. It is well known that implementing agencies and programmes managers can get away easily with time and over-runs or non-fulfilment of targets by attributing these to factors beyond their control. In many cases they are indeed justified as most programmes leave too many loose ends at the planning stage. Nevertheless, several cases of misappropriation of funds meant for anti-poverty programmes have also come to light... This happened primarily because of lack of people's participation; in the implementation of programmes the lack of transparency, of the operation of schemes and inadequacy of the monitoring mechanism. Suitable institutional reforms, for involvement of the people and grassroot level non-government agencies in formulation and implementation are needed to overcome these problems" (Page 120).

The Approach Paper suggests the following policy measures in general and in particular for social sector programmes (Page 122) :

- A genuine push towards *decentralisation and people's participation will be given.* Through institutional reforms a conducive environment for people's participation will be created for strengthening the Panchayati Raj and the different models of people's institutions.
- Reorientation and integration of all village level schemes under the Panchayati Raj to avoid thin spread and wastage of resources.
- The existing schemes whose delivery costs are disproportionately high or which fail to make the desired impact should be considered for reorientation and discontinuation.
- Monitoring and Evaluation of programmes (M&E) will have to be made more effective and purposeful. The Centre, States and the grassroots level organisations/institutions would all have to be involved to ensure the effectiveness of M & E.
- Institutional changes to bring in transparency in implementation and operation of programmes. For this purpose, avoidable barriers to full flow of information must be removed.
- Build in sustainability of outputs and benefits and maintenance of public facilities as a necessary component of project/ programme formulation.

The Ninth Five Year Plan thus puts emphasis on the cost minimisation, accountability and transparency in the policy measures relating to the working project and implementation.

It also emphasises on the people's participation, particularly through decentralized working of Panchayat Raj institutions, by bringing an element of openness and democratic working. However, the document does not spell out changes in the working rules of various institutions which are supposed to bring reduction in transaction cost, promote accountability, bring transparency and more democratic working.

Further, in order to assure people's participation through Panchayat Raj institutions it does not suggest measures to overcome severe problems for realising successful collective action in highly socially and economically segmented Indian Society. There is also a complete lack of awareness of measures to make information more accessible to the people which is awfully lacking in several areas.

The theoretical insights acquired through a review of major theoretical writings in earlier section indicate that institutions could play effective role in economic growth if they are cost effective, equitable in terms of access and are fairly just in the distribution of income gains from economic activities. The equitable access to informations (about the economic opportunities offered by the market and government's interventions), transparency and accountability in the working makes the institution efficient and equitable in seeking access.

In this context significant reforms of various rural institutions in India is necessary.

(a) The working rules of rural bureaucracy and various other organisations and bodies need to be changed in such a manner that its working becomes more cost-effective (reduce transaction cost). These should cover all institutions, related to factor and product markets, and other involved in implementation of several development programmes.

(b) A major reform is necessary in the area of information to the rural people. These include information about all markets, particularly employment, credit, technologies, education and several other areas. More transparent system will help in making information open to people. Therefore, there is need to bring reforms on this front. Giving more programmes to Panchayats as well as provision of informations to them will promote access of information to people at local level.

(c) The theories regarding collective actions and Marxian perspective bring out clearly that in socially and economically segmented and unequal society, and at times socially conflicting interest groups behaviour, the rural organizations and bodies are generally controlled and used by powerful groups. The reforms or regulating provisions which will provide effective participation and also ensure due share to the poor and deprived social groups is, therefore, absolutely necessary.

NOTES

1. N. Nabli and J.B. Nugent (1999), The New Institutional Economics and Its Applicability to Development, *World Development*, Vol. 17, No, 9, pp. 1333-1374,
2. Vernon, W. Ruttan (1989), Institution, Innovation and Agricultural Development, *World Development*, Vol. 17, No, 9, pp. 1375-1387.
3. Vernon, W. Ruttan (1989), Institutional Changes, Chapter 12 in Hans P. Binswanger and Vernon W. Ruttan, *Induced Innovation Technology. Institutions and Development*, John Hopkins University Press, pp. 327-367.
4. Pranab Bardhan (1989), "Alternative Approaches to the Theory of Institution in Economic Development," Clarendon Press, Oxford, p. 7. It is further argued that "under a set of informational constraints and missing markets, a given agrarian institution (say share cropping) may be serving a real economic function, and its simple abolition, as it often demanded on a radical platform, without taking care of the factors that gave rise to this institution in the first place may not necessarily improve the condition of intended beneficiaries of the abolition programme.
5. Similarly, it is pointed out that "The neo-classical institutional economists on the other hand, have the tendency to apply their logic of voluntary contracts to many pre-capitalist forms of production relations (like slavery or coercive labour) ignoring that the sanctions underlying these relationships are often based on extra-economic coercion and the standard maximizing calculus on the part of the agents is somewhat out of place, Pranab Bardhan (1989), *op. cit.*, p. 7.
6. For an overview of this literature, see Stiglitz J.E. (1986). "The New Development Economies", *World Development*, Vol. 14, pp. 257-65 and Pranab Bardhan (1989), *op. cit.*
7. Pranab Bardhan (1989), *op. cit.*, p. 5; Nabli and Nugent (1989), *op. cit.*, agrued that "in the presence of transaction costs, different systems of property rights yield solution of differing efficiency. What is efficient in the presence of transaction costs may be quite different from that which is efficient in the traditional neo-classical economics without transaction costs, p. 1336.
8. Douglass C. North (1989), "Institution and Economic Growth : A Historical Introduction", *World Development*, Vol. 17, No. 9, pp. 1319-1332.
9. For comparison of the information and transaction approaches see Stiglitz (1986), *op. cit.*
10. For detailed discussion on complementarities between Transaction Costs and Collective Action, see Nabli and Nugent (1989), *op. cit.*, pp. 1339-1340.

17

DYNAMICS OF CHALLENGES TO PUNJAB AGRICULTURE

Its Role in the Domestic and Global Markets in the Context of Liberalisation of Indian Economy

Karam Singh

Punjab is a Progressive Agricultural State and a unique example of agricultural led development model which has been in the forefront of agricultural and rural development in India. With the liberalisation of Indian economy, besides remaining tuned to the obligations of meeting the domestic demand for foodgrains, the export competitiveness of its major agricultural commodities has also become the "food for thought" for many. This piece, therefore, explores these roles for Punjab agriculture in the future highlighting the potential for export in the background of relative strength of the Punjab agriculture in the global economy, the scope for specializing in the high value commodities groups in the agriculture sector and the infrastructure and institutional requirements to cope with the dynamics of challenges upcoming with the swings in the market scenario in the wake of domestic and global pressures and upbursts.

Domestic Food Demand and the Role of Punjab Agriculture

With high income elasticities of demand for livestock products (milk : 1.47 rural, 1.01 urban; eggs and meat : 1 04 rural, 0.75 urban) and the economic growth accompanied by targetting reductions in poverty, the escalating demand for milk, eggs and meat will require changes in livestock production methods placing much greater demand for cereals for livestock feed. The 2020 projections with 3 per cent growth rate in income and continuing baseline trends place the total cereal demand at about 280 million tonnes, with poverty removed at about 290 million tonnes and with all Indians fed to Indian Council of Medical Research (ICMR) norms (well fed India) at about 300 million tonnes (Table 17.1). With livestock feeding practices improved to Chinese standards escalates these demand estimates to about 340, 360 and 400 million tonnes respectively. About 5.5 per cent growth rate in real per capita income pushes the projected demand for foodgrains by another 60 million tonnes with Indian feed standards and by more than 160 million tonnes with Chinese feed standards. The startling projection of estimated demand with Indonesian feed standards along with 5.5 per cent growth rate in per capita income is about 760 million tonnes by 2020 of which 440 million tonnes (58%) is required for livestock feed. All said and done, the total demand for foodgrains should be seriously taken around 350 to 400 million tonnes for which we need to plan our agricultural growth (supply) and towards this Punjab shall continue to be relied upon to contribute in a significant way.

On a point to point, peak to peak, long-term basis, the foodgrains production in India increased at a growth rate of 2.4 per cent between 1970-71 and 1994-95 which was entirely due to growth in yield, and the required long-term growth rate upto 2020 to reach a target of 350 million tonnes is slightly less than that, 2.35 per cent, to be precise. In contrast, the growth rate of foodgrains production in Punjab during 1970-71 to 1994-95 was 4.66 per cent of which about 40 per cent was due to growth in area under foodgrains. During 1994-95, Punjab had a share of 11.4 per cent of the foodgrains production in the country and to maintain this level, which it will be required to, it needs to plan for the target of about 40 million tonnes which gives a growth rate of 2.4 per cent. In terms of long-term sustainability problems, which demand an onerous public and private investment in agriculture and in the rural non-farm economy, the area under foodgrains had to be contained which in turn would raise further pressure on pushing the agricultural productivity to a level of 3 per cent plus. This is little higher than the long-term growth rate of 2.9 per cent but far higher than the growth rate of 2.1 per cent obtained during the nineties. That is the challenge. Thus, the Punjab will have to really plan and implement a major stimulus to give a second push to its agricultural economy on to the expansion plan in the context of indegenous Indian market as well as the opportunities opened up in the context of globalization of the Indian economy.

Table 17.1 : Total Cereals Demand, 1990 to 2020 under Alternative Scenarios : India

(Million tonnes)

	Food Coefficients					
	Indian		*Chinese*		*Indonesian*	
	Feed demand (%)	*Total cereal damand*	*Feed demand (%)*	*Total cereal demand*	*Feed demand (%)*	*Total cereal demand*
Baselline						
1990	1.69	147.11	9.57	159.93	12.76	165.76
2020 (3.0 % PCY growth)	3.82	278.48	20.16	335.47	26.46	364.21
2020 (5.5% PCY growth)	6.79	351.51	32.53	485.17	41.41	558.69
Poverty removed						
1990	1.85	154.83	10.39	169.61	13.98	176.67
2020 (3.0 % PCY growth)	4.16	292.58	21.69	358.06	28.54	392.39
2020 (5.5 % PCY growth)	7.42	370.42	34.76	525.70	44.09	613.40
Well-fed India						
1990	5.51	146.28	18.94	170.51	24.73	183.62
2020 (3.0 % PCY growth)	6.60	301.02	30.90	406.83	39.02	461.08
2020 (5.5 % PCY growth)	12.56	362.08	48.62	616.15	58.16	756.74

Note : PCY = Per capita income growth.
Well-fed India : All under-nourished are well-fed per ICMR norms of balanced diet.

Source : G. S. Bhalla and Peter Hazell, 1998. Foodgrains Demand in India to 2020 : A Preliminary Exercise, *Economic and Political Weekly, Review of Agriculture, 32 (52), pp. A-150 to A-154.*

Strength of the Punjab Agricultural Sector

Whatever be the magnitude and nature of the incentives, the sustained performance of the agricultural sector in general and the export performance in particular is essentially a function of the basic structural strength of the agricultural sector. One simple index of such structural strength is that of productivity or yield per hectare. Notwithstanding the scope for minor high value small scale commercially viable level pockets of many enterprises, the Punjab agricultural economy is going to remain the leader of wheat, rice and cotton with 75 per cent of net area sown under wheat in winter, and, about 50 per cent under rice and little less than one-third under cotton in summer; that it is a wheat state in winter and two distinct belts, one of rice and other of cotton in the summer season. The yields per hectare for these important crops of Punjab in comparison with those in India and important countries of the world are given in Table 17.2. Although, India ranks very low in this context and the Punjab, which seems to be shining in relation to India and compares favourably with the comparable situations, but this is not the end of the road. And there are many indicators of resource use inefficiency which need to be given serious attention to improve the relative strength of Punjab Agriculture.

The best spring wheat growing countries that could be more

Table17.2 : Yield of Major Crops in Important Countries, and Fertiliser Use (Best during 1990-95)

(Kg/hectare)

Crop	*Punjab state*	*India*	*World 1*	*World 2*	*World 3*	*World 4*
Rice (Paddy)	5260	2694	6432 (USA) (45)	5962 (China) (260)	6312 (Korea Rep.) (445)	6275 (Japan) (345)
Wheat	4088	2394	6487 (France) (310)	5351 (Egypt) (380)	4187 (Mexico)	3443 (China) (260)
Cotton	570	287	783 (USA) (45)	877 (Pakistan) (380)	652 (Turkey)	790 (China) (260)

Note : Figures in the parentheses are the fertiliser use in nutrients kg per ha of agricultural land.
The fertiliser use in Punjab is 179 kg per ha and in India is 70 kg/ha.

logically compared with Punjab situation are Mexico and Egypt having about 9.5 and 8.8 lakh hectares respectively with best yields during the last five years at 4,187 and 5,351 kg per hectare; the Punjab has about 33 lakh hectares and best average yield of 4,088 kg per hectare. Egypt is endowed with climatic conditions that prevents lodging even at very high level of fertiliser input which is about 380 kg nutrients per hectare compared to about 170 kg per hectare in Punjab. France which grows winter wheat of over 10 months duration with an area of 51 lakh hectares has the average yield of wheat of 6,487 kg per hectare; it also uses above 300 kg per hectare of nutrients. Netherlands, also a winter wheat grower with a small area of 1.3 lakh hectares virtually grows wheat on fertiliser using 665 kg of nutrients per hectare and producing 7,800 kg per hectare. Although in real terms, the comparison for Punjab should include wheat plus rice in terms of paddy which has a productivity level of above 9 tonnes per hectare, but we should tune our research and resource use efficiency to reach the wheat yields of about 6 tonnes per hectare by 2020. And this is something which even at present some farmers do achieve.

In case of rice, important countries for comparison are USA, Japan, Korea and China. Their best average yield during the last five years are 6.0 to 6.4 tonnes of paddy per hectare. Punjab has reached a level of 5.1 tonnes per hectare. Again; the fertiliser in Japan and Korea is more than 400 kg per hectare and more than 250 kg per hectare in China. China has a longer experience in high yielding hybrid rice than Punjab. The productivity in Punjab can be further enhanced by about 15 to 20 per cent with rice hybrids where research needs to be further strengthened. Again, coupled with the promises of research and achieving the resource use efficiencies, removing inefficiencies, paddy yields can be pushed to 7 tonnes per hectare; many farmers even now have these yields. The state needs to push up a stimulus and generate the climate to get a real monsoon of such farmers in the Punjab.

In case of cotton too the situation in Punjab has to be assessed as cotton-wheat system compared with cotton mostly as a mono crop system in important cotton growing countries including Pakistan. The best productivity level during last five years in USA, Egypt, China, Pakistan and Indian Punjab are 783, 877, 790, 652 and 570 kg lint per hectare respectively. The situation is comfortably comparable. Notwithstanding the extremely uncertain and highly variable situation of cotton from year to year in Punjab, there is a further scope to enhance its productivity with the spread of better cotton hybrids and better management of resources particularly the insect pest management and water management in the cotton belt of the state.

An immediate parameter of the scope to improve upon the agricultural productivity can be gauged through the yield variability across regions, across districts, across villages and even across the farmers in the same village. It is also an important indicator of concern for commensurate measures required to improve the strength of the agricultural economy of the state. At the district level, the minimum average yield was 69 per cent of the maximum yield in the case of wheat, 68 per cent in the case of rice, 46 per cent in the case of cotton, 44 per cent in the case of maize and 79 per cent in the case of sugarcane (Table 17.3). In a cost accounting information for 300 farmers from 30 randomly selected clusters of villages for the "Comprehensive Scheme for Cost of Cultivation of Principal Crops in Punjab", the difference between the average yield of the best farmer and the farmer with the lowest average yield (excluding the abnormal observations) was found to be 4,609 kg per hectare in case of wheat, 5,991 kg in case of paddy and 2,450 kg in case of cotton. Even within the same village, the difference between the most efficient and the most inefficient farmers was found to be ranging from 714 to 2,719 kg per hectare in case of wheat, 1,020 to 4,409 kg in case of paddy and 487

Table 17.3 : Yield Variability of Different Crops in Punjab

(Kg/ha)

	Average yield at district level (1993-94)			*Yield gap at farmer level (1991-92)*[2]		
Crop	*Maximum*	*Minimum*	*Gap*[1]	*State*[3]	*Zone*[4]	*Village*[5]
Wheat	4435 (Ludhiana)	3080 (Hoshiarpur)	1355 (69%)	4609 (5823)	3467 (4262)	714 (2719)
Paddy	5898 (Sangrur)	3986 (Gurdaspur)	1912 (68%)	5991 (8000)	2761 (5635)	1020 (4409)
Cotton[6]	495 (Bhatinda)	230 (Ludhiana)	265 (46%)	2450 (2550)	700 (2280)	487 (1993)
Sugarcane	71620 (Sangrur)	56510 (Hoshiarpur)	15110 (79%)	63750 (75000)	50200 (63750)	11750 (49565)
Maize	2598 (Jalandhar)	1148 (Gurdaspur)	1450 (46%)	— —	— —	— —

1. Figures in the parentheses are per cent of minimum yield to maximum yield.
2. *Source :* Comprehensive Scheme for Cost of Cultivation of Principal Crops in Punjab : sample size 300 farmers.
3. Figures in parentheses are the maximum yield recorded in the sample.
4. Main figures and the figures in the parentheses represent the minimum and maximum gap across the three zones respectively.
5. Main figures and the figures in the parentheses represent the minimum and maximum gap across the thirty clusters of villages respectively.
6. The district yields are of lint and the farmers yields are with seed.

to 1,993 kgs in case of cotton. These gaps are significant enough to be bridged by following the development strategies that identify and improve upon the performance of the farmers operating on the lower ladders of efficiency.

Export Competitiveness of Major Agricultural Commodities

In the context of globalisation and increasing the relative participation in the world markets to improve upon the economic power of the country, it is pertinent to compare the relative 'trade economics' in case of major commodities. Two important points need to be mentioned briefly before the comparison. One, the world market prices are fluctuating, whereas the domestic prices, particularly in case of wheat and rice, in rupee terms, are always increasing. Two, the exchange rate, whenever devalued significantly affects the difference between the domestic and the world prices.

The prices of wheat in the world market f.o.b. Gulf and of Punjab wheat f.o.b. Bombay (since the international freight and handling charges to major importers of wheat from India, namely USSR, China and Japan will be about the same from Gulf or Bombay) are given in Table 17.4. It shows that during 1990 and 1991 when world market

Table 17.4 : Export Parity Economies of Punjab Wheat, 1989 to 1998

(Per tonne)

Year	*World market price US wheat to f.o.b. Gulf*		*Punjab wheat price f. o.b Bombay*	*Net margin*
	US$	*Rs.*	*Rs.*	*Rs.*
1989	170.1	2464 (14.49)	2210 (1730)	+ 254
1990	136.8	2278 (16.65)	2330 (1830)	(–) 52
1991	128.9	2313 (17.94)	2760 (2250)	(–) 447
1992	151.1	3772 (24.96)	3070 (2500)	702
1993	141.8	4346 (30.65)	3830 (3250)	516
1994	134.0	4204 (31.37)	4190 (3500)	14
1995	160.0	5021 (31.38)	4400 (3600)	621
Current (1998)	17.0	6645 (38.50)	6000 (4750)	+ 645

Note : 1. Figures in the parentheses in Col. (3) are the average exchange rate.
2. Figures in the parentheses in Col. (4) are the procurement prices of wheat.

prices declined, the Punjab wheat did not have export parity advantage, although it still had an import parity advantage, which was the real situation at that time. But later on since 1992 with significant devaluation; the export parity advantage for Punjab wheat improved considerably. In 1994, the world wheat market prices averaged at US$ 134 per tonne. At these prices, there was little export parity advantage for Punjab wheat. However, with the liberalization of the trade scenario, the future projections are towards improvements in world prices. And at present, the wheat is selling at US$ 160 to 170 per tonne which gives Punjab wheat an export parity advantage of more than Rs. 600 per tonne.

In case of rice, our prices in the world market are about 75 per cent due to quality preferences (except in case of Basmati). The Punjab rice did not have any export parity advantage upto 1991 (Table 17.5). The devaluation in 1992 made the big difference turning to an export parity advantage of above Rs. 200 per tonne during 1992 and 1993. The price in the world market jumped by about US$ 50 per tonne during 1994 to touch a level of US$ 315 per tonne and it gave an

Table 17.5 : Import Parity economies of Punjab Rice, 1989 to 1997

(Per tonne)

Year	*Thai rice f.o.b. Bangkok*		*Punjab rice f.o.b. Bombay*	*Export parity (net margin)*
	US$	*Rs.*[1]	*Rs.*[2]	
1989	320.3	3480	3625 (2050)	(–) 145
1990	287.2	3587	3975 (2250)	(–) 388
1991	314.2	4228	4410 (2500)	(–) 182
1992	287 .4	5276	5070 (2900)	206
1993	267.9	6158	5980 (3500)	178
1994	315.0	7411	6240 (3600)	1171
1995	320.0	7532	6575 (3750)	957
Current (1997)	330.0	9500	8300 (4550)	1200

Note : 1. After adjustment for quality difference at the rate of 75 per cent.
2. Figures in brackets are the procurement prices for superfine rice in terms of paddy.

export parity advantage of about Rs. 1,200 per tonne. As at present, with the world market price at about US$ 330 per tonne, the Punjab rice has an export parity advantage of more than Rs. 1,000 per tonne.

The major exports of rice from India is of basmati variety, which is more than two-third of the total exports of rice in value terms (Rs. 865 crore of basmati out of Rs. 1206 crore of total rice in 1994) And basmati is grown mainly in Punjab and Haryana. Although the domestic economics of basmati is less favourable than the other varieties (net returns Rs. 7,700 per hectare from basmati computed with Rs. 11,400 per hectare from PR 106/PR 108 varictics at normal expectations with improved package of practices), the export parity returns at farm gate are higher from basmati than from other varieties of rice (Table 17.6). Indian traders got f.o.b. Bombay a price of Rs. 1,957 per quintal in 1994 compared with Rs. 739 per quintal for other rice. The export parity returns at farm gate were estimated to be Rs. 15,088 per hectare from basmati which are higher by more than Rs. 1,500 per hectare from other rice which were Rs. 13,552 per hectare, *i.e.* an economic advantage of about 11 per cent from basmati compared with other varieties of rice.

Table 17.6 : Relative Export Parity Economies of Basmati and Other Rice Per Hectare, 1994-95

	Item	*Unit*	*Basmati*	*Other rice*
1.	Export price : f.o.b. Bombay	Rs./qtl	1957	739
2.	Handling charges	"	100	100
3.	Farm gate export parity price	"	1857	639
4.	Yield	qtl/ha		
		Paddy	22.5	64.5
		Rice	15	43
5.	Processing Costs	Rs/qtl		
		Paddy	10	10
		Rice	225	645
6.	Operational costs	Rs/ha	12542	13280
7.	Export parity* returns	Rs/ha	15088	13552

* Farm gate export parity price multiplied by yieldless processing and operational costs per hectare.

In case of cotton, Punjab produces more than one-fifth of India's output. All the cotton is ginned in the state. About one-third of this is processed into yarn in the state, very little of which gets further value-addition in the state. India is a significant partner in the world trade in case of cotton, however, its exports fluctuate considerably and in some years our imports even exceed the exports (Table 17.7).

Both the world and domestic prices of cotton have wide fluctuations. In spite of this, the Punjab cotton has an export parity advantage which reached as high as Rs 1,681 per quintal in 1993. It was Rs. 1,140 per quintal in 1990 and Rs. 835 per quintal in 1994. Even in 1992, when world market prices had reached rock bottom level and India had imported more than it exported during the year, the Punjab cotton had an export parity advantage of about Rs. 120 per quintal.

Table 17.7 : Export Parity Economies of Punjab Cotton, 1989 to 1994

Year	*India (lakh bales)*			*Punjab*	*World price*		*Punjab price f.o.b Bombay Rs/qtl*	*Export parity net margin*
	Prod.	*Exports*	*Imports*	*Prod. (lakh bales)*	*US$ per tonne*	*Rs. per qtl.*		
1989	106.0	1.00	2.30	21.18	1546.5	2240	1770 (1670)	470
1990	135.80	13.70	—	24.54	1712.1	2850	1210 (1600)	1140
1991	117.00	11.90	—	19.09	1573.1	2822	2449 (2329)	373
1992	119.00	0.77	3.00	24.69	1150.6	2872	2753 (2623)	119
1993	130.00	17.88	0.73	23.50	1246.1	3819	2138 (1998)	1681
1994	—	1.77	—	15.15	1746.0	5479	4644 (4494)	835

Note : Price in parentheses are wholesale prices of lint and hence no adjustment for ginning costs has been made.

Export Surplus Potential of Foodgrains from Punjab

At present, Punjab has about 8 million tonnes surplus of wheat out of its best production level of about 14 million tonnes. The future potential projections can be of 10 to 12 million tonnes surplus with about 18 to 20 million tonnes of wheat production. Likewise for rice, the surplus production level can be set to reach a level of 8 to 10 million tonnes compared with the present production levels of about 7 to 8 million tonnes of which 6 to 7 million tonnes is the surplus for domestic and international exports. In wheat, the durum wheat has the better export potential being a better processable variety. One should envisage long term export targets of these commodities and support with the institutions and infrastructure which are efficient to meet the international competitiveness cost effectively. The long term targets of exports on sustainable basis could be 1 million tonnes (m.t.) of durum wheat, 2 m.t. of bread wheat; 2.5 to 3 m.t. of rice of which about 1 m.t. should be of basmati rice. There is a tremendous scope of value additions even in foodgrains, particularly of wheat products. It is a fact that Punjab wheat grains are 'simply' broken outside Punjab into 'dalia' even for the Punjab consumers. The bread and biscuits and pasta products of wheat from outside Punjab also have a better share of the Punjab domestic market than these products being processed to large scale in Punjab.

Potential of Milk and Milk Products

The income elasticities of demand for milk and milk products being more than one is a strong economic pointer of large market potential for which specialized production efforts need a further boost. The present indicators of dairy development in Punjab are much better placed and the scope is even more enormously better (Table 17.8). A milk plant with 5 lakh litres capacity per day (Presently Milk Plant; Ludhiana in the Public sector and Nestle India Ltd. at Moga in the Private sector out of 10 and 7 milk plants in these sectors respectively have a capacity of 4 lakh and 4.5 lakh litres per day) should be envisaged from about 50,000 milch animals producing on the average 10 litres per day. In terms of land (for fodder only), it comes to 5,000 hectares; add 100 per cent for eventualities, nay, inefficiencies of our system and animals, it gives us 10,000 hectares supporting a large milk plant. Instead of thinning the milk shed to more than a district for a large plant, we should identify the specific blocks where the development of needed infrastructure and institutions are envisaged to make the dairy economies relatively much better enterprise at the farm level. Now that the Government of Punjab is again focusing on block level planning, it should better consider this potential at the earliest to set the process in motion at an invigorated speed, for it is nothing new that the Punjab is to venture about.

Tackle the Economic Inefficiencies

Notwithstanding the financial profitability of individuals operating under the market duress, our economic system adds to economic inefficiencies and economic cost escalations to slash our economic competitiveness. I shall cite only two apparent examples. At present, the milk plants at Moga, at Ludhiana and at Karnal, all have their milk collection centres in Dehlon block of Ludhiana district and they

Table 17.8 : Key Indicators of Dairying : Punjab and India, 1992

Indicator		*Punjab*	*India*
1. Population			
Cattle (million)		2.91	204.6
Buffalo (million)		6.01	84.2
Adult female cattle (million) :			
Cross-bred :	In milk	0. 46	4.01
	Dry	0.18	1.78
	Total	**0.64**	**5.79**
Indigenous :	In milk	0.26	27.55
	Dry	0.13	24.45
	Total	**0.39**	**52.00**
Adult female : buffaloes (million) :	In milk	2.28	25.89
	Dry	0.89	14.38
	Total	**3.17**	**40.27**
2. Total milk production (million tonnes)		5.58	58.0
3. Relative contribution to milk production :			
Cows (%)		35	45
Buffaloes (%)		65	52
4. Milk yield per adult famale (litres/day)			
Cows		4.66	0.94
Buffaloes		4.50	1.96
Litres/annum :			
Cows		1701	342
Buffaloes		1642	715

Source : *Indian Livestock Census, 1992* and *Agricultural Statistics at a Glance.* Directorate of Economics and Statistics Ministry of Agriculture, Government of India, New Delhi.

offer a competitive price to the farmers. Competitive price is good, but why add extra transportation costs and also why not achieve the scale economies, and reduce the operational as well as economic costs. The milk plants must have a competition, the one in Ludhiana for Ludhiana (Dehlon) block farmers and the one in Moga for Moga block farmers rather than adding to their costs through spatially spread diseconomies. The second example is that of sugar mills. Transporting cane across the mills over too long distances, stress and crowding on roads, etc. when a large sugar mill too requires only as much area as a milk plant. The economic institutions, economic infrastructure and the economic system must venture into this direction in a way that these inefficiencies and economic cost escalations are removed without jeopardising the competitive spirit and the financial interests of the farmers.

Entrepreneurial Oriented High Value Agricultural Exports

These include honey, mushroom, floriculture (cut flowers and seeds), vegetables and some fruits too. Punjab produces about 2,500 tonnes of honey and exports about 1,000 tonnes. The production potential in the long run is upto as high as 50,000 tonnes of which about 7 to 8 thousand tonnes is not a distant potential. Thus, we should plan for an organised production-processing-marketing and export chain for about 5,000 tonnes annually. Likewise for mushrooms, Punjab producing about 5,000 to 6,000 tonnes which can even reach the present level of India's total production of about 20 to 25 thousand tonnes, majority of which is white button variety that has the export potential. We need the backward and forward linkages developed for matching the export competitiveness requirements. The cut-flowers especially rose to European market in the X-mas season can be a boon. And ideallyflower seeds have even much better potential market which is presently being demonstrated by a few enterprising entrepreneurs in the state without any infrastructural support from the state in the real sense. We need to identify the pockets for each of these potential products and develop the infrastructures and institutions to establish the profitability, cost-effectiveness, quality standards and export-competitiveness for such products.

Role of Public Investment

Investment plays a dominant role in economic development as capacity creator, income generator and pace setter for additional investment. The intensity with which these factors stimulate the economic growth depends upon other factors such as infrastructure, commercial practices, research and development in promoting the trade potential, etc. The mutual interdependence of the agriculture sector with other sectors of the economy, in the investment linkages scenario makes the agriculture industry linkages in the production, demand and supply and savings portfolio operationalise even more significantly. These economic interactions generate 'demand pull' and 'supply push' factors which significantly affect the rural economy. By and large, marketing is an environment for a smoother forward linkage from agriculture to industry, irrespective of the territorial boundaries. Since marketing of agriculture produce is a function of its price, level of output, domestic consumption and reserves as well as cost of production, the production should be increased to allow more marketable surplus to move in assembling centres. This would be a stimuli for derived demands of production inputs and consumption goods. The experience of green revolution in Punjab has demonstrated the role of strong inter-sectoral linkages and marketable surplus potentials. Remember, we can produce small but we cannot market small.

The technology upgradation in agriculture and other sectors of the economy resulted in more roundabout methods of production and a higher use of intermediate inputs, thereby strengthening inter-industry linkages, more so in Punjab. Further, significant increases in per capita income led to higher demand for consumption goods. Since meeting the consumption needs of the people constitutes a major economic activity in the state, the inducement effects of consumption were also quite substantial. Rapid agriculture growth by raising the incomes of an overwhelmingly large proportion of the labour force not only made a deep dent in rural poverty but also led to development of other sectors through forward and backward linkages. It should, however, be noted that the direct and indirect effects of increased economic activity in both agriculture and manufacturing in Punjab have been considerably reduced since the state is a large importer of modern agricultural inputs such as fertilisers, insecticides, diesel fuel and raw materials for manufacturing such as coal, pig iron and metals and also numerous finished goods for consumption. On the other hand, Punjab has benefited immensely from the existence of an assured market for exports of agricultural surpluses and industrial products and from the easy availability of inputs such as fertilisers and diesel fuel at notionally subsidised rates. A comparative analysis of the input-output tables over time shows that besides the agriculture and agro-processing sectors, many machine based and metal based industries as well as Trade, Transport, Banking, Real Estate, and other Services were generating high forward and backward linkages despite import leakages. The Punjab experience demonstrated that it is possible for a region within a large country to enjoy the fruits of specialisation and comparative advantage through trade and integration with the rest of the country.

The importance of the rural non-farm economy in determining current and future incomes and employment in India's rural areas and rural towns multiplies with capital investments in infrastructures which trigger off linkage effects. The growth of the rural and non-farm sector is driven primarily by agricultural growth. It was estimated that each rupee of value added created in agriculture led to Rs. 0.37of direct additional value added in non-farm activities in India's rural areas and rural towns. With feedback effects from non-farm activity back to agriculture, the total indirect income increment became Rs. 0.54. All the evidences suggest that the multipliers would increase over time. Both the production and consumption linkages have grown substantially, buoyed by the rising input intensity of agriculture and the growing incomes which stimulate consumer diversification of spending into non-foods. The magnitude of the growth linkages can be increased through appropriate governmental policies and investments in rural infrastructure like roads, electrification, banking services, etc., which enable enhancing the size of the multipliers. Irrigated agriculture, as that of Punjab has larger multipliers than rainfed agriculture. And the multipliers are further bigger for small to medium sized farms than for the large farms. Appropriate regional and farm targetting of agricultural technology and investments, supported by adequate investments in rural infrastructure, may, therefore, significantly enhance the size of the indirect benefits emanating from agricultural growth.

Areas of Public Investment

Punjab, to an outside reader, and to a macro-expert would seem to be well developed but a flash from the sky would show many 'islands of poverty' amidst this 'ocean of development'. These 'islands' need to be given special public attention. The depressing situation of water resources getting scarcer and costlier and ecological degradation through the emergence of new pests, diseases, increased uses of chemicals, unscrupulous disposal of agricultural and industrial waste need urgent public attention. The marketing system though regulated but still exploits the farmers and public exchequer unbelievably by billions of rupees and is still domestic-oriented rather than export-oriented. The Punjab's surpluses which have to compete in the global market and exploitation of new opportunities with an eye on the global market demand the public investments in the market system to match the export-marketing requirements and standards.

Specifically, some important areas of public investment in Punjab agriculture are outlined here :

Investment in Marketing Infrastructure

The public investment in the marketing system should envisage developing and modernising the markets to meet the export marketing requirements. This has become even more important now that the Indian economy has signed for globalisation. The investment in the marketing infrastructure is also required for high value, highly perishable commodities which often come with special bounties of nature. The gluts of potatoes in some year, of grapes in another year or of kinnows at another place, should not be allowed to rot and rob the farmers; the marketing investments be also planned and made for such gluts in view. Also, effective marketing arrangements should be envisaged for new enterprises like soyabean, sunflower, mushroom, honey, etc. which have vast potential in certain pockets. In fact, this would enable to exploit the pocket-specific specialization in high payoff enterprises which should be the future strategy for diversification of agriculture. And if cut flowers from Punjab have to be exported, a fancy talk by many, it must match, in developing the highly efficient modernised refrigerated road, rail and air marketing system.

Strengthening the Transport and Communication System

In addition to the above specialised agro-based marketing infrastructure system, the state must strengthen extensively its general transport and communication network system. The divided highways of smooth quality and highly disciplined traffic investment system along with an efficient communication network can induce the multiplier effects by increasing the economic activity and attracting the private investment from private sector within the country and from abroad. Specialized dry ports and efficient air-connectivity are the demands of the day.

Investment in Agro-based Industry

The development of agro-based industry to impart value addition to the raw materials is the need of the day to sustain the Punjab agriculture. The necessary infrastructure package for specific industries should be at appropriately identified sites throughout the state. Public investment should also encourage the development of agro-based industry as complete packages of integrated units. For example, a number of products can be prepared from maize. In sugar industry, a composite unit consists of sugar-alcohol-paper-electricity. Likewise, the integrated unit in case of rice is rice-edible oil-cattle feed-chemical (furfural)-electricity-bricks-cement. Specific incentives should be provided to the private sector taking up investments in integrated cost-effective units.

The public investment in the fruit and vegetable processing industry in the potential pockets should be taken up in a planned manner which could be disinvested when still running on profits. The objective should be invest—operate and demonstrate profits-disinvest.

Investment in Water Recharging and Drainage Systems

The water resources of the state are being over-exploited. Water-table is falling at an alarming rate. The tubewells have to be deepened further and further every two or three years. Some areas have already become dark; grey areas are in plenty requiring special urgent attention.

The public investment has to pick up for improvements in water use efficiency and in the savings of water resources of the state. Those who cite the example of Israel doing so much with so little water do not elaborate how much more capital investment is required. Not only that the public investment in recharging the groundwater has to be accorded top priority, but the public investment in a big way in areas prone to flooding and water logging need to be stepped up in such a way that the maximum use of land and water *in situ* is exploited in most efficient and economical way.

Investment in Watershed Development in Shivaliks

The semi-hilly tract of Punjab, popularly known as Kandi belt is a big chunk of under-developed area that outside visitor to this part would hardly believe if it were in Punjab. The investment in watershed development in this tract of Punjab, which is 9 per cent of its geographical area, has been shown to yield high rates of return of 12 to 28 per cent for different activities like afforestation, animal productivity improvement programme, soil conservation, water-harvesting, etc. Although investment has been initiated in the area with the World Bank assistance but the requirement is far too more than being envisaged. Also, the World Bank development projects are for 5 years or extended to 7 years whereas the development of this area is a longer historical process and should not be left to the old vagaries as is usually being done.

Improving the Livestock Productivity

The public investment in improving the livestock productivity in the long-run, not only in improving the breed-stock of animals but also the animal health and management of livestock enterprises is of great significance. The credit facilities for livestock enterprises should be at subsidised rate. The animal insurance should be state funded. The extension advisory service for training and total quality management of livestock enterprises needs to be strengthened. The marketing infrastructure and arrangements with assured and remunerative price should be developed. Specialised dairy development blocks be identified for integrated development of inputs supply, production, marketing, processing and distribution through public investment.

Institutional Credit

The credit flow in Punjab needs to be increased to improve upon not only the credit-deposit ratio but also the total infrastructure in the state. High-tech branches, specialised branches for agriculture, for specialised industries, for export, etc. need to be opened in multi-locations in the state. In fact, the returns to agriculture in the future depend more upon the investment in infrastructure, institutions and at the farm level in highly capital intensive enterprises like 'protected horticulture for export' which demands millions of credit investment per hectare. For the small farm sector, the funds be made available at low rates of interest to take up such potential enterprises as dairy, horticulture, poultry, forestry, etc. with a gestation period for recovery, credit during the intervening period, subsidized insurance of animals, etc. In order to meet some risks, the policies with the objectives of 'interest-insurance credit assurance' and 'credit insurance' should be devised and implemented.

Investment in Agricultural Research

The returns to investment in agricultural research have been reported to be very high ranging from 50 to above 80 per cent in independent studies in early seventies, in eighties and now in early nineties. But the investment in agricultural research, as percentage of net state domestic product from agriculture has been dismally low and is declining. It was 0.55 per cent in 1960s, 0.44 per cent in 1970s, 0.46 per cent in 1980s and 0.44 per cent in 1990s so far. It is even less than 0.4 per cent in 1996-97 as compared to 3 to 5 per cent in advanced countries and the recommendation of one per cent in the Indian situation. There is a real 'contingency constraint' in the research funding which demands that the research must be funded more intensively and specifically from export point of view in farming models of maximum possible investment per hectare of land.

OUR CONTRIBUTORS

K.S. Dhindsa
Professor, Punjab School of Economics, Guru Nanak Dev University, Amritsar.

Indra Nath Mukherji
Professor and Dean, School of International Studies, Jawahar Lal Nehru University, New Delhi.

K.N. Kabra
Professor, Indian Institute of Public Administration, New Delhi.

Karam Singh
Professor, Department of Agricultural Economics & Sociology, Punjab Agricultural University, Ludhiana.

Arun Kumar
Professor, Centre for Economic Studies & Pianning, Jawahar Lal Nehru University, New Delhi.

V. Upadhyay
Associate Professor, Deptt. of Humanities & Social Sciences, Indian Institute of Technology, New Delhi.

Sukhadeo K. Thorat
Director, Indian Institute of Dalit Studies, New Delhi.

G.K. Chadha
Vice Chancellor, Jawahar Lal Nehru University, New Delhi.

Shri Prakash
Ex-Senior Fellow, National Institute of Educational Planning and Administration, New Delhi.

D.N. Rao
Professor, Centre for Economic Studies & Planning, School of Social Studies, Jawahar Lal Nehru University, New Delhi.

Sucha Singh Gill
Professor, Panjabi University, Patiala.

Ashok Mathur
Professor, Centre for the Study of Regional Development, Jawahar Lal Nehru University, New Delhi.

Arun Ghosh
Ex-Member, Planning Commission, New Delhi.

Anju Sharma
Lecturer, Post Graduate Department of Economics, Khalsa College, Amritsar.

Atul Sarma
Professor, Indian Statistical Institute, New Delhi.

Jaswinder Singh Brar
Panjabi University, Patiala

P.K. Mehta
Indian Statistical Institute, New Delhi.

S.S. Johl
Professor of Eminence, Ex Vice Chancellor, Panjabi University, Patiala. Vice Chairman, Planning Commission Board, Punjab.

INDEX